CONSTABULARY LOCA

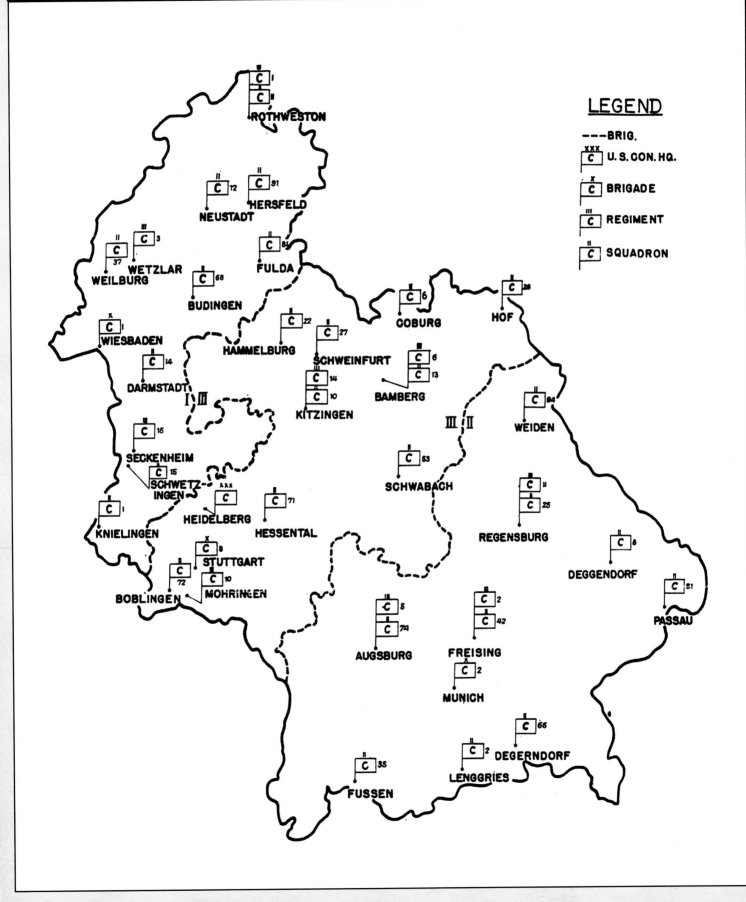

THE UNITED STATES CONSTABULARY

A *History*

Compiled by

William M. Tevington
National Historian
United States Constabulary Association

TURNER PUBLISHING COMPANY
Paducah, Kentucky

TURNER PUBLISHING COMPANY

Publishers of America's History
412 Broadway•P.O. Box 3101
Paducah, Kentucky 42002-3101
(502) 443-0121

Turner Publishing Company Staff
Publishing Consultant: Douglas W. Sikes
Project Coordinator: John Mark Jackson

Designer: David Hurst

U.S Constabulary Association Staff
William M. Tevington, Writer

Library of Congress Catalog No. 98-88041
ISBN: 1-56311-469-0
LIMITED EDITION
Printed in the U.S.A

Contents

PUBLISHER'S MESSAGE

Dave Turner, President

Some of the images persevered for more than two generations before vanishing seemingly in an instant; the incongruity of civilizations vastly diverse but only inches apart, razor sharp wire trimming demarcated "Forbidden zones," cold sentries at "Check Point Charlie" and most ominously, the "Wall", ultimately reduced to rubble by forces more powerful than gunpowder. Other images gradually changed; bombed-out, gutted metropolitan cinders, huddled masses seeking subsistence, a chaotic nation with no remaining law or government to rule its recently suppressed subjects, all giving way to the rebirth of an economic and technological world leader. There were those of us who were aware of it, there were those who witnessed it first hand, and there were those who helped make it happen.

It is of these that we present the story of the United States Constabulary. An innovative military marvel who not only stared WWIII in the eye every day for the decades of the "Cold War", but "With a sword in one hand, and a trowel in the other" kept law and order in a ravaged post-war Austria and Germany so that reconstruction might become an immediate reality.

And just as in performing their duty, "Mobility, Vigilance and Justice" was the theme for the Circle C Cowboys as they labored to prepare this chronicle. We would like to express our appreciation to National Commander, Ray Guillaume and to immediate past National Commander, Mr. Don Purrington, and all previous National Commanders: Bud Groner, Bill Tevington and Bob Jarrett, and all of the members of the U. S. Constabulary Association, especially Trooper William Tevington for his tireless, selfless efforts in compiling and composing this historic volume. We thank them for their efforts and for allowing Turner Publishing Company to have a part in it. Long live the legacy.

Dave Turner
President

FOREWORD

When WW II in Europe ended, Germany was not only defeated, but was demoralized, destroyed and devastated. The country was a shambles.

The victorious nations would jointly assume the occupation of Germany by dividing it into four Zones of Occupation, the Russian, British, French, and United States.

As was the case with the other armies, the United States Army was faced with unbelievably difficult and unprecedented challenges. There was no functioning municipal, state, national, or border police. The beaten country was flooded with refugees and displaced persons. It was the tactical units put in place after the war that initially prevented chaos.

One of these was the Fourth Armored Division. This Division had distinguished itself by spearheading the advance the advance of Gen. Patton's Third Army across Europe. As the war was ending, it had been told that it would be a PERMANENT occupation Division.

After VE Day, the battalions of the Division were spread throughout its occupation zone, and were bringing law and order to the communities and assisting the German citizens to get their lives back together.

During the war I was a Tank Battalion Commander, but after as the occupation began, I eventually became Chief of Staff of the Division. We were smoothly accomplishing our assigned mission when, without warning, we were hit by a combination hurricane, cyclone, tornado.

We were told that the Division which had won fame during the war in Europe would be summarily deactivated, would be a division no more. This was staggering, unbelievable news. What came next was even more astonishing. We learned that as the division was being deactivated, its units would become the nucleus of a brand new, unique, specialized force, so special and so unique that none like it had ever before existed in our Army. It was to be a force especially created for the special needs of a successful occupation of Germany. It would be called The United States Constabulary

We were seized with an unprecedented sense of urgency. Thousands of tasks, it seemed, had to be done at once. As Chief of Staff, together with the direction and the guidance of the Division Commander, Maj. Gen. Fay B. Prickett, and the support and cooperation of the division staff and the commanders and staffs of all subordinate units - it was our responsibility to get the job done. And what a big job it was !

The division immediately had to divest itself of all the items that had made it a fearsome power during WW II - - its tanks, halftracks, armored artillery — its hundreds of trucks, engineer and maintenance equipment.

Even more important was the psychological change. There had to be a different mind set. No longer were the tactical troops warriors, fighters. Yes, they were still soldiers, but now they would have to learn to be soldier policemen—Constabulary Troopers.

Tremendous coordination had to be effected with the 1st Infantry Division. They would take over the 4th's area of responsibility. Their units throughout had to be in place as units of the 4th withdrew.

VI Corps Headquarters would furnish the nucleus of the Constabulary Headquarters, but the 4th Armored Division became the nucleus for much of the rest. Division Headquarters became the 1st Constabulary Brigade, Combat Command A the Second Brigade and Combat Command B the Third Brigade.

Something new came into being — three Regimental Headquarters in each of the Brigades. And under the Regiments were battalion sized units called (after the Cavalry) Squadrons. All battalions of the 4th Armored, regardless of what they had been before became Squadrons and were scattered in all three Brigades. Tremendous planning and coordination had to be effected in the creation and organization of these units.

There were not enough battalions in the 4th to flesh out all the Regiments. So tank, field artillery, antiaircraft battalions were gathered throughout the Theater, and integrated with battalions of the 4th.

As all of this was taking place, each unit had to shuck its TO/E (tables of organization and equipment), and had to be equipped according to the Constabulary TO/E. Simultaneously every soldier turned his back on his specialty —tanker, infantryman, artilleryman, and each one trained hard in his new role — that of a soldier/policeman.

And almost at once — everywhere it seemed — on every vehicle, every sign, and on the shoulders of every trooper appeared the now famous yellow circle with the blue "C" crossed by the red bolt of lightning.

At the outset the mission seemed impossible, the challenges more than daunting. Amazingly, the mission was accomplished. The reason above all else — the Constabulary Troopers. The warriors of WW II, the "high pointers", had returned home. They were replaced by 18, 19, and 20 year old "kids" with limited military experience and service. These would become the backbone of the Constabulary. They faced a situation that had never existed before. They were confronted with unbelievable, unprecedented, demanding challenges. They were given tremendous responsibilities and the freedom to use their judgement and initiative, as they operated far and wide in small groups with, often, little guidance or supervision. These fine young Americans more than met the challenge, and insured the success of the United States Constabulary.

The United States Constabulary—the special, unique Corps sized unit formed in less than six months — from a concept to reality in six months — a most ambitious undertaking. A one time deal and it worked!

During its period of existence the United States Constabulary accomplished the United States Army's mission of insuring the success of the American occupation of Germany.

Albin F. Irzyk
Brig. Gen. USA (Ret)

Note: Lt. Col. Albin F. Irzyk was S-3 of the First Constabulary Brigade. He later commanded, in the 1960's, one of the former Constabulary Regiments. The 14th Armored Cavalry Regiment in Fulda.

Escort Duty by 820th Constabulary Police Company.

THE UNITED STATES CONSTABULARY
CHAPTER 1: "A BEGINNING"

The word "CONSTABULARY" was not new to the U.S. Army, having been first used in the Philippines in the early 1900's. The concept and design of the force that was to be needed to occupy both Germany and Austria was the subject of discussion as early as November 1944. The 15th U.S. Army undertook a study for the purpose of determining a basis for the troops and organizations required. As a result of this study, recommendations were made looking into the division of troops between "City Garrison and Frontier Command Troops". The Frontier Command were intended for control of personnel moving across the western borders of Germany by means of fixed posts, road blocks and motor patrols. On the 15th of April 1945 the 15th Army directed the establishment of the Frontier Command, which may be considered as the prototype of the U.S. Constabulary insofar as its methods of operation were concerned.

The term "CONSTABULARY" made its first appearance in September of 1945 in connection with the planning for the reorganization of the occupation forces in the European Theater. District Constabularies were formed in the Eastern and Western Military Districts, in the Berlin District and in the American Zone in Austria. Special markings first made their appearance at this time, a three inch high "DC" in yellow on helmets of the units so designated. The 15th Cavalry Group was designated as the District Constabulary for the Western Military District (7th U.S. Army), except the Bremen Sub-District which used on company from the 311th Infantry Regiment reorganized as a Cavalry Reconnaissance Troop (Mechanized) and under the command of the 15th Cavalry Group. On 30 November 1945, 3rd U.S. Army established a District Constabulary consisting of the 2nd and 6th Cavalry Groups with the following units; 2d and 42nd Cavalry Reconnaissance Squadrons (Mechanized) and the 6981st Provisional Rifle Company. On the 28th of November 1945, U.S. Forces attached the 4th Cavalry Group less one troop to the 83d Infantry Division and authorized it to employ this force as a District Constabulary. This Group comprised the 4th and 24th Cavalry Reconnaissance Squadrons (Mechanized), one troop of the 24th being attached to the Vienna Area Command as a District Constabulary for that area. Berlin District designated the 16th Cavalry Group with a Provisional Cavalry Reconnaissance Squadron (Mechanized) consisting of the Reconnaissance Troop, 78th Infantry Division, Anti-Tank Company, 310th Infantry Regiment as its District Constabulary.

Allgau Kaserne, Fussen, Germany Home of the 35th Constabulary Squadron.

Bucca and Cabral, Berlin 1946.

Troop Ship USAT George Washington, October 1946, destination America. Seasoned Troopers on the way home.

CHAPTER 2: "LET'S GET TO IT"

Traffic maze at the "Burg."

Judo class in the "Burg's" gym.

Review of the 2nd. Regiment troops by Gen. Ike Eisenhower, Munich, Oct. 10, 1946.

A preliminary memorandum was distributed to Staff Sections at Headquarters, U.S. Forces, European Theater on 3 November 1945 which set forth the tentative estimate of the strength of the "Constabulary", outlined the type of training, and the duties which it was expected to perform. This was followed on 24 November 1945 by a formal directive issued by Theater Headquarters which required the G-1, G-2, G-3, G-4 Divisions, the Office of Military Government, and the Theater Signal Officer to proceed with planning for the police type occupation. This directive defined the police type occupation as a method of controlling the population of an occupied territory by means of a "ZONE CONSTABULARY."

The mission of the "Zone Constabulary" was defined by the planning directive as that of maintaining general security in the United States occupied zones of Germany and Austria by means of an active patrol system is assistance to the military government by conducting routine motorized patrols, covering the entire occupied area, operating permanent and temporary road blocks, participating in large scale raids, cooperating with the German Police to back-up minor reprisal action and to act upon requests from the Counter Intelligence Corps, and to perform other duties as might be required in the execution of the mission.

Total strength of the "Zone Constabulary" previously estimated at 38,000, would be broken down completely and the prospective locations and areas of individual units delineated. The general organization of the units were to be along the line of mechanized cavalry. Practical recommendations for changes in the Table of Organization and Equipment (T/O&E) with particular regard to items of signal, mechanized and motorized equipment were to be made by the "District Constabulary".qqqDate of organization of the "Zone Constabulary" was tentatively set for 1 April 1946 and the date of operations as 1 July 1946. It was directed that a training program be planned to include pre operational training during the months of April, May and June 1946, and a plan for continuous training following the commencement of operations.

CHAPTER 3: "THE RIGHT MAN"

History was repeating itself again. After World War I the people clamored for the boys to come home. The Army had the feeling that every voter back home was shouting "Bring the boys home." Congress naturally, reacted to the desires of its constituents, and the War Department had no choice but to comply. In Europe, as relations with the Russians grew increasingly tense, American demobilization moved into high gear. But even that wasn't fast enough to satisfy either the Congress or the people at home. Military morale, slovenly dress and appearance plummeted. General Eisenhower, because he was more interested in working on a point system that provided the blueprint for who got to go home and when. He spent so much time with this that before long the Army had a couple of million troops roaming Europe, basically, as they pleased and getting into trouble. General Eisenhower was returned to the States to succeed General George C. Marshall as Chief of Staff, U.S. Army. He left behind Lieutenant General Joseph McNarney as American Military Commander in Europe.

At approximately and in the same time frame, Maj. Gen. Ernest N. Harmon's XXII Corps was moved from Czechoslovakia to Germany. General Harmon figured that its deactivation was close at hand so he asked for and received a leave to return to the United Staes for a short period of time to spend the holidays with his family. He returned to Europe shortly after the New Year for reassignment. When reporting to General McNarny he found the General had real trouble on his hands and was informed he was to become one of the troubleshooters. Discipline had sunk so low that some of the American troops had become a mob of brawling, catcalling GI's and had marched on General McNarny's Headquarters shouting "We want to go home"

General McNarny said to General Harmon, "Harmon, you are going to be head of the Constabulary." A more logical choice could not have been made. General Harmon had Commanded both the 1st and 2nd Armored Divisions, as well as the XXII Corps during the war. He was a gruff, no nonsense, spit and polish, individual and when he spoke you knew he was in command. His first reponse was, "Whats that" knowing of only one constabulary that he could recall was the Philippine Constabulary created after the Spanish-

Major General Ernest N. Harmon, Commanding General, United States Constabulary. Organizer, and first CG.

American War. General McNarny laid out the picture, he was to develop an elite force of about 35,000 men designated to exercise broad police powers over civilians and American military personnel. They would also set an example of soldierly dress and discipline. The deterioration in the behavior of the U.S. Military was so severe that the existing military police forces no longer could cope with it. The period of time to get the unit up and functioning was six months, 1 July 1946.

On 10 January 1946 Major General Ernest N. Harmon assumed command of the United States Zone Constabulary of which he, at that time, was the only member. He made his headquarters at Bad Tolz, which at the time was Third Army Headquarters. The task assigned was to organize a type of police force that would be large and mobile enough to maintain order in an area the size of Pennsylvania. The area was the home to sixteen million Germans, one-half million plus refugees, and hundreds of thousands of our own troops. This was the task and it was to be accomplished until a German Police force could be trained and become operational.

CHAPTER 4: "THE RIGHT MEN"

The Colors of the 35th Constabulary Squadron on Parade.

The "Right Man" then had the task of assembling a team of the "Right Men." Colonel Lawrence Dewey to be Operations Officer, Colonel Harley Maddox to be Chief of Staff, and then good fortune smiled on Harmon when Colonel J. H. Harwood, a former state police commissioner of Rhode Island joined the staff. Harwood handled the publication of the very comprehensive and easy to read "Troopers Handbook" that gave our prospective troopers a step-by-step guide to their duties. Colonel Dewey and General Harmon drew up, from scratch, the Constabulary's tables of organization and equipment.

The staff and General Harmon set out to design a distinctive uniform for the Constabulary that would clearly mark the troopers as members of an elite force. The uniform was to become an important symbol, as it bespoke a worthy soldier's pride in his appearance. Quite possibly, General Harmon was reacting to what he considered a preposterous decision by the War Department in assigning General James Doolittle the job of revising the Army's system of discipline and military courtesy. He considered General Doolittle a brave and highly decorated officer: but he had a long record as a careless and indifferent officer. General Harmon's ideas on discipline were honed after World War I , where he led one of the last cavalry charges, and afterwards where he had various assignments. He was also concerned with the morale of his troops remembering that in combat the men had little time to waste and that there due to the pressure maintained discipline at a high level . He was always stressing neatness, alertnesss, promptness, and swift, precise compliance with orders.

Lt. General Lucius D. Clay inspects his honor escort at Wiesbaden Airport.Troopers are from the 14th Squadron stationed at Darmstadt.

Headquarters Detachment Mess Personnel, 1948-1950.

General Prickett speaks with Pfc Otto Mann of Winnewod, Oklahoma.

General Maxwell D. Taylor inspecting an early border patrol section.

GEN HOBART R. GAY

CHAPTER 5: "THE UNIFORM"

The Constabulary uniform, considering it was designed from items readily available, was a very definite eye-catcher. The patch round in design with a cavalry yellow backround, blue border and a large "C" with a red lightning bolt slashing through the "C". These distinctive colors represented the cavalry, infantry, and artillery and were the backrounds the troopers had. The standard uniform of the day was modified, depending on availability of certain supplies. The boots were also different, smooth brown leather adapted from enlisted cavalry boots and called "Boots, Cavalry, Modified Lace Top. Many troopers also purchased "Paratroop Boots" because from the beginning the men assigned, and later the members of the Women's Army Corp took a great deal of pride in their appearance. A brilliant yellow scarf, Sam Browne leather, a helmet liner bearing the Constabulary insignia and stripped in yellow and blue. A blouse was also provided instead of the usual "Ike Jacket". This is when many troopers heard the words "Leather doesn.t shine it glistens." Many hours were spent polishing leather and brass, and even simonizing the helmet liner. The Constabulary colors and markings were applied to just about everything; General Harmon's train (Formerly Hermann Goering's), jeeps, motorcycles, M-8's, M-24's, _ Tons, 2 _ Tons and anything else that moved. The Constabulary would be noticed and they were, the populace never knew when or where the would see the "Blitz Polizei". The Germans gave the name and also some others, the Constabulary was respected by the Germans. Because of training and pride in their unit and themselves, they deported themselves with dignity were honest, firm and compassionate in the daily dealings doing a difficult assignment. Also, at this time and it should always be thought of as part of the uniform, the motto was devised "Mobility, Vigilance, Justice" and became a way of life for all the units of the Constabulary. The need to be fast moving was necessary to ensure that no part of the American Zone was without the police power it needed, to be ever alert for trouble, especially on the borders; and to be fair and impartial in dealing with everyone.

Officer, 2nd Cavalry, dress uniform   Trooper, field service uniform

UNITED STATES CONSTABULARY · 1950

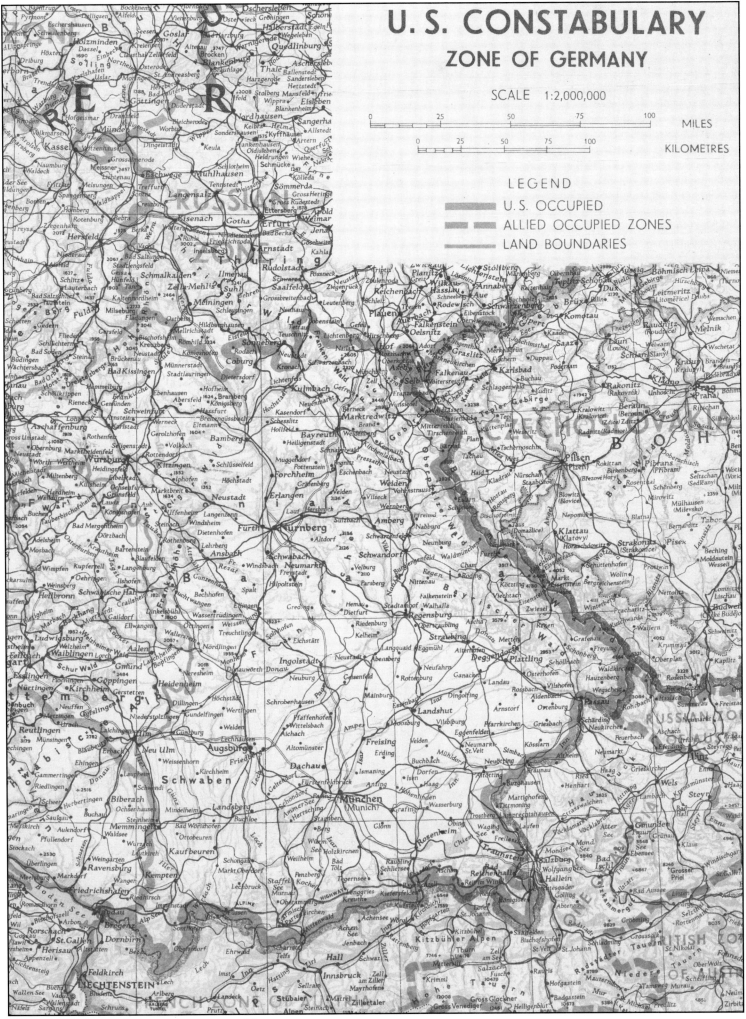

U. S. CONSTABULARY
ZONE OF GERMANY

SCALE 1:2,000,000

MILES

KILOMETRES

LEGEND
U.S. OCCUPIED
ALLIED OCCUPIED ZONES
LAND BOUNDARIES

U.S. Constabulary Troopers road map, US Zone of Germany.

CHAPTER 6: "TRAINING AND LOGISTICS"

In February 1946 staff plans were sufficiently advanced to allow the move to Bamberg and the first Headquarters of the Constabulary and to begin the training, so necessary to achieve goals that were now in place. In March 1946, at Sonthofen in the Bavarian hills, the Constabulary School was opened. An institution that soon became known, irreverently, as "The West Point with the Dehydrated Curriculum." One look at the spacious courtyard and to honor our fallen comrades from the Japanese War we named it "Corregidor Quadrangle."

The most difficult problem faced in the creation of the Constabulary, and one that was never really solved, was the availability of qualified men, and, once they were fully trained, to hang on to them. It goes without saying that the Constabulary was peculiarly dependent upon the good judgement, sensitivity, and the honesty of the individual trooper. It was not unusual for the police work to be carried on by two or three troopers operating away from their headquarters. They had to possess unusual powers of arrest, search, and seizure. The temptation was frequently presented for bribes, as Europe was fillied with desparate people willing to pay high prices for permission to cross borders illegally or to deal in black market goods. The idea was to attempt to attract and keep the more mature combat veterans. They were increasingly hard to come by as the rotation system swept them home for discharge and most of the replacements were 18 to 22 year old draftees with little or no experience. This was also true for competent junior officers.

Despite or in spite of these difficulties the Constabulary became operrational 1 July 1946 as scheduled. The American Zone was divided into three states, or "Lander", for administrative purposes. General Harmon tailored the commands to match the civilian divisions. Each state was the responsibility of a brigade, each brigade had three regiments, and each regiment had three squadrons. Every month Sonthofen graduated 650 students. It was extremely difficult to keep the ranks filled with properly trained men. As an example, in the first two months of operation the Command lost over 14,000 men, which was close to half of what was authorized and had to settle for green troops as their replacements.

Considering the emphasis the Constabulary placed on discipline and the traditional forms of military courtesy it soon was swimming against the tide. Other commanders found it difficult to resist pressures from their drafted enlisted men and the voters back in the United States to relax customary Army standards. It is important to remember that before 1946 Americans had no experience with a peacetime army that was not entirely composed of volunteers, and those mainly career men. Much of the restlessnessof the postwar draftees in Europe could be laid at the door of the soldier newspaper, The Stars and Stripes. The paper carried (The widely read) column called "The B Bag" to which the editors invited discontented enlisted men to submit their gripes about their commanders. This was fine for civilians but in the military it could wreak havoc. From the first days of Constabulary, General Harmon made it plain that the men under his command would not use "The B Bag", instead that the military code entitled each man to send his commanding officer any complaint he might have. Also, he let it be known that if the problem was with a superior, a letter to him personally and he would investigate. Only one trooper ever violated the ban on "B Bag". A man attached to the regiment in Karlsruhe and the punishment came swiftly as the General's schedule was rearranged. A parade formation was called the man was called front and center his insignia was removed and he was immediately dismissed from the Constabulary. As can be guessed this incident came to the attention of several American newsmen, probably tipped off by the Stars and Stripes. They went to General McNarny and asked what he intended to do about a situation in which one of his commanders was curbing the right of free speech. McNarny gave the a brief answer: "Harmon can run his own show." General McNarny never asked General Harmon for an explanation either privately or publically. The public vindication was appreciated. General Harmon received thirty to forty request a month and acted on all of them.

Constabulary Troopers acting as "Aggressors" during maneuvers 23 June 1948.

Most of the colonels we recruited to command our brigades and regiments were extraordinarily good. At one time a colonel came to General Harmon complaining about the handling of some administrative duties by some of unit commanders. Knowing that they had distinguished war records as combat leaders and that many of them had been promoted in the war, Harmon did not hesitate in saying; "If they were good enough to advance in wartime they can handle Constabulary units. It's up to you to set up classes, train them in the handling of their paperwork and administration. If you can't do it I'll get another colonel that can". The complainer took the hint and soon found himself to be a better teacher than he realized.

In researching items for this history the writer made the following discovery: The initial concept, the assignment of General Harmon, his choice of staff left a lasting and enduring presence of the first Commanding General that lasted, in many ways, to December 1952 when Constabulary was absorbed by Seventh Army. All those that were priveleged to wear the "Circle C" can be proud of the type of leadership we always enjoyed from our Constabulary Commasnding Generals. We were blessed with "LEADERS" and not the managers that later came along.

General Harmon set himself the task of visiting each of the twenty-seven squadrons at least once a month. Arrivals were carefully timed so that maximum attendance was at the stations. Honor Guards, and a surprisingly large number of civilians. The people in Munich referred to the arrival of the train as "The second coming." Subordinate commanders joined in the high ceremony of these inspections with gusto. One humerous event event happened, at precisely 8 A.M. the General disembarked from the train and in addition to the troops lined up for inspection there were seventeen tanks. After inspecting the men it became time for the tanks, they were shined and gleaming in the sunlight in their Constabulary blue and yellow. Sniffing the air, a tank is a marvelous weapon, but - to be blunt - it stinks. To prepare for the visit the tanks were driven to the spot drained of gasoline, painted inside and out and not quite ready for combat. Many red faces that day.

Signal Corps Radio SCR-399 consisting of PE-95 Power Unit on 1 ton trailer. The Radio is installed in a HO-17 which is mounted on a 2 1/2-Ton Truck.

Troops of the 42nd Constabulary Squadron on patrol.

General Clay, Military Government, inspecting Troops.

CHAPTER 7: "SOME PROBLEMS"

With time drawing near, preparations went into high gear. One major, and very pressing, problem was the number of highway accidents that claimed fifty to sixty lives in the American Zone. The roads were narrow and twisting in the towns and country side. But Germany had, and still has, one of the world's finest finest high speed highways better known as the *"The Autobahanen"*. It seemed to bring out the "Barney Oldfield" in any one that had access to a "Jeep". The "Jeep" was the great World War II workhorse but it certainly wasn't designed for high-speed highway travel. When accelerated beyond a reasonable speed they had a tendency to turn over and kill the occupants with great regularity. The Constabulary, without shame, established speed traps along the autobahns and speeders caught in them were severly punished. Mobile Summary Courts were organized under Constabulary auspices moved up and down the highways and dispensed speedy justice at the roadside. A man convicted of driving ten miles over the speed limit lost his driving permit on the spot, less than ten, his permit was annotated and if it happened again he lost his permit.

General Harmon personally stopped two soldiers driving 6X6's and racing. They had their permits pulled and it was probably a difficult explanation to their commanders because they had to send out replacement drivers. What good were the "Governors". those devices that were supposed to keep the vehicles legal? One could find a decent hill, start down, take it out of gear and then "Pop the clutch" and supposedly deactivate the governor without any visible outside signs of tampering. Harmon wanted his "Troopers" to get back home in one piece, and he was up to any program that would insure that.

Generally, the German civilians caused fewer problems than did the displaced persons and the American soldiers, the closing months brought a disturbing rise in incidents that evidenced a resurgence, or possibly a last gasp, of Nazism. In most cases they amounted to nothing more than the display of swastika flags and emblems, and the posting of derogatory notices. Of greater concern were reports of sabotage and attempted sabotage to communication and transport lines, unprovoked attacks on American military personnel, and several instances of wires, designed to decapitate the unwary, being strung across roads.

Part of Constabulary's responsibility was to build a new German police force orginized along the lines found in an American state police organization. With the able assistance of a German nobleman, Count von Henneberg, civilian police were soon

A "Speed Trap"

Patrolling the Autobahn, 74th Sq.

ready to go on the job. The activation of a civilian police force permitted the Constabulary to concentrate its efforts on border control and law enforcement among displaced persons and American servicemen. But we remained on call to work with the German police when needed. Working jointly with von Henneberg's force, the Constabulary devoted its most intensive antisubversion efforts to the investigation of a series of three, possibly four, simultaneous explosions on the night of 19 October 1946, in Stuttgart and Backnang. These explosions caused extreme damage to the town halls in the cities and to a jail in Stuttgart. A small fire in a displaced persons camp in Backnang which broke out at the same time was believed to have been ignited by a similar explosion. A month later agents of the Constabulary Counter-Intelligence Corps Detachment at Stuttgart organized a raid on several homes that had been under surveillance and arrested eleven person who subsequently confessed to the bombings. The leader of the group, Siegfried Kabus, was a former commander of Storm Troopers; most of the others said they had been leaders of the Hitler *Jugend*, the Nazi youth movement.

The principal weapon against criminal activity in the refugee camps was the lightning raid. Staged in cooperation with the U.N. Relief and Rehabilitation Administration (UNRRA), the agency responsible for the camps. November 1946 saw a raid on the D.P. camp at Bamberg. A seizure of $45,000 worth of morphine, codeine, and penicillin was made by 676 Troopers, the residents could not explain nor account satisfactorily for having. In addition, a large quantity of GI clothing and live ammunition was discovered. A total of eighty-four persons were turned over to military

government for trial on charges of black marketing and other offenses.

One of the most elaborate raids was conducted by units of the First Constabulary Brigade, though the results were not conclusive. Wildflecken had a D.P. camp which housed 15,000 persons, mostly from Poland. The rumor was that "Wildflecken is providing a hiding place for numerous fugitives, wanted for everything from theft to murder". In addition, the camp security officer in Landkreis Fulda told the authorities that he had seen men in the camp openly wearing sidearms in defiance of the prohibition against all firearms. More than 1600 Troopers entered the camp on the day of the raid, but the contraband found was not impressive; one carbine, a few pistols, several liquor stills, and very inconveniently, a bull, a number of pigs and several horses that appeared to belong to the neighboring farmers. Approximatey 500 person were detained but could only arrest and charge fifteen.

One of the many responsibilities of the Constabulary was the policing of 1,400 miles of international and interzonal boundries that ringed the American sector in Germany and the control of international travel through the Zone. Only two trains crossed through the American sector in 1946. One of them was the Orient Express, found in many detective and spy

novels, which ran from Paris to Istanbul; the other ran from London (With boat connections across the English Channel) to Switzerland. It was soon discovered that many of the trains' passengers were not properly documentated to enter the American Zone. The solution was simple, not by prohibiting transit passengers but by assigning Troopers to ride the trains as they passed through the sector. The Troopers job was to examine the papers of those that sought to board or alight at stops in Germany.

Another problem was that the American Zone was a powerful magnet to blackmarketeers and other criminals as well as to refugees simply seeking a better life. Illegal immigrants were a steady challenge to the Constabulary's honesty and patrolling skills. Between July and December operations the Constabulary turned back 26,000 entrants that lacked the proper papers. Another 22,000 person that did slip by illegally were apprehended by Troopers who intensively patrolled a ten-mile strip immediately inside the border.

The Constabulary operated 126 border posts General Harmon determined that these these posts would serve to command respect for the United States. Insisted that they be maintained with the same attention to appearance demanded in troopers' uniforms'. There was a blueprint furnished on how each

Checking Passes at the Lamarr Bridge near Garmisch near the Austrian Border are Germans and Americans working together.

Making it difficult for "Black Marketing" to be carried on. Random checks were the order of the day.

Checking for proper documentation to preclude unauthorized person from entering the American Zone.

Military Police of the 820th M.P.'s conduct a search for contraband.

Pfc William Rommer of Hoboken, N.J. checks identifications on a train between Austria and the American Sector.

Pfc Gerry Plakinas (L) and Sgt John G. Humm shown as they discover a suitcase of Morphine during "Operation Camel" in Bamberg. Narcotics, at that time, had a value of $45,000.

Border Checkpoint in operation.

post was to be laid out: there would be three small quonset huts, one for sleeping, one for eating and one to serve as an office. Neatly trimmed grass would surround the buildings and the Stars and Stripes would fly proudly from the flagpole in each installation.. One post failed to comply with orders, no flagpole and no grass. The squadron commander and unit commander were relieved immediately. The regimental commander was given forty-eight hours to comply with orders in every detail. Where did he find the sod, but grass was there and a flagpole and Harmon was happy.

The stickiest border problems the Constabulary encountered were along those sections facing areas under Communist control, the German States of Thuringia and Saxony, which were in the Soviet Zone and Czechoslovkia. Czech diplomats were a constant source of irritation and worry.

They maintained a constant stream of complaints to Constabulary Headquarters about Trooper "Discourtesy" which usually consisted on noithing more than pointing out to the diplomat that that no one, and this included diplomats, were allowed to bring prohibited items across the border.

CHAPTER 8: RUSSIAN RELATIONS

The worsening of U.S. - Soviet relations started early on and many difficulties were encountered in reaching solutions to relatively simple problems along the boundry between the Russian Zone and our American Zone. Apparently Moscow had clearly decided that Germany was to be the main scene of the struggle for power between the East and the West, with Moscow giving the orders. General Harmon while in Czechoslovakia the year before had very few problems with the Russians.

It took many weeks of negotiating before Harmon could meet with his opposite number, General Prosnick. Then when the conference was arrasnged Harmon met Prosnick at the Russian line and was taken to a house six miles inside the Russian Zone. Around the long conference table sat many unsmiling Russian officers. Proposals for straightening out our border difficulties were made. A number of incidents of promiscuous shootings on both sides. No one had as yet been hurt, but the situation was quite tense and real trouble could break out very easily. All these conversations were handled by interpretters. The interpreter for the Russian was a young, frowning major who it developed was a graduate of New York's City College. Prosnick agreed in principle to Harmon's proposals, but he had to get the final authority from his government. Finally the Russian Goverment agreed.

Harmon, on numerous occasions, invited Prosnick to visit him on the American side, but, with one polite excuse after another, he was never able to make it. The reason was discovered in a rather amusing way during Harmon's, second and last, meeting with Prosnick, when the major interpreter was called away to the phone. Suddenly those at the table were not only smiling but also speaking English. The major was the commissar and was Moscow's watchdog.

Initally American-Russian relations were excellent, the swapping of American cigarettes for Russian Vodka happened up and down the border. Then things changed and it became a game that could have become very serious. Not only the random shootings but the moving of border markers and signs. Americans were, in the beginning, very trusting and tney followed orders as to have far from markers they were to be. But, when the markers were moved further into the other zone, Americans were "Detained" and ransom paid. This ransom, usually, consisted of American cigarettes and/or whiskey.

Once we could talk and be friendly.

ABOVE: A Russian tank.

LEFT: Lt. Beckner, 25th Sq. inspecting rail shipment.

CHAPTER 9: HARMON LEAVES

In September the Constabulary was showing that it had reached a point where it was running very smoothly so Harmon decided to cut down his hours to more peacetime standards. He urged his wife to join him in Bamberg, shortly thereafter they moved to Heidelberg when the Third Army was transferred to Austria. Harmon then assumed Third Army responsibilities to go along with his other duties.

Their first anniversary of the operational phase was rapidly approaching. Harmon pointed out to the Pantagon that he had been overseas approaching five years and he requested an assignment in the United States. His request was granted by General Lucius Clay, who had succeded General McNary. Clay came to Harmon's final review of the Constabulary in Heidelberg and used the occasion to present Harmon with his fourth Distinguished Service Medal.

Travel plans were laid on and the Harmons' utilized the Constabulary train for the last time to Bremerhaven. Departure was set for 7:30 A.M. the streets of Heidelberg were lined with Germans bidding him a last farewell. This wholly spontaneous turnout was eloquent testimony that the Constabulary had and was doing its job of bringing impartial justice to Germany, and that the effort was appreciated. Harmon was Constabulary Commander from 10 January 1946 to 1 May 1947

Major General Withers A. Burress, Second CG

Major General I. D. White, Fourth Commanding General and the one that was responsible for implementing the change in mission. General White was responsible for the insignia of Armored Cavalry to be the M-26 Tank superimposed on crossed sabers.

CHAPTER 10: THE UNITS

Many organization provided units that made up the Constabulary, these units came mainly from the First Armored Division and the Fourth Armored Division. Also units from various Army and Corps were assigned. These units were not geared to accomplish the assignment but General Harmon had in appoximately three months after coming under Constabulary control, started and completed a training program, they became operational.

After the end of World War II there was a need for occupational forces. However, the need was for mechanized units as opposed to infantry. The need was really for a highly mobile security force with a flexible oreganization, and for this reason cavalry and armor units were not only available but more adaptable. The Constabulary initially consisted of the Headquarters, the 1st, 2nd, and 3rd Constabulary Brigades and the 1st, 2nd, 3rd, 4th, 5th, 6th, 10th, 11th, 14th, and

the 15th Constabulary Regiments. Most regiments had three squadrons. Also, each regiment had a light tank troop, a motorcycle platoon (25 Motorcycles), and a horse platoon (30 Horses). In addition the Constabulary School Squadron, the 97th Constabulary Signal Squadron, and the 820th Military Police Company were assigned. One should be aware the the 16th Cavalry Group was redesignated and reorganized as the 16th Constabulary Squadron and was assigned to the 4th Constabulary Regiment with duty station, Berlin. Women's Army Corps personnel were also assigned at this time and saw duty with Constabulary Headquarters and the various Constabulary Brigades. Also assigned at this time were the following support units: 12th Transportation, Truck Company, 19th Medical Detachment, 85th Car Company, 427th CIC Detachment, 7827th MI Company, 2nd Recoiless Rifle Company, 2nd Special

Services Company, and 114th Constabulary Band. Each regiment had an Army Ground Forces Band attached.

After the "Berlin Blockade" began the need became evident that additional troops was going to be needed. At this time the 70th, 74th, 517th, and 519th Armored Field Artillery Battalions were assigned. At approximately the same time the 370th, 371st, and 373rd Armored Infantry Battalion along with the 54th and 547th Combat Engineers, 73rd

Armored Ordnance Maintenance Battalion, 40th Ordnance Depot Company, 93rd Engineer Bridge Company and the 552nd Pontoon Bridge were assigned. The need was soon seen that a medical unit was needed and the 51st Armored Medical came under Constabulary Control. The 7732nd Field Artillery group and the 555th Engineer (C) Group were activated for control. .

RIGHT: Mounted troops of the 16th Constabulary Squadron Berlin.

BELOW: Mounted Troopers were used to patrol difficult border areas.

A view of the Burg Sonthofen.

Another view of the "Burg" with the Constabulary insignia on the tower.

Retreat Ceremony. Please note that prior to change in mission troopers wore the blouse, Sam Browne leather, distinctive helmets and 'Trooper Boots" (Leather does not shine leather glistens, as can be seen in this picture.

CASA CARCOCA, Garmish, Germany. An unusual building designed by two engineer officers, who used local labor and fellow soldiers. They almost finished before being caught. As the Army needed recreation for the troops, they decided to complete it. As the photos show, the roof could be opened for a view of the mountains and the dance floor could be retracted for ice shows.

nstein Castle, Füssen, Germany. Courtesy of Al Sallustio of D Trp, 42d Sqdn.

CHAPTER 11: UNITS AND LINEAGE

HEADQUARTERS UNITED STATES CONSTABULARY

Organized 23 July 1918 in the Regular Army as Headquarters VI Army Corps. Reconstituted 27 July 1944 as Headquarters VI Corps. Reorgaiized and redesignated 1 May 1946 as Headquarters, United States Constabulary. Inactivated 24 November 1950. Units that had been assigned to Constabulary then came under 7th Army Control, <u>BUT,</u> they continued to wear the Constabulary patch and had (US Constabulary) after unit designation until 15 December 1952. As of summer 1946 the Headquarters were located in Heidelberg. The following locations of the various units were also as of summer 1946.

Headquarters, First Constabulary Brigade

Organized 15 April 1941 as 4th Armored Division. The combat record of this division includes the following campaigns, Normandy, Northern France, Rhineland, Ardennes-Alsace and Central Europe. Redesignated Headquarters, First Constabulary Brigade 1 May 1946. Location was in Wiesbaden.

The Second Constabulary Brigade traces its lineage to two separate units as follows:

Headquarters, Second Constabulary Brigade
INITALLY ASSIGNED

Organized 8 January 1942 as Headquarters and Headquarters Detachment, Combat Command A, 4th Armored Division. Reorganized and redesignated Headquarters Company, Combat Command A, 4th Armored Division. Converted and redesignated Headquarters and Headquarters Troop, Second Constabulary Brigade 1 May 1946. Inactivated 20 May 1949 in Germany and returned to 4th Armored Division. Location was in Munich.

AND THEN ASSIGNED

Constituted 29 August 1917 in the Regular Army as Headquarters, Second Cavalry Brigade, as an element of the 15th Cavalry Division. Relieved from assignment 12 May 1918. Reconstituted 20 August 1921 as Headquarters and Headquarters Troop Second Cavalry Brigade an element of the 1st Cavalry Division. Converted and redesignated 20 May

1949 as Headquarters and Headquarters Troop, Second Constabulary Brigade. Inactivated 15 December 1951 in Germany. Location was also in Munich.

At the time of the deactivation of the 2nd Constabulary Brigade most, if not all, of the Constabulary units had been under its control.

Headquarters, Third Constabulary Brigade

Organized 8 January 1942 in the Regular Army as Headquarters and Headquarters Detachment, Combat Command B, 4th Armored Division. Reorganized as Headquarters and Headquarter Company, Combat Command B, 4th Armored Division. Converted and redesignated Headquarters and Headquarters Troop, United States Constabulary. Inactivated 20 September 1947 in Germany. Location was in Bad Cannstatt.

1st Constabulary Regiment

Activated 28 July 1943 as the 11th Tank Group which entered Europe and combat 31 July 1944. Came under Constabulary Control

Constabulary Headquarters Horse Platoon formerly the 2nd Regiment Horse Platoon. Under the leadership of T/Sgt Junius Leonard at the first Horse Show in Heidelberg. Many events were held 12 October 1947.

Picture taken at Camp Perry, Dotzheim (Wiesbaden), home of the First Constabulary Brigade Left to right : 1st Lt., John C., Burney Jr, Sgt Charles McCarthy, M/Sgt William Gibb, 1st Sgt James M. McMillian, Sgt Ollie Crenshaw and Sgt John Weisner. Picture on the wall is of Brig. Gen. Arthur Treadeau, CG 1st Constabulary Brigade. Of Note: Gibb is wearing "Bloused trousers with Boots Cavalry, Modified Lace Top."

French Troops cross the to meet Troopers coming from other direction.

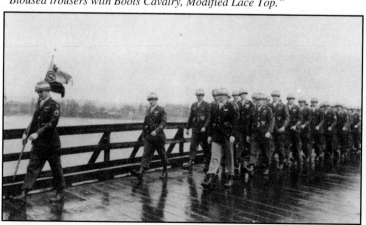

American Troops go to meet the French.

16 February 1946. Redesignated 1st Constabulary Regiment 1 May 1946. The Regiment was stationed at Rothweston and was a unit of the lst Constabulary Brigade. The Squadrons assigned and their Headquarters location were 11th Constabulary Squadron; Rothweston, 12th Constabulary Squadron; Neustadt, and the 91st Constabulary at Hersfeld. This was the first of many Constabulary units that could be said of "They were in the Fulda Gap."

2nd Constabulary Regiment

Constituted 23 May 1836 in the Regular Army as the 2nd Regiment of Dragoons. Redesignated 5 March 1843 as the 2nd Regiment of Riflemen and dismounted, Remounted and redesignated 2nd Regiment of Dragoons 4 April 1844. Redesignated 2nd Cavalry 3 August 1861. On 15 July 1942 personnel and equipment transferred to the 2nd Armored Regiment. Regiment broken up 22 December 1942 asnd its elements reorganized and redesignated as Headquarters and Headquarters Troop, 2nd Cavalry Group, Mechanized, and the 2nd and 42nd Cavalry Reconnaissance Squadrons, Mechanized. These units came under Constabulary control 1 April 1946 and were redesignated 1 May 1946 as the 2nd Constabulary Regiment, the 2nd Squadron became the 2nd Constabulary Squadron and the 42nd Squadron became the 42nd Constabulary Squadron. In addition the 66th Constabulary Squadron, formerly the 66th

Armored Field Artillery Battalion, was redesignated along with the other 2nd Regiment units. The Regiment was initially strationed at Freising, with the 2nd Squadron Headquarters at Langgries, the 42nd at Freising, and the 66th Squadron Headquarters at Degendorf. The Regiment and its Squadrons were under the 2nd Constabulary Brigade.

3rd Constabulary Regiment

The 3rd Constabulary Regiment was ioriginally Combat Command A, 1st Armored Division. The history of the 1st Armored Division is its history. It came under Constabulary Control 20 March 1946 and was redesignated 1 May 1946 as the 3rd Constabulary Regiment. The Regiment was stationed at

The 114th Anniversary 2nd Constabulary Regiment. Reviewing Lt. Gen Clarence Heubner CG, US Army, Europe; Col. Franklin Wing, Maj. Gen. Frank Milburn, Deputy CG US Army Europe and Maj. Gen. I. D. White, CG, US Constabulary. 9 May 1950.

Augsburg, 9 May 1950 2nd Constabulary Regiment celebrating 114th Anniversary.

T/Sgt Bill Lester, 3rd Constabulary Regiment, found the items displayed.

General Prickett presents Boxing Award to T/5 Joseph Motzi of the 3rd Constabulary Regiment.

The two man Russian Zonal Border Patrol at Morles, Germany, Pvt Gus Jones and T/5 Robert Pippin members of the 3rd Regiment Horse Platoon.

T-5 Francis Murray, 3rd Constabulary Regiment's Horse Platoon. Checks papers of a person crossing border.

Wetzlar and was also a unit of the Ist Constabulary Brigade. The Squadrons assigned and their headquarters locations were: 37th Constabulary Squadron at Weilberg, the 68th Squadron at Budingen, and the 81st Squadron at Fulda. The 81st Squadron had the honor of being one of the first units that would engage anyone coming down the "Fulda Gap"

4th Constabulary Regiment

The War Department authorized ten Constabulary Regiments for the occupation of Germany and Austria. Because of a different command structure the 4th Regiment came under the operational control and command of the Area Commander in Austria as was also the case with the 16th Squadron that came under Berlin Command. The "Tables of Organization and Equipment were the same as their counterparts in the US Zone and the various Constabulary Commanders were often at their locations.

Constituted 3 March 1855 in the Regular Army as the 1st Cavalry. Redesignated 3 August 1861 as the 4th Cavalry. Reorganized and redesignated 16 April 1942 as the 4th Cavalry, Mechanized. The Squadrons were also redesignated and reorganized the 1st Squadron became the 4th Cavalry Reconnaissance Squadron, Mechanized, and the 2nd Squadron as the 24th Cavalry Reconnaissance Squadron, Mechanized. Converted and redesignated 1 May 1946 as the 4th Constabulary Regiment, the Squadrons were also redesignated and reorganized as 4th Constabulary Squadron and the 24th Constabulary Squadron. At the same time the 16th Cavalry Group, Mechanized, wes redeignated, reorganized and assigned to the 4th Constabulary Regiment. The 4th Constabulary Regiment was inactivated 1 May 1949 at Salzburg, Austria, The 4th Constabulary Squadron was inactivated 1 April 1949 at Linz, Austria. The 24th Constabulary Squadron was relieved from assignment 4th Constabulary Regiment 1 April 1949 and was assigned to the United States Constabulary and replaced the 22nd Constabulary Squadron at Hersfeld. The 16th Constabulary Squadron in Berlin was relieved from assignment 4th Constabulary Regiment and assigned US Constabulary 1 February 1949.

Initial assignments of the 4th Constabulary Regiment and its Squadrons' Headquarters were as follows: 4th Constabulary Regiment, Linz. 4th Constabulary Squadron, Linz, 24th Constabulary Squadron, Bad Schallerbach. The 16th Constabulary Squadron, Berlin. The 16th Constabulary Squadron also added (Separate) to its designation. The 16th also wore three different distinctive unit insignia while stationed in Berlin, the 4th Regiment, Two Berlin Bears facing each other on the lapels and the 16th Regiment's.

The 16th Constabulary was inactivated 27 November 1950 at Grafenwohr. The 24th Constabulary Squadron was inactivated 15 December 1952 at Hersfeld, one of the last units that wore the "Circle C".

The 4th Cavalry had a distintive record in Viet Nam.

5th Constabulary Regiment

Activated 1 September 1942 as the 6th Tank Destroyer Group, began combat assignment in France as the XIII Corps antitank section. Came under Constabulary control and command 5 March 1946. Redesignated 5th Constabulary Regiment 1 May 1946 and under the 2nd Constabulary Brigade with the following Squadrons assigned 8th Constabulary Squadron, 35th Constabulary Squadron, and the 74th Constabulary Squadron.

Initial assignments of the 5th Constabulary Regiment and its Squadrons' Headquarters were as follows: 5th Constabulary Regiment, Augsburg, 8th Constabulary Squadron, Deggendorf, 35th Constabulary Squadron, Fussen, 74th Constabulary Squadron, Augsburg.

6th Constabulary Regiment

Constituted 4 May 1861 in the Regular Army as the 3rd Cavalry. Redesignated 3 August 1861 as the 6th Cavalry. Assigned to

ABOVE: 2nd. Cav. Regt., the old Dragoon's color guard.

LEFT: Outside the PX in Munich.

3rd Cavalry Division 15 August 1927. Reorganized and redesignated 21 July 1942 as the 6th Cavalry, Mechanized. Regiment broken up and its elements reorganized and redesignated as follows Regimental Headquarters became 6th Cavalry Group, 1st Squadron became 6th Cavalry Reconnaissance Squadron, Mechanized, and the 2nd Squadron as the 28th Cavalry Reconnaissance Squadron, Mechanized. These units were reorganized and redesignated 6th Constabulary Regiment and the 6th and 28th Constabulary Squadrons. The 6th Constabulary Regiment had the 53rd Constabulary Squadron assigned. The Regiment and its subordinate units were under the 3rd Constabulary Brigade.

Initial assignments of the 6th Constabulary Regiment aand its Squadrons' Headquarters were as follows: 6th Constabulary Regiment, Bayreuth, 6th Constabulary Squadron, Coburg, 28th Constabulary Squadron, Hof, and the 53rd Constabulary Squadron, Schwabach.

10th Constabulary Regiment

On 1 March 1943 the 10th Tank Group was organized. Redesignated 28 November 1943 as the 10th Armored Group. Committed into battle as CCR, 8th Armored Division. Came inder Constabulary control and command 15 February 1946. Redesignated 10th Constabulary Regiment 1 May 1946. The former 4th, 13th, and the 771st Tank Battalions became the 72nd Constabulary Squadron, the 13th Constabulary Squadron and the 71st Constabulary Squadron. All former Tank Battalions that were assigned to the 10th were

also redesignated Constabulary Squadron 1 May 1946. The 10th Regiment and its subordinate units were under the 3rd Constabulary Brigade.

Initial assignments of the 10th Constabulary Regiment and its Squadrons' Headquarters were as follows: 10th Constabulary Regiment, Moehringen, 13th Constabulary Squadron, Bayreuth, 71st Constabulary Squadron, Hessential and the 72nd Constabulary, Boeblingen.

11th Constabulary Regiment

Constituted 2 February 1901 in the Regular Army as the 11th Cavalry. Reorganized and redesignated 11th Cavalry Group, Mechanized 19 April 1943. Come under

Constabulary command and control 20 February 1946. Reorganized and redesignated 11th Constabulary Regiment 1 May 1946. The former 25th Cavalry Squadron, the 51st Armored Infantry Battalion, and the 94th Armored Field Artillery Battalion also were reorganized and redesignated as the 25th Constabulary Squadron, the 51st Constabulary Squadron and the 94th Constabulary Squadron on 1 May 1946. The 11th Regiment and its subordinate units were assigned to the 2nd Constabulary Brigade.

Initial assignments of the 11th Constabulary Regiment and its Squadrons' Headquarters were as follows: 11th Constabulary Regiment, Regensberg, 25th Constabulary Squadron, Straubin, 51st

A 10th Constabulary Regiment's Horse Mounted Trooper and an inquisitive horse.

Troops of the 10th Constabulary Regiment stand in review for Maj. Gen. Ernest Harmon at Wetzlar, Germany 28 May 1946.

Constabulary Squadron, Passau, 94th Constabulary Squadron, Weiden.

On 17 May 1972 the 11th Armored Cavalry Regiment relieved the 14th Armored Cavalry Regiment at Fulda. This assignment was after having spent time in combat in Viet Nam, and after having participated in numerous engagements.

14th Constabulary Regiment

Constituted 2 February 1901 in the Regular Army as the 14th Cavalry. Reorganized and redesignated 14th Cavalry Group, Mechanized 12 July 1943 with the 18th and 32nd Cavalry Reconnaissance Squadrons assigned. Entered combat 14 October 1944. Came under Constabulary control 20 February 1946 Reorganized and redesignated 14th Constabulary Regiment. Units assigned were the 10th Armored Infantry Battalion, the 22nd and 27th Armored Field Artillery Battalions. Which became the 10th, 22nd and 27th Constabulary Squadrons 1 May 1946. They were assigned to the 3rd Constabulary Brigade.

Initial assignments of the 14th Constabulary Regiment and its Squadrons'

Headquarters were as follows: the 14th Constabulary Regiment, Kitzigen, 10th Constabulary Squadron, Kitzigen, the 22nd Constabulary Squadron, Hammelberg and the 27th Squadron, Schweinfurt, .

15th Constabulary Regiment

Constituted 2 February 1901 in the Regular Army as the 15th Cavalry. Reorganized and redesignated 15th Cavalry, Mechanized 22 March 1942. Reorganized and redesignated 15th Cavalry Group, Mechanized ,12 March 1944 and its Squadrons redesignated as follows: 1st Squadron as the 15th Cavalry Reconnaissance Squadron, Mechanized and the 2nd Squadron as the 17th Cavalry Reconnaissance Squadron, Mechanized. Cam,e under Constabulary control and command 1 April 1946. Reorganized and redesignated 15th Constabulary Regiment 1 May 1946. The 15th Cavalry Reconnaissance Squadron mechanized became the 15th Constabulary Squadron. Assigned was the 1st Tank Battalion and the 14th Armored Infantry Battalion which became the 1st and 14th Constabulary Squadrons. The Regiment and its Squadrons

were assigned to the 1st Constabulary Brigade.

Initial Assignments of the 15th Constabulary Regiment and its Squadrons; Headquarters were as follows: 15th Constabulary Regiment, Weinham, 1st Constabulary Squadron, Karlsruhr, 14th Constabulary Squadron, Darmstadt and the 15th Constabulary Squadron, Mannheim.

NOTE: As of 16 November 1948 the 2nd Constabulary Regiment became the 2nd Armored Cavalry Regiment (US Constabulary). On 20 December 1948 the 6th and 14th Constabulary Regiments became the 6th Armored Cavalry Regiment (US Constabulary) and the 14th Armored Cavalry Regiment (US Constabulary).

The 15th Constabulary Squadron along with the 24th Constabulary Squadron carried the Constabulary designation until 15 December 1952. The three Regiments and their Battalions until 15 December 1952 had (US Constabulary) after their unit designations. They along with the 2nd, 6th, and 14th Armored Cavalry Regiments were considered the finest "Armored Force anywhere".

ABOVE LEFT: Review in honor of BG Fay B. Prickett, Commanding General First Constabulary Brigade With Colonel Edward Maloney, Commanding Officer 14th Constabulary Regiment. BG Prickett was soon to depart to Zone of Interior.

ABOVE RIGHT: Crossing the Rhine with dignity.

LEFT: Mex a Border Guard Dog. When the "Wall" came down later owned by Kevin Tevington.

CHAPTER 12: THE RUBBER MEETS THE ROAD

The various headquarters commands did what all headquarters are fond of doing. Passing information to some lonely outpost members, telling them, basically how to do their jobs. The majority of times they had no idea of what was going on and they were sure they could predict the outcome of any type encounter. The various G-4's and S-4's could not maintain the proper supply channels and this became more evident between the departure of General Harmon and the assuming of command by General I.D. White. Most probably this was due to the rapid rotation of troops and most of the depots were also having losses plus records were in disarray. The items, most probably in Europe but where. For example no frieze liners for either the field jacket or the parka troopers were issued; try sleeping in the frigid weather on the border in the "Summer Sleeping Bag", nothing but a blanket with a poplin cover. Troopers took this and did their jobs; and yes, during this same period Korea started so all the promotions for enlisted personnel became "Frozen". Promotions came when someone was reduced. This was the way it was; not everything was "Peaches and Cream".

Considering all of this the Constabulary Trooper not only did his job but did it, not only with distinction but, with attention to detail not usually found. This happened because in the line units were the officers and non-commissioned officers that cared. The individual Trooper had pride in himself or herself and had a tremendous amount of integrity.

Now let us get to the heart of the Constabulary the various Squadrons, Battalions and Companies the made up the United States Constabulary.

Constabulary School Squadron

Activated 15 October 1942 as a separate Coast Artillery Battalion; the 465th Anti-Aircraft Weapons Battalion (Mobile). Entered combat area 30 July 1944. Came under Constabulary control and command 14 February 1946. Redesignated Constabulary School Squadron 1 May 1946. Duty station Sonthofen. The first group of instructors were assembled at Bad Tolz on 23 January 1946 at this time General Harmon outlined the mission of the school, the subjects to be taught, the high standards that would be maintained and the problems that most likely to be encountered. On 23 January 1946 the initial group of instructors departed for Sonthofen to begin the initial work of organization, preparation of curricula, and the table of organization. The curriculum of the school was organized related subjects under six departments: The Department of Geopolitics; the Department of Police; The department of Tactics; The Department of Motor Transport; The Department of General Instruction; and The Department of Communications.

1st Constabulary Squadron

Constituted 2 March 1833 in the Regular Army as the *United States Regiment of Dragoons*. Redesignated 15 May 1836 as the 1st Regiment of Dragoons, Redesignated 3

ABOVE: Completed Uniden steel bridge constructed by CoC, 54th Ba. (C) to cross the 2nd Armored Cav. Regiment. T across the Danube River, Sept. 1950.

RIGHT: Keeping in touch with headquarters.

August 1861 as the 1st Cavalry. Reorganized and redesignated as 1st Cavalry, Mechanized 16 January 1933. Redesignated 1st Armored Regiment, Light. Regiment less the 2nd Battalion reorganized and redesignated 1st Tank Battalion. Converted and redesignated 1st Constabulary Squadron and assigned 15th Constabulary Regiment. Inactivated 20 January 1948.

The 1st Regiment had an illustrious history from the Mexican, Civil, Indian Wars plus the War with Spain, World War I and II. This unit as a Constabulary Squadron lived up to those that served before them and maintained the high morale and faithfullness that the unit was noted for.

2nd Constabulary Squadron

Redesignated 22 December 1943 from 1st Squadron, 2nd Cavalry Regiment, (Mechanized) to the 2nd Cavalry Reconnaissane Squadron (Mechanized). Came under Constabulary control and command 1 April 1946. Redesignated and reorganized 1 May 1946 as 2nd Constabulary Squadron.

4th Constabulary Squadron

On 21 December 1944 the 1st Squadron, 4th Cavalry Group was redesignated 4th Cavalry Reconnaissance Squadron (Mechanized). Arrived combat area, France, 6 June 1944. Had a distinguished tour of service culminating in being redesignated the 4th Constabulary Squadron and being one of two Constabulary Squadron assigned to US Forces Austria on 1 May 1946.

6th Constabulary Squadron

Formerly the 1st Squadron, 6th Cavalry Regiment redesignated 6th Cavalry Reconnaissance Squadron (Separate) on 1 January 1944. Arrived combat area (France) on 10 July 1944. Came under Constabulary control and command 1 April 1946. Redesignated 6th Constabulary Squadron 1 May 1946. Assigned to the 6th Constabulary Regiment.

8th Constabulary Squadron

Constituted 13 January 1941 in the Regular Army as the 3rd Battalion, 5th Armored Regiment (Light). Redesignated 8 May 1941 as the 3rd Battalion, 35th Armored Regiment. Reorganized and redesignated 8th Tank Battalion 10 September 1943.Came under Constabulary control and command 20 March 1946. Converted and redesignated the 8th Constabulary Squadron, and assigned to the 5th Constabulary Regiment 1 May 1946. Inactivated 11 December 1951.

10th Constabulary Squadron

Parent unit 51st Infantry Regiment organized 22 May 1917 from personnel from the 11th Infantry Regiment. Assigned to 4th Armored Division 13 January 1941. Redesignated 51st Armored Infantry Regiment 1 January 1942. 2nd Battalion, 51st Infantry Regiment redesignated 10th Armored Infantry Battalion 10 September 1943. Came under Constabulary control and command 25 February 1946. Redesignated 10th Constabulary Squadron 1 May 1946. Assigned to the 14th Constabulary Regiment.

Note: Along with the 373rd Armored Infantry Battalion the 10th's Distinctive Unit Insignia or Crest references the units assignment to the Constabulary.

11th, 12th and 14th Constabulary Squadrons

Constituted !1 January 1812 as the 11th Infantry Regiment. Consolidated between March and October 1815 with the 25th, 27th, 29th and 37th Infantry Regiments to form the 6th Infantry Regiment. Redesignated 6th Infantry Regiment (Armored) assigned to 1st Armored Division. Reorganized and redesignated 20 July 1944 as follows: 1st Battalion as the 6th Armored Infantry Battalion, 2nd Battalion as the 11th Armored Infantry Battalion and the 3rd Battalion as the 14th Armored Infantry Battalion. Relieved from 1st Armored Division 1 May 1946 and concurrently reorganized, converted, redesignated, and resaasigned as follows: 6th Armored Infantry Battalion as the 12th Constabulary Squadron, assigned to 1st Constabulary Regiment, 11th Armored Infantry Battalion as the

11th Constabulary Squadron, assigned to the 1st Constabulary Regiment and the 14th Armored Infantry Battalion, assigned to the 15th Constabulary Regiment.

11th and 12th Constabulary Squadrons inactivated 20 September 1947 at Fritzlar, Germany. The 14th Constabulary Squadron converted and redesignated 14th Armored Infantry Battalion 20 December 1948 and reassigned to 1st Armored Division.

13th Constabulary Squadron

Parent unit constituted 2 February 1901 in the Regular Army as the 13th Cavalry. Reorganized and redesignated as the 13th Armored Regiment (Light) and assigned to 1st Armored Division, 15 July 1940. Regiment broken up 20 July 1944. Regimental Headquarters and Headquarters Company, Service Company, and Companies D, E, and F,

reorganized and consolidated to form the 13th Tank Battalion. Came under Constabulary command and control 15 February 1946. Converted and redesignated 13th Constabulary Squadron 1 May 1946, and assigned to the 10th Constabulary Regiment. Inactivated 20 September 1947 at Coburg, Germany.

15th Constabulary Squadron

The 1st Squadron, 15th Cavalry Group was redesignated 15th Cavalry Reconnaissance Squadron on 12 March 1944. Arrived combat area 5 July 1944. Came under Constabulary command and control 1 April 1946. Redesignated 15th Constabulary Squadron 1 May 1946. The 15th Constabulary Squadron remained on the border continuously until 15 December 1952 when all remaining Constabulary units lost the Constabulary designation.

16th Constabulary Squadron

Constituted in the Regular Army as the 16th Cavalry, 1 July 1916. Rdesignated as the 16th Cavalry, Mechanized 15 June 1942. Regiment broken up 22 December 1943 and its elements reorganized and redesignated as follows: Headquarters and Headquarters Troop, 16th Cavalry, Mechanized redesignated Headquarters and Headquarters Troop, 16th Cavalry Group, Mechanized; 1st Squadron redesignated 16th Cavalry Reconnaissance Squadron, Mechanized; 2nd Squadron redesignated 19th Cavalry Reconnaissance Squadron, Mechanized. Attached to 78th Infantry Division during later part of World War II. 16th Cavalry Group, Mechanized redesignated 16th Constabulary Squadron and assigned to the 4th Constabulary Regiment 1 May 1946. Relieved from the 4th Constabulary Regiment and assigned to the United States Constabulary 1 February 1949. Inactivated 27 November 1950 at Grafenwohr, Germany.

The 16th Constabulary Squadron had many unusual happenings while stationed in Berlin. The Horse Platoon particapated in numerous "Four Power" horse shows. During the Berlin Blockade they stood eye to eye and never blinked.

22nd Constabulary Squadron

Constitued 18 May 1918 in the Regular Army as a Separate Battalion of Mountain Artillery. Reorganized and redesignated 1 July 1921 as the 1st Battalion, 22nd Field Artillery. Assigned to the 4th Division 23 July 1929, the 6th Division 7 December 1929. Reorganized and redesignated 13 January 1941 as the 22nd Field Artillery Battalion. Reorganized and redesignated as the 22nd Armored Field Artillery Battalion and assigned to the 4th Armored Division, 1 January 1942. Came under Constabulary command and control 25 February 1946. Converted and redesignated 1 May 1946 as the 22nd Constabulary Squadron and assigned to the 14th Constabulary Regiment. Inactivated 20 May 1949 at Hersfeld, Germany

25th Constabulary Squadron

Redesignated 10 September 1943 from 84th Reconnaissance Battalion to the 25th Cavalry Reconnaissance Squadron, Mechanized. Entered combat area 24 February 1945. Came under Constabulary command

and control 20 February 1946. Redesignated 25th Constabulary Squadron 1 May 1946. Assigned 11th Constabulary Regiment.

27th Constabulary Squadron

Constituted in the National Army as the 27th Field Artillery, 5 July 1918. Reconstituted in the Regular Army 24 March 1923. Redesignated as the 27th Field Artillery Battalion and assigned to the 1st Armored Division, 15 July 1940. Reorganized and redesignated as the 27th Armored Field Artillery Battalion, 1 January 1942. Came under Constabulary command and control 20 March 1946. Converted and resignated 27th Constabulary Squadron 1 May 1946. Assigned 14th Constabulary Regiment. Inactivated 20 December 1948 in Germany.

28th Constabulary Squadron

Formerly 2nd Squadron, 6th Cavalry Regiment on 1 January 1944 redesignated 28th Cavalry Reconnaissance Squadron (Mechanized). Entered combat area 10 July 1944. Came under Constabulary command and control 1 April 1946. Redesignated 28th Constabulary Squadron 1 May 1946. Assigned 6th Constabulary Regiment.

35th Constabulary Squadron

Constituted 13 January 1941 in the Regular Army as the 2nd Battalion, 5th Armored Regiment (Light) and assigned to the 4th Armored Division. Redesignated 8 May 1941 as 2nd Battalion, 35th Armored Regiment, and assigned to the 4th Armored Division. Consolidated 10 September 1943 with Regimental Headquarters reorganized and redesignated as the 35th Tank Battalion. Came under Constabulary control and command 5 March 1946. Converted and redesignated as the 35th Constabulary Squadron 1 May 1946. Assigned to the 5th Constabulary Regiment. Inactivated 20 September 1947 at Augsburg, Germany.

37th Constabulary Squadron

Constituted 13 January in the Regular Army as 1st Battalion, 37th Armored Regiment (Light) and assigned to the 4th Armored Division. Consolidated 10 September 1943 with Regimental Headquarters reorganized and redesignated 37th Tank Battalion. Came under Constabulary command and control 10 March 1946. Converted and redesignated 37th Constabulary Squadron, 1 May 1946 and assigned to the 3rd Constabulary Regiment. Inactivated 20 September 1947 at Weilburg, Germany.

42nd Constabulary Squadron

Redesignated 22 December 1943 from 2nd Squadron, 2nd Cavalry Regiment (Mechanized) to 42nd Reconnaissance Squadron (Mechanized) Entered combat area 20 July 1944. Came under Constabulary command and control 1 April 1946. Redesignated the 42nd Constabulary Squadron, 1 May 1946.

51st and 53rd Constabulary Squadrons

Parent unit constituted 15 May 1917 as the 51st Infantry Regiment After numerous assignments through the years with various Infantry Divisions assigned to 4th Armored Division, 13 January 1941. Redesignated 51st Armored Infantry Regiment, 1 January 1942. Regiment broken up and redesignated 10 September 1943 as follows: Regiment (Less 1st and 2nd Battalions) as 51st Armored Infantry Battalion; (1st Battalion as 53rd Armored Infantry Battalion; and the 2nd Battalion as the 10th Armored Infantry Battalion. The 51st came under Constabulary command and control 20 February 1946, the

53rd the 28 February 1946. Both units redesignated 1 May 1946 as the 51st Constabulary Squadron assigned to the 11th Constabulary Regiment and the 53rd Constabulary Squadron assigned to the 6th Constabulary Regiment. The 51st Constabulary Squadron was inactivated 20 December 1948.

66th Constabulary Squadron

Constituted in the Regular Army as thre 66th Field Artillery and assigned to the 4th Armored Division 16 December 1940. Reorganized and redesignated 1 January 1942 as the 66th Armored Field Artillery Battalion. Came under Constabulary control and command 25 February 1946. Reorganized and redesignated 66th Constabulary Squadron and assigned to 2nd Constabulary Regiment 1 May 1946. Inactivated 20 December 1948.

68th Constabulary Squadron

Constituted 1 October 1933 in the Regular Army as the 68th Field Artillery. Redesignated the 68th Field Artillery (Mechanized) 1 March 1940. Redesignated 68th Field Artillery (Armored) and assigned 1st Armored Division 15 July 1940. Reorganized and redesignated as the 68th Field Artiley Battalion 1 January 1942. Came under Constabulary command and control 20 March 1946. Converted and redesignated 68th Constabulary Squadron and assigned to the 3rd Constabulary Regiment. Relieved from the 3rd Constabulary and assigned to Headquarters, US Constabulary 24 September 1947. Relieved from Headquarters, US Constabulary and assigned to 2nd Constabulary Regiment 10 February 1948. Inactivated 20 December 1948.

71st Constabulary Squadron

Constituted 13 January 1941 in the Regular Army as the 1st Battalion, 5th Armored Regiment (Light) and assigned to the 4th Armored Division. Redesignated 8 May 1941 as 1st Battalion, 35th Armored Regiment. Relieved from the 4th Armored Division,

reorganized and redesignated 771st Tank Battalion. Came under Constabulary contro;l and command 25 April 1946. Reorganized and redesignated 71st Constabulary Squadron and assigned to 10th Constabulary Regiment 1 May 1946. Inactivated 20 September 1947 at Hessenthal, Germany.

72nd Constabulary Squadron

Constituted 2 Februarey 1901 as the 3rd Squadron, 13th Cavalry. Reorganized and redesignated as the 3rd Battalion, 13th Armored Regiment (Light), and assigned to the 1st Armored Division, 15 July 1940. Reorganized and redesignated as the 4th Tank Battalion 20 July 1944. Came under Constabulary control and command 25 Februasry 1946. Converted and redesignated 72nd Constabulary Squadron and assigned to the 10th Constabulary Regiment, 1 May 1946. Inactivated 20 September 1947 at Boeblingen, Germany.

74th Constabulary Squadron

Activated 15 November 1942 as a separate Coast Artillery Battalion the 474th Anti-Aircraft Artillery, Automatic Weapons Battalion (S-P). Redesignated from Coast Artillery 1 February 1943. Arrived combat area, France -ETO, 6 June 1944. Came under Constabulary command and control 20 March 1946. Converted and redesignated 74th Constabulary Squadron and assigned to the 5th Constabulary Regiment 1 May 1946.

81st Constabulary Squadron

Activated 12 May 1941 as the 1st Armored Reconnaissance Battalion. Arrived combat area North Africa 21 December 1942, Italy 28 October 1943 where redesignated 81st Cavalry Reconnaissance Squadron (Mechanized) 20 July 1944. Came under Constabulary control and command 20 March 1946. Redesignated 81st Constabulary Squadron assigned to the 3rd Constabulary Regiment 1 May 1946.

91st Constabulary Squadron

Constituted in the Regular Army as the 91st Field Artillery, 1 October 1933. On 1 January 1943 redesignated as the 91st Field Artillery Battalion and assigned 1st Armored Division. Came under Constabulary control and command 20 March 1946. Converted and redesignated 91st Constabulary Squadron and assigned to 1st Constabulary Regiment 1 May 1946. Inactivated 20 September 1947 at Hersfeld, Germany.

94th Constabulary Squadron

Constituted in the Regular Army 1 October 1933 as the 94th Field Artillery. Redesignated as the 94th Armored Field Artillery Battalion, 1 January 1942; and assigned to the 4th Armored Division on 6 January 1942. Came under Constabulary control and command 20 February 1946.

Converted and redesignated as the 94th Constabulary Squadron and assigned to the 11th Constabulary Regiment 1 May 1946. Relieved from the 11th Constabulary Regiment, converted and redesignated as the 94th Field Artillery Battalion, 6 January 1948.

97th Constabulary Signal Squadron

Constituted 10 April 1942 as the 97th Signal Battalion. After approximately two years of training by the "Cadre of eight officers and twenty-four enlisted men and with additional and also advanced training at various military schools. The intergrated Battalion was manned per the Table of Organization and Equipment by this time the Battalion was

already overseas and stationed at Waymouth, England. They departed for the combat area during the later part of 1944. The Battalion was assigned to the XVI Army Corps and had the difficult task of setting up communications for

all three US Armies, the 1st, the 3rd, and the 9th. Came under Constabulary control and command 1 March 1946. Redesignated 97th Constabulary Signal Battalion on 1 May 1945. Duty station for the Battalion was Boeblingen.

Additional units were assigned and came under the heading of "Special Troops" among them were:

Original Designation	Constabulary Designation	Constabulary Control & Command
85th QM Car Platoon	85th Constabulary Car Platoon	15 February 1946
114th Army Band	114th Constabulary Band	15 February 1946
820th MP Company	820th Constabulary MP Co.	18 February 1946

Playing of the National Anthem, 20 Sep 1947 Augsberg, Germany.

A BRIEF HISTORY OF THE
16TH CONSTABULARY SQUADRON (SEPARATE)
BERLIN, GERMANY

In accordance with the Yalta Agreement when Germany had been defeated by the Allies, the former Deutsches Reich was to be divided into four zones of occupation: USSR, USA, Great Britain and France. The great capitol city of Berlin was to be an enclave within the Soviet Zone, divided into three sectors and occupied by the USSR, UK, and USA. The Soviet Army fought a bitter battle to take Berlin from the still loyal, fanatical Nazi defenders. The Soviets occupied the city from early May, 1945 until July 4, 1945. On that date the US, UK and French forces were authorized to move into their assigned sectors of Berlin. (France was added to the occupation forces by agreement. A portion of the British Sector was assigned to them). The first major US unit assigned to occupy Berlin was the 2nd Armored Division, then followed by the 82nd Airborne Division, followed by the 78th Infantry Division, each for a period of approximately 90 days.

The first American troops in Berlin found the city in virtual total ruin; looted by the Soviets of all moveable machinery, supplies, transportation, and some key people. There was no electricity, heat, water, food and marginally adequate shelter. There were no tools for the inhabitants to dig themselves out and bury thousands of Berliners entombed by bricks and cement from the fallen buildings. The collapse of Berlin (before the war the fourth largest city in the world) was total. The suffering was further intensified by the fact that they were not allowed to leave and that no German from the outside could enter the city. There was no money since most of the banks were destroyed and there was no government to back a currency.

The U. S. Military found Berlin in dire need of medical services. Several US medical units immediately set up first aid stations in the Grunewald. They later moved to Berlin's Pathological Institute on Unter den Eichen in a 19th Century German complex of medical clinics. These clinics were later consolidated to become the 279th Station Hospital. US Quartermaster units brought with them tons of "U" rations and set up impromptu kitchens. These facilities were later taken over by US occupation units supplied with rations arriving daily via trucks and trains. Of special help was the US 36th Combat Engineer Battalion who brought to Berlin badly needed tools and motorized equipment to move rubble, begin reconstructing and repairing first their own and other units' billets and headquarters, then taking care of buildings soon to be occupied by various agencies of the new administration of the City of Berlin.

Accompanying the US 2nd Armored Division at the time of the initial quadripartite occupation was the 16th Cavalry Group composed of the 6th and 28th Cavalry Reconnaissance Squadrons. This light, armored, mobile force initiated patrols of the devastated US Sector and sustained contact with the British, French and Soviet forces. The 16th Cavalry Group remained in Berlin during the rapid rotation of the 82nd Airborne Division and 78th Infantry Division. However its effectiveness was diminished by the rapid departure of combat weary officers and men under the point system of US demobilization. By late 1945 the 78th Division created a temporary and provisional light armored, mobile force designated the 78th Infantry Division Provisional Squadron to patrol the devastated streets of Berlin in the American Sector to replace the 16th Cavalry Group.

After the unconditional surrender of all enemies of the US after V-J Day the vast US Army, Army Air Corps and Navy stationed in Western Europe underwent a precipitous deactivation and demobilization. Combat units that had defeated the Axis virtually dissolved as fast as air and sealift could move men (and some equipment) to the United States. It was clearly apparent that there would be an inadequate combat force remaining to execute the occupation of the large American zone of Germany. To fill this void a decision was made in Washington to create a unique provisional organization to be called the US Zone Constabulary. This 35,000 man force would assume the mission of overwatching the long border between the US and USSR zones of occupation, demonstrate the military presence of the US, and where necessary preserve law and order. Under the command of a dynamic, combat experienced Armor/Cavalry officer, MG Ernest N. Harmon, the US Zone Constabulary was created in the US occupation zone in early 1946.

Organization and equipment for the Constabulary Force was based on the Armored-Cavalry Squadrons and Groups that had played such an important role in the defeat of the German Wehrmacht. Concurrently the US Berlin Command requested and gained approval that one such Constabulary Squadron be activated in Berlin as a component of the US Occupation Force there. A skeleton planning staff was formed in early 1946. On May 1, 1946 the 16th CONSTABULARY SQUADRON (SEPARATE) was activated from the remaining units of the 78th Infantry Division Provisional Squadron and fleshed out from draftees called to duty in late 1945 to early 1946. Units designated were:

> 16th Cavalry Group Hq Hq, Hq & Sv Troop
> 78th Div. Cav. Recon. Trp A Troop
> Anti-Tank Co. 310th Inf. Regt B Troop
> Anti-Tank, Co. 309th Inf. Regt C Troop
> Cannon Co. 310th Inf. Regt D Troop
> Co. "A". 771 Tank Bn E Troop

The 16th Constabulary Squadron was not under the command of the US Zone Constabulary. It was one of the two combat units assigned to the Berlin Command. Tables of organization and equipment (TO&E) and most operational and administrative procedures were those quickly developed for the Zone Constabulary.

At the time of the activation informal arrangements were made to associate the 16th Constabulary with the 4th Cavalry Group, then part of the occupation force in Austria. There was no command relationship. However the 16th Squadron was authorized to wear the distinctive insignia (DI) of the distinguished 4th Cavalry Regiment (see insignias below).

The primary missions initially assigned to the 16th Constabulary Squadron (Separate) were:

1. To patrol at random all main streets of the American Sector thereby representing the presence and strength of the US occupation force in Berlin.

2. To patrol daily the autobahn from Berlin to Helmstedt (the place where the autobahn left the Soviet zone and entered the British occupation zone of Germany).

3. To support when needed the newly activated Berlin police force.

4. To support as needed special missions requiring US combat forces e.g., refugee control, CIC searches, and humanitarian relief.

5. To organize and equip a para-military German Civilian Guard Detachment assigned static security of selected US installations in Berlin.

6. To maintain on continuous 15 minute alert a force of one mechanized platoon to respond to any emergency in Berlin.

These missions were subsequently modified to accommodate the withdrawal of the USSR from the Berlin Allied Kommandatura (the Inter-Allied Authority in Berlin), the restoration of the Berlin Police Forte, the massive Berlin Airlift named "Operation Vittles", and numerous international crises impacting on Berlin. When the seven convicted NUREMBERG trial prisoners were brought to Spandau Prison in Berlin the 16th Constabulary Squadron furnished the first prison guard detachment. Every fourth month thereafter this duty was repeated in rotation among the four occupying nations. On occasion the entire squadron or parts thereof was deployed within Berlin to control actual or threatened civil disturbances. Such actions were normally in close collaboration with British and French occupation forces. Relations with the USSR rapidly deteriorated as opposing concepts for the occupation and restoration of Berlin emerged. An elite platoon of 30 horse mounted troopers performed innumerable ceremonial duties for all levels of US occupation forces in Berlin. On occasion the Horse Platoon made random mounted patrols of heavily wooded segments of the US-USSR sector boundary.

The 16th CONSTABULARY SQUADRON (SEPARATE) on May 1, 1946 wore the insignia of the parent Regiment, (Fig. 1) the 4th Cavalry Group. However at a later date they wore the Berlin Bears (Fig's 2). On February 1, 1949 the squadron was identified as heir to "Strike Hard", the 16th Cavalry Group insignia (Fig. 3).

All troopers assigned to the Constabulary proudly wore on the left shoulder sleeve of their uniform the new Constabulary insignia (shoulder patch). The organization of the Constabulary is symbolized in the basic disk of Cavalry yellow, bordered by a ring of Infantry blue. The dominant letter "C" for CONSTABULARY, also in Infantry blue, is pierced by a bolt of lightning in Artillery red. The lighting bolt is symbolic of speed and armored power inherent in the Constabulary and was especially appropriate for the 16th Constabulary Squadron whose origin is traced to the 78th Infantry Division, "The Lightning Division". After successfully completing a brief, special training program and meeting certain disciplinary standards members of the 16th Squadron were awarded a "flash" or "tab" reading "CONSTABULARY. worn 1/2 inch above the "Circle C". It was perpetuated by the "BERLIN" tab added to the US Army Europe shoulder patch worn by the Berlin Brigade until it was inactivated in 1994.

On activation the 16th Squadron was assigned a German Luftwaffe Anti-Aircraft Kaserne and an adjacent smaller Vehicular Repair and Maintenance Kaserne called "Emerick". Both had been severely damaged by repeated aerial bombardment and further abused by the first Soviet occupation force. No utilities functioned. Bomb craters pot-marked the entire area. Concurrent with the first occupational mission was a self-help reconstruction project. US Army engineers (mentioned earlier) plus civilian contractors subsequently took over the rehabilitation. These Kasernes were in the area of Berlin called Lankwitz, part of the bezirke (borough) of Tempelhof.

US Berlin Command selected the name "Patton Barracks" for the Squadron's Kaserne complex. Shortly thereafter headquarters US European Command named a major installation in the US Zone of Occupation after Gen. George S. Patton Jr. of WWII fame. The 16th Constabulary garrison was re-named "Oliver Barracks" in honor of LTC Francis McD. Oliver, a distinguished Cavalry Reconnaissance Squadron commander killed in action in France in early August 1944. In 1948 the Squadron was moved to a larger, more modern US complex named "McNair Barracks", formerly a major headquarters and electronics manufacturing plant of Telefunken, one of Germany's larger firms.

In addition to the 16th Constabulary Squadron there was a battalion (subsequently a regiment) of Infantry stationed in Berlin. The two combat units plus the entire Berlin complex were supported by the traditional US Army combat support and service support units of varying size. These included battalions, companies, detachments of: Signal Corps, Corps of Engineers, Military Police, Ordnance, Quartermaster, Transportation, Medical, Army. Security Agency, Counter Intelligence, Adjutant General, Judge Advocate General, Tempelhof Airfield was a US operational air base under an independent Army Air Corps commander.

The Squadron maintained close operational contact with the infantry unit and was dependent on the day-to-day service support of these technical service units. A small aviation detachment of light (observation) aircraft was part of the 16th Constabulary Squadron. The total Army occupation force in Berlin was assigned to the US Army Berlin Command headed by a major general. Also in Berlin superior to Berlin Command was the office of Military Government for Germany (US), "OMGUS", under Gen. Lucius D. Clay. By early 1947 there was a growing community of several thousand American spouses and children of American servicemen living in Berlin. Security and support. for these dependents was part of the mission shared by the 16th Constabulary Squadron.

Patrols of the US sector streets of Berlin were usually accomplished by a team of one M-8 armored car and two 1/4 ton trucks ("Jeeps"), seven soldiers commanded by an NCO. On occasion an officer commanded; the strength of the patrol was increased; occasionally decreased to one or two "Jeeps". Routes and timing were continuously varied. The duration of a patrol averaged about four hours. Night patrols were less frequent than in daylight. A basic load of ammunition accompanied each patrol; each maintained continuous contact by radio with the squadron operations center. Fraternization with native Berliners was prohibited; courtesy and emergency assistance were required. Some sample actions by a patrol were:

a. Report, investigate a traffic accident.

b. Transportation of an ill or injured German to a hospital.

c. Pursuit of a fleeing criminal.

d. Escort; assistance to a Berlin policeman or police patrol.

e. Apprehension of intoxicated Allied personnel.

f. Break up street fights.

g. Dispersal of unauthorized crowds.

With occasional exceptions 16th Constabulary patrols were well received. Violent incidents decreased as Berlin began its tortuous recovery.

In addition to metropolitan street patrols the 16th Constabulary Squadron patrolled the 110,-mile autobahn eastward to the British zone several times a week. Composition of the patrol varied: normally one armored car and two "Jeeps". British and French mechanized patrols alternated with the US Army in this long, usually boring drive through the Soviet zone of occupation. Incidents of harassment by Soviet military forces varied in frequency and seriousness. In late 1948 the USSR attempted to isolate the American, British and French forces in Berlin by blocking all roads, rail and canal routes into the city. This resulted in the famous Berlin Airlift. The 16th Constabulary Squadron's major effort switched to supervising the rapid unloading of cargo from aircraft arriving at Tempelhof Airfield 24 hours every flyable day. Additionally the Squadron maintained static security over the stored fuel, food, medical supplies, clothing, etc. stocks at Tempelhof before they were distributed to local ration points. Prior to the task being assigned to a US MP Battalion the 16th Constabulary Squadron provided security guards aboard the US railroad train between Hamburg and Berlin/Bed in-Hamburg. This procedure was considered necessary to preclude interference by Soviet forces as the train passed through the Soviet zone of occupation. Harassment (usually creating delays) occurred sporadically.

As the western (Allied) sectors of Berlin recovered, rebuilt, and created traditional government functions the missions of the 16th Constabulary Squadron were reduced.

"E" Troop, the Squadron's light tank unit, was transferred out of Berlin in 1948.

The Squadron Horse Platoon survived as one of the last mounted units of the US Army. It was absorbed into the 579th Military Police Battalion in late 1950 and was inactivated in 1953.

The 16th Constabulary Squadron (Separate) was deactivated on November 27, 1950 at Grafenwohr, Germany. Most remaining missions were assumed by a re-enforced MP Battalion. The majority of the 16th Constabulary Squadron's officers and enlisted personnel were absorbed into the 6th Infantry Regiment which was newly reactivated in Berlin. At the time of deactivation many official and unofficial commendations were written and spoken about the four and one-half years of exemplary performance of duties under the US Zone Constabulary credo of "Mobility, Vigilance and Justice". The forty-nine years of US occupation of Berlin ended on September 8, 1994. The long, sometimes critical, always sensitive force that performed that mission was modeled on the standards of excellence of the first mobile, light armored 16th CONSTABULARY SQUADRON (SEPARATE).

Research and original text written by
Al Solosky, Headquarters, 16th SQDN S-3
Reviewed by Samuel McC. Goodwin
Brig. Gen. US Army, Ret
First 16th Squadron Commander

Horse Plt., 16th Constabulary Sq., on parade, Berlin, July 1947.

Captain Victor Shantz, CO, 15th Constabulary Regiment's Horse Platton, 7 June 1948.

May Day, 1 May 1950. Berlin's 16th Squadron usual duty on May Day.

CHAPTER 13: MAJOR REORGANIZATION

After the advent of the Berlin Blockade the mission of the United States Constabulary changed. Additional units were added to what remained of the Constabulary. At this time it would be prudent to say that instead of lightly armed and equiped units patroling to maintain control of borders the Constabulary became a lean, mean, fighting machine, ready to provide an armored force without equal in the free world. Added units were of Infantry, Artillery, Ordnance, Medical, Combat Engineers, and Counter Intelligence Corps and Military Intelligence Detachments. Many of the units lack having a history listed here. The reason, many of the museums and libraries do not have any information on units. The Constabulary Association has attempted to provide information on Constabulary Units where possible to these museums and libraries.

7732nd Field Artillery Group

The 7732nd Field Artillery Group, located at Sonthofen, was organized in May 1948 to supervise the training of and to exercise control of and to exercise general supply contro;l supervision of the United States Constabulary field artillery units. It was in effect the Artillery Section of Constabulary Headquarters.

70th Armored Field Artillery Battalion

Constituted 16 December 1940 in the Regular Army as the 70th Field Artilllery Battalion. Inactivated 9 December 1945. Activated 15 December 1948 at Fussen, Germay and assigned US Constabulary. Reorganized and redesignated 15 October 1951 as the 70th Armored Field Artillery Battalion.

74th Armored Field Artillery Battalion

Constituted 13 January 1941 in the Regular Army as the 74th Field Artillery Battalion. Inactivated 31 October 1946. Activated 15 December 1948 at Landshut, Germany and assigned US Constabulary. Reorganized and redesignated 15 October 1951 as the 74th Armored Field Artillery Battalion.

517th Armored Field Artillery Battalion

Constituted 5 July 1918 in the National Army as the 1st Battalion, 35th Field Artillery and assigned to the 12th Division. Demobilized 8 February 1919. Reconstituted 22 July 1929 in the Regular Army. Activated 10 February 1941. Reorganized and redesignated on 1 March 1943 as the 976th Field Artillery Battalion. Inactivated 6 March 1946. Redesignated as the 517th Field Artillery Battalion, 5 February 1947. Activated 20 May 1949 at Sonthofen, Germany and assigned US Constabulary. Reorganized and redesignated 10 September 1951 as the 517th Armored Field Artillery Battalion. Inactivated 20 May 1955 at Budingen, Germany.

519th Armored Field Artillery Battalion

Constituted 5 July 1918 in the National Army as the 2nd Battalion, 35th Field Artillery and assigned to the 12th Division. Demobilized 8 February 1919. Reconstituted 22 July 1929 in the Regular Army. Activated 10 February 1941. Reorganized and redesignated 1 March 1943 as the 977th Field Artillery Battalion. Inactivated 8 January 1946. Redesignated 519th Field Artillery Battalion 5 February 1947. Activated 20 May 1949 and assigned US Constabulary 20 May 1949 at Sonthofen, Germany.

370th Armored Infantry Battalion

Activated 15 October 1942 and assigned to the 92nd Infantry Division. Participated in the Aisne-Marne and Oise-Aisne operations in World War I, and the occupation of the St, Mihiel and Aire Sectors. Arrived combat area, Italy, 24 July 1944. Saw action in the Rome-Arno, North Appenines and Po Valley campaigns. Inactivated 27 November 1945. Reactivated 5 October 1948 as the 370th Armored Infantry Battalion, Kitzigen, Germany and assigned to US Constabulary Note: The Distinctive Unit Insignia of the 371st includes the circled black buffalo which was the 92nd Infantry Division's shoulder patch.

371st Armored Infantry Battalion

Activated 15 October 1942 and assigned to the 92nd Infantry Division. Arrived combat area, Italy, 18 October 1944. Saw action in the Rome-Arno, North Appennines and PO Valley Valley campaigns. This unit decorated by two foreign goverments, Italy and France.

Reactivated and redesignated as the 371st Armored Infantry Battaliion, Kitzigen, Germany and assigned to the US Constabulary, 5 October 1948.

373rd Armored Infantry Battalion

Constituted 9 September 1948 as the 373rd Infantry Battalion. Actvated 5 October 1948 at Kitzigen, Germany and assigned to US Constabulary with duty station at Giessen, Germany. Redesignated 373rd Armored Infantry Battal;ion, 19 July 1951.

Note: The blue shield with the Constabulary colors golden orange and black on the fess indicate the attachment of a basically Infantry unit.

51st Armored Medical Battalion

The 51st Armored Medical Battalion, located in Boeblingen, was activated at Fort George C. Meade, Maryland in 1940. In World War II the unit participated in the assault landing on Sicily, and the Naples -Foggia, Rome-Arno, Tunisia, and Algeria-French Morocco Campaigns.

7767th Constabulary Tank Training Center

The 7767th Constabulary Tank Training Center was established at Vislseck in the Grafenwohr area, in the fall of 1948. The primary mission of the school was to make each student a qualified tank gunner and driver. To give each student a complete asnd well rounded backround necessary to make him a better tank crewman, The courses included gunnery, driving, maintenance, tactics, and communications.

555th Engineer Combat Group

The 555th Engineer Group was located at Russelsheim. The commanding officer of the Group was responsible for the planning and supervision of administrative, tactical and technical training and operations of the US Constabulary engineer units. Attached to US Constabulary on 3 March 1950. 54th Engineer Combat Battalion

The parent unit of the 54th Engineer Combat Battalion was the 42d Engineer Battalion, which was constituted 2 December 1917. The Battalion participated in the following campaigns: Algeria-French Morocco, Tunisia, Sicily, Normandy, Northern France, Ardennes-Alsace, Central Europe, and the Rhineland campaigns of World War II.. The unit was assigned to the US Constabulary September 1948 as the 8th Engineer Combat Battalion and later redesignated the 54th Engineer Combat Battalion and was stationed in Boeblingen, Germany.

CHAPTER 14: "THE GENERALS"

"There wasn't a bad one in the lot" so said a Trooper that spent the entire time the US Constabulary was in existence in one of the line units. As has been said before most all of the Constabulary Officers were "Leaders" and this went also for the General Officers.

Commanding Generals and their times of command:

Major General Ernest N. Harmon	10 January 1946 to 1 May 1947
Major General Withers A. Burress	1 May 1947 to 5 April 1948
Major General Louis A. Craig	5 April 1948 to 21 May 1948
Major General I. D . White	21 May 1948 to 7 March 1951

Deputy Commanding Generals:

Major General William Schmidt	Brigadier General Gallagher
Brigadier General E. Collier	Brigadier General Edmund B. Seebree

During January 1946 Brigadier General Halley G. Maddox was appointed Chief of Staff of the Constabulary Planning Group.

BRIGADE COMMANDING GENERALS
First Constabulary Brigade
Brigadier General F.B. Prickett
Brigadier General Arthur G. Trudeau
Brigadier General George W. Reed Jr.

Second Constabulary Brigade
Brigadier General Hobart R. Gay
Brigadier General Edmund B. Sebree
Brigadier General Bruce C. Clark

Third Constabulary Brigade
Brigadier General Thomas Harrold
Brigadier General Bruce C. Clark

Notes: General Harmon became the President of Norwich University. He brought about a remarkable change not only to the staff but also to the physical plant. He found that in addition to everything else, he was also one thing that was very necessary as a university president the knack to raise money and start foundations. General Burress was awarded his third star and became First Army Commander.

General White insisted upon and had the M-26 Tank superimposed on the Cavalry Sabers for the branch insignia for Armor. General White ended his career as Commander-in-Chief, United States Army, Pacific.

General Clark was the moving force behind the Constabulary NCO Academy which later became the 7th Army NCO Academy.

Troopers of the 27th Constabulary Squadron. Fifth from the right is George Reimler of St. Mary's, Kansas and a member of Outpost #8.

T/4 Albert Bathon, radio communication, Ottobeuren, Germany, June 1946.

Sgt. Harold Green of the 15th Constabulary Regiment's Motorcycle Platoon.

A Trooper of the 16th Constabulary Squadrons Horse Platoon in the Grunewald Forest.

CHAPTER 15: EQUIPMENT PECULIAR TO THE U.S. CONSTABULARY

No one that that served in the early days of the Constabulary can forget that vehicle that was so associated with patrolling, and with the "Show of Force" that was essential to the mission of the Constabulary as the M-8 Armored Car.

General Harmon had definite ideas as to what this vehicle should look like and how it was to be maintained. Painting was of primary importance. The vehicle had a high gloss olive drab body. The markings were as follows: a three inch blue strip sandwiched between two each three inch stripes. Between the front and second set of wheels were the USA numbers (USA 1234567) on both sides. On each side of the turret were thirty inch Constabulary insignia. Front of vehicle also a thirty inch Constabulary insignia, a yellow circular bridge marker with the black numeral seven (Load limit), unit designations were on a light tan rectangle with O.D. letters and numbers, right side Regiment and Squadron and the left side Troop and vehicle number on the rear the same markings with regiment and squadron on the left side and troop and vehicle number in the right side as you look at the back of the vehicle but there was no special background. In addition to the M-8's there were M-24 and M-26 Tanks and they were painted in many ways similar to the M-8's, There were many instances that American and Russian Tanks were eyeball to eyeball. Especially in Berlin when the "Blockade" started. The Troopers of the 16th Constabulary Squadron met the Russians on their terms and they did not blink. At no time did any Constabulary unit, either in the Zone or in Berlin, give an inch. This page in American History has not been told and the men not only of the Constabulary but also of the First Infantry Division deserve the recognition and rewards for a "Job Well Done" Another means of patrolling was the "Harley 45" a motorcycle with all the Constabulary markings, on fenders, and tank.

We can not forget the "Horse". That means of getting into rather difficult places when on border patrol. There were many areas where M-8's, motorcycles, and or jeeps could not travel. One thing to note during the early days of the Constabulary there were multinational horse shows one particular one was held in Berlin and was a Quad Meet. Another vehicle to be considered that was somewhat different was the "Airplane" initially there had been assigned "Light Observation Aircraft, L-4's and L-5's" later on more modern versions were included on the Tables of Organization and Equipment.

There were the usual assortment of three quarters, two and one halves, five tons, tractors with trailers, and at times many of the units even had half tracks, some even with quad fifties that must have come from some anti-aircraft units. Some of us in the "Fulda Gap" area thought this would be an extremely helpful addition to what we had on the border.

Communications equipment went from EE-8 Telephones to SCR-399 Radios (Signal Corps Radio mounted on a two and one half truck in a Shelter HO-17 and pulling a trailer with a PE-95 Power Unit). Switchboards, both BD-71 and BD-96, repeating coils and any type of equipment that would allow units to communicate up and down the chain of command. Not to be left out were the Signal Corps Radios that were mounted in the jeeps, three quarter ton and the armored vehicles Signal Corps Radios such as the voice radios SCR-300's, SCR-508 and SCR-528's for voice communications and the SCR-506 for CW or Continuous Wave (Morse Code). Message Centers in addition to delivering messages had the ability to code or encode messages using Code Machine M-209 or One Time Message Pads.

The one thing that really stood out was the special equipment that early on the Constabulary Trooper wore. Instead of an "Ike Jacket" each Troopers wore the old brass button blouse, Sam Browne leather equipment, Boots, Cavalry, Modified Lace Top, Yellow Scarf, and a specially painted and highly polished Constabulary Helmet Liner. Two things should be noted at this time "Leather Does Not Shine, Leather Glistens and all Constabulary Helmet Liner needed constant Simonizing". On patrol, on pass or in the Kaserne the Constabulary Trooper was expected to be an example.

The Trooper was not a number, the Trooper was a very necessary tool in bringing about the changes that were necessary in big picture. When patrols came in or shifts on duty were over there were always food waiting, sometimes only hot coffee and sandwiches but there was a cook and others that did not think it was an imposition to be there at midnight or later. Troopers did look out for each other. Squads, platoons, and Troops were family and it was believed that they lived up to what General Harmon said just before 1 July 1946 "They will know us by the integrity of our Troopers"

Aircraft of the United States Constabulary.

Pfc. Chris Bucksmith, second from right, HQ co., 1st Bn., 6th A/C, mortar platoon, 81mm 1950.

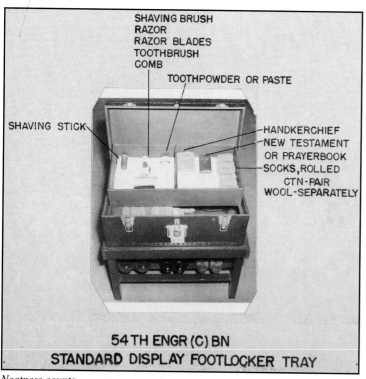

SHAVING BRUSH
RAZOR
RAZOR BLADES
TOOTHBRUSH
COMB

TOOTHPOWDER OR PASTE

SHAVING STICK

HANDKERCHIEF
NEW TESTAMENT
OR PRAYERBOOK
SOCKS, ROLLED
CTN - PAIR
WOOL - SEPARATELY

54 TH ENGR (C) BN
STANDARD DISPLAY FOOTLOCKER TRAY

SWEATER, WOOL KNIT
WOOL UNDERSHIRT
WOOL DRAWERS
UNDERSHIRT, CTN
SHORTS, CTN
TOWEL, BATH
TOWEL, FACE
WASH CLOTH

REAR OF LOCKER
GLOVES & ATHLETIC
EQUIPMENT
MISC. PERSONAL ITEMS

O'SHOES OR
SHOEPACS
LOWQUARTERS
ATHLETIC SHOES

54 TH ENGR (C) BN
STANDARD DISPLAY FOOTLOCKER
W/O TRAY

Neatness counts.

Motor Pool. SSgt. Joe Tokach, Ottobeuren, German, June 1946.

An M-24 of the 37th Constabulary Squadron.

Aircraft of the United States Constabulary.

LEFT: The ever faithful Jeep.

Sgt. Jones and Cpl. Ross on live fire.

An M-8 of the 37th Constabulary Squadron.

D Co., 2nd Bn, 2nd ACR, on a field excercise.

16th Constabulary Sq., M-8's on parade, Berlin, 1949.

CHAPTER 16: TRAINING PROGRAMS

Beginning on 1 April 1946 the Constabulary began its unit training program with the following objectives:

1. Training of all units that were detailed or about to be detailed to the Constabulary except those units assigned or detailed to the District Constabulary. Training was culminate with on the job training during the period 1 to 30 June 1946.

2. Additional training for District Constabulary for attainment of the highest standards of performance of Constabulary duties.

3. Achievement by each individual of the highest standards of discipline, appearance, and military and professional qualifications that would enable each trooper to act as a well oiled part of the Constabulary mission.

4. Development of a high esprit de corps in keeping with the establishment of the United States Constabulary as an elite body of soldiery.

5. Development of leaders and their indoctrination.

The period of eight weeks from 1 April to 31 May 1946 was designed to prepare the Constabulary for its mission of on-the-job training. Because of the rotation of many troops back to the Zone of Interior, Regimental Commanders were assessing the personnel available to them and tailoring training to the quality of what he had. The first four weeks were to be used for basic subjects and the second four would have the emphasis placed on subjects peculiar to the Constabulary. The District Constabulary did many of those items in which they were not proficient and utilized their operational time also as on the job training. Then came small unit, platoon, troop and squadron training. All of this led General Harmon to say, "Troopers will be known for their integrity". Many troopers on the various raids were offered bribes and the author never heard of any takers. Many soldiers that were not in the Constabulary requested transfers to Constabulary units. A Constabulary Trooper gained a presence from this training and whether or not the Trooper remained in service or returned to civilian life this presence remained.

Another provider of training was "The United States Constabulary School" at Sonthofen. In determining the curriculum emphasis was upon those subjects believed to be essential to the operation of a mobile occupational force, normal military training did not cover those subjects that were to be taught. Some of the subject matter included, but was not limited to: Tactics on riot duty, raids and searches, guard and care of prisoners, mounted patrols, employment of air liaison sections, security, and the use of Constabulary Weapons. Police training on the duties of duties, responsibilities and jurisdiction of the Constabulary Trooper, techniques and mechanics of arrest, operations of a Constabulary command post, elements of crime, laws of arrest, rules of evidence, interrogations, confessions and statements, court room demeanor and giving testimony collection and preservation of evidence, passes and permits, traffic control and accidents, and border control. Geopolitical training on the German psychology and background, German political parties, international relations, organization, functioning and relationship of the Constabulary to other military agencies. General instruction to include self defense, map reading, report writing, geography of Germany. The course of instruction was continuously being updated.

The Constabulary School was closed in June 1948.

CHAPTER 17: WAR DEPARTMENT & DEPARTMENT OF DEFENSE ORDERS

The following are excerpts from numerous War Department and Department of Defense General Orders. The orders listed are the only ones that have been recovered from various sources. Any one desiring additional information on items listed in this chapter are welcome to query either the National Historian U. S. Constabulary or the United States Cavalry Museum at Fort Riley, Kansas.

On 6 April 1946 the following order was published: AG 322 (3 Apr 46), AO-I-GNCT-M SUBJECT: Redesignation, Reorganization, and Assignment of Units For Constabulary Force in Europe.

On 17 June 1946 the above War Department Order was amended to include the assignment of an Army Ground Forces Band to each Regiment by AG 322 (11 Jun 46), AG-I-GNGCT-M.

On 19 March 1947 by AGAO-I 322 (5 Mar 47). The following units were deactivated: Light Tank Troops of the 1st to 6th, inclusive, 10th 11th, 14th, and 15th Constabulary Regiment and the Light Tank Platoon, Constabulary School Squadron.

On 24 September 1947 the Department of the Army issued AGAO-I 322 (5 Sep 47) CSGOT-M SUBJECT: Inactivation and Redesignation of Certain Constabulary Units. This affected the following units: 3rd Constabulary Brigade, 1st, 3rd, 5th, and 10th Constabulary Regiments. With their Squadrons as follows: 11th, 12th, 91st, 37th, 81st, 8th, 35th, 74th, 13th, 71st, and 72nd. The Headquarters and the Service Troops of the Regiments also were deactivated as was the Headquarters Troop of 3rd Brigade. In addition the 68th Constabulary Squadron was relieved from assignment to 3rd Constabulary Regiment and assigned to Headquarters, United States Constabulary.

On 10 February 1948 Department of the Army issued AGAO-I 322 (23 Jun 48) The following units were constituted as of 23 January 1948: Recoiless Rifle Troop, 2nd Constabulary Regiment Headquarters, Special Troops, U S Constabulary , and the

Constabulary Flight Detachment. The following units were deactivated. Service Troop of the 4th, 6th, 14th, 15th, 11th and 2nd Constabulary Regiments and Service Troop of the Constabulary School Squadron.

Units that were to be redesignated and reorganized: 85th Transportation Car Platoon to 85th Constabulary Car Platoon, 820th Military Police Company to 820th Military Police Platoon, Headquarters & Headquarters Troop, 97th Constabulary Signal Battalion to Headquarters and Headquarters Detachment, 97th Constabulary Squadron. All Regiment and Squadron Headquarters & Headquarters Troops of the remaining Constabulary units were redesignated as Headquarters, Headquarters & Service Troop, _____ Regiment or Squadron.

On 16 November 1948 Department of the Army issued AGAO-I 322 (15 Nov 48) CSGOT-M SUBJECT: Reorganization of Constabulary Units. An Assault Gun Company was assigned to each Battalion in an Armored Cavalry Regiment. The 2nd Armored Cavalry Regiment had the Service Company added. The 15th Constabulary Regiment and the 15th Constabulary Squadron were inactivated. The Assault Gun Companies were inactvated per AGAO-I 322 (25 Aug 49) 26 September 1949. NOTE: On the above date the four remaining Constabulary Regiments became Armored Cavalry Regiments. At the same time the 11th Armored Cavalry Regiment was deactivated leaving the Constabualry with three Armored Cavalry Regiments and a mission change to become a combat ready as soon as possible.

On 10 April 1950 Department of the Army issued AGAO-I 322 (7 Mar 50) GI-M SUBJECT: Reorganization of certain Constabulary Units; Headquarters Troop, US Constabulary

to Headquarters Company, US Constabulary; 85th Constabulary Car Platoon to 85th Transportation Car Company (US Constabulary); Constabulary Flight Detachment to Flight Detachment, US Constabulary. Activated was the 19th Medical

Detachment (US Constabulary) with an authorized strength of two Officers and eleven Enlisted.

On 24 May 1950 per Department of the Army Orders AGAO-I 320.2 (4 May 50) SUBJECT: Activation, Inactivation, Redesignation and Reorganization of Units in the European Command. The following Constabulary Units were affected the 54th and 547th Engineer Combat Battalions each lost Medical Detachments, the 97th Constabulary Signal Squadron lost both officers and enlisted in Headquarters Detachment and in all troops. The 19th Medical Detachment was reassigned to Seventh Army as well as Flight Detachment, U S Constabulary which became Flight Detachment, Seventh Army. The 427th CIC Detachment also went to Seventh Army.

On 16 February 1951 per Department of the Army Orders AGAO-I 322 (13 Feb 51) SUBJECT: Activation, Redesignation and Reorganization of Certain Units in the European Command.. The 2nd Constabulary Recoilless Rifle Troop was inactivated. The Assault Gun Companies of the 2nd, 6th and 14th Armored Cavalry Regiments are redesignated as Howitzer Companies of the 2nd, 6th and 14th Armored Cavalry Regiments, respectfully, will remain active unfilled. In addition the following Constabulary units were reorganized: 555th Engineer Combat Group, 547th Engineer Combat Battalion, 552nd Engineer Pontoon Bridge Company, the 519th Armored Field Artillery Battalion. and the 51st Armored Medical Battalion.

On 15 August 1951 the First Constabulary Brigade was inactivated the remaining units that were still classified as Constabulary the 2nd, 6th, and 14th Armored Cavalry Regiment (US Constabulary) were placed directly under SEVENTH ARMY command and control. It is noted with much pleasure and pride that many in the Brigade Headquarters reluctantly removed their Constabulary patch. The Regiments along with the 15th and 24th Constabulary Squadron continued to wear the Constabulary patch until 15 December 1952.

CHAPTER 18: GERMAN YOUTH ACTIVITIES

During the demilitarization period the Allied Control Council directed that all; sports and military athletic organizations be disbanded as of 1 January 1946, prohibited the conduct and development of all military athletics in educational institutions, and prohibited all youth activities above the level of the Land Kreis. On 1 April 1946, the Office of Military Government initiated a new youth activity program. Active encouragement was to be given to the formation of volunteer groups of young people for cultural, religious and recreational purposes. This program had as its objective the constructive use of leisure time and the successful development of democracy in terms of ideas, initiative, responsibility, and the practice of democratic procedures. Activities of a military nature were definitely prohibited while no uniforms or emblems were to be worn without the approval of the Land Office of Military Government. On the 15th of April 1946, General McNarney, European Theater Commander, expressed the desire that the program be extended by all practical means.

Local commanders were directed to survey existing athletic and recreational facilities in their areas with the idea of making them available on a part time basis. They were encouraged to take an active part in assisting the German Youth Committees working in their areas, even to the extent of using qualified military personnel to participate in the program in order to demonstrate the application of the highest democratic ideals to the German Youth.

During the Summer Session of the Theater Athletic School held in Stuttgart in June 1946, the demonstration of games, coaching methods, and actual participation in athletic contests were afforded German youths by the school faculty. The enthusiastic response of German youth and sports leaders to this program clearly indicated the desirability of sponsoring similar schools throughout the US Zone with recommendations from General McNarney that all youth activities within a major command be coordinated by the Senior Commander present.

On 6 August 1946, General Harmon directed that all Constabulary Commanders of Brigades, Regiments, and Squadrons take immediate steps to organize athletic schools or clinics for German children. He recommended that those sports for which there was adequate Class X and surplus equipment be emphasized. He also indicated that every effort should be made to select personnel interested in, and capable of conducting this program.

Headquarters, United States Constabulary, on 8 August 1946 issued instructions as to the number and grade of personnel to be assigned to German Youth Activity programs. Brigades were to provide one full time field grade officer and at least two full time non-commissioned officers. At regiments level one officer was to designated German Youth Activity Officer in addition to his other duties while one senior non-commissioned officer would serve as full time assistant. Squadrons and troops were to be represented by a full time noncommissioned officers with one officer in the squadron as German Youth Activity Officer in addition to his other duties. At a conference of Brigades and Regimental German Youth Activity Officers, means and methods of carrying out instructions of higher headquarters in regard to German Youth Activity programs and in the rendition of reports, were discussed at great length. Conferences were held on the regimental level for squadron and troop personnel during the period 3 to 5 September 1946.

As a former athlete, General Harmon believed in the German Youth Activity Program and his his Constabulary Headquarters published a directive on 11 September 1946. This directive gave specific instructions on the implementation of the program. Explicit instructions on the requirements and duties of unit commanders, German Youth Activity Officers and non- commissioned officers. Personnel so assigned were to maintain liaison with their respective Military Government Youth Representatives and to meet with Kreis Youth Committees in order to acquaint these local Youth Committees with the availability of Army assistance. Each troop was directed to establish and conduct a sports clinic if there was not one in operation in their respective area. Youth Centers were to be established in as many towns as possible. Now a typical Harmon order: Each squadron was to have at least one Youth Center operating by the end of September. All squadrons were directed to establish a tent camp in order to facilitate the German Youth Activities in the area. Local School Principals were to be contacted in order to obtain their cooperation and assistance in regard to out-of-school activities and sport classes held inside the school buildings. The success of the German Youth Activity program depended largely upon the action and wholesome participation of the individual trooper. Every effort was put forth to publicize the program. Many troopers not only gave of their time but also were known to contribute for additional equipment.

This would be the proper time and the proper place to acknowledge that many programs became easier to recruit the youths to participate because of the interaction of troopers patrolling the towns and their conduct during raids. Children and young people were always a favorite of the Constabulary Trooper. Most, if not all, carried candy and gum which was shared with German Youth.

NOTE: Many people do not know that during some of the most dangerous times during the "Berlin Blockade" a unit of the United States Constabulary and a unit from the First Infantry Division played a football game with the proceeds devoted to the "Children of Berlin". The Constabulary won the game but the Constabulary and the First Infantry Division were the units that made sure that the "Kids Won".

Children of the German Youth Activities are the leaders of Germany today. A Germany that has the highest living standard and the highest salaries of any Country in Europe. Many of the programs of the German Youth Activity most probably helped in not only teaching democracy but also a way of life. The Constabulary Trooper can be proud of the part they played and their reward will be coming.

6th Armored Cavalry Regiment, Security Platoon, Straubing, Germany, 1949, being inspected by Maj. Gen. I.D. White (CG, US Constabulary) 1Lt. Edwards, platoon leader, left front. Rear, Cpl. Tracy, Pvt. Sanderfoot, Pvt. Huether, Pfc. Bennett, Pfc. McCann.

6th Armored Cavalry Regiment, Security Platoon, Straubing, Germany, 1950, being inspected by (front to rear) 1Lt. Lucien C. Benton, Gen. Bruce C. Clark, Col. George A Rhem. Rear, Col. Tracy, Pfc. Bennett, Pvt. Martindale, Pvt. Hagan.

6th Armored Cavalry Regiment, Security Platoon, Straubing, Germany, 1951. Kneeling, 1Lt. J.M. Christensen, MSgt. B.C. Harmon. 1st row, Sgt. Tracy, Pfc. Oberlander, Pfc. Percell, Cpl. Irby, Cpl. Pritchett, Pvt. Laquino, Pvt. Weisberg, Pfc. Swanson, Cpl. Dill, Sgt. Hubbartt, Sgt. Brokaw. 2nd row, Cpl. Salzieder, Cpl. Hagan, Cpl. Wilcox, Pvt. Meyers, Cpl. Huether, Pfc McCann, Pvt. McKeon, Pvt. Zamrok, Pfc. Masterss, Cpl. Haynes, Cpl. Zupan, Pfc. Masters, Cpl. Haynes, Cpl. Zupan. 3rd row, Sgt. Anzelc, Cpl. Martindale, Pvt. Lunden, Cpl. Schultz, Pvt. Bennett, Cpl. Dixon, Cpl. Girard, Pfc. Caltrider, Sgt. Lee, Cpl. DeWitt.

CHAPTER 19: "CONSTABULARY'S LAST COMMANDING GENERAL"

The task of going from a police type unit to a dominant combat unit was the Constabulary's task in 1948. Again the right man was found for the job, Major General I. D. White. A man that had commanded the 2nd Armored Division after General Harmon, a man of the "Old School", a leader and not a manager.

On his last day as Commanding General the troopers of Headquarters, United States Constabulary presented him with a large, locally produced keepsake of his time with Constabulary. Today it can be found in the U.S. Cavalry Museum at Fort Riley.

The written portion follows:

UNITED STATES CONSTABULARY
1946-1951

MAJ GEN ERNEST N HARMON	— 1 JULY 1946	— 1 MAY 1947
MAJ GEN WITHERS A BURRESS	— 1 MAY 1947	— 5 APRIL 1948
MAJ GEN LOUIS A CRAIG	— 5 APRIL 1948	— 21 MAY 1948
MAJ GEN I D WHITE	— 21 MAY 1948	— 7 MARCH 1951

THE U.S. CONSTABULARY WAS BORN IN GERMANY FOLLOWING WORLD WAR II. THE COMBAT EXPERIENCED VI CORPS, 1ST AND 4TH ARMORED DIVISIONS FORMED THE NUCLEUS OF THIS NEW OCCUPATION FORCE. A UNIQUE FORCE IN THE ANNALS OF THE U.S. ARMY. THE CONSTABULARY WAS CHARGED WITH THE MILITARY AND CIVIL SECURITY THROUGHOUT THE U.S. ZONE. THIS FLEXIBLE, HIGHLY MOBILE, CAVALRY- TYPE ORGANIZATION MAINTAINED LAW AND ORDER IN SUPPORT OF MILITARY GOVERNMENT DURING THE TURBULENT POST-WAR YEARS OF 1946 AND 1947

THE CONSTABULARY TROOPER WITH HIS DISTINCTIVE UNIFORM CONSISTING OF A CAVALRY-YELLOW SCARF, HIGHLY POLISHED TROOPER BOOTS, A COLORFULLY STRIPPED HELMET LINER, AND THE NOW FAMOUS "CIRCLE C" INSIGNIA SO IMPRESSED THE CIVILIAN POPULACE THAT IT RESPECTFULLY ACKNOWLEDGED THE FORCE AS THE "BLITZ POLICE" OR "LIGHTNING POLICE" AND SOON RECOGNIZED THAT THE CONSTABULARY MOTTO, "MOBILITY — VIGILANCE — JUSTICE APTLY DESCRIBED ITS PERFORMANCE OF DUTY.

THE CHANGING WORLD CONDITIONS IN EARLY 1948 MADE ORGANIZATIONAL AND MISSION CHANGES IN THE CONSTABULARY DESIRABLE. THE MISSION OF THE CONSTABULARY WAS EXPANDED TO INCLUDE THAT OF COMBAT READINESS. UNDER MAJOR GEN I. D. WHITE, THE CONSTABULARY WAS TRANSFORMED ONTO THE LARGEST ARMORED FORMATION IN THE U. S. ARMY. THE FAMOUS 2ND, 6TH, AND 14TH CAVALRY REGIMENTS REORGANIZED AS ARMORED CAVALRY REGIMENTS — PROVIDED THE ARMOR COMPONENT OF THE NEW COMMAND AND WERE SUPPORTED BY FOUR ARTILLERY BATTALIONS, THREE INFANTRY BATTALIONS, TWO ENGINEER BATTALIONS, THE EQUIVALENT OF TWO ORDNANCE BATTALIONS, TWO SPECIAL CONSTABULARY BORDER SQUADRONS, AN ARMORED MEDICAL BATTALION, A SIGNAL SQUADRON AND MISCELLANEOUS SPECIAL TROOPS. THE FAMOUS 1ST AND 2ND CAVALRY BRIGADE HEADQUARTERS — REORGANIZED AS CONSTABULARY BRIGADES FORMED THE MAJOR SUBORDINATE TACTICAL HEADQUARTERS.

AT THE CLOSE OF 1950 THE UNITED STATES CONSTABULARY CONSTITUTED ONE OF THE TWO PRIMARY COMBAT FORCES IN THE EUROPEAN THEATER AND THE LARGEST TRAINED ARMORED FORCE IN THE ARMY.

RECOGNIZED BY MILITARY AND CIVILIAN LEADERS ALIKE AS "OUTSTANDING IN TRAINING, MORALE, EFFICIENCY, AND EFFECTIVENESS', THE U. S. CONSTABULARY GAINED ACKNOWLEDGMENT IN THE CONGRESSIONAL RECORD OF THE 81ST CONGRESS AS "PROBABLY THE KEENEST AND MOST VIGILANT EYE WE POSSESS - - - - READY TO FULLY LIVE UP TO (ITS) MISSION"

Right: General I.D. White observing units of the 14th Constabulary Regiment.

BELOW: Changing of the Guard, Berlin/Spandau prison, Germany, 1952.

Lt. Guy K. Troy jumping Constab horse at horse show in Frankfurt, 1950.

Gen. I.D. White (center) and staff officers viewing a winter demonstration, Munsingen, Germany, 1948

ACKNOWLEDGMENTS

This narrative on the United States Constabulary could not have and was not done alone. The input from many by giving and loaning of information was greatly appreciated. I know that of the many that contributed some will be forgotten and for that I apologize.

The number of Troopers that I have met and talked to has greatly increased my knowledge of the Constabulary. The Troopers of all the Constabulary Units living and dead have all made a contribution to this "History of the United States Constabulary". This history was compiled from information in "The Establishment and Operations of the United States Constabulary 3 October 1945 - 30 June 1947 by Major James M. Snyder, Major, Cavalry; Combat Commander, Autobiography of a Soldier by Major General E. N. Harmon, USA (Ret.) with Milton MacKaye and William Ross MacKaye; Military Review, Volume XXVI, March 1947, Number 12 an article titled Mobility, Vigilance, Justice, A Saga of the Constabulary by Lt. Col. A.F. Irzyx, Cav. Military Review, Volume XXIX, October 1949, Number 7 an article titled A Progress Report on the United States Constabulary by Capt. H. P. Rand, FA. Also numerous publications by James A. Sawicki on lineage of some Constabulary Units. A "Special Thanks" must go to the following: Terry Van Meter, Director, U.S. Cavalry Museum, Fort Riley, Kansas Past National Commander Robert Jarrett; Colonel (Ret) Robert L. Hoffman; Wesley G. Stapleton, Brigadeer General (Ret) Albin F. Irzyk, Frank L. Stephenson, Bill Strub, Vincent Bucca, and the countless others that called with information and support that made this history possible. This could not have been done without the whole hearted support of my wife, Dita. I thank all of the members for putting up with me and my not answering of my mail as quickly as I wanted or that you deserved. For that I am truly sorry As a former member of the 14th Constabulary Regiment and the 14th Armored Cavalry Regiment I leave you with this. May we all be together at the last "Roll Call", Troopers of every United States Constabulary Unit. "SUIVEZ MOI"

Dedication of the Constabulary Monument at Ft. Knox, Kentucky, at the Patton Museum, September 16, 1994. Buell B. Smith

U.S. Constabulary - The Early Days

by Dr. James O. Whittaker, T/5
Constabulary HQ, 1946-47

When World War II ended, Germany was a mess. Saturation bombing by the Allies had destroyed one-fourth of all the housing; 20 million refugees had fled westward ahead of the advancing Red Army; several million German POWs were in camps all over the country. Slave laborers forced to work in German industry were in camps run by the United Nations Relief Organization; American GIs who had fought in combat were still wearing side arms and wanted to "go home." Nazi war criminals were still at large, as were many thousands of SS who had been involved in atrocities unimaginable in past wars.

Something had to be done and fast. One of Patton's generals, Ernest Harmon, was chosen to head up a new outfit intended to put some "spit and polish" into the occupation of Germany. A headquarters was set up at a Wermacht Kasserne in Bamberg, and three Brigade Headquarters were established in Munich, Frankfurt and Stuttgart. Eventually a total of 55,000 men would wear the special helmet liner with the gold stripes and lightning bolt through the gold "C." Special gold parachute scarves at the throat and paratrooper boots completed the outfit.

General Harmon even had his own special "Honor Guard" consisting of three Harley Davidson motorcycles, followed by a jeep with a .50 caliber machine gun, an armored car, the general's car, another jeep, and three more Harleys bringing up the rear. Each of the motorcycles had a Thompson sub-machine gun in a special holster on the front wheel. With sirens wide open and roaring at top speed through the city streets, everybody stood wide-eyed at this new sight in Germany. Each member of this special honor guard was an MP and they were all virtually the same height. General Harmon himself was a striking figure. Although not very tall, he was resplendent in pink riding breeches, burnished cavalry boots, a beautiful tunic with ribbons that stretched from his pocket to his epaulet. Finally, the riding crop he always carried completed the uniform of the man we all referred to as "Old Gravel Voice," behind his back of course.

There was in addition, his own special train consisting of locomotive and three streamlined passenger cars. Its previous owner, Herman Goering, also had given up a huge Mercedes armored limousine with bullet-proof glass. So heavy was this car that it required five forward speeds and three in reverse to get it moving. Finally, for longer distance travel, the general had his own DC-3 airplane, with appropriate Constabulary insignia.

I enlisted in the Regular Army on 20 February 1946 on Market Street in downtown San Francisco. At that time one could enlist for 18 months, so desperate was the need for replacements in both Germany and Japan. A train ticket took me across country to Fort McClellan where I went through infantry basic training - but a basic that had been reduced to only six weeks. Most everyone was scheduled to depart for Japan. By sheer luck I had trained in a heavy weapons company, and we went to Germany.

From Camp Kilmer in New Jersey we went to New York City then on a Liberty ship bound for France. Some of the guys were seasick as soon as they set foot aboard ship. I felt great - until we got one day out in the Atlantic. Then, like most everyone else, "mal de mer" overtook me. We slept four deep and heaven forbid if you had the bottom bunk and the guy on top was sick. Ash cans filled with guess what, were everywhere. Those who could eat, stood up to do so in the mess, there were no seats. On deck, the desperately seasick wrapped themselves from head to foot in their blankets against the cold. Lying stiff on deck they looked exactly like bodies laid out to be buried at sea.

It took 10 days for this rolling, pitching tub to reach France. At Cherbourg we saw first signs of the war, the superstructures of sunken ships were everywhere in the harbor as we docked. Most of the buildings were in ruins. Frenchmen rowed out in boats begging for cigarettes, candy, and anything else. GIs threw half the ship to them.

We boarded old French passenger cars, those kind with all the doors down the side of the car. Late that night we pulled out of Cherbourg for our journey across France. Next morning one could see no sign at all of the war, only the peaceful, rolling French farm land so typical of western France. At each town the train stopped and hundreds of French civilians surrounded the train looking for handouts. We think they radioed ahead to the next town that the "goodie train" was on its way.

Not until we got close to the German border did we again see signs of the war: burned out tanks, entire trains lying on their sides next to the track, locomotives with holes shot in their boilers. Saarbrucken was the first German city we saw, a sobering sight. Ruins were everywhere; destruction virtually complete. No more civilians came to our train as we entered Germany.

We rolled on to Amberg, Germany and the "repple-depot" where I was assigned to Constabulary Headquarters. By July I was on duty in G-3 and very nervous at first. We had been shown films of the "Werewolves," the Nazi underground movement, while still at Camp Kilmer in the States.

These supposedly fanatic Nazis were portrayed as sneaking up on unsuspecting GIs and cutting their throats on German streets. I understand that there was one attempt to assassinate General Harmon at his quarters in Bamberg, but other than that I never heard any reports of "Werewolf" activity anywhere in the U.S. Zone.

Our G-3 office in the Headquarters worked 24 hours a day, seven days a week, 365 days a year. We had direct phone lines to each of our brigade headquarters. Any serious incident occurring anywhere in the U.S. Zone was reported up the chain of command and finally to our office in Bamberg. We prepared written reports of these incidents for the general. Next door to our office was the general's map room, and in that room there were large floor-to-ceiling maps of the entire U.S. Zone of Occupation. Different maps showed different facts. On one I remember, colored pins were stuck in the towns where serious incidents had occurred. Some towns were masses of pins, each color representing a different incident: murder, rape, fatal vehicle accident, etc.

At that time the American Army was still segregated. There were no Black (or as they were called then "Colored") troops in the Constabulary. Few Blacks had served in combat units during the war. Most had been in motor pools or served in graves registration units. When the war ended, Black units with their white officers were assigned to specific towns in Germany. Whether because of poor leadership or the simple fact of segregation, many became involved in serious incidents. The other group which showed up on our maps were the so-called "displaced persons" or DPs. These were the "slave laborers" of German industry, mostly people from eastern Europe who were forcibly brought to Germany. When the war ended, most did not want to return home to Communist states in the East. Betwixt and between, they were unwanted in Germany, did not want to return home, and were denied entry to most western countries including the United States. They were also involved in many serious incidents. I should add that any incident involving Jews was considered a "serious incident."

One has to remember that we were an Army of Occupation, not an Army that liberated Germany. We did not abuse the local civilian population but there was no pretense that we had come as liberators. We wore Army uniforms at all times. There was a curfew from midnight to 8:00 a.m. and we had no American money at all for the entire year I was there. The Black Market was virtually the only market in Germany. No stores were open. Every city was in ruins. Most of the bridges in the towns lay broken in the streams and rivers where they had been blown up by retreating Wermacht forces.

American forces had captured over 70 tons of Nazi documents in Berlin including the membership lists of the Nazi Party for the entire country. Anyone who had been a party member was subject to arrest until cleared by a "Spruckhammer," a de-Nazification court. Former Nazis could not work in government or even assist United States forces which constituted the "government" of Germany. They could not even play musical instruments in our clubs if they had been party members.

The SS had been declared a "criminal organization" by the Nürnberg Tribunal. Consequently, anyone who had served in the SS was subject to automatic arrest. Much of the activity of the units of Constabulary in the field was aimed at finding such people. I remember reports of Constabulary units surrounding entire towns and blocking all road access. They then systematically searched every room in every house looking for Nazi materials, weapons, pictures of Hitler, or anything else forbidden to German civilians by the Occupation authorities. SS members had been branded in the left armpit with the double lightning bolt insignia of the organization. Suspected individuals were easily identified when told to remove their shirt and hold up their left arm.

There were SS prison camps all over our Zone of Occupation. These men received special attention, and unlike members of the Wermacht typically released quickly when the war ended, SS members were held for long periods until they could be cleared or otherwise dealt with. These were the activities that Constabulary was involved with, long before the Berlin Airlift and the Cold War.

Life was hard for the Germans. The winter of 46-47 was one of the coldest in a hundred years. I spent many evenings in German apartments huddled around those ceramic space heaters they had in those days. When the little charcoal we could secure burned up, we wrapped blankets around our shoulders and continued talking. Many became fast friends and to this day I regard Germany as a second home; I am always amazed at how quick my German returns whenever I visit the country.

In G-3 we worked two weeks from 8:00 a.m. to 5:00 p.m., one week from 5:00 p.m. to midnight and one week midnight to 8:00 a.m. We then received a three-day pass. By taking another person's shift, say from 5:00 p.m. to midnight and working through to 8:00 a.m., we managed to get five days off every month instead of just three. I took advantage of it and visited every major capitol in Europe. By the time I was 19 years old I had seen the Bunker in Berlin where Hitler ended his life, visited the Vatican and shook hands with the Pope, and in general, saw more of Europe than 98% of the American population, I was ready to begin college.

Constabulary Border Tales

by 2nd Lt. William A. White,

This is the story of one border tour of a Constabulary Platoon from 1946-47. We had been on several border controls prior to this time and each trip was an adventure. But this one covers a gamut of experiences.

Usually a troop was sent to a border location and patrols were run from there by the platoon. 1st Platoon, E Troop, 6th Squadron was different. The troop commander usually put my platoon by itself to cover a different area. In this instance the troop went to Kronach with the 1st Platoon dispatched to Steinach, about 45 minutes away right on the border to control the crossing point.

What follows is the events of my three month tour, October, November and December 1946.

The platoon consisted of 2nd Lieutenant William A. White, platoon leader; Tech Sergeant Stan Wahala, platoon sergeant; 1st Section Sergeant Hendry, section sergeant with eight men; 2nd Section Sergeant Nicholson, section sergeant with eight men; 3rd Section Sergeant Gift, section sergeant; Operations Sergeant Sensha with seven men; technicians, Tech 4 Poolmon and Cook; Tech 5 Raymer, mechanic; Tech 5 Reid, radio operator; Private First Class Nolhstern, medic. As you can see, we were set up to be a completely operational unit.

We arrived at the border crossing about two miles from town, right on the border. Our home was a Gasthaus that belonged to a German family living nearby. The frau was a known black marketeer and an illegal border crosser. She was one of our targets.

The Gasthaus was a three story building. The bottom level consisted of two large dining rooms with bay windows overlooking a stream that ran by the house. There was a large kitchen and a room we converted into our CP. Outside there was a shed-type building for the mechanics and a parking area for our jeeps and one 2-1/2 ton truck. Second floor was quarters for the men. Each sergeant had a room by himself. The enlisted men were two to a room. There was one large squad-type room for the eight German border police that worked with us. I had a penthouse on the third floor, consisting of a bedroom, bath, sitting room and balcony over the stream. It's good to be king! After getting settled in I made an inspection of the German police area. It was a mess! I got the German sergeant and told him to clean it up and that I would inspect the next day, GI style. He apologized and said the previous officer hadn't paid any attention to him. I told him he was now a part of the platoon, and I would expect him to soldier as a part of the unit. At inspection the next day the Germans stood tall for a white glove inspection, which they passed,

In the meantime I contacted the Steinach mayor and chief of police and asked them to meet me at the railroad station at 4:00 p.m. that day. When they arrived I said, "I will point out certain females that you will put up in town and not bother." They objected, but we were in charge. These were girlfriends of some members of the platoon, in spite of the "No Fraternization Rules."

We setup one of the dining rooms for dances. The other was the platoon mess. The NCO and I had a table in that part of the dining room that overlooked the stream. Every night the truck went into town, picked up the girls and band and brought them to the Gasthaus for a dance. At 11:30 p.m. a truck loaded up and took the girls back to town, along with any trooper that had a pass. The trooper had to be back by noon the next day. If a trooper had a patrol he could not attend the dance, as patrols were on alert two hours before a patrol and one hour after for briefing and debriefing.

Patrols consisted of two kinds. Jeep patrols, usually four to six hours and foot patrols two to four hours. We usually had two to four German border police with us. We did something other units did not do. The border police were part of our units, taking part in calisthenics and other activities, even to taking part in boxing matches. The first time this happened the border police sergeant said, "Lieutenant I can't fight an American soldier with boxing gloves." I told him that if he didn't I would fire him. Troopers had a great respect for the border police once they knew them, and the border police liked the idea. We had no trouble in the unit like some units of the Constabulary had.

After we had been at the outpost for about a week the mayor visited me and said, "Lieutenant I have some beer for you." I, of course, told him we couldn't accept. He then said, "You don't understand, it's a brewery. You Americans came through here and told us to brew beer for the Army and we did. I told him I would let higher headquarters know and get back to him. However, I started drawing beer for my troops in the evenings. Later in the week I went back to troop headquarters and was getting ready to leave for my platoon area, when the captain said, "Bill, there is something going on up there." So I finally told him about the brewery. He replied, "Don't tell anyone, don't let squadron know and I'll start sending my trucks up to get some. We won't tell squadron until we leave the border" (which was about two months later).

One day when I was on patrol, driving by myself, villagers in a small town stopped me and said that Russian soldiers had been in town and taken one of their town police with them when they went back across the border. I headed for the border and saw them on a small hillock on their side. I drove up to the border, left my jeep with a machine-gunner and told him to cover me and shoot if necessary. I walked across the border to where the Russian soldiers were and told them to give me the policeman. There was a slight argument until I waved to my driver. They decided they didn't want to fight. The German policeman accompanied me back to the jeep and we drove back to town. As we started up the road for our command post, I saw four jeeps approaching at max speed. They passed me and pulled to a stop, and I joined them. It was my platoon sergeant and a couple of squads with machine guns loaded. I asked what was going on. Sergeant Wahala said, "Lieutenant, we heard the Russians had you and we were coming to get you, even if we had to fight." This was the spirit of the 3rd Platoon.

Earlier, I told you that the lady owner of the Gasthaus was a border crosser and blackmarketeer, although we had been unable to catch her. Our cook had been going with one of her daughters from the day we first arrived. We had been there about six weeks when one afternoon, about 3:00 p.m., Tech 4 Poolmon came to me and said, "Lieutenant she is across the border and expected back very soon." I immediately covered the border with the troops and caught her on her return. I was in on her capture. A trial was held by the American Government and Court for our area. During the time I was testifying she blurted out what she thought of me, and there was a price on my head for what I had done.

Another time a large truck approached our checkpoint to cross (our point was a closed crossing). I went out to see what was happening as my guards had a gun aimed at the truck. Approaching I could see two Chinese in the front. They spoke English so we got into a conversation. The general idea was that if I turned my back and, let them cross I would get paid well. I told them where to go and notified troop of the incident and sent them toward the troop command post.

Oh yes, one more thing. The troops, except for the driver, had warm feet while on patrol. I had some firebricks heated in the oven, then placed on the metal floor of the jeep. The troops not driving could put their boot soles on them and keep warm for several hours.

As a separate platoon we drew rations from the company weekly but also added to our rations locally. I would get the local German kids to furnish us with trout and we paid them one cigarette for each trout they brought us. Needless to say we always had trout. We could also get geese and chickens in the same manner. We had German border police assigned to the border units. Some or all us constabulary units treated them badly. When I had a squad with me I made them soldier with my troop and was trusted with respect by my men. They respected me for that. In one location I took over, I inspected their part of our barracks and it was said that I told the sergeant that I would be back that afternoon for an inspection and expected it to be GI. He understood, that afternoon it was better than my own troop. They took part in patrols, PT, even boxing, as we had boxing gloves and sometimes needed them to settle arguments. The first time it was hard to convince them to box with a GI. While on the border most of the time it looked as though I didn't carry a weapon, however, I had a hide out German 32 Walther. One night my platoon sergeant and one other man plus myself went on a patrol, and about a half hour up the trail we stopped to listen. Shortly we heard footsteps so

we slipped off the trail to catch some illegals. However, it was the German police sergeant and a couple of his men. I stopped him and chewed him out then asked him what he was doing. His answer was because I was unarmed and didn't carry a weapon, he was back up in case of trouble. I ordered him back to the outpost after I got back, and in my office I showed him my hide-out weapon.

He told me that he had worked in that gun factory and it was a fine weapon and he wouldn't worry as much. I went around seemingly unarmed a lot of the time to show the German populace that I wasn't scared.

At Nordhalben, our first border assignment in 1946, I was sent to set up a control point with orders to look over a good location for observation across the border, as well as a good platoon location to take over any buildings or what ever we needed. I met with the town mayor and police chief, told them why I was there and what we would set up etc. We found a good three story building that met our needs and told the people to evacuate. One of the people in the building, the leader, said to me, "Lieutenant why do you pick on us. We were in the concentration camp and many of us died; why don't you look at the building up the street a block, it is better than this one." I took a look and it was a two story modern mansion and owned by a doctor. I knocked on his door, told him I had just confiscated his home and he was outraged. I gave him until that afternoon to move and said we would help him. He went for the mayor and I told the mayor that he had no say in the matter and to get him out to another place. We moved him out and look over the house which made a great outpost. When we did this we made sure no damage was done to the property. At this location we had good relations with the Russians. I have pictures where we traded uniforms. We made patrolling line on the border fun.

Many years later when I again met with my platoon sergeant he stated, "Lieutenant you were tough but you gave us a job to do and then got the hell out of the way and let us do our job."

I was on one patrol where we caught some border crossers. One of them was a Russian lady who had a police dog that was part wolf. She kept the dog under complete control. She spoke excellent English, was very good looking and wanted to get away from the Russians. When she got ready to get on the truck to be transported to headquarters she asked me to take her dog and care for it, so it would not be mistreated. I told her I didn't speak Russian. She stated that the dog understood German, so I said okay. She stooped down, gave the dog a hug, then handed me the leash and spoke to the dog. I took the leash and said "Come." The dog looked back then followed me to the jeep. It became my constant companion, friend and guard. It was a beautiful German police and wolf. Later when the family

came over, it stayed with the wife and daughter. When I left Germany I turned the dog over to a friend, Lieutenant Whiteside.

Later in late 1947. I became Battalion S-2 (Intelligence) and sent a number of intelligence items to regiment. One such one was the first info that the Russians were going to blockade Berlin. I was also on the Czech border when the Yugoslavia's invaded and took over Czechoslovakia; the regimental commander, Colonel Hamilton, ordered me to that check point. During the period leading up to the take over, many agents (mostly British but some Egyptian) came through, and when they used a certain phrase or word they would be taken aside and I would interrogate them then pass the info back to regiment. We knew when the Yugoslavians would take over. Late at night about 1:00 a.m., I got a call from the local Border German police; they had a building surrounded but the person wanted to talk to an American officer. I drove down there and they gave me a fill in on the situation. I told them to get back. I had the lights on my jeep to shine on me, then removed my pistol, laid it on the ground and strode up to the front door of the cottage. As I entered I said in German and English, "American officer coming in." I entered and no one was there in the main room. I again stated in a loud voice, "American officer alone and unarmed." No answer. I walked loudly to the bedroom door, opened it and immediately had a gun stuck in my gut. The Czech immediately recognized me as an officer and reversed the pistol. He handed it to me and immediately gave me a big hug. He was icy wet, disheveled and almost blue from the cold. I immediately covered him with a blanket from the cottage bed and evacuated him to my quarter where I interrogated him. He was the Czech Minister of War. When the Yugoslavian had come in to the capitol, he had jumped out a window and started his escape. The Jugs had followed him with dogs but didn't quite catch up to him near the border. He had swam an ice covered lake and crossed into Germany. At my quarters, which was warm, we had some schnapps and talked until dawn. We both slept until about noon, then talked some more before I took him to "Shangra La" for further interrogation by the CIC who, needless to say, were a little put out because I had not reported in earlier. I told them that if I had they would have had a corpse. About six months later I was again asked to report to regiment for a party. When I entered the party he was there, I again got a big hug and he told everyone I had saved his life. I can't remember his name.

I enjoyed border patrol and hated garrison duty. At one outpost I was relieved by the commander general of the Constabulary, General "Pop" Harold. He had inspected three different border control points in about a 60 day period and I had been there. He drove up and I was there standing tall when he got out of the sedan and yelled, "Lieutenant what are you doing here?" He turned to the battalion CO and said "relieve him immediately." Here I am a little perplexed, wondering what the hell did I do. He then walked up to me, returned my salute and said, "Didn't I see you at op 3 about 6 weeks ago." I said "Yes Sir." "Didn't I see you at Nordhalben three weeks ago?" I said, "Yes Sir and now here." "Colonel, this man will go stir crazy serving with so much time on the border." After the inspection I followed them back to the kasserne. Later in 1952 while in Japan after the 1st Cavalry was relieved from Korea and sent to Japan, I was a again inspected by General Harold and reminded him of the Constabulary and the border incident, and I was able to explain why I liked the border. I have a lot more tales of the border that could fill a book, all as interesting as the one above.

Battalion officers took over a hotel in the middle of Coburg, across from the Banhoff (railroad terminal), and we each had a room of our own: senior officer at that time 1st LTC, three captains, one first lieutenant day officer, hotel manager and about 20 2nd lieutenants. The hotel had a large plush dance area and officers mess. Dinner was served at precisely 7:00 p.m. after a cocktail hour from 6:00-7:00 p.m. Every officer dressed in class A (pinks and green). The only officer excused were those on the border or the OD at the kasserne. The LTC Battalion CO came in and sat down followed by the other officers who took their designated places. The staff ate at the "old mans table." We had dinner music during our meal played by local musicians. Dinner was served in courses, after dinner we sat there and had coffee. No one could depart until the Battalion CO left. This was every night. We also had dances every Saturday night in spite of the non-fraternization laws; dances ended promptly at midnight with *The Pledge of Allegiance* and *The Star Spangled Banner*. Sometimes we would have our meals and dances at the castle on the hill in a club just outside the walls.

About the 1st of 1947 dependents were allowed to come over. We were lucky not living in a kasserne like most troops. We took over houses in the city of Coburg and these houses were in different locations within the city. Usually two houses and yards side by side or back to back; again, in spite of the non-fraternization rules, we had to meet with the Germans as well as having to use maids and firemen to maintain the furnaces. We had a special ceremony for meeting the wives. They were met in Bamburg at the train station by a limousine and husband. The limousine stopped at an area just outside of Coburg where an escort met them with the Battalion CO who welcomed them and gave them a bouquet of flowers. They were then escorted to the hotel for a welcome with other officers and wives. After this they were escorted to their new home in Germany. My daughter was about 3-years-old and our maid had a daughter the same age. They played together and many a weekend Joan stayed with the maid at her home. One incident that occurred with my daughter was when I was escorting a colonel from regiment around the town. I stopped at the town square to show him Queen Victoria's Palace, a Tudor style layout. Her husband being Prince Albert or Gotha who was the Prince at that area. As we stopped this little ragamuffin, dressed liked the other German kids in the area, runs over to the jeep, looks up and says "Hello Daddy." I bent down kissed her and said "Run along and play now, daddy is busy." The colonel was flabbergasted saying, "Is that your daughter." Is she German? What is this?" I explained that she was not German but always played with the Germans. He then said, "Aren't you afraid she could be kidnapped or harmed." I told the colonel "If you touched her every German here would protect her." Nothing more was said but I'm sure he discussed it with the CO. But that was how we lived. It was much different than other units in Germany.

At Newstadt, one of our border crossing points, I was given permission to visit the Russian CP on the other side, and he visited my CP from time to time. In this area we had the electric and gas works and they had the coal field. The coal trucks went through the two check points several times a week, each truck and driver was checked and the load was looked at. One day he came over to my check point and watched us check the trucks through. After our check he said he had his men get up on each truck and prod it a dozen times or so with iron prods. I told him I didn't think it necessary and it was very dirty work for anyone. He stated that was the idea. I didn't understand his sense of humor. Another time at this location I was patrolling with a German Border Police Sergeant on skis. He was a tall blond athletic person and looked like the perfect skier. We noticed a border crosser not being a very good skier. I reached down, run-skipped my skies and took off on foot, the snow not being that deep. The border police sergeant did the same. After we had rounded up the illegal crosser, I asked him why he took off his skis. He stated he didn't ski either. Even though he sure looked the part.

Another time the CIC people were having a clandestine meeting with some operatives from the other side in a Gasthaus on our side near the border. Our job was to cover their operations in case anything got out of hand. We were dressed in white parka and blended into the snowy back ground. It was a tough job. Here they were in this warm Gasthaus having hot food and drinks while we were outside in the cold night air and low freezing weather. Several hours later after the conference broke up they didn't even give us hot coffee.

Visiting a historical castle overlooking the town of Coburg, Germany was an old Feudal Castle of Prince Albert of Gotha, Queen Victoria of England's husband. The local Germans always stated that it had not been taken by enemy forces since 1066 when William the Conqueror had done so. It had a marvelous collection of ancient art, chandelier of Dresden china and many delicate pieces of art. I took my platoon of GIs there for a tour using one of the American Red Cross Ladies as guide and interpreter. While she was getting the German curator who was in charge, I got the 20 GIs in a group. I told them I was going to give them an order they would probably not hear again, "Put your hands in your pockets and keep them there. If I see anyone with his hands out of the pockets or touching a piece of art. I will rap your knuckles." As an officer we always carried a swagger stick about 18" long with the battalion crest on it. The tour took about an hour and a half and was enjoyed by the GIs. After the tour the curator told the Red Cross lady how pleased he was the way we had conducted our tour and nothing had been touched or broken. Of course quite a chuckle ran through the GI group. After we left the Red Cross Lady said, "Bill I know something went on there, what was it?" My answer was "You don't want to know."

I had been in the 6th Battalion 6th Regiment Constabulary for 2-1/2 years and was due to rotate back to the States on the 24 July 1948. On the 23rd the German population in Coburg had rioted against the police. They had it surrounded and were throwing bricks and threatening the police. The Battalion CO needed someone to calm the situation down. I had performed this service several times during my service as platoon leader and as the Battalion S-2, and I had trained a person for over three months to take my place. I went into hiding as I did not want to get hurt the day before going home. The colonel sent people looking for me. Finally Major Lucey, the Battalion Provost, found me and said "Bill the "old man" wants you for this last time." I told him I was afraid of getting hurt and I wouldn't be able to go home. Finally he convinced me and I went in and saw the old man saying I would do the job. He said I could have as many men and what ever I needed to do the job. I told him I needed only two sergeants who had been with me before on this type of operation. Their job was to protect my back. I also had a platoon on call at the downtown CP. I then approached the mob on foot and with my body guards I strode into the mob and in a loud voice said, "The Prussian is coming through, stop what you are doing." I had to push a few out of the way rather roughly. (The towns people as well as many Germans had nicknamed me the Prussian because of the stern direct way I did things when challenged). I got to the door of the police station and went in. After I was inside there was some more rock throwing and I had a police man hand me their bull horn. I stepped out on the balcony and told the rioters they had a half an hour to break up their actions and go home or I would have to bring in troop and someone was sure to get badly hurt. After about 30 minutes or more I walked outside and the people went home. As a show of force I had one of the jeeps come by and pick us up. I then reported to the CO and he thanked me. I left the next morning at 5:00 a.m. for home. Two years later I was recalled for action in Korea.

Memorable Assignments

by Dominic P. Licastro

I enlisted in the U.S. Army at Worcester, MA, 1 February 1946, was inducted at Fort Devens, MA and took my basic training at Fort McClellan, AL.

I was assigned to the U.S. Constabulary in Marberg, Germany in June 1946 and sent to the 820th Constabulary Military Police Company in Bamberg, Germany.

Our duties were as guards to General Harmon's train and also at his home; we escorted visiting VIPs; patrolled the U.S. Army dependents areas, the town and highways. We were also assigned to the German Police Headquarters and conducted raids on civilian homes, hotels and camps for displaced persons. We were also in charge of the military stockade at the Panzer Kaserne near the Constabulary Headquarters.

While in Bamberg I and my buddy, Virgil I. Moss from O'Fallon, MO, were sent to the Constabulary Training School in Sonthofen. We trained in police procedures, desk and record keeping, judo classes, traffic control and investigations. We were situated in the Allgau Alps region, a beautiful area. This school originally was a German youth training school before the Americans took it over.

A year later the U.S. Constabulary Headquarters moved to Heidelberg and took over the 7th Army Headquarters. The 820th Constabulary Military Police Company was assigned to civilian homes for their headquarters, a few months later the 820th MP Company was reduced to a platoon.

At this time our commander, Lieutenant James Vaught, was looking for a volunteer to work with the newly organized GYA, an Army sponsored German youth activities group springing up all over Germany. I volunteered to work with the GYA in Heidelberg. We started with 45 children, ages 9-16 years, in a small former restaurant. We grew so fast that we had to open a civic center in the center of the city. The organization grew to 3,000 children from 9-19.

I organized a boys baseball team, called The Black Raiders, who played other GYA teams around the Heidelberg area. WACs from Constabulary Headquarters were in charge of a girls softball team. I organized a show group consisting of teenage boys and girls. We also had an orchestra for dancing and show group activities. All were members of the GYA Center.

The ski club was named White Lightening

and we organized a wrestling team and a basketball team. A cabinet shop was set up in the basement of the Civic Center where we repaired broken furniture. All work was done by the youth of the center and we were able to furnish a three floor boys center and a two floor girls center in Heidelberg.

We played games of Bingo and gave candy bars for prizes. We had dancing for the members, crafts, English lessons, radio classes and camping trips.

Our show group traveled to other towns and cities to perform shows and other GYA show groups would do the same. Tap dance lessons were given by Tech 5 Roberta Milabella, from Headquarters WAC Detachment. Tech 4 Margaret M. Lindeman, also from Headquarters WAC Detachment, was the first enlisted WAC to join our group at the center. The first officer was Lieutenant Anne Bradford; the first volunteers at the center were Major William R. Kuder, 1st Lieutenant Lowell Beilsmith, Lieutenant Anne Bradford and Lieutenant Bertha Hunter. German civilians who volunteered were Hilde Teidermann and house mother Mrs. Brown.

Master Sergeant Royal Tipton, Corporal Edward R. Jones, Tech 4 George Bell also worked with the GYA. Later, Tech 3 William E. Willoughby, WAC Staff Sergeant Naomi Sanders and others were assigned to our GYA group.

While in Heidelberg our mascot dog, Master Sergeant Spike, was killed by two boxer dogs. I had a coffin ready for Spike because he was getting along in years and was suffering the effects of old age. We received permission to bury Master Sergeant Spike at retreat. We put his coffin on the hood of our jeep and gave him a military escort to his grave which was on the side of our barracks at Headquarters. Spike was picked up in France by a GI coming through. He was a war veteran, going through Paris, Luxembourg, Rottack, Badoltz, Regensberg, Berlin, Bamberg and Heidelberg. He was sorely missed by the GIs in the area.

After one year in Heidelberg, the Constabulary Headquarters moved to Stuttgart. I spent my last eight months in Vaihingen, Germany. While there I flew to England to meet my pen pal whom I had been writing to for two and a half years. After meeting my pen pal Dorothy Jean Radford, we decided to get married. We were married in Plymouth, England July 24, 1948 and celebrated our 49th wedding anniversary in 1997.

In November 1948 I left Germany for Fort Dix, NJ where I was discharged. I joined the Reserves unit and became an active reservist when I joined the 201st Military Intelligence Unit. We were recalled to service on 11 September 1950 and sent to Fort Holibird, MD, from there we were separated as a group and I went to Fort Bragg, NC where I was assigned to the 3420 ASU and worked as a desk sergeant in the main post stockade. Later I was assigned

as an assistant provost marshal investigator. I was discharged from the U.S. Army 10 April 1952.

In August 1953 I was appointed to the police department in the town of Southbridge, MA. I retired from the force in February 1976 after 22-1/2 years of service.

I was appointed in 1980 the chief of security at Harrington Memorial Hospital, Southbridge, MA, where I retired in February 1995 after 15 years of service.

I was appointed a Justice of Peace in 1985, a post I still hold. I have been a notary public for 35 years. I belong to several veterans organizations and several police organizations. I am also a member of the U.S. Constabulary Association.

I served in the U.S. Navy in 1942 (medical discharge), U.S. Maritime Service and Merchant Marine from 1943-45 and my Army career ran from 1946-52.

My Time in The U.S. Constabulary

1946-48

by SMSgt Harry F. Miller

I served in the 740th Tank Battalion during World War 11 and when it was deactivated in July 1946, I was assigned to the 39th Infantry Regiment, 9th Infantry Division. It too was deactivated in December 1946 in the realignment of forces in Germany.

I had requested reassignment to a tank unit just prior to the deactivation of the 9th Division and in November 1946, I was reassigned to the 2nd Constabulary Regiment at Freising, Germany, which is approximately 35 miles north of Munich. I was the only one assigned to the 2nd Regiment from the 39th Infantry Regiment at that time and, as such, I traveled alone via jeep to Munich then by train to Freising.

Upon arrival at Freising, it was noted that the Bahnhof (train station) had been completely destroyed during the war and nothing remained except for the train platform where a small wooden shack stood housing the RTO (Railway Transportation Officer). I reported in with the RTO and was told that transportation would be arranged for me to the Vimy Kaserne where the 2nd Constabulary Regiment was housed. A jeep soon arrived with bright yellow and blue stripes with a Constabulary logo in place of the white star commonly used on U.S. military vehicles of the era. The driver drove me to the kaserne and entered the main gate where we were stopped by a guard and told to dismount and await the OD (Officer of the Day). After a short wait, the OD appeared and stated that he wished I had not arrived at this time as they were expecting an inspection by Major General Ernest N. Harmon, C.G., U.S. Constabulary. I, of course, saw no reason for this to be of concern to me, however, I was in no position to complain. The OD therefore told me that he would put me up in an empty room and asked that I stay out of the way and hidden until General Harmon completed his inspection when the OD would have me sent to my assigned unit, which was still unknown to me.

My "hide-out" was in an empty cold room that had only a GI cot in it and nothing else. I was there only a short while when I heard a car door slam beneath my window. I peered out and saw the great man (Harmon) emerge from his sedan whereupon he stretched and looked up at the flag pole where he noticed that the gate guard had raised the flag upside down. Needless to say, Harmon came unglued. He chewed upon the guard, the OD, the greeting officer and everyone else that he could find. Harmon was well known for his fiery temper and gravelly voice which we was not timid to use.

Later on that day, a review of the regiment was to be held. Harmon, the regimental commander, Colonel Charles H. Reed (a relative by marriage to General George S. Patton and president of the Reed Tobacco Company of Virginia. Reed was also the officer that had organized the burial for Patton upon his untimely death), and Reed's staff were all on the reviewing stand. The review was to be led by the Light Tank Troop which was equipped with the M-24 Chaffee light tank. The idea was for the tanks to make a high speed pass through the main gate (which was always kept open), pass in review past Harmon and the others, drive around the quadrangle and the secondary gate (which was always kept closed and locked) and back through the main gate. For some reason however, the lead tank broke through the secondary gate and passed in review with the iron gate hanging from the main gun in the turret of the tank. Not deterred, the tank kept going the wrong way, rounded the quadrangle and passed out through the main gate. Of course this was too much for Harmon who again went into orbit and turned beet red in the face as he swore and obviously had words for Colonel Reed.

The remainder of the review went off without a hitch. I was told, however, that Harmon and Reed had a long conversation in Reed's office before Harmon left the area.

Colonel Reed was of a different time, as was Patton. Reed became unhappy one day when he discovered that the German's would buy only Pall Mall cigarettes, a longer cigarette than most of the day. To combat this, Reed had his tobacco company send over cases of his premiere brand called Piedmont and had all Pall Malls taken from our PX counters. One pack of these convinced GIs and Germans alike that they were not good cigarettes. There was a steady flow of troops into Munich to purchase their cigarette rations after that until Pall Malls returned to the local PX counters.

Colonel Reed's wife was the first dependent to arrive in Freising. Being the highest ranking woman (yes, they really believed they held their husband's rank), she made her appearance one day in our PX. The PX was in a gray building across the street from the main gate of the kasserne. While in the PX, Mrs. Reed had the misfortune to be standing near a few GI mechanics who had just crawled out from under vehicles in the motor pool and had gone to the PX for their cigarette ration. Mrs. Reed proceeded to berate these men because of their filthy fatigue uniforms. They tried to explain that their job was a filthy one and that they were bound to get dirty. The next day, the edict was passed that a class "A" uniform only could be worn to the PX. This meant that from then on, instead of taking 10 minutes to go to the PX for the mechanics, they now had to go to their quarters, take off the dirty fatigues, take a shower, get into a class "A" uniform, go to the PX, return to their quarters and change back into fatigues and return to work some 30 to 45 minutes later.

But I digress:

Two days later and still waiting in my "hide-away," I began to get weary of hiding and decided to walk around the kasserne to see what kind of a place I had been assigned to after having learned that it was not very well schooled as best as I could tell. As I walked down the sidewalk near the Regimental Headquarters, I heard a voice yell "Trooper!" several times. Not knowing what a trooper was other than a state policeman or paratrooper, I kept walking when suddenly the voice changed and yelled "Soldier!" I certainly knew what that was since I felt that I was a soldier and a good one at that. I stopped, turned around and saw the face of a Constabulary Major glaring at me. "What outfit are you in soldier?" he bellowed. "I have no idea Sir," I said. "Well where is your brass and your shoulder patch and your stripes," he asked. "I don't have any, Sir, we could never get them in the 9th Division where I came from," I told him. "Well, why are you here," he asked, "Because I was sent here" I replied. "So what outfit are you in now," he asked. "I have no idea, I've been hiding in an empty room for two days waiting for someone to tell me." With that, the major threw up his hands and walked away. As I walked back to my hiding place, I wondered what kind of an outfit I had been assigned to and what on earth I was doing there. I later learned that the major was Major Steinmetz, the regimental provost marshal - more about him later).

Eventually, someone remembered that I existed and came to release me and sent me to Headquarters Troop of the Regiment for duty as message center chief. The same duty I had performed in my earlier career.

One incident that I recall happening while I was at Freising happened on the Austria-Germany border along the Autobahn between Salzburg, Austria and Munich, Germany. Our 2nd Constabulary Squadron was manning the border check point along the Autobahn when a large captured German Army truck, bearing a red star on the cab, barreled through the arm that was lowered across the road to stop traffic. The check point always had an M-8 armored car standing by to pursue speeders, so the guards dispatched the M-8 after the offending truck and brought it to a halt. The two soldiers in the truck were Russians. One was a sergeant and the other a private. Since the GIs in the armored car could not speak Russian, they took the two offenders to the Regimental Headquarters in Freising where I heard this story and saw the results. No one at regiment could speak Russian so an interpreter was called from the Counter Intelligence Corps. As it happened, the interpreter could not communicate with the two men and resulted in speaking broken, GI German with the two Russkies. Meanwhile, contact was made with the Russian representative to the Dachau War Crimes Trials taking place at the former Dachau Concentration Camp. A Russian colonel arrived shortly at the Regimental CP (Command Post) and interrogated the two Russian soldiers. When he finished, the soldiers were red faced and standing at attention. The Russian colonel explained to us that the two soldiers had been given a truck with evidence for the War Crimes Trials and had been told to go to Dachau and not to stop for anything! This they did.

Major Steinmetz, the regimental provost marshal mentioned above, had a bad habit of hiding in a dark place at the corner where the street to the kasserne intersected with the main street of Freising. The main street had been "The Adolf Hitler Strasse before and during the war. It was now called the Captain Snow Strasse, named for the first military governor in Freising. Captain Snow's son was in our unit at this time, but back to Steinmetz. One night our troop had a party at the Weinstephen Brewery in Freising. After much beer drinking and hilarity, my Communications Platoon personnel were walking back to the kasserne. When we rounded the corner to go up the hill to the kasserne, we decided we should relieve ourselves in the dark. As we stood on the curb, wetting the cobblestones, Major Steinmetz appeared out of the dark commanding us to "put those things away and come with me!" About this time, several members from the horse platoon came running around the corner laughing and yelling into the arms of Steinmetz. "You men, come with me!," said the major. At this point, my friends and I ran past the major and up the steep hill to the kasserne and never heard a word from the major. The funny part of this was that we all worked in the Message Center next to Steinmetz' office and he never recognized us nor was anything ever said to us. I was relating this story to a former member of the horse platoon at a reunion in 1996 and learned that he had been one of the members that saved us. He also related what happened to him and his comrades. Ironic after 49 years to have learned the rest of the story - which I leave to him to tell.

It is a little known fact that some of us banded together, pooled our resources (cigarettes and coffee) and paid the brew meister at the Weinstephen Brewery (the world's oldest) in Freising to obtain the proper ingredients to make 23 percent beer. It was lovely stuff and self supporting. We had been having trouble with the 3rd Army MPs in the form of the 508th MP Battalion in Munich. Each time we went to Munich, they spotted our shoulder patch and gave us fits. Delinquency reports were sent in on us continually. One day, the MPs learned that we had the 23 percent beer and wanted to purchase some from us. We told them that they could not have any due to their treatment of us while in Munich. They called a truce and we sold them a truck load of our precious beer. From that day forward, we could do no wrong in Munich and several incidents occurred that were overlooked by them.

Around the middle of 1947, the Yugoslavs decided that they wanted to take Trieste from the Italians. The Trust Troops (Trust meaning Trieste, U.S. Troops) were inadequate for the job of fending off the Yugoslavs, so we were alerted to go to their assistance. As it turned out, the Yugoslavs relented and all was calm again without the 2nd Regiment. We were pleased to say the least.

Not long after the above incident, we were told that the 2nd Regiment was to deactivate. Some of Colonel Reed's devotees maintained that it was not deactivated, however, we underlings were told that it was and were told that Reed took the Regimental colors back to the States with him. This of course was the rumor, however, it has been substantiated by other members. Be that as it may, some of us were shipped to the 5th Constabulary Regiment and its subordinate units; many went to the 5th Regiment Headquarters; however, I went to the 35th Constabulary Squadron in Fussen, Germany, near the location of the Neuswanstein Castle which is seen on nearly every travel poster for Germany. I was again assigned as message center chief and was there only briefly. This was a more military organization and much better led with officers that were respected more than those we had in Freising, in my opinion. I recall that at retreat ceremonies we were required to have condoms in one pocket and a prophylactic kit in the other. This was assured by the commanding officer passing us as we were lined up for retreat. As he passed, we pulled out condom in one hand and pro-kit in the other. That was about as far as they could go without actually watching us use them.

The 35th Squadron soon moved en masse to Augsburg and about the same time the 5th Regiment was redesignated 2nd Regiment and the 35th Squadron was redesignated 42nd Squadron. This placed the entire newly re-activated 2nd Regiment in three Kasserns in Augsburg. While in Augsburg we trained and trained hard for a combat role which I feel

created higher morale than our previous mission did. We accomplished 100 mile hikes and spent six months combat training in the field at the Graffenwohr Training Area. My communications officer was 1st Lieutenant Walter Cunningham, the best officer I ever knew in the Army. I met Walt again at the first reunion of the Constabulary in Helen, GA in 1993. I left the 42nd Squadron in July 1948 and returned to the States; four months later, I was in Tokyo, Japan.

I remained in the Army until 1953 when after Korean War service, I left the Army as a sergeant first class and immediately joined the USAF and was given the rank of technical sergeant, which was the equivalent of the sergeant first class rank that I held in the Army. I served until January 1966 as a communications operations superintendent and retired from the USAF as a senior master sergeant during the Vietnam War. I spent a total of 10 years in Germany during my service and 16 years of my 20 years service was spent overseas.

My Constabulary years were some of the best I experienced in the Army with the exceptions of the SNAFU's mentioned above. Isn't it strange how we remember the ludicrous and forget the serious?

After retirement, I worked as a private investigator for seven years covering the area of west Texas, New Mexico and Colorado. I then worked as the director of security and safety at a Santa Fe, New Mexico Hospital where I remained for five years. My last working years were at The University of Texas at Arlington where I was employed as a safety inspector and from which I retired in January 1989.

My wife Helen and I have been married 21 years and have five children between us. We have spent our retirement years traveling (mostly to Europe) and dancing. Helen sings with a local musical group and I schlepp the speaker and equipment.

Speed Trap

by Guy K. Troy

One of the stories I remember most was with the 15th Constabulary Squadron. I was in C Troop and periodically we were detailed to conduct speed traps on the major highway to control speeding. Our squadron S-3 was a Major Darrah and he designated C Troop to set up a speed trap between Schwabisch Hall and Stuttgart.

The traps were conducted by stationing two teams a mile apart hidden some distance from the officer. The teams were in each direction from the officer to catch any one speeding in either direction. The teams had radios and the first one to have a car pass their location would make a call on the radio, and the next person would check the time it took to go

the mile. The office would then consult the chart and determine if there had been a speeding violation and if so flag the car and award a ticket.

On one particular day we were doing business as usual with not much traffic. Suddenly a civilian car exceeding the speed limit passed and was duly flagged. I marched up to award the citation when suddenly I saw the driver with a major and snapped to attention. The major was Major Darrah who had posted our trap. I don't know who was most embarrassed, he or I. Since all of the tickets went to the S-3 office anyway, I remember I wrote him a ticket. We had laughs about it later.

Another memory was during the exchange of reich marks to deutsche marks in 1948. The reich mark was worthless at this time. Many lieutenants in the squadron were suddenly called in the middle of the night to report to the kasserne. We were each formed into two machine gun jeeps and one on 2-1/2 ton truck teams. We then convoyed to Frankfurt and were isolated in a large warehouse building. It was only then that we were told our mission which was to carry the new deutsche mark to various banks.

At a specific time I took my team to the main bank in Frankfurt which was heavily guarded at this time. We loaded the truck with boxes of deutsche marks and one German from each of the banks we were going to. We took off with me leading in one jeep, the trucks and the other jeep protecting the rear. My two objectives were the two main banks in Kaufburen and Hempten. We traveled with reasonable speed directly to the banks, backed the 2-1/2 tons to the door and quickly unloaded the trucks, all the while posting the machine gun jeeps appropriately. This was the deutsche mark used today. The German civilians were allowed to exchange a limited amount of riech marks only for the deutsche mark.

We also had a mission to police and monitor the thousands of displaced persons (DPs) which remained after the war. In many cases large numbers were housed in abandoned kassernes or any large apartment building left standing. These became DP camps and were usually surrounded by barbed wire fences. In many cases they became a hot bed for contraband, although I don't remember exactly what. Periodically, they were searched. One such raid occurred at Heidenhiem south of Schawabisch Hall. The squadron moved out in the early morning hours and we surrounded the DP camp before dawn. While some troops kept the security, most were divided into small teams of three to four soldiers for search. Our mission was to search the entire camp. We began at the top floors and entered every room and had every occupant open all closets doors, cabinets, underbed, etc. It was an extremely thorough procedure. It was long after dark when we finished and I was in the last M-8 covering our withdrawal. As I said I don't remember exactly what we were searching for or whether we were successful, but we certainly got a good view of how the many displaced person were living.

My Big Motorcycle Crash

by Ronald B. Johnson

When I went to Freising in June 1946, I was put in a replacement barracks with others I'd traveled with down from Erlangen. We were waiting for assignment to one of the units that were to be part of the U.S. Constabulary, either the 2nd Regiment Headquarters Squadron or the 42nd Squadron. (It was also where we were called out onto the parade ground for the ceremony that officially made it the 2nd Constabulary Regiment on 1 July 1946.)

A couple of others and I were called into a room where a sergeant in boots and breeches waited to talk to us. He said he was in the Motorcycle Platoon and they were looking for men over six feet tall who wanted to ride bikes (Harley 45's to be exact). He said they would train us to ride them, so I quickly agreed; mostly, I think, because I was so glad to find somebody who wanted me.

I really needed the training, because I didn't know how to drive anything. I had been through the Mechanized Cavalry training in Fort Knox, but I still couldn't really drive. When we drove cross-country in M-8s, it didn't seem to matter much when you ground the gears or whatever. We had only eight weeks of basic training and I spent most of it on KP or guard duty (ours was the only troop in training in the whole regiment, so we pulled duty for the whole outfit).

I was 16 years old (I lied about my age), not knowing how to drive, which I also had to do on jeep patrol, and having to learn about riding a bike. Again, it was pretty much okay as long as we were in the fields or on the hills; but when we got on the road, as we eventually did, it was another story.

The problem was the clutch. It has a rocking motion that was totally different from the push for the brakes, which I was still working on with some difficulty. I kept stalling the bike, because I didn't want to give it enough gas.

After several stalls, my section sergeant said, "Dammit, just give it a lot of gas and jam in the clutch." Being a dutiful soldier, and scared as hell, I did, and it worked. The only problem was that I was not facing downroad, but toward the other side of the road. About 10 feet from the road were some trees and, as I found out later, a barbed wire fence.

Being as I'd given it a lot of gas, I was across the road immediately. I tried to steer in between two trees; only problem was that they were only about two feet apart. The net result was that the front wheel got through, but the rest of the bike and I didn't.

The only real harm done, other than a slightly bent handle bar, was a small cut on my left nostril, about an inch from my eye, caused by the barbed wire. They called me Lucky Johnson for a while after that.

A Soldier's Story

by William K. Jackson

Though I was fortunate to miss actual combat with all its accompanying horrors and sufferings, I was proud to serve in its aftermath as a member of the specially picked forces known as the U.S. Constabulary. Those of us who served know that the 30,000 troopers were to join an outfit that would be in force from early 1946 to 1952. We were to police and maintain the peace in a Germany that had been bombed and whipped into submission. The troopship had brought me from the east coast to Le Havre, France, then by train across that country to Kitzingen in southern Germany.

Though I had been introduced to what war does to the destruction of a city when I had originally landed in Manila, the Philippines, it was nothing compared to what I now saw. I was a 19-year-old soldier. I had been born on a peaceful, little tropical island and came to the treeless plains of southwestern Kansas in 1937. Now, in Schweinfurt, Germany, all I saw about me was total destruction. It seemed like the bottom of hell with not a building untouched. At least it was a hell with all the fires finally put out and no longer smoking. Fortunately the military kasserne where we were billeted was in fair shape and had been shot up with mostly just small arms fire. Due to the shortage of personnel and my knowledge of tanks (I had had 22 weeks of training at Fort Riley, KS) I was quickly promoted to tech 4 sergeant and found myself either driving, or in command of an M-24 light tank assigned to the 14th Constabulary Regiment. Our job was to make surprise raids on towns or sections of cities, seal off the roads leading in so other troopers could enter and make searches for illegal weapons or activities. The next nine months were some of the most interesting of my life. We went on weekend passes to cities such as Heidelberg that had no destruction at all. It seemed out of place among all the other bombed out towns. Some of us had the opportunity to visit a session of the Nürnberg trials where all the Nazis were on trial. We were seeing and being a part of history without realizing it. That's how it is with youth.

My wife and I flew to Germany 50 years later and drove about that country as well as several surrounding it. I did not recognize Schweifurt. It was difficult to find the kasserne where we troopers stayed. Why? Because, in the entire city, not a brick was out of place. In 1946 I had learned to get about by recognizing a certain building with the roof missing, the front destroyed, three stories missing, an entire block gone, and on and on. You see what I mean. The Germans had put it all back together.

Constabulary Days

by John Hollern

I first learned of the U.S. Constabulary while thumbing through a magazine while home on delay en route to be stationed in Germany in March 1947. After reading the article I thought, boy would I like to be assigned to that outfit. On the train ride from Bremerhaven to the Marburg Replacement Detachment, I rode in a compartment of six. Four of the soldiers were returning to Germany. During the trip there was one stretch of road that ran parallel to the tracks and there was a Constabulary patrol riding in the same direction. One of the returning veterans said "some Circle C Cowboys." The conversation that then took place about the Constabulary was what a great job they were doing, always looking sharp and on the ball.

After hearing those vets talk about the Constabulary I definitely wanted to be a Circle C Cowboy. Thank God I was assigned to the 6th Constabulary Regiment in Bamberg. I knew then that my time in occupied Germany would not be wasted time.

In Bamberg I went through a month training to learn to be a trooper. Although I only saw him a few times during training, First Sergeant James K. Brinsfield set the standard for uniform and dress. After a week or so of training the first sergeant said we would be allowed a pass if we could pass his personal inspection. His standards were boots to shine like glass, a short GI haircut, a clean shirt and trousers with creases like a knife and of course a condom and pro-kit in pocket. I ran across Sergeant Brinsfield later in my career and it was always in a show place assignment. All this just re-enforcing my thought that the best available were our trainers.

Upon completion of regimental training I was assigned to the 13th Squadron which was stationed in the same kasserne as Regimental Headquarters. When I reported in to C Troop with a few other troopers we were given an indoctrination by the troop commander. To this day I have never received as thorough and inspiring welcome to a unit as then given, even though there were only about five of us.

I enjoyed the pomp and ceremony of formal guard mounts every Friday and the Sunday church formation every Sunday. One Sunday when the churchgoers were to break ranks and go to the location of services of their choosing, I did not fall out as usual. I had to pack to leave that afternoon for Signal School in Ansbach. After the church-goers had departed, the squadron left the parade ground and double-timed back to the troop area the long way. After formation I asked my buddy what that was all about, and he replied "where in the world have you been? We do that every

Sunday to encourage us to attend church." I personally thought it was good idea that someone was also caring for our morals.

When I attended the Signal School it was but one of many schools I was to attend. The *Constabulary Lightning Bolt* had an article in it entitled "School Boy Holleron Off Again." I also attended the Constabulary basic course, advanced course, and non-commissioned officers course all at the Berg in Sonthoffen. Later there was the administrative clerks course at the Quartermaster School in Darmstadt with a promise from my troop commander, Captain Goldsmith, that he would not assign me to a clerk's position. He assured me I would always be glad to be able to type. He was absolutely right. My worry was to be assigned to an inside type job. Just the year before I had convinced the Cook Board, whose job it was to interview and place or promote personnel according to their MOS, that I wanted my basic cavalry MOS not Radio Operator MOS as my primary. I said I wanted to be a real trooper. Remember, at that time we used CW Morse Code at the lower levels of the unit, not voice.

Troop information was a required weekly subject and as I had reached the rank of corporal I was then sent to the U.S. Army Troop Information and Education School at Buedingen. Again I knew that I was serving with the best as the first sergeant for the school troops was the same person who was my first sergeant when I first was assigned to C Troop, 13th Squadron. First Sergeant Robinson was the same one who at each troop formation would encourage us to do right, tell us we were improving, and that smart troopers do not get in trouble.

In the fall of 1948 the 13th Squadron was moved to Coburg and shortly thereafter we were redesignated the 6th Squadron which I believe had been inactivated by mistake. Our area of operations now included our old area plus what had been the 6th Squadron and the 27th Squadron.

I really loved the job we were doing and volunteered for every patrol, road block, and anything in line of Constabulary duty. My platoon sergeant, Tech Sergeant Clemons, used to volunteer for all the week-end patrols because when the unit moved to Coburg most of the dependents were still living in Bamberg. This was his way of making up for not being available on short notice after hours. There were two other troopers in the platoon who were drivers and loved their jobs also and always volunteered. By us four always ready to go, it was easy to get two more to volunteer because the other troopers rotated amongst themselves knowing they had a good thing going for them.

On one road block that we set up south of Bamberg a German tried to run through it on a bicycle. Trooper Byers had to chase him down with a jeep and run him off the road. When the man appeared in military court in Coburg it wound up the only reason he had not stopped

was because he did not like Americans. He said like all the German ex-soldiers said at that time, that he had served on the Russian Front. I believe he received 90 days in jail for the offense and had the court and time to do in Coburg because that is where we were stationed, although he lived south of Bamberg.

Another incident which happened east of Bamberg at a road block was that a Mercedes ran through the entrance point but did stop at the exit point. Tech Sergeant Clemons had the occupants dismount and gave them a real dressing down by explaining how serious the situation was to run a Constabulary road block. He then pointed to me and the machine gun and explained that the gun would have been used had they continued on. After he checked the Germans identification cards and license, he really laid onto the German who had been riding in the back seat. It wound up that he was a member of the Landerat. Sergeant Clemons then told him that Democracy demanded that all people obey the laws, not just the ordinary people. The official apologized and we really felt he had both learned a lesson in Democracy and meant it when he said he was sorry.

While at the Constabulary School the Weapons Department taught pistol and sub-machine gun firing. The instructors were the 1946 European champs. After the instruction there and for the rest of my career, I always fired expert with any weapon with only two exceptions. From that instruction I learned my lesson well enough that I was later able to compete in the National Matches at Camp Perry, OH. Those Champions bred more champions.

I can attest to why Americans first started to need to have a hunting or fishing license when doing those sports. It was the spring of 1948 and my platoon was in Schirding for border patrol duty. In the arms room were ten 03 Springfields for the purpose of hunting. Two troopers wanted to hunt and asked me if I would be the NCOIC for the party. Lieutenant Jack Schramm okayed the hunt. While we were hunting one trooper hit a doe and wanted to bury it. Instead we loaded it up and returned to the platoon building. I explained to Lieutenant Schramm what had happened. He had me take the doe to the Burgermeister.

About two weeks later, while I was on desk duty, in came the local military government officer, an interpreter, the Jaegermeister and the Burgermeister. They told Lieutenant Schramm that about a week ago some Germans had reported that it sounded like there was a small war in the woods and then saw some Americans leaving. After several days there, two does were shot and one had a young one in her. When Lieutenant Schramm turned to me and asked what had happened, I reminded him that this incident had taken place after I had been NCOIC and that a T-4 had been the NCOIC.

From regiment came orders of no more

hunting or fishing until further notice. After three months the ban was lifted and that now Americans must also have a license when hunting or fishing. I also found out the ban had been EUCOM wide, not just the regiment.

I served in war and I have served in peace. I even came out of retirement to serve in Vietnam, but to me my proudest service was with the U.S. Constabulary. We were the best Uncle Sam had.

My Story
by Albin F. Irzyk

I consider myself one of the important midwives who attended the "birthing" of the U.S. Constabulary.

During combat in Europe, I commanded the 8th Tank Battalion of the 4th Armored Division. Toward the end of combat, but before it ended, the 4th Armored had already been informed that even though most divisions would redeploy back to the States, the 4th would remain in the Occupation of Germany.

Shortly after V-E Day the battalions of the division were spread throughout its occupation zone. I was the commander of a Kreis called Vilsbiburg. My job, along with that of my troops, was to bring law and order to the Kreis, and to assist the German citizens to begin getting their lives back together. We began the steps that the military government units would continue when they arrived. All members of the division assumed that they would continue what they were doing well on into the future.

Subsequently, I was ordered from my battalion to division headquarters where I eventually became chief of staff of the division. We were smoothly accomplishing our assigned mission when, without warning, we were hit by a combination hurricane, cyclone, tornado.

We were told that the division, which had won fame during the war in Europe, would be summarily deactivated and would be a division no more. This was staggering, unbelievable news. What came next was even more astonishing. We learned that as the division was being deactivated, its units would become the nucleus of a brand new, unique, specialized force, so special that none like it had ever existed in our Army. It was to be a force especially created for the special needs of a successful occupation of Germany and would be called the U.S. Constabulary.

We were immediately hit with an unprecedented sense of urgency. Thousands of tasks it seemed had to be done at once. As chief of staff with the guidance of the division commander, Major General Fay B. Prickett, the support and cooperation of the division staff and the commanders and staffs of all the subordinate units, it was my responsibility to get the job done, and what a big job it was!

The division had to immediately divest

itself of all the items that had made it a fearsome power during World War II; its tanks, half tracks, armored artillery; its hundreds of trucks and jeeps; its engineer and maintenance equipment.

Even more important was the psychological change. There had to be a different mind-set. No longer were the members of the division tactical troops, warriors, fighters. Yes, they were still soldiers, but now they would have to learn to be soldier policemen-Constabulary Troopers.

Tremendous coordination had to be effected with the 1st Infantry Division. They would take over the 4th's area of responsibility. Their units throughout had to be in place as units of the 4th withdrew.

VI Corps headquarters would furnish the nucleus of the Constabulary Headquarters, but the 4th Armored became the nucleus for much of the rest. Division headquarters became the nucleus for the 1st Brigade, Combat Command A of the 4th the nucleus of the 2nd Brigade, Combat Command B of the 4th the nucleus for the 3rd Brigade.

Something new came into being - three Regimental Headquarters in each of the brigades, and under the regiments were battalion sized units called (after the cavalry) squadrons. All battalions of the 4th Armored, regardless if they had been tank, armored infantry, or armored artillery battalions became squadrons, and they were scattered in all three brigades. Tremendous planning and coordination had to be effected in the creation and reorganization of all these units.

There were not enough battalions in the 4th to flesh out all the regiments, so tank, field artillery, antiaircraft battalions were gathered throughout the theater and integrated with the battalions of the 4th.

As all this was taking place, each unit had to shuck its TO/E (Tables of Organization and equipment), and to be integrated, equipped according to the Constabulary TO/E. Simultaneously, every soldier turned his back on his specialty, tanker, artillery man,

infantryman, and each one trained hard in his new role, that of soldier-policeman.

At the outset the mission seemed impossible. The challenges were certainly more than daunting. Amazingly the mission was accomplished. This special, unique, unprecedented corps sized unit was formed in less than six months. From a concept to reality in six months, a most ambitious undertaking and a most successful one.

During its period of existence, the U.S. Constabulary accomplished its mission of insuring the success of our occupation of Germany.

Because of that, I take great pride and satisfaction in the role that I played. I was able to pull the strings that initially put many of the major pieces in place that held until the Constabulary had finished its job.

Thus, I was a "Charter Member" of the "Constabulary." Along with other members of the 4th Armored Division's staff, we became members of the 1st Brigade. General Prickett became the commanding general, and I his S-3 and later his executive officer.

My Sport Story

by Albin F. Irzyk

Constabulary duty was most demanding and challenging. The hours and days were long. Nevertheless, time was found to have some fun.

Early on, a squadron level baseball program was initiated, leagues were formed, and play would soon start.

Late one morning, there was a knock on my door, and when I opened it, there stood an obviously uncomfortable sergeant. He introduced himself as Sergeant Bryant and explained that he was the captain of the baseball team of Headquarters and Headquarters Troop of the 1st Brigade. He further explained that the troop was in a squadron baseball league, and, because of its small size, was heavily undermanned and needed all the help it could

get. He had heard from someone that I had been a baseball player and wondered if I could come out for practice (obviously to check me out). My job was most demanding but I checked with General Prickett about going out. He, a great sports fan, urged me to go. I went to practice and must have passed muster for I was invited to be the team's shortstop.

The away games would be the problem. Again, General Prickett and I found a solution. A substitute outfielder was a pilot. I would work until the last possible moment. Then Lieutenant Flanagan in an L-5 would fly me to the game.

After I joined the team, I learned that Sergeant Bryant was known as "Pappy" Bryant. He was the oldest man in the troop and a talented pitcher.

The upshot: we more than held our own in the squadron league and had a most successful season.

One lasting memory: we were playing a doubleheader at Fulda against a very good team. I was having a particularly good day at the plate. After two hits in the second game, I came to the plate for the third time. As I stepped into the batter's box, a loud, raucous voice yelled, "Get the old man out!" At the time I was a 28-year-old lieutenant colonel.

Pappy was considerably older than I and we were playing with 19, 20 and 21-year-old youngsters. This story had a happy ending for the "old men." Both Pappy and I were selected to the All-Star Team at the end of the season.

M-8 Armored Car, Special Edition

by T-4 Clifford Gubler

Early in 1948 the 68th Constabulary Squadron stationed in Augsburg allowed me to have an M-8 Armored Car. (A speedy six wheeled monster mounting a 37mm cannon.) On my own I paid to have it professionally painted and detailed by a German firm.

It came back beautifully finished with lacquer and stretched the limits of military specifications. Vehicle number "B-25" was a magnificent beast. She was Troop B's flagship and participated in many patrols and raids. Road blocks were her specialty as you could spot her a mile away.

That year, B-25 was almost in the history books when the Autobahn to Berlin was first blockaded. A small team of us was ordered to get ready to drive to Berlin to contest the closure. We made a test run to Munich to see if the vehicles would hold up for a long trip. As usual, "B-25" purred and was raring to go. Fortunately our trip was canceled at the last moment. I guess they figured that razzle-dazzle wouldn't have impressed the bad guys.

Old "B-25" first got in trouble while on maneuvers with the 1st Infantry Division in Grafenwhohr. As "Aggressors" and in the spirit of disrupting "Enemy" communications, she

2nd Constabulary Regiment 1948 Boxing Champions

Top Row (L to R) Arnold McKee, Bantamweight; Kirasuki Higa, Featherweight; Thomas Thompson, Lightweight; Gilbert Carlos, Welterweight; and James Brown, Middleweight. (Bottom Left) Herb Coon, Light Heavyweight. (Bottom Right) Tony Bersani, Heavyweight.

literally called off the war. It seems as though someone had placed a large number of ground laid telephone wires in "B-25's" pintle tow hook and told me to drive off. A few days later, MPs came to pick up my lieutenant. He had inadvertently ordered the dragging away of many of the enemy's switchboards that had been attached to the wires. No one was seriously hurt by this careless act.

I lost my friend, old "B-25," when an envious regiment spirited her away. (I'll never forgive 1st Sergeant Williams for the way she was taken.) I later heard that a picture of her was featured in the *Military Government Times*.

Railroad Checkpoint Duty

by T-4 Clifford Gubler, Trp. C, 37th Constabulary Sqdn.

In the summer of 1946, just the U.S. Constabulary manned the Border Checkpoint at the Lorch Railyard. All trains were halted at the border as anyone entering or leaving the American Zone was subject to checks. As the trains came through day and night, our small eight man detachment could only provide for just two troopers per shift for border control. It wasn't until the Fall when we got some German Border Police in to help. Nevertheless, our shifts began when a train steamed in and we halted it for usually an hour. Hundreds of passengers would usually get off, spread themselves out all over the yard and quietly await our inquiries. By their sides, many had all their worldly goods packed in blankets and battered suitcases.

Our job was to wade through this sea of humanity and randomly check papers. My three years of high school German served me in good stead. I made a special effort to check the papers of anyone who glowered at me. One man that we detained for lack of identification said that we were just like the SS.

The Orient Express came through about once a week but didn't have to stop for customs. A trooper usually just swung aboard and rode it to the next stop. By "Showing the Flag," I met many gracious people who wondered who we represented.

Being Constabulary Troopers, we were never concerned with our isolation. If we ever needed a backup, the rest of our small detachment was located in our Gasthaus billets, a good half mile away.

The Terrible Trains

by T-4 Clifford Gubler

In the spring of 1946, the 37th Constabulary Squadron was involved in enforcing the Big Three's edict of returning DPs (Displaced Persons) to their country of origin.

The DP Camp in Wetzlar housed a horde of persons who for the most part did not want to be repatriated. Black market activities and gangs kept the camp in constant turmoil.

One of the 37th's jobs was to slowly clean out the camp and put these unfortunate people on trains headed for their home countries. I'll always remember one fine Spring morning when the 37th swoops down and cordons off the rail yard and DP Camp. Troopers were all over the place. Hundreds of DPs are collected and taken to the rail yard. We hustle these poor souls on to the waiting railroad cars. Most are quietly resigned to their fate. The loading process is completed with little protest or resistance.

Whistles blow, doors are slammed shut and another terrible train pulls smartly out of the yard picking up speed. Logic indicating that reluctant passengers tended to stay aboard fast moving trains.

We later learned that some of the DPs were seriously injured when they jumped off the train a few miles away. Many of these people must have had an idea of the bleak futures they would have faced in the Russian Zone.

History books tend to gloss over Constabulary operations like this. Sadly enough, I was there.

How American Soldiers Are Duped

From Soviet Official Publication PRAVDA *#79, 19 March 1948*

In the foothills of the Alps, in the region of Garmisch, lies a little mountain village, Oberammergau. It is famous the world over for the Passion Plays which have been held there for centuries, and which have attracted visitors from all parts of the world. Hence we proceeded to this village. However, there instead of the passion plays, we discovered an American Espionage School for spies and saboteurs who were eventually to be sent to work in Eastern European countries. American Intelligence Agents, together with German Fascist Generals and other criminals train Polish Andersmen, Ukraninian Nationalists, Jugoslav Chetniks, and other fascist scum accepted into the American Army in the arts of espionage, sabotage and provocation.

The Big Switch

by Sam Zafran, Outpost 6

The call came early in the morning, Armored Cars M-8 and M-20 Crews, move out in two hours. Full combat gear, basic load of ammo, destination to be revealed later. Rest of the troop to follow later as the armored cars would slow down the other wheeled vehicles.

Once out of the kasserne, we pulled over to the side of the road on the Autobahn. Destination, Rhien Main Airbase, Frankfurt, Germany. Engine hatches were pulled back and steel balls and heavy paper clips were inserted, off we roared down the Autobahn at full clip.

After bedding down that night with the rest of the troop, we arose the next morning, went through the hurry up and wait period, then observed trucks entering the area. Boxes were unloaded from the trucks and then loaded into the turret compartments and crew compartments of the armored cars. One M-8 and one M-20 were teamed up to two machine gun jeeps and the individual teams were dispatched to predetermined destinations; 37s were loaded with buckshot rounds, 30s and 50s were belted and half-loaded.

Our first inkling as to what was occurring was when we made our first stop in the city at a large imposing building, guarded by German police. A number of boxes were unloaded, and we proceeded to our next destination, following the same routine. We finally realized they were delivering the New German Deutch Mark to replace the old Reich Mark then being used. Of all the many and varied duties ie speed traps, DP camp raids and border patrols, this was one of the most memorable incidents in my U.S. Constabulary career.

DIES IN BATTLE

WASHINGTON - (AP) - The Army announced Wednesday the award of the Medal of Honor posthumously to 1st Lieutenant Richard T. Shea Jr., husband of Mrs. Joyce E. Shea of New Milford, NJ, and son of Mr. and Mrs. Richard T. Shea, Portsmouth, VA. Lieutenant Shea won the IC4 a cross-country, championship three straight years while at West Point.

He was killed 8 July 1953, little more than a year after he was graduated from West Point.

When the Communists launched an attack on an outpost held by Company A of the 17th Regiment of the 7th Division, Shea, its executive officer, volunteered to lead the counter-assaults.

In the first night's fighting Shea killed two Chinese with his trench knife and directed American fire on enemy positions. The following day Shea led his men in further advances.

Shea was wounded during the second day, but refused to be moved and continued to lead his men. Once when the enemy held up the Americans by heavy machine gun fire, the lieutenant charged the position, throwing grenades, firing his carbine and killed three Chinese.

On the third day the reinforced enemy attacked with great force. Shea led a counter-attack and was again wounded. Shea was last seen in close hand-to-hand combat with the enemy. He was 26 at the time of his death.

The United States Constabulary Squadrons, 1946-52

by 2nd Lt. Thomas O. Dinackus

When the War In Europe ended In 1945 the US Army was faced with the difficult task of providing an occupational force to enforce military government in Germany, while the American public was clamoring for the quick demobilization of the armed forces now that hostilities had ended. A large traditional occupation force was out of the question; the solution arrived at was the U.S. Constabulary, an elite mechanized police force which possessed a significant combat capability. The Constabulary became operational on 1 July 1946 and the command was active until 1950, with some individual Constabulary units remaining active until the end of 1952.

The backbone of the Constabulary was the Constabulary Squadron. As initially organized, each squadron was authorized a headquarters and headquarters troop, three mechanized troops and two motorized troops. The mechanized troops were designed to conduct mounted patrols and were equIppe4 with M-8 Armored Cars and jeeps with .30 cal. machine guns. The motorized troops had a limited amount of transport and were used to conduct dismounted patrols in urban areas and to man station positions.

The squadrons were assigned to the Constabulary Regiments on a basis of three per regiment. Nine Constabulary Regiments were stationed In Germany and comprised the U.S. Zone Constabulary. These regiments were organized into three Constabulary Brigades which reported directly to Constabulary Headquarters. A separate regiment, the 4th, was headquartered in Austria and had its subordinate units in Austria and West Berlin. In addition to the 30 "line" squadrons in the 10 regiments, two special squadrons existed which were assigned to the Zone Constabulary-the Constabulary School Squadron ran the Constabulary School and the 97th Constabulary Squadrons were created by the redesignation and conversion of various mechanized units on occupation duty in Europe. Most of the 1st and 4th Armored Divisions became Constabulary units, along with elements of the seven mechanized cavalry groups in Europe and various other armored, tank destroyer and self-propelled antiaircraft units.

Chart #2 U.S. Constabulary Squadrons, 1 July 1946

U.S. Zone Constabulary - Germany
1st Constabulary Brigade
1st Constabulary Regiment
1lth Constabulary Sqdn - Kassel

Chart #1 - Origin of the Constabulary Squadrons

All redesignations occurred 1 May 1946

Constabulary Unit	Previous Designation	Previous Assignment
1st Constabulary Sqdn	1st Tank Bn	1st Armd Div
2nd Constabulary Sqdn	2nd Mecz Cav Recon Sqdn	2nd Cav Gp*
4th Constabulary Sqdn	4th Mecz Cav Recon Sqdn	4th Cav Gp*
6th Constabulary Sqdn	6th Mecz Cav Recon Sqdn	6th Cav Gp*
8th Constabulary Sqdn	8th Tank Bn	4th Armd Div
10th Constabulary Sqdn	10th Armd Inf Bn	4th Armd Div
11th Constabulary Sqdn	11th Armd Inf Bn	1st Armd Div
12th Constabulary Sqdn	6th Armd Inf Bn	1st Armd Div
13th Constabulary Sqdn	13th Tank Bn	1st Armd Div
14th Constabulary Sqdn	14th Armd Inf Bn	1st Armd Div
15th Constabulary Sqdn	15th Cav Recon Sqdn, Mecz	15th Cav Gp*
16th Constabulary Sqdn	HQ and HQ Trp,	16th Cav Gp —
22nd Constabulary Sqdn	22nd Armd FA Bn	4th Armd Div
24th Constabulary Sqdn	24th Mecz Cav Recon Sqdn	4th Cav Gp*
25th Constabulary Sqdn	25th Mecz Cav Recon Sqdn	4th Armd Div
27th Constabulary Sqdn	27th Armd FA Bn	1st Armd Div
28th Constabulary Sqdn	28th Mecz Cav Recon Sqdn	6th Cav Gp*
35th Constabulary Sqdn	35th Tank Bn	4th Armd Div
37th Constabulary Sqdn	37th Tank Bn	4th Armd Div
42nd Constabulary Sqdn	42nd Mecz Cav Recon Sqdn	2nd Cav Gp*
51st Constabulary Sqdn	51st Armd Inf Bn	4th Armd Div
53rd Constabulary Sqdn	53rd Armd Inf Bn	4th Armd Div
66th Constabulary Sqdn	66th Armd FA Bn	4th Armd Div
68th Constabulary Sqdn	68th Armd FA Bn	1st Armd Div
71st Constabulary Sqdn	771st Tank Bn	GHQ Unit
72nd Constabulary Sqdn	4th Tank Bn	1st Armd Div
74th Constabulary Sqdn	474th AAA AW Bn (SP)	GHO Unit
81st Constabulary Sqdn	81st Cav Recon Sqdn, Mecz	1st Armd Div
91st Constabulary Sqdn	91st Armd FA Bn	1st Armd Div
94th Constabulary Sqdn	94th Armd FA Bn	4th Armd Div
97th Constab Signal Sqdn	97th Signal Bn	GHO Unit
Constabulary School Sqdn	465th AAA AW Bn (SP)	GHO Unit

*Technically, these squadrons were attached and not assigned to the Cavalry Groups; however, they served with their parent group throughout the campaigns in Europe

Note that for the majority of the cavalry squadrons, official sources disagree as to whether they were designated "Mecz Cav Recon Sqdn" or "Cav Recon Sqdn, Mecz" before their redesignation as Constabulary Squadrons.

The U.S. Zone Constabulary began a one month test period on 1 June 1946, and became fully operational on 1 July. The Constabulary units in Austria and Berlin also became operational at about the same time.

12th Constabulary Sqdn - Bad Nauheim	42nd Constabulary Sqdn - Munich
91st Constabulary Sqdn - Kassel	66th Constabulary Sqdn - Munich
3rd Constabulary Regiment	5th Constabulary Regiment
37th Constabulary Sqdn - Lollar	8th Constabulary Sqdn* Regensburg
68th Constabulary Sqdn - Frankfurt	35th Constabulary Sqdn - Regensburg
81st Constabulary Sqdn - Fulda	74th Constabulary Sqdn - Augsburg
15th Constabulary Regiment	11th Constabulary Regiment
1st Constabulary Sqdn - Seckenheim	25th Constabulary Sqdn - Regensburg
14th Constabulary Sqdn - Darmstadt	51st Constabulary Sqdn - Regensburg
15th Constabulary Sqdn - Seckenheim	94th Constabulary Sqdn - Regensburg
2nd Constabulary Brigade	3rd Constabulary Brigade
2nd Constabulary Regiment	6th Constabulary Regiment
2nd Constabulary Sqdn - Bad Tolz	6th Constabulary Sqdn - Bamberg

28th Constabulary Sqdn - Bayreuth
53rd, Constabulary Sqdn - Nuremberg

10th Constabulary Regiment
13th Constabulary Sqdn# - Stuttgart
71st Constabulary Sqdn - Stuttgart
72nd Constabulary Sqdn - Stuttgart

14 Constabulary Regiment
10th Constabulary Sqdn - Kitzingen
22nd Constabulary Sqdn - Kitzingen
27th Constabulary Sqdn - Fulda

Assigned directly to U.S. Zone Constabulary:
97th Constabulary Signal Sqdn - Bamberg
Constabulary School Sqdn - Sonthofen

Independent of HQ, U.S. Zone Constabulary:
4th Constabulary Regiment
4th Constabulary Sqdn - Linz, Austr1a
16th Constabulary Sqdn -West Berlin
24th Constabulary Sqdn - Linz, Austria

*Attached to the 11th Constabulary Regiment
#Attached to the 6th Constabulary Regiment

The biggest problems faced by the Constabulary were the shortage of personnel and the high rate of turnover. By early 1947 the personnel shortage had forced a reorganization which included the inactivation of one "line troop per Constabulary Squadron. In Spring 1947 the European Theater experienced a troop cut and the Constabulary was greatly reduced in size as a result. One third of the squadrons were inactivated and virtually every squadron was affected by the reorganization, which began on 1 July 1947. In addition, within the squadrons all motorized troops were eliminated and each squadron reorganized to consist of a headquarters and headquarters troop and four mechanized troops. When the reorganization was completed, 11 of the 32 Constabulary Squadrons had been eliminated.

Chart #3 - U.S. Constabulary Squadrons, 3 November 1948

U.S. Constabulary - Germany

1st Constabulary Brigade
14th Constabulary Regiment
10th Constabulary Sqdn - Frtizlar
22nd Constabulary Sqdn - Hersfeld
27th Constabulary Sqdn - Darmstadt

15th Constabulary Regiment
1st at Constabulary Sqdn - Knielingen
14th Constabulary Sqdn - Boblingen
15th Constabulary Sqdn - Schwabisch

2nd Constabulary Brigade
2nd Constabulary Regiment
2nd Constabulary Sqdn - Augsburg
66th Constabulary Sqdn - Degerndorf

6th Constabulary Regiment
6th Constabulary Sqdn - Coburg
28th Constabulary Sqdn - Schweinfurt
53rd Constabulary Sqdn - Schwabach
11th Constabulary Regiment
25th Constabulary Sqdn - Straubing
51st Constabulary Sqdn - Landshut
94th Constabulary Sqdn - Weidon

Assigned Directly to U.S. Zone Constabulary:
68th Constabulary Sqdn - Augsburg
97th Constab Signal Sqdn - Heidelberg
Constabulary School Sqdn - Sonthofen

Independent of HQ, U.S. Zone Constabulary:
4th Constabulary Regiment
4th Constabulary Sqdn - Wels, Austria
16th Constabulary Sqdn - West Berlin
24th Constabulary Sqdn - Horsching, Austria

In 1948 the final major reorganization of the Constabulary took place. Up to this point the Constabulary had been strictly an internal security force. However, by early 1948 it was becoming obvious that the USSR posed a threat to the West and the role of the Constabulary began to change to reflect this. In April 1948 the constabulary troops began to reorganize as tactical units equipped with M-8 armored cars, light machine guns, recoilless rifles and mortars. Then, in the Summer of 1948, the 2nd, 6th and 14th Constabulary Regiments began to reorganize as Armored Cavalry Regiments. By the end of 1948 this reorganization was complete; the three ACRs were assigned to the Constabulary and provided the majority of its combat power. The Armored Cavalry Regiments were responsible for guarding the border and providing a mobile reserve while the few Constabulary Squadrons left continued the internal security mission.

Chart #4 - U.S. Constabulary Squadrons, 3 January 1949

Assigned to U.S. Zone Constabulary:
22nd Constabulary Sqdn - Hersfeld
53rd Constabulary Sqdn* - Weiden
97th Constab Signal Sqdn - Boblingen

Independent of U.S. Zone Constabulary:
4th Constabulary Regiment
4th Constabulary Sqdn - Horsching, Austria
16th Constabulary Sqdn - West Berlin
24th Constabulary Sqdn - Horsching, Austria

*There is some doubt as to whether the

53rd Squadron was still active as of 3 January 1949, although it is listed in official sources as active.

In the Spring of 1949 the 4th Constabulary Regiment was inactivated and its 4th Squadron was redesignated as a reconnaissance unit. The 22nd and 53rd Squadrons had already been inactivated, while the 15th Constabulary Squadron, which had been inactivated earlier, was reactivated. On 1 July 1949, three years after the Constabulary had become fully operational, the command consisted of two Brigade Headquarters, three Armored Cavalry Regiments, a Field Artillery Group, several combat engineer, ordnance, transportation, etc., units, and four Constabulary Squadrons:

15th Constabulary Sqdn - Welden
16th Constabulary Sqdn - West Berlin
24th Constabulary Sqdn - Hersfeld
97th Constab Signal Sqdn - Boblingen

All of these units were assigned to Headquarters, U.S. Constabulary.

The Headquarters, U.S. Constabulary was inactivated in November 1950 and used to provide personnel for the newly-activated headquarters, U.S. 7th Army. With this reorganization, the U.S. Army Europe concluded its period as an occupational force and reoriented itself as a defensive army protecting its section of West Germany. However, the requirement for Constabulary units still remained; the last two Constabulary Squadrons to see service in Europe were the 15th and 24th Squadrons, which soldiered on for two years after the inactivation of Constabulary Headquarters until the inactivation on 15 December 1952. For six and a half years the squadrons of the U.S. Constabulary had performed their special mission as the mechanized police force in occupied Germany and had admirably lived up to their motto, "Mobility, Vigilance, Justice."

Selected Bibliography
Stanely Russell Connor and Mary Lee Stubbs, *mor-Cavalry Part 1: Regular Army and Army Reserve*, Army Lineage Series (Washington: Office of the Chief Military History, 1969).

The U.S. Constabulary, Occupation Forces in Europe Series, 1945-46 (Frankfurt am Main: Office of the Chief Historian, European Command, 1947).

Major James M. Snyder, *The Establishment And Operations Of The U.S. Constabulary, 3 October 1945-30 June 1947* (n.p.: Historical Sub-Section G-3, U.S. Constabulary, 1947).

Major General Ernest N. Harmon, "U.S. Constabulary," *Armored Cavalry Journal*, Vol. 55, No. 5 (1946) pp. 16-18.

Lieutenant Colonel A.K. Irzyk, "Mobility, Vigilance, Justice - A Saga of the Constabulary," *Military Review* Vol. 26 No. 12 (1947) pp. 13-21.

Captain H.P. Rand, "A Progress Report on the U.S. Constabulary," *Military Review*, Vol. 29, Nov. 7 (1949), pp. 30-38.

Various U.S. Army Station Lists, especially those for:

1 July 1946

2 September 1947

3 November 1947

3 January 1949

2 May 1949

1 July 1949

Memories of the

16th Squadron (Separate)

Berlin, Germany 1946-48
by CSM William C. Strub, USA Ret.

I was sent to Berlin as a replacement assigned to the 78th Division. Seven or eight weeks later it was announced the 78th was going to be a carrier unit for all personnel being returned to the States. All replacement personnel were to be transferred to other units.

I was assigned to a newly activated unit called the Constabulary. Assignment was to C Troop, 16th Constabulary Squadron (SEPARATE), and that was a key suffix. This was to be my home for the next 31 months. The 16th was part of the 4th Regiment with headquarters in Austria. Physically we were stationed a few miles away in Berlin and were under the control of Berlin Command Headquarters. While everyone still looked like soldiers, we were now called troopers.

Getting settled and acquainted with a new group of people was a bit of a task, but the good news was that we had better living quarters. Only four men to a room and we each had our own foot and wall locker. The bad news, we had to get up, stand a formal Reveille and go back to some basic training. It was training, motor maintenance, guard duty and motorized city patrols. And more bad news, more men were being sent home or reassigned so that we were operating at 50% strength. We started to meet ourselves coming off one duty and going on to another. The only thing that broke the routine was the periodic ultimatums from the Russians, "You have 72 hours to get out of Berlin or else."

In the Spring of 1946 I and one other volunteer were picked to go with two mechanics from Headquarters Troop to Kitzingen in the American Zone to pick up a wrecker for the squadron motor pool. Driving several hundred miles with four men in a jeep, pulling a trailer full of five gallon gas cans, is an experience, and once is enough.

This trip did point out to me quite clearly that Berlin was an island in the middle of the Russian Zone of Occupation. So now, when I heard the Russians gave us an ultimatum to, "Get out of Berlin in 72 hours, or else," I had a better feel for the statement. This happened several times in 1946 and once (maybe twice) in 1947. We stayed and things were smoothed over by the high commands. Although one time we got to the point where we were briefed on our assignment and were about to move out when we got the signal to stand down. We never spoke about it, but some of us thought there would be a showdown someday. While slightly outnumbered, we all felt, we're here and we're going to stay. We were all young and bulletproof in those days.

About this time the Helmstedt Patrol was added to the duty assignments of the squadron. This was a patrol of the Autobahn from Berlin to Helmstedt in the British Zone, 108 miles (plus .2 or .3 more). In discussions and articles I have heard varied distances quoted, but I guarantee the correct distance is 108 miles. There was an American Aid Station 27 miles out from Berlin and a British Outpost 66 miles out of Berlin. Many patrols would terminate at the British Outpost and return but on some occasions the patrol would go all the way to Helmstedt - and back.

It was a cold Thanksgiving Day (1946) that I had the good/misfortune to be in charge of the Helmstedt Patrol. We had a wonderful Thanksgiving Dinner in the mess hall with the other members of the troop, where a German photographer took pictures of everyone. I think the prize one was me biting into a turkey drumstick. Then it was off in the cold night to the Autobahn. If you speak with someone today who was in Germany during the Winter of 1946-47, they will recall, without hesitation, that it was the worst winter they have ever encountered.

We took off in two jeeps and an armored car, bundled up in our winter gear, which we knew from guard duty wasn't the most protective. We stopped at the American Aid station to thaw out a bit, then went on to the British Aid Station. By the time we reached that point we were frozen stiff and the British soldiers had to undress us to thaw us out. At that time I received a call from the Berlin Duty officer who chewed me out for being two hours behind schedule. I tried to explain that we could not drive fast because of the cold and our inability to hold the steering wheel or feel the accelerator, but he wanted no excuses, get moving and get back to Berlin fast.

I wrote up the incident in the patrol log, in what might be considered unmilitary like terms, and noted that we were not goofing off but were trying our best under very severe circumstances. About a week later I was summoned to the squadron commander's office and he questioned me about the report. I recounted what happened. When asked about wearing the proper clothing, I explained that our issue wasn't the best for the weather we were up against.

Our squadron commander carried the report to Berlin Command and apparently did a little chewing of his own. As a result all Berlin Command G-2 Officers and key NCOs had to make the Autobahn Patrol. Our colonel made it a point to be the first officer in the squadron to make the run and the squadron executive officer was the second. Later, I learned a report was submitted requesting better cold weather gear. I have never forgotten the colonel and the manner in which he backed our patrol.

Christmas (1946) is remembered for the troop Christmas tree and my leave in Switzerland. I was delayed in Frankfurt and by the time I got to Karlsruhe I missed my connection and spent Christmas Eve sleeping on the wooden bench in the Bahnhof. A very memorable Christmas.

In February and March of 1947, Berlin Command assigned the Constabulary the additional responsibility of guarding the trains passing through the Russian Zone. I had a five man detail to guard the Munich Train while another platoon sergeant had a 20+ man detail to guard the Frankfurt train. I never did find out if the Frankfurt train was more important or if my team was considered more efficient.

About this time we started to get some replacements. As with any group, you get some good ones and a few complainers. Whenever I ran the Helmstedt Patrol I always had the men load the full complement of ammunition per orders. Some of the NCOs in the squadron only loaded one box of ammunition for each machine gun. I doubt they even took any 37mm rounds. And, I always got one or two who would ask why we had to load all the ammo, after all, nothing ever happens.

One night in Spring 1947, it was my turn to lead the patrol. We lined up the jeeps and armored car and I told them to load up. Two men asked, "Do we have to take all that ammo?" The gunner that night was from Texas and you couldn't take enough ammo for him, so I had him oversee the loading. It was a normal, routine patrol. The temperature was in the 50s and it looked like a nice night for a ride down the Autobahn.

We were signing out at the MP checkpoint when I was approached by a Swiss officer. He told me he was waiting for a supply truck. It had been fired upon on the Autobahn, and would I escort the truck back to Berlin? This was a first. Did I forget to mention that whenever I was in charge of a detail something happened?

I called the squadron duty officer and reported the request. He had received a report from our aid station where the truck was waiting for us. We were told to escort the truck to Berlin. It was fired upon but it was only small arms. I often wondered how I would react when faced with a firefight. But I was so intent on briefing the patrol and issuing instructions to check their side arms, the head space on the machine guns and to take the grenades out of the canisters, that I never did think about it. What I enjoyed most was when one of the complainers came to me and asked, "Do you think we have enough ammunition Sergeant?" I couldn't resist replying, "We'll soon find out, won't we?"

We rolled out and didn't encounter anyone till we drove about 15 miles. There we saw a light being waved on the road. My driver slowed down and stopped. Then out of the dark a Russian soldier came into our headlights. He was holding a rifle at port arms. I told the driver to stay in the jeep and keep his weapon handy. I took the order board, printed in four languages, and went out to meet the Russian. I tried my German asking, "Was ist los? Wir ist Americanish Soldat." There was no response. I showed him the order board with the Russian language page, but I doubt he could read. He looked confused and I could see things were going down hill. The only reassuring thing was that he kept the rifle at the port position.

The driver of the second jeep was of Slavic descent so he came forward to help. He tried some Slavic expressions, then reverted to Americanish Soldat and showed the Russian the chevrons on my arm. No response. He kept looking at us and then at the vehicles. It was only 3 to 5 minutes that we were standing there, but it seemed like an eternity. Finally one of his comrades called and he turned and walked away.

The driver told me that he thought they were AWOLs on a binge and were probably the ones who fired on the truck. If that was the case we should have done something to stop them, but what? Surely the Russians would turn that into an International incident. So we decided to go on to the aid station, get the truck and return to Berlin, and on the return trip, no stopping. Luckily, that is what happened. We escorted the truck back without any problem, and that was all right with me. I didn't know it at the time, but I had nothing to worry about. My Texas gunner had a round in the 50 caliber and the Russian dead in his sights.

In October 1947 I was sent to Intelligence School with four other troopers. While we were getting settled in the barracks we introduced ourselves to other classmates and noted two NCOs wearing the Berlin Command insignia. We mentioned we were from the Constabulary in Berlin. One NCO replied that they didn't like the Constabulary. When we asked, "Why?" He replied, "Because some sergeant in our squadron complained about being cold and as a result, we had to ride the Autobahn Patrol." I did not think that was an appropriate time to tell him I was responsible for his winterized training.

These were some of my key memories. The duties and assignments appeared routine and did not seem important at the time. It was only after many years that you look back at the big picture and realize the Constabulary was an important part of history. On our 50th Anniversary trip to Germany the German people received us warmly and expressed their appreciation for our being there and standing tall against all odds. They stated, on more than one occasion, they would not be there today if we weren't there then. And that makes those memories all the more important.

2nd Regt. EC football champs. Dragoons, 1947 Class A Title Holders.

W.C. Strub.

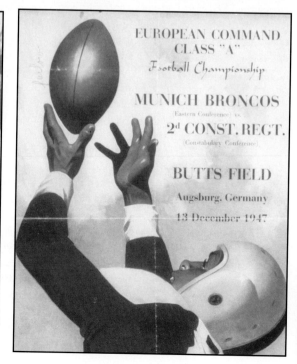

Platoon Headquarters, Gasthouse, Falkenstein.

Lt. White, 1946-47.

Headquarters, Constabulary, Heidelberg.

S/Sgt. Richard T. Shea.

Front, M/Sgt. Ritchey, Sgt. Ruscito, Sgt. Freeman, Cpl. Wells, Cpl. Kirchmayer. Back, Sgt. Wilson, Sgt. Baker, Sgt. Lanza, Cpl. Wicka.

Old Heidelberg, 1947.

Cabral, Bucca, Cinaglia.

Troop A, 24th Constabulary, Eblsburg, Austria, Aug. 1947.

BAD HERSFELD

BAD KISSINGEN

Semper Custos

FULDA

51st Med. Sq. 1st: Ryan, DeChant, Anderson, McDerminth. 2nd: Casanovas, Wach. 3rd: Cramer, Lt. Lowell, Guest, Milbrandt.

November 1945.

Outpost at Bad Reichenhall, C Trp., 66 Cnst. Sq., 2nd Regt.

Ralph F. Miles, Lt. Col., Armor, Deputy Commander.

24th S-1 section. M/Sgt. Ted L. Handy, Sgt. Joseph D. Scott, Pfc. Myron P. Bennett Jr., Pvt., Woodrow Joiner, Pfc Randall A. Zechman, Pvt. Joseph E. Drury, Cpl. Frank B. Kennedy Jr., Sfc. Elmer M. Bailey.

Constabulary School: large buildings above the town.

24th S-2 and S-3 sections. Front: M/Sgt Alfred D. Gionet, Pvt. James E. Tallyn, Sgt. Roger R. Guillame, Pvt. Jaroslav MArtyniuk, Pfc. Charles Hager. Back: Sgt. Roger J. Thellen, Pfc. Thomas E. McNamara, Pvt. Richard Kirk, Pvt. Joseph Procino.

24th 3rd. Platoon-B Troop. Front: Cpl. Edward J. Trainer, Pfc. Roosevelt Thomas, Sfc. Henry Ontiveros, Cpl. John D. Juillerat, Cpl. George H. Lamb. 2nd.: Sfc. Paul R. Berry, Sgt. Roland L. Plott, Pfc Charles Brogdon, Cpl. Anthoney J. Boulbol, Sfc. Julius Sumrall. BAck: Sgt. James E. KAil, Sgt. Hanry R. Lavoie, Pfc. Berl Litton, Pfc Eearl H. Richardson, Cpl. Richard Ronaldson.

"Battledown," first originated at Ft. Know, KY, by Lt. Col. Ralph F. Miles. In 1943 it was used as a training medium, to provide soldiers with training in hand-to-hand combat tactics. It was held each week during the operation of the battle training for all the troops stationed at Ft. Knox until 1944 when the battle training was discontinued. Battledown reappeared in 1949 among the troops of the US Army at a sports carnival at Camp Hood. Lt. Col. Miles, "the father of Battledown", put on this event, and eventually provided detailed plans for the activity to the Special Service Branch.

M/Sgt Buster sweats it out after 9-day AWOL escapade. Buster, a three and one half year old boxer went AWOL while on Excercise Rainbow. The America Red Cross apprehended him.

Silver Cup presented to Officers and Men of the 24th Constabulary Squadron at a special ceremony in Wolfenbuttel, Germany, 11 October 1952.

Third headquarters, Stuttgart, Germany, 1948.

Headquarters, Bamberg.

Outpost #8. 35th Sq., members of the baseball team, Fussen, Germany, 1947. George Doris, Ralph Moriarity, Ray Perkins, L. Nagel, civilian, W.W. Wilson, A. Sallustio. Squatting: M. Eichert, mascot Slewfoot.

Ft. Riley, KS, 1945. Front: Gorgan, Bruce, Squire, Fletcher, Snook, unk. Back: Shade, Oberg, Ohren, Peterson. Top: Canoe.

Gerard "Jerry" Mckenna and Robert "Bob" Lemke. Germany Court Reunion, 66 Constabulary. Sq., E Troop, 1966.

Headquarters, Heidelberg, 1947.

14th Armd. Cav., 2nd. Bat. F Troop. Schweinfurt, Germany, 1950-1951.

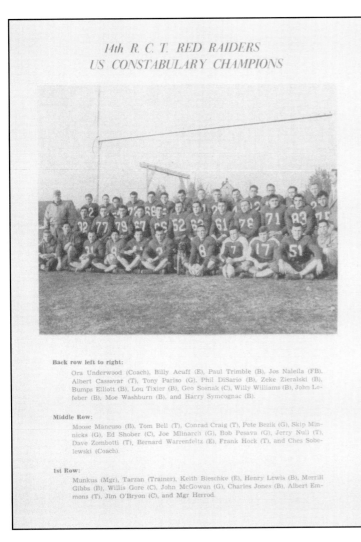

14th R. C. T. RED RAIDERS
US CONSTABULARY CHAMPIONS

Back row left to right:

Ora Underwood (Coach), Billy Acuff (E), Paul Trimble (B), Jos Naleila (FB), Albert Cassavar (T), Tony Pariso (G), Phil DiSario (B), Zeke Zieralski (B), Bumps Elliott (B), Lou Tixier (B), Geo Sosnak (C), Willy Williams (B), John Lefeber (B), Moe Washburn (B), and Harry Symcognac (B).

Middle Row:

Moose Mancuso (B), Tom Bell (T), Conrad Craig (T), Pete Bezik (G), Skip Minnicks (G), Ed Shober (C), Joe Mlinarch (G), Bob Pesava (G), Jerry Null (T), Dave Zombotti (T), Bernard Warrenfeltz (E), Frank Hock (T), and Ches Sobelewski (Coach).

1st Row:

Munkus (Mgr), Tarzan (Trainer), Keith Bieschke (E), Henry Lewis (B), Merrill Gibbs (B), Willis Gore (C), John McGowan (G), Charles Jones (B), Albert Emmons (T), Jim O'Bryon (C), and Mgr Herrod.

2d HQS Constab Brigade basketball team, Munich, winter 1949-1950. Lt. Troy, coach.

2d HQS Constab Brigade basketball team, Munich, winter 1949-1950.

1949 U.S. Constabulary Champs, 14th Regt. Red Raiders beat Rhine Main Rockets 14-13.

6th Armored Cavalry Rgmt., Unicorns. Southern Conference Basketball Champions, Straubing Germany 1950-1951. Front: John Henderson, John Nichols, Dean "Diz" Worger, Cletus Jone, Conception Martinez, Bill Wade coach. Back: John McMahon, Jim Tracy, Luther Dillard, Glenn Percell, Jimmie Pritchett, Glenn Torbleson.

6th Armored Cavalry Rgmt., Unicorns, 1957. Southern Conference Basketball Champions, Straubing Germany. Left row, bottom to top: J.M. Christensen, coach; George Hoffmaster, coach; Jim Tracy, coach; Sammy Parise, trainer; Al Inman, player/coach.

U.S. Constabulary Southern League Baseball Champs, 1950. Front: Lt. Lynn, Sgt. Russell, Sgt. Daniels, Cpl Kraft, Cpl. Billowitch, Cpl. McMillan. 2nd: Cpl. McHenry, Cpl Patricelli, Cpl. Reboli, Cpl. Smith, Sgt. Porter, Cpl. Pinto. 3rd: Cpl. Hellubroik, Cpt. Callahan, Pfc. Meyers, Sgt. Durain, Sgt. Mamalito, Sgt. Cottle, Pfc. Green.

15 Constabulary Sq. Baseball team, Spring 1948. Lt. Troy, standing on left.

Hotel Alpenhof gegen Kramer.

Biographies

15th Constabulary Sq. Special Police/Honor Guard Platoon, Welden, Germany 1950. Standing: Sfc. Fry, Cpl. Wood, Cpl. Jarrell, Sgt. Williams, Cpl. Hale, Cpl. McFarland, Pfc Reighley, Pfc Brace. Kneeling: Cpl. Kitchen, Sgt. Weber, Cpl. Epperson, Cpl. Morrow.

JAMES A. ADAMS, born Sept. 27, 1928, St. Marys, OH, inducted into service Feb. 8, 1946, Ft. Hayes, OH. Military locations and stations: Kitzingen Germany; Milrickstat, Germany.

Discharged June 1947. His awards include the National Defense, Good Conduct, Army Occupation Medal and WWII Victory. He is single and retired.

JOHN DEWEY AID, born Oct. 21, 1921, Ava, MO, joined the Army Nov. 17, 1943, Jefferson Barracks, St. Louis, MO. Basic training Camp Dodge, IA.

Duties: WII CBI Australia French Indo China 1944-45; Korean War 1950-52; Vietnam 1967-68.

Occupation duties: Germany 1946-1946: 11th Constabulary border patrol Russian Zone, Witizenhausen, Eschinege, Eichenberg Station, Kassel, Hofgeisman, Bamberg, Coburg, Bad Soden,  Allendorf, Warburg, Bad Hersfeld, Fulda, Bebra.

Korea occupation duty 1965-66; 1970-1971, Seoul. Korean War 1950-1952. Yalu River November 1950 G-4. Pusan to Yalu River; Wonju wounded Feb. 2, 1951. Germany occupation/Austria. France Italy 1953-1958; 1961-1965.

Retired Dec. 7, 1972. His awards include the Army Commendation second award, seven Good Conducts, Army Expedition Medal, Korea, Over Seas Service Bar (8), Senior A/C Badge, National Defense Service Medal, w/OLC, three Purple Hearts, Combat Infantry Badge, seven Battle Stars.

First marriage in 11th Constabulary, May 15, 1948, Kassel, Germany to Hilde Böddiger. They have a son and daughter and two granddaughters. Currently marshall on golf course 10 years. Enjoying life, Ocala, FL with wife Hilde.

G. THOMAS ALLOTTA, born and raised in the Italian section of South Philadelphia where he was drafted into the US Army in 1945. After basic training he "shipped out" to Sonthofen, Germany where he served as cadre in D&G troops of the US Constabulary School until returning to the US in 1947. He was an early member of the Constabulary where he achieved the rank of "buck" sergeant. Earned the Good Conduct Medal, European Theatre of Operations Medal and the WWII Victory Medal.

Upon returning to Philadelphia Tom married Bessie and they have two daughters. Tom worked as a operating engineer of heavy equipment from which he retired. He is a member of the Union of Operating Engineers and the Roman Catholic Church in Jamison, Bucks County, PA. He is collector of WWII guns, an active member of the US Constabulary Association. Tom is a life member of the Veterans of Foreign Wars in Philadelphia.

TONY ALVAREZ, born May 24, 1929 Santa Monica, CA, inducted into service November 1948, Ft. Ord, CA. Military locations and stations: Ft. Ord, departed Camp Kilmer, NJ; Fussen, Germany; Nurenburg, Germany. Discharged at Camp Roberts, CA; Service Btry.; 70th FA.

His awards include the Occupation and Good Conduct.

Married Donna Dailey, July 6, 1974. They have no 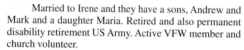 children. Retired after 35 years of service at McDonnell Douglas Co. where he worked on all planes produced, missiles and satellites. Raced first Yamaha motorcycle in

the US. Collect military memorabilia. Currently owns four cannons and participates in Civil War Reenactments. He has traveled across country three times to reenact the Battle of Gettysburg (twice) and the Battle of Manasas. Has traveled to Germany three times, once purchasing a BMW motorcycle in Munich, touring the country. The motorcycle was then shipped home. He still enjoys riding.

LESTER CLYDE (ANDY) ANDREWS, born Sept. 11, 1928, Wheeler, NY. Joined the Army June 28, 1948. Military locations and stations: Ft. Dix, NJ; A Troop, 25th Constab., Straubing, Germany. Served with Tank Co., 1st Bn., 6th Armd. Cav. as platoon sergeant. Discharged June 1954 as sergeant first class.

Served in the Germany occupation and received the Good Conduct Medal.

Andrews is married to Sharon B. Andrews and they have children: Monica, Barry and Jerry and grandchildren: Christopher, Breanne, Cody, Scott and Marcus. Employed with Taylor Wine Co. and retired April 1985.

ANDREW ANDREYKO, born July 12, 1928, Swedeland, PA, inducted into service January 1947, Philadelphia, PA. Military locations and stations: Ft. Bragg, NC; Fitzsimmons GH, CO; Camp Pickett, VA; Camp Kilmer, NJ; Weiden; Coburg; Ft. Indiantown Gap; Valley Forge GH, PA.

SFC Andreyko was ischarged in January 1953 and received Good Conduct Medal, Occupation Medal and National Defense Service Medal.

Married to Irene and they have a sons, Andrew and Mark and a daughter Maria. Retired and also permanent disability retirement US Army. Active VFW member and church volunteer.

ANTHONY ANGELINI, born Sept. 9, 1927, Italy. Entered service Jan. 18, 1946, US Army. Received basic training, Ft. McClellan, AL (Inf.) Schwabish Hall, West Germany. E Trp., 71st Constab. Sqdn., 10th Regt., 3rd Bde., Ft. Dix, NJ separation.

Enlisted August 1948 in the USAF, assigned to Kelly AFB, TX. October 1948, England (UK) for support to the Berlin Airlift. 1952, Westover AFB, MA. May 1953, separated from active duty and assigned to the AF Reserve. October 1957 recalled to active duty and assigned to Niagara Falls Municipal Airport, NY; Pagwa AS, Ontario Canada; Highlands AFS, NJ; Bucks Harbor AFS, ME; North Truro AFS, MA; Phu Cat AB, Vietnam; Plattsburg AFB, NY; McGuire AFB, NJ.

Retired September 1975. Awards include the Army Good Conduct Medal w/3 Loops, Occupation Medal (Germany), WWII Victory Medal, National Defense Service Medal w/2BSS, AFLSA w/4 OLC, Republic of Vietnam Campaign Medal and Small Arms Expert Marksmanship Ribbon.

His hobbies include trap shooting, hand gun target shooting and reloading his own ammunition.

WILLIAM DONALD ARMSTRONG, born April 18, 1928, Whitehall, IL, enlisted in Regular Army, Feb. 21, 1946, East St. Louis, IL. Received basic training, Ft. Knox, KY, medium tank crewman. Discharged December 1948. Used two months furlough.

Duties: US Constabulary, Budigan and Augsburg, Germany; Constabulary School, Wetslar, Germany E and D Troop, 68th Constab. Sqdn. converted from 68th Constab. Armd. Field Arty. Bn., 1st Armd. Div. to 3rd Constab. Regt., May 1, 1946 to HQ US Constabulary-Augsburg September 1946 to 2nd Constabulary Regt., Feb. 10, 1948.

Service schools attended: 7712 European Theater Intelligence School; US Forces, European Theater, Obermmergau, Germany; Army Ordnance School, Eschwege, Germany; Demolition School, Chemical Warfare School, Airborne training.

Outposts duty "E" Troop Fulda "D" Troop, Hanau, Kastel Bridge, Schluchtern (railroad).

His awards include the WWII Victory and Occupation Medal, Germany.

Married Shirley Ann Ballard Dec. 15, 1950 and they had one son, (deceased), one daughter, Patricia, two grandchildren, Joshua Armstrong Hall and Amanda Lynn Hall.

Graduated Illinois College Class of 1953. Supervisor 31 years for McDonnell Douglas, St. Louis, MO. A supervisor on the team of the US Pioneering Space Programs of Projects Mercury and Gemini, hailed as among the most important and successful explorations in the history of mankind.

Received the National Aeronautic Space Administrations Skylab Achievement Award in appreciation of dedicated service to the nation as a supervisor on the Skylab Team which expanded man's knowledge and capabilities in space.

A past master of Franklin 25 Masonic Lodge, a Shriner and member of American Legion, VFW, Geneological Society.

ROBERT B. (BOB) BAEHR, born Feb. 19, 1928, Plainville, CT, graduated high school, joined the Army Feb. 15, 1946. Commissioned June 15, 1947. His military locations and stations: Munich, Germany; Ft. Devens, MA; South Post, Ft. Meyers, VA. Served with 7001st ASU HQ 2nd Constab. Brig. MDW Det. 1, as truck driver. Drove for Maj. Gen. Gay in Munich. Drove Chafer in Pentagon Washington, DC. Discharged Jan. 20, 1950 as corporal E-4.

His awards and medals include the WWII Victory Medal and Army of Occupation Medal.

Married to Jeannine J. Baehr and they have children: Robert C. Baehr and James M. Baehr; grandchildren: Adam Baehr, James Baehr and Danielle Baehr. Employed as inspector of materials in MRC. Went in the Army and was trailer driver for 38 years. After discharge from Army retired in 1989.

RICHARD LEE BAKER, born July 4, 1927, Greensboro, NC, entered military service Sept. 13, 1945.

Duties: Woodrow Wilson General Hospital, Staunton, VA, September 1945-February 1946; US Army Hospital, Ft. Monroe, VA February 1946-January 1947; 16th Constab. Sqdn., (HQ Troop & Horse Plt.), Berlin, Germany, January 1947-November 1950; 279th Station Hospital, Berlin, Germany, November 1950-April 1951; 351st MASH, Ft. Bragg, NC, May 1951-October 1951; 351st MASH Landstuhl, Germany, October 1951-October 1954; Seventh Army NCO Academy, Munich, Germany, July-August 1953; USA Dispensary, VHFS, Warrenton, VA, October 1954-December 1955; US Army Hospital, Ft. Belvoir, VA, December 1955-March 1958; US Army Medical Service Gp., Okinawa, March 1958-August 1961; 714th Preventive Medicine Unit, Ft. Stewart, GA, August 1961-March 1964; Medical Field Service School, Ft. Sam Houston, TX, March-June 1964; 5th Preventive Medicine Unit, Korea, July 1964-July 1965; 714th Preventive Medicine Unit, Ft. Bragg, NC, July 1965-April

1966; 44th Medical Bde., Vietnam, April 1966-April 1967; Walter Reed Army Medical Center, Washington, DC, April 1967-July 1971; Walter Reed Army Institute of Research, Washington, DC, July 1971-August 1975; civilian employment, Tawam Hospital, United Arab Emirates, November 1979-March 1985.

Baker retired Sept. 1, 1975. He received several medals during his career, including the Legion of Merit, Bronze Star, Meritorious Service, Army Commendation, Good Conduct w/3 Silver Loops, WWII Victory, Army of Occupation w/Berlin Airlift Device, Humane Action, National Defense Service w/OLC, Vietnam Service, Vietnam Campaign, Republic of Vietnam Campaign Gallantry Cross Unit Citation w/Palm and Meritorious Unit Citation.

Married Jane M. Browne. They have three sons and one daughter. Member, North Carolina Army Retiree Council, American Legion, VFW, DAV and US Constabulary Association. He is an avid reader and travels as much as possible.

ALEXANDER P. BARANOWSKI, born Sept. 8, 1925, Hanover Township, PA, Volunteered for the draft Dec. 11, 1945. RA Dec. 13, 1945. Arty. basic, Ft. Sill, OK, 1946 Germany 1AD, 447 IPW Team, (3 A Mil Intel Course). July 1, 1946 327th CHID; squadrons-1, 27, 28, 2/14AC. Promoted SFC August 1949. Duties: Observer at Nuremberg War Crime Trials-MI REP during entries to Jewish DP Camp Bamberg and Polish Camp Wildflecken, visit border outposts. Training/Schooling: Combat and Counter Intel. Aerial Observer, 7A NCO Academy. Constructed 1:25,000 Relief Map Series, made of Plywood & Plastic Wood, overall size 3/4 meters (last seen at V Corps HQ Frankfurt 1995). Returned 5/51 to ZI.

RO Status: Completed 10-20-30 Series, Ord School (2d Lt. to Cpt. May 1953-May 1960). Served Acting O positions (as EM-RO): Schools O, 30 Inf. & CTC, Ft. Benning, GA 1953-54; S2-S3-27 Ord. Bn. 1st Cav., Japan, 1955-56; S3 & Asst. (OPN MASS), 181st Trans. Bn., Mannheim, Germany, 1957-58; Officers Amphibious Course, Little Creek, VA 1961; JV & V Rifle and TRI-ATH PISTOL Team Coach, LaSalle College, Philadelphia, PA 1961-64; Air Ground Opn School USAF, GY, 1964, Helicopter Act O, HQ USAREUR, November 1955-May 1966. Retired EM, Aug. 1, 1966-RDY RES-03. MOB Alert O, September 1982; rescinded July 13, 1984; ending a 42 year Army commitment. Education: BS Trenton State College, NJ; 24 hours graduate studies, CMU; current microcomputer Crs. Comm Col.

Memberships: USCON, DAV, N.O. TRENCH RATS Association, REC MGRS and ADMIN, Statue of Liberty Foundation; life member, 1 AD & ROA.

THOMAS E. (TOM) BARRY, born Feb. 20, 1928, Detroit, MI, joined the service March 7, 1946. Military locations and stations: Degerndorf, Brannenburg, Rosenheim, Traunstein, Freising, Keifers Felden. Served with B Troop, 66 Constab. Sqdn.

Discharged Aug. 13, 1947 and T/5 and received the Army of Occupation Medal, WWII Victory Medal and a lapel button.

He enjoyed his time with the Constabulary. Married Bernice and they have children: Bob, Ray, Richard and Carol and two grandchildren. Employed with the city of Pontiac and County of Oakland, Department of Aviation and Transportation. Retired March 13, 1993 after 37 years.

MIKE BASOZKI, born Jan. 5, 1929, Jefferson Township, PA, grew up in Windsor Heights, WV. Enlisted in the Regular Army, Jan. 8, 1946; completed basic training at Camp Robinson, AR. Assigned to Co. F, 39th Inf. Regt., 9th Inf. Div., Bad Tolz, Germany April-December 1946.

Assigned to the US Constabulary December 1946-October 1952: 22nd Constab. Sqdn., Hammelburg, 1946-1947; B Trp., 10th Constab. Sqdn., Wurzburg, 1947; Prov. Trp. 14th Constab. Regt., Kitzingen, 1947; B Trp. 71st & 15th Constab. Sqdn., Hessenthal, 1947-1948; A Trp., 42nd Constab. Sqdn., Augsburg, 1948-1950; Co. E, 2nd Bn., 2nd Armd. Cav. Regt., Augsburg and Bamberg, 1950-1952.

Other assignments: 47th Inf. Div., Camp Rucker, AL, 1952-54; 3rd Inf. Div., Ft. Benning, GA 1954-56; Co. H, 3rd Bn., 6th ACR, Regensburg, Germany, 1956-57; 593rd FA Bn. and 83rd Arty., Budingen, Germany, 1957-60; 4th Inf. Div., Ft. Lewis, WA, 1960-62; 7th Inf. Div. Korea, 1962-63; Advisor to 116th ACR, National Guard, Twin Falls, ID, 1963-65; 1st Sqdn. 2nd ACR, Bindlach, Germany, 1965-68; 2nd Sqdn. 1st Cav. 4th Inf. Div., Vietnam, 1968-69; USA Training Center, and 9th Inf. Div., Ft. Lewis, WA, 1969-72; 2nd Sqdn., 11th ACR, Bad Kissingen, Germany, 1972-74.

Retired Sept. 1, 1974 as command sergeant major at Ft. Lewis, WA. He was awarded the Combat Infantry Badge, Meritorious Service, 12 Air Medals, Army Commendation w/OLC, Good Conduct w/8 knots, WWII Victory, Germany Occupation, National Defense w/OLC, RVN Service w/4 Battle Stars, RVN Campaign, KPUC, RVN Gallantry Cross w/Palm and w/SS, RVN Civil Actions and three Overseas Bars.

While stationed in Augsburg, met and married Rita Blau, born in Riga, Latvia. They have a son, Steve, a daughter, Joyce and a grandson, Bryce. After retiring from US Army in 1974, pursued career as an accountant for Army Civil Service, and retired for a second time in 1992. Resides in Spanaway, WA. Enjoys fishing, traveling and cruising, and is an avid coin collector.

GEORGE WADE BATES, born June 22, 1926, Meridian, MS, inducted into service Oct. 3, 1944, Camp Shelby, MS. Military locations and stations: Ft. Knox, Central Germany, 3rd Armd. Div., 1st Armd. Div., 13th Tank Bn., 13th US Constab. (HQ Troop).

Discharged Aug. 7, 1946, Ft. Bragg, NC. His awards include campaign and service ribbons.

Married and has five children (one deceased). Attended University of Tennessee. Received BS in electrical engineering in 1950; Massachusetts Institute of Technology, Sloan Fellow, MS Industrial Management, 1962. Retired from South Central Bell Telephone Company in 1987. Currently resides in Mountain Brook, AL.

RAYMOND R. BATTREALL, born Sept. 19, 1926, St. Joseph, MO, joined Army Specialized Training Reserve Program (ASTRP) for Aviation Cadet training Oct. 13, 1943. Basic training, Sheppard Field, TX, USMA, West Point, NY, 1945-49.

Duties: 14th ACR (USCON), August 1950-August 1953; 11th ACR, Camp Carson, CO and Ft. Knox, KY, 1953-54; University of Pennsylvania (MA) 1955-56; Instr.,

Department of English, USMA, August 1956-June 1959; 1 Cav. Div., Korea, 1959-60; 3rd ACR, Ft. Meade, MD and Germany, 1960-63; HQ, USAREUR, 1963-64; C&GSC, 1964-65; Adv, ARVN Armor, 1965-66; AFSC, 1966; CO, 3/3 ACR, Germany, 1967-68; Tac Dpt., USMA, 1968-70; Sr. Adv., ARVN Armor Cmd., 1971-72; Army Adv. Gp., MACV, 1972-37; SOUTHCOM, CZ, 1973-75; Saudi Arabia, 1975-77; Ft. Knox, KY, 1977-79.

Retired July 1979 and received four Legion of Merit, three BSM, Purple Heart, three MSM, ARCOM, several VN awards.

Married Nancy Dickens, June 25, 1950 and they have two daughters, two granddaughters, and one grandson. Married Ann Hannigan, Oct. 21, 1991 and has three stepsons, one stepdaughter, two grandsons, and four granddaughters. He is a Chamber of Commerce volunteer and extensive traveller.

ELDRED (BILL) C. BEALE JR., born Jan. 10, 1923, Suffolk, VA. Drafted AUS Feb. 14, 1946. Received basic training, Ft. Knox, KY.

Duties: 2nd US CAV/Constab., Degerndorf, Germany, May 1946-September 1950; 6th Inf. Regt., Berlin, Germany, September 1950-January 1954; Ohio State University ROTC Staff, April 1955-January 1958; OHARNG, January 1958-December 1964; 80th Inf. Div., December 1964-October 1977-September 1983.

Retired Sept. 30, 1983. Recalled to active status for Desert Storm. Retired June 30, 1991.

Received several decorations during career, including: Legion of Merit, Army Commendation, WWII Victory, WWII Occupation, National Defense Service 2nd AWD, Armed Forces Reserve, Army Reserve Components Achievement w/OLC, Army Good Conduct w/Clasp, NCO Professional Development, Army Service Ribbon, Overseas Service Ribbon, Southwest Asia Service, Army Lapel Button.

Married Frankie Graham and they have three sons, two daughters, four granddaughters and one grandson. They enjoy traveling.

GORDON G. BELD, a native of Grand Rapids, MI who served in the S-2 section of the 66th Constab. Sqdn. during 1946-47, later earned a BA degree from Hope College and an MA from the University of Michigan. He was a high school teacher, academic advisor at Davenport College, writer for Grand Rapids newspapers, and director of news services and publications at Alma College. His freelance articles, mostly on historical topics, have been published in many newspapers and magazines. Active in church and community organizations, he is particularly interested and involved in efforts to assist refugees who resettle in the US.

He and his wife, the former Martha Debbink of Wauwatosa, WI, have three children. They enjoy traveling, especially to the Basque Country of northern Spain where their only two grandchildren live. They presently reside in Holland, MI.

WILLIAM D. (DOUG) BELL, born Sept. 29, 1930 in Lindsborg, KS, and reared in Hugo, OK. His military career, which spanned 27 years, started in 1947 with Co. F, 180th Inf. Regt., 45th Div., Oklahoma National Guard. Attended summer camp in Ft. Sill, OK and joined the Army in 1948; attended basic training and Cooks & Baker's School at Ft. Ord, CA, with subsequent assignment to Service Btry., 91st FA Bn., 2nd Constab. Div. (later designated 519th) at Sonthofen, Germany, December 1948.

Old acquaintances will remember him for his character part in the USO sponsored Soldier Show in 1950 and the "Hill Top Roller Rink", a skating rink, whose conversion, of the old Enlisted Club, was planned, supervised and operated by him until he returned to the US in July 1950. Doug re-enlisted in the Air Force and served in Alaska, Pakistan and England for a total of 11 years overseas. Some of his awards include the Meritorious Service Medal (twice), the Air Force Commendation Medal (three times), the Good Conduct Medal (five times), the Air Force Good Conduct Medal (three times), the Defense Service Medal (twice) and the Outstanding Unit Citation three times. He was retired at Lackland AFB in February 1974, where he served as the base food service superintendent over one of the largest military food service operations in the world with over 26 facilities in the production of 50,000 meals per day.

Doug holds an associate of science degree from Cisco Junior College and is very active in the Toastmaster International Club of America. He is also involved in the Veterans of Foreign Wars, having served various offices at the post and district, and is now serving the Department of Texas as the state senior vice commander.

He is married to Jeanie, his wife of 46 years, and they have a son, Douglas and two grandchildren.

RALPH EDWARD BEMIS, born Dec. 11, 1927 in Helena, MT, entered the US Army, Oct. 26, 1945.

Military locations and stations: Basic training, Camp Lee, VA 1945; US Constab. HQ Trp., 2nd Constab. Regt. Horse Plt. October 1946 to February 1947; February 1947-July 1947 HQ Trp., 2nd Constab. Regt. Freising, Germany; Augsburg, Germany, D Trp., 74 Constab. Sqdn., July 1947-Sept. 20, 1947. Transferred to D Trp., 2nd Constab. Sqdn. September 1947 to February 1948; HQ and Service Trp., 2nd Constab. Sqdn. Dec. 2, 1948; HQ and HQ Co., 1st Bn., 2nd Armd. Cav., US Constab. to April 1949; May 1949-May 1950, 536th Engr. Maint. Co., Ft. Bragg, NC; August 1950 to Korea, 23rd Inf. Regt., 2nd Inf. Div. Heavy Mortar Co., September 1951 to 1952, Madigan Army Hospital; then to F Co., 5th Regt., Combat Team 1952-53; Ft. Lewis, WA 1953-56; 1956-1960, 23rd Inf. Regt., Ft. Richardson, AK; 1960-1964, Ft. Ord, CA, HQ 10 3rd Bde., 1964-November 1965, 5th Tank Bn., Munich, Germany. Retired Nov. 1, 1965.

Fought battles and campaigns in Korea 1950-51 and 1952-53. Discharged Nov. 1, 1965 and received the Combat Infantry Badge, O.M.G WWII Victory Medal, NDSM, Good Conduct Medal, Korean Service Medal, Korean Presidential Unit Citation, UN Defense, UN Off, Chinese Intervention, Bronze Service Star and three Battle Stars.

Married Nona Gayle and they have five daughters, one son, 16 grandchildren and one great-grandson. Employed as a service station owner. Driver combination local delivery.

ANTHONY C. BERSANI, born May 24, 1927, Detroit, inducted into service Dec. 5, 1945. Military locations and stations: Ft. Bragg, NC; Munich, Germany; Fussen, Germany; Augsburg, Germany, Korea.

Discharged Dec. 18, 1948. Awards and medals include the United Service Medal, Good Conduct Medal, Army of Occupation Medal w/Germany Clasp, Korean Service Medal w/Bronze Star, Sharp Shooter Badge, WWII Victory Medal, Honorable Service Lapel Button, WWII National Defense Service Medal, Republic of Korea Presidential Unit Citation Badge. He is now retired.

DONALD BIRKHOLZ, born July 8, 1929, Charles City, IA, entered the US Army September 1948. Military locations and stations: Ft. Knox, (basic) APG Maryland (School), Straubing, Germany (duty). Served with B Co.,

73rd Ord. Bn., 8th Ord MM Co., inspector 7th Army IG-Eucom IG (small arms). He achieved the rank of staff sergeant and was discharged June 1952. Awards include the Army of Occupation and Good Conduct.

Memorable experience: Basic September 1948 to December 1948; APG School (Small Arms December 1948-March 1949); Germany (Straubing) March 1949 to May 1952. Working with IG team and traveling all over Germany with team. Being a member of small bore, big bore and skeet team.

Married to Dolores and they have children: Kay Ann, Toni Lynn and Michael E. Birkholz and grandchildren: Nicklous E. Bernat (Kay's son). Employed 35 years in wholesale heating and air conditioning business as operations manager and assistant manager. He retired July 1991.

ROBERT A. BOBACK, born Scranton, PA, April 28, 1927, entered Army June 25, 1945 at New Cumberland, PA, 1946, Camp Pickett, VA. Enlisted Camp Pickett, VA until March 1947. Ft. Dix signed up for Reserves Feb. 19, 1947 until Feb. 11, 1950. Signed up April 4, 1954 until April 3, 1957. While in Germany he was a truck driver and auto serviceman. Traveled to Wetzler, Paris, Belgium, Manheim, Stuttgart. Traveled up and down the Autobahn. When first entered Army he was in the 1st Armd. Div. He then changed over to HQ Trp., 3rd Constab. Regt.

Received Army Occupation Medal and WWII Victory Medal. At the present time he is a commander VFW Post in Quakertown, PA. Retired from Reading Railroad and Conrail. Employed as engineman for 33 years. He is a 8th degree black belt and judges tournaments in two states.

GORDON C. BOCK, born March 26, 1929 lived his life in and around Flint, MI. He was one of eight children. His three brothers also served in the services. They were told that he did not tell his true age when he enlisted.

Served in the Trp. 10th Constab. Sqdn. from March 27, 1946-Dec. 29, 1948, specialty mechanic 014. Stationed in Fritzlar, Germany. He also served one year in Michigan National Guard. Met a young German girl from Kassel, Germany. They were married November 1948 in Kassel. On returning to Flint, he started working for General Motors at the Buick City complex. Retired after working for 40 years. He loved working on cars and tinkering around the house. He was always willing to help out family and friend when needed.

Bock had two daughters and a son. And was the proud grandfather to one granddaughter and four grandsons. He also has two stepgrandchildren and four step-great-grandchildren. He had been married 46 years at the time of his death, Nov. 7, 1994.

FRANK J. BONGIORNO, born July 17, 1927, Bound Brook, NJ, entered service Aug. 29, 1945. Military locations and stations: Inducted Camp Dix, NJ; basic training, Camp Croft, SC; Ft. Knox, KY. Served with HQ Troop, 15th Constab. Landed in LeHavre, France, March 1946.

Traveled by boxcar to Stuttgart, Germany. They were se[nt] from Stuttgart to Weinheim to receive additional Hors[e] Cavalry training. After finishing their training, they we[re] then sent to a cavalry camp on the outskirts of Karlsruh[e] for permanent duty. He remained there on duty until Janu ary 1947.

Discharged March 11, 1947 as sergeant. His award[s] include the Army of Occupation and WWII Victory Medal.

Memorable experiences: Patrolled Rhine River on horse back. Enforced military law and order; checked il legal entry into Occupied Zone; mounted parades, care[d] for, fed and groomed horses in their care.

He has been married to Joan for 45 years. Employe[d] as president of Frank J. Bongiorno and Associates (insur-ance and real estate firm). President of Manville Nationa[l] Bank, Manville, NJ. Retired Jan. 1, 1991.

He is past president of Somerset County Board o[f] Realtors, Somerset Valley Visiting Nurse Association, Manville Chamber of Commerce. Director of First National Bank of Central Jersey, National Westminster Bank, Raritan Valley Chapter of American Red Cross, Somerset Crippled Children Treatment Center.

Received Community Service Award of Somerset County Board of Realtors, Manville Lodge 2119, Elk of the Year.

RICHARD T. (DICK) BOSMA, born Jan. 2, 1930, Whitinsville, MA, entered the Army in 1948. Military locations and stations: Germany-Scheinfurt/Flukeplatz Conn Barracks, and Bad Kissengen/Mantauefel Kaserne.

Served with D Co., 2nd Bn., 14th Armd. Cav. Discharged as private first class June 23, 1952 achieved the rank of corporal.

Trained in defensive tactics, and performed partial border patrol; held over his hitch during the Korean Conflict for an extra nine months (Trumans Year).

His awards and medals include the Occupation of Germany Ribbon, Weapons Expert Badge for M-1 Garand, M-2 Carbine, 45 auto pistol, Thompson Sub Machine Gun, 45 cal. grease gun, 30 cal. Browning light machine gun.

Memorable experiences: while on border patrol around Sonnheim they lunched at a border barrier he apprised the sergeant that four Russians were approaching their position two tommygunners in the trees and an officer and one enlisted on the road, he walked to the barrier to meet them while he scoped the area and saw a machine gun in a barn loft and another on a hill to the right of them, he told the sergeant and they asked the officer about them he replied "Com See Com Sah" Needless to say they left the area post haste. He served Honor Guard to Gen. White two times.

Married for 41 years to Alice E. and they have children, David William and Deborah Eve and grandchildren: Dakota, Vincent, Dante and Samantha.

Civilian employment and positions held: machinist first class, machine tool repairman, facility maintenance specialist, plant superintendent, plant engineer, master machinist, and aerospace technician for Martin Marietta.

EDWARD JOSEPH (FRENCHIE) BOUTIN, born Oct. 30, 1928, Bennington, VT. He joined the U.S. Army in 1945 and served overseas with the U.S. Constabulary in various locations in France, Germany and Austria.

They had good times
nd bad times. He partici-
nted in the raid on the
Danube River with Troop D,
5 Sqdn. He was there for
ght days. They went aboard
23 Dungerain vessels and
ok everything they had; it
as Black Market in
egendorf. They couldn't go
nt at night because the Ger-
mans were beating up the GIs and sometimes killing them.
Ve were on 24 hour alert at all times.

Discharged July 21, 1947 as PFC. Awards include
ne ETO, Good Conduct, WWII Victory Medal with Germany Clasp, Army of Occupation Medal and National
nefense Service Medal.

Has been retired since 1982.

GEORGE BERNARD BOWDREN, born Oct. 18,
1927, Mineola, NY, drafted Jan. 22, 1946, infantry basic
raining, Ft. McClellan, AL, retired Oct. 1, 1971.

From 1946 to 1952 HQ 6th Constab. Regt., Bayreuth,
Bamberg, Schweinfurt and Straubing. Advanced from private, tank crewman to master sergeant, personnel sergeant;
Ft. Jackson, SC June 1952-October 1956. Appointed second lieutenant USAR Feb. 23, 1955, remained on AD as
master sergeant; Korea November 1956 to March 1958;
Ft. Sill, OK April 1958-April 1959; Advisor Army Reserve Schenectady, NY April 1959-January 1961; SETAF
Italy February 1961 to June 1964. Ordered to active duty
n reserve grade first lieutenant Sept. 28, 1961; HQ MDW
Washington, DC July 1964-February 1966; Army Concept Team, Vietnam March 1966-June 1967; Army Postal
Service, Washington, DC July 1967-September 1971.

Retired Oct. 1, 1971. Received the following med-
als during his almost 26 years of active service: Legion of
Merit, Bronze Star Medal, Army Commendation Medal
w/OLC, Good Conduct Medal (5th Award), WWII Vic-
tory Medal, National Defense Service Medal w/OLC,
Army of Occupation Medal, Vietnam Campaign Medal,
United National Service Medal and two Overseas Service
Ribbons.

His service schooling included 7th Army NCO Academy, Munich, Honor Graduate Number 1 Class Number
10; Series 10 Extension Courses; Associate Adjutant General Course; US Navy Air Traffic Management Course;
LaSalle University Computer Programmers Course; Defense Computer Institute Command and Control Course;
and the first firing of the 20mm atomic shell during the
atmospheric nuclear weapons tests, Nevada.

Married Elisabeth Theresa Renghart, Jan. 30, 1962;
Past Chapter Commander, Retired Officers Association;
Editor, United States Constabulary Association Lightning
Bolt.

PATRICK O. BOWMAN, born Sept. 1, 1913 Derry
Township, Hershey, PA, entered service from Pittsburgh,
PA April 4, 1941. Basic training, Ft. Belvoir, VA then as-
signed to Co. D, 21st Avn. Engrs., Langley Field, VA.

Duties: Co. supply sergeant, Army maneuvers Louisiana, Lake Charles Airfield. NCO supply coordinator for
laying first huge runway 150 x 3000' interlocking steel
plates atop mountain ridge near Ft. Bragg, NC; an engineering feat acclaimed by Gen. Henry Arnold as a great
aviation achievement in 1941. Following Pearl Harbor
moved to Mitchell Field, LI, NY, constructed protective
sand bag revetments and connecting runways.

1942: Battalion supply sergeant then NCO instructor rifle marksmanship, Langley Field. NCO instructor live
ammunition combat range Ft. Eustis, VA. Platoon sergeant
in practicing shore assault and beach landings at Virginia
Beach.

Commissioned second lieutenant OCS Ft. Lee, VA.
Completed supply course in armored force warfare and
assigned August 14 to 5th Armd. Div. on maneuvers

Mojave Desert, CA. Served as training officer desert war-
fare, Battalion transportation officer, Division PX officer.
At Camp Cooke: Div. Athletic and Recreational Officer.
MG Jack Heard was the division commander.

1943: Completed Special Service Administration and
A.E.S course at Washington and Lee University, Lexington, VA. 1st Lt. Maneuvers with 5th AD in Tennessee,
operated 18 Mobile Branch PX's. Moved to Pine Camp,
NY, training and preparation deployment overseas. Completed and assisted in administering censorship course,
pistol, carbine, infiltration close overhead MG Fire. Moved
with division to Ft. Indiantown Gap, Lebanon County, PA.
MG Lunsford Oliver became the 5th AD commander in
March.

1944 Captain. Sailed with division from port of New
York February 10, docked Liverpool England, February
24. As PX officer operated 15 B/branch exchanges supplied by US Warehouse Reading England. Member of inspection team at Marshalling Camps accommodating invasion assault troops for D-Day. Class B finance officer
for invasion troops. With division departed Southampton
England July 26 and landed Utah Beach France. With other
units in the Patton's 3rd Army the 5th led breakout from
Normandy pursued German Army to Falaise Gap, rolled
through France, Belgium, liberated Luxembourg and was
the first allied unit to pierce the Siegfried line and fight on
German soil, September 11. Assigned to HQ CCA Div.
took heavy casualties in Huertgen Forest bitter fighting.
BG. Eugene Regnier was CCA commander.

1945: with CCA crossed the Rhine River and reached
Elbe River at Tangermunde Germany April 12 about 50
miles from Berlin. The bridge was blown and CCA over-
ran Stendal and secured the area. After the German surrender CCA moved HQ to Erfurt. At this point Bowman
was transferred to 3rd Armd. Div. and became the Div.
PX officer in the occupation of Germany. Then assigned
to HQ 7th US Army, AES Section as operations and later
as executive officer. Promoted to rank of major.

1946: Transferred to HQ 3rd US Army. Executive
officer Army Exchange Service. Then to HQ US Constab.
in Heidelberg as special staff officer, AES.

1947: Separated from service at Frankfurt on Main
Germany to accept civilian employment in the American
Occupation Zone. Also managed and closed out the AES
buying section in Bern Switzerland. Military Occupational
Specialty is 4210. Awarded five Bronze Service Stars for
Normandy, Northern France, Rhineland, Central Europe
and Ardennes Campaigns, also WWII Victory, Bronze Star,
Army of Occupation, Army Commendation, EAME Cam-
paign and American Defense Medals.

Married Dorothy Elizabeth Reinthaler, have three
daughters, two sons, six grandchildren.

He was marketing director (domestic and export)
for 36 years with Lebanon Ball Co. Retired: devoting time
and energy to family, Rotary Club, PA Sports Hall of Fame,
VFW, Quentin Riding Club, genealogy and other activities.

GEORGE WESLEY BOYLE, born April 26, 1926,
Escondido, CA. Military loca-
tions and stations: Ft. Knox,
KY September 1944-Febru-
ary 1945; Co. A, 771st Tank
Bn. Germany, various loca-
tions April 1945-March
1946; Troop E, 16th
Constab. Sqdn., Berlin,
March 1946-July 1946.

Discharged July 30,
1946 Camp Beale, CA. His
awards include the Central
Europe Campaign Medal, Good Conduct, WWII Victory
and Army of Occupation Medals.

Married Renness Cook, July 24, 1949. She died July
18, 1997. They had three daughters, three granddaughters
and three grandsons. Retired and former motor carrier and
rail freight forwarder, management and sales. Ordained
Presbyterian elder, regular cardiac rehab exercise program
attendee. Plans to travel.

JOHN W. BRADSHAW, born Oct. 6, 1927,
Burlington, Alamance County, NC, joined the Army Air
Corps, Oct. 6, 1945. Military locations and stations: Kessler
AFB, Biloxi, MS; HQ Sqdn., 441st Trp. Carrier Gp.,
Eschborn, Germany; HQ 61st Trp. Carrier Sqdn. Rhine
Main, Germany Pope, AFB, NC; Camp Pieri, Dotzheim,
Germany; Camp Kilmer, NJ; Ft. Jackson, SC; Ft. Knox,

KY; Molesworth AFS, En-
gland; Knoxville, TN; Otis
AFB, MA; Tyndall AFB,
Panama City, FL; Cape
Newenham, AK (AF re-
mote); Hulman Field, Terre
Haute, IN. Retired at Pope
AFB, NC.

Served with Army Air
Corps, US Constab., USAF,
(22 years). Discharged May
31, 1967 as staff sergeant. His awards include the Good
Conduct Medal, WWII Victory Medal, Army of Occupation Medal, National Defense Medal, Air Force Professional Military Education Grad. Ribbon, Air Force Longevity Service Award and Air Force Outstanding Award.

Memorable experiences: July 1946 while in the
Army Air Corps he was transferred from Eishborn to Rhine
Main Air Station, for rebuilding and opening of Rhine
Main.

Married 44 years to Mary and they have children:
Sharon Bradshaw Reeves, US Army (ret.), Hugh L. and
Richard Bradshaw; grandchildren, Melissa Reeves and
Bradley Reeves. Volunteer at Durham, NC VAMC and the
VFW VAVS representative, 17 years as a volunteer. Di-
agnosed with cancer while on active duty. He was restored
with a 100 percent permanent disability.

JAMES OLIVER BRADY, born March 22, 1925, Bir-
mingham, AL, enlisted RA Sept. 27, 1940, Ft. Benning,
GA. Retired Ft. Gordon, GA,
Nov. 1, 1970.

1940-43: Ft. Benning,
GA; 1943: Ft. McClellan, AL;
Ft. Rucker, AL, Tennessee
maneuvers. 1944: Tennessee
Maneuvers, Ft. Gordon, GA;
England, France, Luxem-
bourg, Belgium. 1945: Germany, Ft. Campbell, KY.
1946: Ft. Campbell, KY.
1947-48: Berlin, Germany
(first sergeant, HQ Trp., 16th Constab. Sqdn. (Sep); 1949:
Ft. Jackson, SC; Ft. Benning, GA. 1949-1951; Ft. Benning,
GA; Korea. 1952-26: Ft. Belvoir, VA; Germany. 1956-62:
Rock Hill, SC; 1962-66, Germany; 1966-67: Vietnam.
1968-70; Ft. Gordon, GA.

Served on AD as sergeant major, CW4 and LTC.
Awarded Meritorious Service Medal, Bronze Star w/OLC,
Purple Heart and Army Commendation Medal.

Married Eleanor C. Thomas, May 5, 1946, Augusta,
GA and they have one daughter, one son and three grandchildren.

ERNEST L. (TEX) BRIGHT JR., born Jan. 14,
1929, Galveston, TX, entered the Army August-Septem-
ber 1946. Military locations and stations: Germany,
Coburg, Swabach, Karlshrue, Sweinfurt, Bamburg, Japan,
Korea two tours; Ft. Campbell, Ft. Bliss. Served with 6th
Constab. Sqdn., 53rd Constab. Sqdn., 48th AAA AW Bn.
(SP), 21st AAA as chief radio operator.

Discharged February 1953 as staff sergeant. His
awards include five Battle Stars, Korean Service Medal,
UN Service Medal, European Occupation, Berlin Airlift,
Good Conduct w/OLC.

Memorable experiences: drinking Cokes with Russian officers at Neustadt border crossing point. Being
evacuated by USN from Hungnam-HamHung Korea
(Christmas 1950) 7th Div. Soldier of the month at Coburg,
1947.

Married Nancye Carolyn and they have children:
Robert, Kelly, Timothy and David. Employed with the
Coca Cola Company and Lone Star Beer Co. Retired De-
cember 1990 and then unretired September 1993. He is
now back to work with the United Ministry Port of
Galveston, Inc. Member of VFW, American Legion, Noon
Optimist, US Constabulary Association and Men's Pro-
peller Club.

ALVAN DOUGLAS BROOKS, born June 1, 1928
and entered the service Sept. 27, 1946 and was stationed
at Fort Banks, MA; Camp Kilmer, NJ and Aberdeen, MD.

Shipped overseas to Bremerhaven, Germany; assigned to 74th Sqdn. Constabulary; shipped to Augsburg
for classification and assigned as clerk typist (405). After
all personnel was evacuated he was transferred to the 35th
Constabulary Sqdn., Fussen.

Two weeks later transferred to 1st Div. HQ for lifeguard training. Upon qualification transferred back to 35th in Fussen. One of his assignments was a 100 mile hike over a short period of time. The best assignment was getting a workable knowledge of the M8.

Discharged Feb. 25, 1948. He received the ETO Occupation Medal.

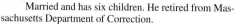

Married and has six children. He retired from Massachusetts Department of Correction.

CHARLES C. BROSIUS, born Oct. 25, 1928, Chicago, IL, enlisted in service Feb. 5, 1946, Ft. Sheridan. Military locations and stations: Ft. Knox, February-May 1946; Constabulary May 1946-February 1949; OSC Ft. Riley, 1949; Okinawa and Korea, 1950-52; UK, 1953-56; Germany 1959-62; Korea 1964-65.

Discharged April 1, 1966 and received the Commendation Medal. Married and has one son. Now retired vice president, Chicago Bank.

SIMMS M. BROUILLETTE, born Nov. 15, 1927, Ville Platte, LA, received a BA from the University SW LA. Joined the Army Nov. 15, 1945. Military locations and stations: Basic training Camp Jos. Robinson, AR; Weiden; Passau; Regensburg; Landshut. Attended Constabulary School Santhofen. Served with HQ TR 11th Regt., B Trp., 51st Constab. Sqdn. Discharged as T-5 October 1948.

Memorable experiences: Served for a short time in the horse platoon in Weiden and later served in PM Section. Transferred to 51st Sqdn. Enjoyed duty on Czech border at Eisenstein.

Married Mary Jane and they have a son, Stanley Brouillette and grandson, David Brouillette. Employed as classroom teacher (mathematics) for 32 years. Retired in 1986.

GARY G. (BROWNIE) BROWN, born April 1, 1932, Edgewood, MO, entered the RA Feb. 21, 1950. Military locations and stations: Ft. Dix, NJ training; Bad Hersfeld, Germany. Served with B Trp., 24th Constab., later 7th Army, as patrol leader.

Discharged March 14, 1953 as corporal. His awards include the European Occupation Ribbon, Good Conduct Ribbon and Border Legion Certificate.

Married Juanita J. Beamer June 11, 1955. They have children: Gary Jr., Wayne and Dina and grandchildren: Natalie, Kenneth, Julie, Cameron and Kayla. Employed with Chrysler Corp., Newark, DE for 41 years. Retired Dec. 31, 1993.

HENRY W. (HANK) BROWN JR., born Sept. 23, 1927, Providence, RI, received an associate degree in Business Science.

Joined the US Army Feb. 7, 1946. Military locations and stations: West Germany, June 1946-December 1949; Fulda; Bad Hersfeld; Fritzlar; Wiesbaden (Dotzheim). Served with B Trp., 81st Constab. Sqdn; HQ 14th Regt., HQ 1st Bde.

Discharged March 20, 1950 as corporal (E-4). His

awards include the WWII Victory Medal and Occupation Medal Germany WWII.

Memorable experiences: Extended border-duty assignments as a radio operator, combined with German-language immersion, developed into highly educational experiences; still memorable.

Married Martha R. Brown and they have children: Kristina B. Hayes and Rebecca O. LePage and grandchildren: Sarah, Nicholas and Tristan Hayes; Jennifer and Justin LePage. Employed as federal administration worker; state and local welfare-outreacher worker. Retired Dec. 1, 1984.

MAURICE C. BROWN JR., born Feb. 14, 1926, Bath, ME, inducted into service July 11, 1944, Ft. Devens, MA. Military locations and stations: Ft. Bragg, 1944; Ft. Meade, 1944; Camp Miles Standish, 1944; 808th FA Bn., December 1944; 3rd AFA Bn., 1945; 16th AFA Bn., 1945; Troop B 51st Constab. Sqdn. Passau, July 1946; Trp. E 6th A/C November 1946; ROTC Phoenix, AZ, 1951-54; Co. B, 723 Tank Bn., Camp Irwin, CA, 1954-55; HQ Co., 35th Tank Bn., 2nd AD, Germany 1955-59; Co. E, 40th Armd. 1st Cav. Korea, 1959-60; G Trp., 6th A/C Ft. Knox, KY, 1960-62; B Trp., 3rd Sqdn., 12th Cav., 3rd AD Germany 1962-67; HQ General Support Gp., Ft. Ord, CA, 1967, until retirement Oct. 31, 1967.

His awards include the Army Commendation, Good Conduct Ribbon, ETO Ribbon, WWII Victory, Germany Occupation and National Defense.

Married Dorothea Figert, Landshut Germany, Sept. 6, 1950. Now retired and travels a great deal.

HILTON N. (BROX) BROXTON, born Nov. 10, 1920, Waycross, GA, joined the US Army Feb. 17, 1939. Military locations and stations: Ft. Benning, GA; Ft. Belvoir, VA; Ft. Monmouth, NJ; Ft. Lewis, WA and seven training camps in Louisiana, Mississippi and Arkansas.

Overseas during WWII, served in England, France, Luxembourg, Belgium and Germany. After WWII, served in France, then in Army of Occupation in Germany and Austria. Last, served in Greece as a military advisor to the Loyalists during the Greek Civil War in the early part of 1948.

Discharged for service connected disabilities at Percy Jones General Hospital, Battle Creek, MI, Nov. 15, 1948.

VINCENT J. BUCCA, born April 28, 1927, inducted into service 1945, Boston, MA. Military locations and stations: Camp Croft, SC; Berlin, Germany 1945-47; 1945 Camp Croft, SC training then to Germany December 1945, 78th Div. 1946; 16th 1947-47.

1945-46 First assignment, 7th Inf. Div., 310th Inf. Bn., F Co., 5th Plt. The division left on points to the US in 1946.

1946-47, volunteered to the Horse Plt., 16th Constab. Sqdn. Squadron commander, 1st Lt. Quinn. Although his stay in the constabulary was most rewarding he found it quite challenging, growing in the city, having to learn to ride a horse.

Most of his duties were centered on either parade duty for the upper echelon or guard duty on the outskirts of Berlin. With the change in relations between the US and Russia he thinks much of the contact that they had with their counterparts while on duty. While patrolling the outskirts of the perimeter it was not uncommon to meet,

ride side by side and speak with each other in broken German.

Being young and away from home he found it was incredibly difficult to see the German people scrape for food, cigarettes and even soap. He hopes that being one of the first occupation squadrons stationed in Berlin made a positive impact on the German people.

Through the years he has had many fond memories of the camaraderie that was shared with others in the squadron. He hopes that maybe through the Constabulary he may be able to establish contact with some old buddies.

Discharged in 1947 and received American Defense Medal, Good Conduct, ETO, Victory Medal and Army of Occupation. Married and father of three. Two girls and one boy. All married. Retired from US Post Office.

CHRISTOPHER T. BUCKSATH, born Sept. 5, 1929, Dalton, MO, enlisted in the Army September 1948, took basic and leadership training at Ft. Knox. From February 1949 through June 1952 he was assigned to Co. E, 1st Bn., 6th A/C Regt., at Straubing, Germany. Attended University of Missouri, 1952-54. Reenlisted December 1954 and assigned 1st Bn., 6th Inf. (Berlin); 20th Engr. Bn., (Ft. Devens) 1957; 62nd Engr. Co., (ADM) (Vicenza Italy) 1958-61; G3 Operations, Ft. Leonard, MO July 1961 December 1962; MAAG Vietnam 1963; S3, 5th Engr. Bn. FLW 1964-65; Opns SGM, 1st Engr. Bde, FLW 1967-68, Construction Directorate, MAAC Vietnam July 1968-June 1968; CSM 1st Bn., 1st Engr. Bde, FLW 1969-June 1972; CSM, 130th Engr. Bde, Hanau, Germany 1972-October 1975; CSM 937th Engr. Gp. (Ft. Riley) 1975-April 1976.

Retired April 1976. His awards include the Meritorious Service Medal w/2 OLC, Bronze Star, Commendation Medal, Expert Infantry Badge, and other service/campaign medals. Bucksath has three sons and a daughter. Robert retired in February 1998 as a CW5 warrant officer. Mark retired as SGM from the Special Forces in February 1997. Kristen and Chris J. enjoy the civilian world.

Bucksath enjoys all sports and bowls four times a week (owns three-300 games). He was a member of the SETAF (Italy) team that won the USAREUR Bowling Championship in 1961. He golfs and pitches horseshoes. In horseshoes won championships at SETAF Italy; USAHAC Vietnam and several times at Ft. Leonard Wood was the Singles and Doubles Champion.

He owns the Victory Bar in Moberly, MO and is very active in the Fraternal Order of Eagles.

JOHN DAVID BUFFINGTON, born Nov. 1, 1930, Union Bridge, MD, inducted into service November 1948, Camp Pickett, VA. Military locations and stations: Camp Pickett, VA; Fussen; Nurenburg, Germany; Ft. Meade, MD.

Discharged May 1952. Married Charlotte A. Overholtzer and they have son, Michael. Enjoys camping, traveling, restoring old tractors and working on cars.

JOHN A. BUSTERUD, born March 7, 1921, born Coos Bay (Marshfield), OR. Received BS from the University of Oregon, 1943; LLB Yale Law School, 1949.

Joined the Army Aug. 9, 1943 and commissioned Jan. 14, 1944. His military locations and stations: Ft. Benning, GA; Camp Hood, TX; ETO.

Served with the 90th Div. (3rd Army); 4th Armd. Div. (3rd Army); 1st Constab. Bde. Commands held: Battalion Command; Inspector General, 4th Armd.; ACT's GI, 4th Armd., adjutant, 1st Constab. Bde. (1st incumbent).

Participated in battles in Rhineland and Central Europe. Discharged October 1946. His awards and medals include the Bronze Star, Commendation Ribbon, DOD Meritorious Service Medal and Combat Infantry Badge.

Memorable experiences: discovery of Gold and Art Treasures at Merkers in April 1945; organizing 1st Constab. Bde., Wesbaden.

Married to Anne and they have children: John W. and James P. Busterud; Mary Busterud Dunlap and grandchildren: Holt, Spencer, Ellie Dunlap; Rebecca and Thomas Busterud. Employed as attorney, state legislature; chairman, president's council on environmental quality; president, Resolve. Retired Mil. Res. 1961.

ROBERT H. (BOB) CAMPITELL, born June 9, 1927, Norristown, PA, attended Villanova University, 1950-55.

Joined the service US Army July 1945. Attended basic training Camp Wheeler, GA. Assigned 416th military Government Co., Norristown, PA; 358th Civil Affairs Bde., Norristown, PA; 2059th USAR School, Bethlehem, PA. 79th ARCOM NCO Academy, Ft. Indiantown Gap, PA, commandant; 1st US Army NCO Academy, Ft. Pickett, VA, assistant commandant; 817th P&A Bn., Chester, PA, command sergeant major; 358th Civil Affairs Bde., Norristown, PA, command sergeant major. Federal Emergency Management Agency Region III Philadelphia, PA, CSM; Army Reserve Personnel Center, St. Louis, MO, Liaison to Ft. Dix, NJ.

Retired June 1987, 24th Div., Ft. Stewart, GA. Recalled to active duty, March 3, 1991, Operation Desert Storm. Retired for second time Sept. 27, 1991, Ft. Meade, MD.

Spent 43 years total service includes three overseas tours: US Constabulary, 1946-47, Germany; 358th CA Bde., 1973 NATO-Belgium, Germany, Norway; 817th P&A Bn., 1980, Germany, 21st Sup. Com, Kaiserlauten.

His awards and decorations: Expert Infantry Badge, Legion of Merit, Meritorious Service w/4 OLC, Army Commendation, Army Achievement w/OLC, Good Conduct, Army Reserve Component Achievement w/2 OLC, Victory Medal, Army Occupation, National Defense Service, Humanitarian Service, Overseas Service Ribbon (2), Pennsylvania Commendation Medal and numerous other service and ribbon awards, certificates and citations including "the four Chaplains Legion of Honor" award.

Fifteen years serving on Ft. Dix Retiree Council, Ft. Dix, NJ; 30 years with Boy Scouts of America; 20 years #1 boat "Washington Crossing the Delaware" Christmas pageant, Washington Crossing, PA; 4th degree, Knights of Columbus.

He is a life member VFW since 1947. Life member Retired Sergeants Major and Chiefs Association. Presently vice commander Outpost #2 US Constabulary Association. Hobbies: Log home in Poconos Mountains, PA and jazz piano.

Married to Midge and they have children, Eric Campitell and Carol Brame and grandchildren: Patrick Brame and Rachel Brame. Employed at Coopers Creek Chemical Corp., West Conshohocken, PA as sales manager. Retired December 1995 after 43 years with company.

LOUIS T. (SMOKY) CARACCIOLO, born Feb. 26, 1928, Scranton, PA, entered the Army Jan. 30, 1946. Military locations and stations: basic training, Ft. McClellan, AL; ETO April 1946, assigned to 39th Inf., 9th Div., Prien, Germany. Moved to Bad Aibling to guard last POW camp. Sent to Constabulary School August 1946 to Deggendorf, Passau and Landshut with B Troop, 51st Sqdn.

Reenlisted July 1950 sent to Austria with 350th Inf., 88th Div. until June 1953.

Memorable experiences: escorting soldiers from the Ukranian lions who fought with the Nazi's back to the Russians. Qualified to shoot on Eucom Rifle Team. Taking POWS to Dachau for Denazification and discharge.

Married Jenny and she died in 1975. He is remarried to Anna Mae and they have children: Louis, Gina, Mary Ann, Carol, Angela, Michael and Christopher; grandchildren: Gena, Daniel, David, Megan and Hardy. Employed with the US Post Office as letter carrier, retiring Jan. 3, 1993.

GILBERT I. (GIL) CARLSON, born July 8, 1930 in Plymouth, MA, joined the service July 25, 1949. Military locations and stations: Ft. Dix, NJ; Ft. Devens, MA; Fritzlar and Fulda Germany. Served with 9th Div., 39th Inf., HQ & HQ Co.; 1st Bn., 14th A/C, 24th Constab.

Held positions as radio operator; net control station regiment also taught Morse Code and radio procedure. He achieved the rank of private first class and discharged Nov. 28, 1952.

Served in skirmished with East German police while on boarder patrol.

He was awarded the National Defense, Occupation of Germany and Good Conduct.

Memorable experiences: Berlin airlift and May 1 show of force parades also working with the MPs to break up riots.

Married to Mildred Carlson and they have children: Deborah, Judith, Sandra (all married); grandchildren: Dana, Mikel, Jullie, Alicia, Paul, James, Alana.

Employed as Station A installer repairman for New England Telephone Co., also a security guard for a local hospital for seven years (1985-1992).

ROBERT P. (BOB) CARPENTER, born Dec. 30, 1925, Laporte, PA, received a BS degree from Lockhaven University Pennsylvania; MED Shippensburg University, (PA).

Joined the US Maritime Service January 1945 in Safety Seamanship Div. teaching abandon ship drill.

Served in HQ combat command (1) 1st Armd. Div., then 3rd Regt. Constab. Trained Radio School, Ft. Bragg, ended up county clerk, 3rd Constab., Service Troop.

Mayor of Laporte, PA since 1969 and just won (1997) reelection. End of next term - 31 years as mayor.

Married Nancy June 1950 and they have a daughter Carol Insinger and grandchildren: Laurie Beth and Lisa Ann Insinger. Employed 15 years as a high school science teacher and 15 years as high school guidance counselor. Retired June 1982.

PETER CARROLL, born July 23, 1931, Clifton, NJ, enlisted in service Sept. 10, 1948. Military locations and stations: 3rd Bn., 14th Armd. Cav. Regt., December 1948-October 1950; Coburg, Germany; Heavy Motor Co., 6th Inf. Regt., Berlin October 1950-May 1952.

Married Alma Desantis Oct. 23, 1954 and they have one son, Kevin, a daughter, Kathleen and two grandchildren.

Retired sergeant at arms in US Constabulary Association. Traveling, returned to Germany September 1996 for 50th anniversary of US Constabulary.

WILLARD CHAPIN, born June 7, 1927, Levering, MI, joined the US Army Sept. 11, 1945. Military locations and stations: Basic, Ft. Bliss, TX and Freising, Germany.

Served with Constab. 2nd Regt. HQ as personnel sergeant major. Discharged June 1947 as staff sergeant.

Married to Mary F. and they have children, Beth Borchard and Dennis Chapin; grandchildren: Sara Chapin, Brian Chapin and Andrew Borchardt. He was owner of Chapin Chevrolet, Inc. and retired March 15, 1987.

JOHN ROBERT CHERRY, born Sept. 26, 1930, Blount City, entered the US Army June 3, 1964. Constabulary, the best unit in the US Army. Started off as the 68th Provision FA Bn., in 1947 then became the 70th FA Bn. in Fussen, Germany. They moved to Nurnberg in 1950. In 1952 they came under the 7th Army. He was with the 7th Army and the 70th FA Bn. longer than any trooper. Their motto was "move shoot and communicate" and they did better than any other FA Bn. in the Constabulary. Rotated back to the States March 1954. Discharged April 1955. He was with the 70th and HQ Btry., A Btry.

Married Wilma and they have children: Robbie, Doyle, Robert and Arnold; grandchildren: Joshua, Dylan, Jessica and Zachary. Employed with Birmingham Water Works as a service rep. Retired May 1, 1991.

BILLY J. (SKINHEAD) CHESNUT, born Nov. 17, 1927, London, KY. Entered the US Army, Jan. 10, 1946. Military locations and stations: Ft. Knox, Ft. Polk, Ft. Holabird; AP Hill, Ft. Dix, Camp Atterbury, Camp Kilmer, Kassel and Fritzlar Germany. Served with 1st Constab. Regt., 14th Armd. Cav., 241st Armd., CIC 201st Engr., 149th Inf.

Discharged July 2, 1977 as 1SG E-8. Memorable experiences: entire time with US Contabulary.

Married Effie R. Chesnut and they have children, Mary Anne and Billy Joe, Jr. and grandchildren: Carrie, Brandon, Holly and Jordan. Employed with KY ARNG Tech as shop foreman, OMS. After retirement drove tanker with hazardous material. Retired Nov. 17, 1992.

EDMUND J. CHMIEL, born June 11, 1931, Chicago, IL, attended Constabulary School, Sonthofen, Germany.

Entered US Army Oct. 23, 1946, serving until March 1948. Served with the Illinois Air National Guard June 1, 1949-July 23, 1952; USAF, Activated Air Guard April 1, 1951-July 23, 1952.

Military locations and stations: US Army basic training, Ft. Knox, KY, POE Camp Kilmer, NJ; Marburg, Boblingen and Ulm Germany, 1947-48; Illinois Air National Guard, Midway Airport Chicago, IL; USAF, Midway Airport, Chicago, IL, April 1, 1951-July 1, 1951; Pope Field, Ft. Bragg, NC, July 1, 1951-Sept. 1, 1951; Langley Field, VA, Sept. 2, 1951-Nov. 1, 1951; Merignac AFB, Bordeaux, France, November 1951-February 1952; Laon, France, February 1951-July 1952.

United served with A Trp., 14th Sqdn., 15th Regt., Army USAF, 108th Light Bomb Sqdn. and 126th Light Bomb Sqdn.

Awards include the Victory Medal, Occupation of Germany, Good Conduct, UN Service Medal, Overseas Service Ribbon and Army Lapel Button.

Three honorable discharges: US Army, USAF, Illinois Air National Guard.

ANDREW B. (ANDY) CISNEY, born June 14, 1927, Orbisonia, PA, entered the US Army Dec. 18, 1945. Military locations and stations: Ft. Knox, KY; Ft. Meade, MD; Stuttgart, Germany; Wetzlar, Germany; Dillenburg, Germany; Marburg, Germany. Served with 4th Armd., A Trp., 37th Constab.

Held commands as chauffeur for company commander, Capt. Gail B. Lee and discharged March 17, 1947.

Married Beulah M. Cisney Dec. 9, 1950 and they have a daughter Connie Lee Shatzer Fittry and Rick Cisney and grandchildren: Scott Shatzer, Jennifer Shatzer, Amy Cisney, Joe Cisney, Andy Cisney and Cristie Cisney.

Employed as trucking owner/operator for 15 years, American Can Co.; mail clerk, store clerk, maintenance dispatcher, shipping dispatcher, James River Corp., purchasing agent. Retired from James River April 12, 1994.

HAROLD VINCENT CLARK JR., born Aug. 27, 1932, Pittsburgh, PA, enlisted in the regular army, March 2, 1948. Basic training, Ft. Dix, NJ. After basic went to 82nd AB, Ft. Bragg, NC June 1948-November 1948. Put on orders for ETO, US Constab. Co. C 373rd Armd. Inf. Bn., Giessen, Germany, Verdun Kaserne, then changed to Miller Barracks, graduated from US Constab. NCO Academy in 1950, Munich, Germany. Left Germany April 1951. Arrived at Ft. Dix, NJ as instructor in automatic weapons, where he gave Vito Farinola aka Vic Damone movie star and singer, instructions on light 30 cal. and 50 cal. machine guns.

Left Ft. Dix, arrived in Camp Stoneman, CA February 1952 put on orders for Korea (EVIL) made amphibious landing at Inchon Harbor. Joined up with 1st Cav. Div., 5th RCT involved in one major battle campaign, pulled back to guard POWs on Koje Do Island, returned to Japan, Hokkaido, Chitose 1. Went to Honshu, Sendai, Japan to 50th Signal Bn. as teletype operator, then motor pool sergeant.

He received Combat Infantry Badge, Parachute Infantry Badge, Army of Occupation Medal, Korean Campaign Medal w/Bronze Star, UN Medal, Syngman Rhee Citation, National Defense Medal and Good Conduct Medal.

Widowed 1989 and they have two daughters, one son and 10 grandchildren.

Retired from steel mill in Pittsburgh, PA. After 35 years moved to Augusta, GA in 1990. Currently vice commander Post 505 Augusta, GA, service officer, VFW Post 3887 and 11th District historian, American Legion, Georgia.

LOUIS W. CLINE JR., born Sept. 1, 1930 Williamstown, NJ, graduated Glassboro High School 1948. Enlisted US Army Sept. 21, 1948, Philadelphia, PA. Basic training Camp Breckenridge, KY.

Assigned to A Btry., 70th FA Bn., US Constab., Fussen, Germany February 1949. Honorably discharged

as sergeant first class, Sept. 22, 1953. Served three years New Jersey National Guard discharged as master sergeant. He was in construction for four years, New York Shipbuilding for 10 years.

Cline was with the Department on Navy at Philadelphia Naval Base for 26 years. Retired in January 1994 as an engineering technician.

Married Martha Weese in Nurenberg Germany. They have one daughter, Barbara, and two granddaughters, Jill and Kate. He is a member of the American Legion Post 252 The Raymond Cline Post, Williamstown, NJ.

While stationed with the 70th FA in Fussen, Germany. He gave Hershey bars every payday to the small children of Ziegelwese a small town just outside of Fussen. The children waited for their candy bar.

Years later on a visit to his wife's family. He went to the local bank to exchange dollar for D-Marks. As he approached the teller the young lady said, "May I help you Sgt. Cline?" As he did not give her his name, he looked surprised. She then said, You do not remember me do you?" And he replied, "No!" She then said she was one of the children that you gave candy bars to. He was very surprised to be remembered just by giving candy and being nice to the children.

ERNEST C. COFFONE, born Dec. 7, 1924, Worcester, MA. Inducted into service Feb. 19, 1946, Ft. Devens, MA. Discharged July 13, 1947.

His military locations: Wetzler, Germany; Weilburg, Germany; Camp Kilmer, NJ; Dillenburg, Germany; Bad Schwalbach, Germany; Stuttgart, Germany.

Awarded Army of Occupation Medal and the WWII Victory Medal. Widowed in February of 1994. He has one daughter, three grandchildren and one great-granddaughter. He also has two sisters and three brothers. Coffone enjoys playing pool, cards, babysitting. Likes sports and visits West Point four times a year. Retired from 35 years at Norton Co., Worcester, MA as a mason worker.

ALFRED B. (CHARLIE) COMINGORE, born May 23, 1923, Lafayette, IN, received a BS from Newberry College 1984; (at age 1961); Listed Who's Who 1984.

Joined US Army 1944 and USAF, 1961. Military locations and stations: US Army, 12th Armd. Div., France and Germany. Discharged September 1946. USAF Indiana-Illinois; Germany; North Carolina; Taiwan; New York; Italy; England; Texas and South Carolina. Served with 12th Armd. Div., 92nd Cav. Recon, 3rd Constab. Regt. (S-4 Sgt.).

Retired March 1980 as master sergeant. His awards include the Air Force Commendation Medal, Presidential Unit Awrd, Air Force Outstanding Unit Award, American Campaign Medal, ETO Campaign Medal, WWII Victory Medal, Army Occupation, National Defense Service Medal, Expert Marksmanship, Air Force Longevity Ribbon w/4 clusters, Air Force Good Conduct w/4 clusters and Army Good Conduct Medal.

Memorable experiences: retired at age 56. Last 10 years managed officer and NCO clubs. Honor graduate "Open Mess Management - 1978"

Married to Barbara and they have a son, Bob Pitts and grandchildren Brian Larsen, Brian Pitts and Brad Pitts. Employed as executive director, Senior Catering, Inc., serving "Meals on Wheels" 1984-1986. Retired 1986.

RICHARD EDMUND CONDON, born Dec. 6, 1928, Detroit, MI, enlisted in the USMC May 1946. Medically discharged June 1946. Enlisted in US Army July 1946, basic training, Ft. Bragg, NC.

Duties: Korea, November 1946-1948 with 31st Inf. Regt., 7th Inf. Div.; May 1948 US Constab., 6th Constab. Regt. HQ Trp., Schweinfurt, Germany (later designated) 6th Armd. Cav. Regt.; 1952-53 Korea Co. I, 9th Inf. Regt., 2nd Inf. Div.

June 1953-December 1954 Nebraska Military District MP Detachment, Omaha, NE. Accepted into the Criminal Investigation Div. December 1954. December 1954-July 1960 Ft. Wayne, MI; 1960-1964 7th Army Training Center, Grafenwohr, Germany; 1964-65 Ft. Campbell, KY; 1966-1967 Uijongbu, Korea, 19th CID; 1967-68 Ft. Ord, CA and was appointed warrant officer in 1968; 1968-1971 Sandia Base, Albuquerque, NM 46th CID with additional duties at the Defense Atomic Support Agency, Inspector Generals Worldwide inspection team. 1971-72 Vietnam, Det. C, 8th Military Police; CID; 1972-1977 Ft. Ord, CA. Retired Nov. 3, 1977 as a CWO-3 with over 31 years service.

He received several medals and awards throughout his career, including: Combat Infantry Badge, Legion of Merit, Bronze Star, Army Commendation Medal w/OLC, Army Good Conduct (six awards), WWII Victory Medal, Occupation Medal for (both) Germany and Japan, Korean Service Medal w/2 Battle Stars, Vietnam Campaign Ribbon, Vietnam Service Medal w/3 Battle Stars, United Nations Medal, National Defense Service Medal w/cluster and Army Expeditionary Forces Medal.

Married Peggy Ann, June 22, 1953 and they have five children and six grandchildren.

Member of DAV, VFW, US Constabulary, 2nd Infantry Division, 9th Infantry Regiment, Korean War Veterans and CID Agents Association.

After military retirement he joined the Las Vegas, NV Metropolitan Police Dept. as an investigator with the Special Investigation Section. He retired January 1991 for his second and final retirement.

He is a fourth degree member of the Knights of Columbus, likes to read, travel and visit an occasional casino.

DUDLEY F. CONEY, born Oct. 28, 1914, enlisted in regular army June 6, 1938. Married to Constance D'Antone March 14, 1942, she passed away April 25, 1993.

Duties: Panama Canal Zone, platoon sergeant and supply sergeant 1938, 1939 and 1940. Camp Grant, IL Reception Center 1941, 1942; OCS Ft. Knox, November, December 1942, January 1943; 749th Tank Bn., Camp Bowie, TX 1943; England January-June 1944; Normandy and Central Frances 1944-45; Ft. Knox 1945-46; US Constab. June 1946, 1947, 1948, 1949; Ft. Knox 1949; Camp Gordon 1950-1951; Ft. Bragg, 1952; Ft. Campbell 1952, 1953; Korea 1954; Japan 1954-1955; Ft. Sam Houston 1956, 1957, 1958; Ft. Leonard Wood 1959, Bremerhaven, Germany 1960, 1961, 1962; Ft. Gordan, GA, 1963-1964.

Colonel Coney retired Dec. 31, 1964. His medals include the Bronze Star, w/V and two clusters, Purple Heart, Commendation Medal, Occupation Medal, European Service w/3 clusters, Far East Service w/cluster, Korean Service and Airborne Jump Senior Badge.

JAMES F. CONNOR, born Jan. 7, 1929, Butler, PA, inducted into service March 17, 1947, Butler, PA. Military locations and stations: Ft. Bragg, NC; Ft. Myer, VA; Hersfeld, Germany; Ft. Lee, VA; La Rochelle, France; Ft. Hood, TX; Ft. Polk, LA; Ft. Bliss, TX; Homestead AFB, FL; Korea. Retired Aug. 1, 1967, El Paso, TX.

His awards include the Commendation Medal, Occupation Ribbon (Germany), Good Conduct, National Defense Service and Expert Infantry Badge.

Married Nenette Zubiarrain, LaRochelle, France and they have a daughter, Patricia and a son, James. Fully retired after 26 years as a Department of Army civilian. Total federal service 46 years.

CLIFFORD E. (CLIFF) COOPER, born Sept. 13, 1930, Onied, TN, entered the US Army, Oct. 26, 1948. His military locations and stations: basic training, Ft. Ord, CA, Schweinfurt and Bad Hersfeld. Served with the 22nd and 24th Constab. Sqdns. Discharged June 13, 1952 as private first class.

Married to Marguerite and they have children: Anthony, Teresa and Lawrence and grandchildren: Delaney and Ashley. Employed as driver ONC Motor Freight, secretary-treasurer, Teamsters Local 962; Secretary-Treasurer Joint Council #37. Retired Jan. 31, 1987.

EDWIN CORDEIRO, born Nov. 6, 1926, New Bedford, MA. Joined the Army Feb. 27, 1945 and took basic training at Fort Bliss, TX with Btry. D, 56 AART BN.

Arrived in LeHavre, France Jan. 7, 1946. Duties with 467 AAA and 390 AA HQ, 3rd Army, Bad Tolz; U.S. Constabulary, Augsburg, Germany, C Troop, 74th Sqdn. 5th Regt; Patch and Sheridan Kasernes then changed to the 2nd Constabulary Regt.; Constabulary School, August-September 1946, Sonthofen, Germany, Desk and Records Course #2.

In Germany was assigned to 2nd Bde., Munich; 5th Regt., 74th Sqdn., A Troop in Augsburg; B Troop, Donauworth; C Troop, Gunzburg-Ottenbeuren; D Troop, Gablingen; E Troop, Memmingen.

Arrived back in the States in September 1948 and discharged at Camp Kilmer, NJ, Sept. 20, 1948. Awards include the Bronze Star Medal, Meritorious Unit Emblem, Good Conduct Medal, Army of Occupation Medal w/Germany Clasp, WWII Victory Medal, Korean Service Medal w/Silver Star, National Defense Service Medal, UN Service Medal, Expert Rifle Badge, Overseas Service Ribbons and Army Lapel Button.

Member of U.S. Constabulary Assoc., 2nd Cav. Assoc., Korean War Veterans Assoc., VFW and American Legion.

Recalled to active duty for Korea in August 1950, and assigned to 95th MP BN, 8th Army. Separated Aug. 20, 1951,

Married Mary Garcia June 22, 1952 and they have three children: John, Leann and Jayne, and three grandchildren: Jordan and Jared Cordeiro and Joseph Ramanazzi. Self-employed, 21 years, TriValley Grower, equipment manager. Retired Dec. 31, 1996.

HARRY F. CORRADI, born June 29, 1928, Brooklyn, NY, entered the service 1947, 27th Constabulary, stationed in Darmstadt, Germany. Served with 14th Constab., Manheim and 27th Constab. Darm.

Discharged 1948 as corporal and awarded Germany Occupation and Good Conduct.

Memorable experiences: hunting wild boar and deer ray buck in Stuttgart Black Forest, also Deberg Elk, Hersh.

Married Doris and they have children: Harry Corradi Jr., Susan, Gail, Loretta and 15 grandchildren. Employed as Merchant Marine, farmer, NR Association, Hunter Ins. Safety NA Rifle Association, gunsmith, hunting guide. Retired 1978 as NYC TA pump inspector.

JOSEPH FRANKLIN CORRIGAN, born July 29, 1926, Williamsburg, PA, was drafted into the Army November 1944. Took basic at Camp Croft, SC, sailed to unknown destination March 1945. April 1 landed in Naples, Italy as replacement for 5th Army. Took AIT outside Naples. Later moved to Rome, took two weeks engineering training. Returned home July 1942 and went to Camp Chaffie, AR. Reenlisted August 1945. Went to France March 1946. After going through Camp Lucky Strike he left for Germany. Stopped at Schwabech outside Nurenburg in April he went Armd. Cav under 4th Armd. Div. July 1946 they went Constabulary, later called 53rd Sqdn., 6th Regt. He was with them until July 1948. Returned home and was discharged. Stayed in Reserves until September 1950, then was called up for Korea.

He believes the most important job he helped with while in the Constabulary, besides the daily routine patrol was setting up and maintaining road blocks around Nurenburg during the war trials.

Married Betty J. Reed, April 14, 1951 and they have children: Sue, Deborah, Linda, James and Kenneth and 11 grandchildren. Employed as rewind operator at Appleton Papers, Roaring Spring, PA. Retired February 1989.

RAYMOND C. CRAMER, was with the 71st Sqdn., E Trp. at Swabish Hall in 1946, then transferred to 10th Regt., Light Tank outside of Stuttgart. Returned to the 15th Sqdn., Med Det. until late 1948. Later served with 68th FA at Fussen, Germany.

JAMES M. CROSS, born Nov. 22, 1930, Hagerstown, MD, entered military service Sept. 16, 1948 and had basic training at Camp Breckenridge, KY. Arrived in Bremerhaven BOE January 1949 and was assigned to C Btry., 70th FA Bn. as a cannoneer, driver and company clerk. Transferred to Sonthofen with an FA Gp., transferred to Boeblingen at a tent city and last transfer put him in Vaihingen (Stuttgart) as chief draftmans for the Artillery Section for 7th Army. Discharged in 1954. Joined the

Hagerstown, MD Department of Police where he stayed for 24 years, then retired. Moved to North Carolina in 1984 and finally retired as chief of security with the Gaston County Dyeing Machine in Mt. Holly, NC. He earned the Good Conduct Medal, Army of Occupation (Germany) and the National Defense Medals.

Cross married Norma C. Ard after the death of his first wife. He has two sons and a daughter. Jim collects police shoulder patches from North Carolina and also collects East and West German Police insignia. He currently lives in Bessemer City, NC.

CHRISTOPHER J. CUNNINGHAM JR., born Sept. 25, 1927, Albany, NY. Enlisted US Army Oct. 2, 1944 at 17. Stationed at Ft. Bragg, Ft. Riley, Ft. Dix, Ft. Benning and overseas at LeHavre France; Freising; Munich; Stuttgart; Heidelberg; Laufen; Bad Reichenall Germany; Yokohama Japan.

Served with the 2nd Cav., 2nd Constab. Horse Plt., 7766th Horse Trp., attached to Constabulary HQ, 7th Base Post Office in Japan.

Discharged September 1948. Volunteered for the Korean Conflict May 1952. Discharged May 1954. His awards include WWII Victory, Army of Occupation, Korean Service, UN Service and National Defense Service Medals.

Memorable experiences: seeing first hand the devastation and destruction wrought by war as well as the indignities the civilian population had to suffer because of the actions of their leaders; seeing man's inhumanity in the way the concentration camps were run, and their inmates disposed of like old rags. On the plus side were the friendships that were formed in the Horse Plt. that still endure to this day.

Widowed in 1992 and has four children, eight grandchildren and one great-grandchild. Worked for Albany Newspapers for 42 years and retired as national adv. manager January 1993. Now engaged to be married to Lorraine Heeran (former high school sweetheart) in the spring of 1998.

JOHN M. (JD) D'AMICO, born Feb. 4, 1927 Coatesville, PA, attended Radio-TV Institute 2 1/2 years.

Entered and commissioned into the army June 11, 1945. Military locations and stations: New Cumberland, PA; Camp Wheeler, GA; Camp Pickett, VA; Wieden, Germany; Passau, Germany. Served with 4th Armd. Div, 51st Constab. Div. Radio operator in armored car.

Discharged Jan. 29, 1947 as technician fifth grade. His awards include the Good Conduct, ETO, Occupation and Victory Medal.

Memorable experiences: went overseas on the USS *West Point,* at the time it was the third largest ship in the world. In peace time it was the SS *America* the largest in the USA.

Married Mary J. D'Amico for 35 years and have a son, John M. D'Amico Jr. and wife, Susan. He owned and operated radio TV, VCR sales and service stores for 36 years. Retired June 1, 1990.

GUY L. DAVIS, born Aug. 15, 1927 in Tennessee. Entered service October 1944. His military locations and stations: Camp Wheeler, GA; Germany; Belgium; Camp Hood, TX; Ft. Lawton, WA 1984; Karlsruhe; Schwabisch

Hall, Fussen Germany 1951. Served with 759th FA March 1945-November 1945; 529th FA, November 1945-November 1946; November 1946-May 1950. Constabulary duties February 1948-May 1950; 70th FA B Btry.

Discharged May 1950 as corporal. His awards include the EAMET Ribbon, Bronze Service Star for the Germany Campaign.

Married Joyce and they have children: Jerry, Larry, Faye and Robert and grandchildren, Mandy and Jarad. Employed as life and health insurance business district manager. Retired May 1994.

SAMUEL CHARLES DE BONO, born July 11, 1928, Bronx, NY, entered service March 25, 1946. Attended HQ US Constabulary School, Constabulary EM Basic Course, Sept. 8, 1947-October 1947, Sonthofen Germany. Constabulary EM Advanced Course, Nov. 17, 1947-Dec. 13, 1947, Sonthofen Germany.

Military locations and stations: basic training, Ft. Knox, KY. Landed Bremerhaven Germany, July 1946. Served with E Trp., 6th Sqdn., 53rd Sqdn., 91st FA Bn., which was part of a group artillery. Discharged Jan. 14, 1949 as T/5.

His awards and medals include the WWII Victory Medal and Army of Occupation Medal.

Married Joan and they have children: Nancy, Samuel C. Jr., and Kenneth and grandchildren: Christopher, Jessica, Robert, Craig, Jillian and Devan. Employed as US Postal Service clerk and retired from the post office 1986.

WILLIAM J. (BILL) DEELEY, born March 22, 1928, Chicago, IL, received BA in public administration; AA Police Science.

Joined the Army Sept. 21, 1948. Military locations and stations: Ft. Ord, CA; Stuttgart/Via Hingen, Germany. Served with 820 MP Plt.; US Constab. Provost Marshal's Office. Held positions as operations sergeant; US 7th Army Provost Marshall's Office.

Discharged June 17, 1952 as SFC, and awarded Good Conduct Medal of Germany Occupation.

Memorable experiences: marrying his wife on Dec. 1, 1951 in Stuttgart, Germany.

Married to Helga P. and they have children, Kevin and Michelle Ann and grandchildren: Kyle, Sean and Jack. Employed with Employment Development, Department State of California; supr. investigator; Sealbeach Police Department; Signal Hall. Retired Dec. 1, 1991.

ADOLPH (AL) DESTEFANO, born Nov. 3, 1927, Rutland, VT, joined US Army March 1946. Military locations and stations: March 1946-July 1948, HQ 10th and 15th Constab. Regt., Stuttgart, Germany; July 1948-January 1949, 70th FA Bn., Fussen, Germany; January 1949-June 1950, Army Transportation Command, Ft. Hamilton, NY; July 1950-September 1950, 2nd Inf. Div. Engrs., Korea; September 1950-May 1951, Valley Forge Army Hospital, PA; May 1951-October 1952, Army Transportation Command, Ft. Hamilton, NY; 2998th Engr. Float

Bridge Co., Korea, October 1952-March 1954; 65th Inf. Regt., 8th Inf. Div., Ft. Carson, CO, March 1954-March 1955; 226th Transportation Co., Vassincourt, France, March 1958-March 1958; Army Advisory Gp., NJNG, March 1958-March 1960; CMAG, Okinawa, Taiwan, March 1960-January 1961; Army Advisor Gp., Massachusetts, NG; January 1961-October 1964; USAREUR Trans. Gp., Kassel, Germany; MACV, CICV, Vietnam, October 1965-January 1967.

Discharged January 1967 as first sergeant (E-8). His awards and medals include the Army Commendation Medal w/OLC, Purple Heart, Good Conduct Medal, Occupation Medal, Korean Service Medal w/3 Battle Stars, UN Medal, Vietnam Service Medal w/3 Battle Stars, Distinguished Service Medal, Korean Unit Citation, National Defense Service Medal, WWII Victory Medal and Vietnam Cross of Gallantry w/Palm.

Married to Alice and they have children, Craig and Christine. Employed as Allstate Insurance Co., RO supply supervisor. Retired April 1987.

WILLIAM G. DEWEESE, born May 31, 1927, Alma, IL, inducted into service Aug. 4, 1945, Ft. Sheridan, IL. Military locations and stations: Ft. Knox, KY; Camp Pickett, VA; Camp Kilmer, NJ; Camp Phillip Morris; LeHavre, France.

Served with 771st Tank Btry., Camp Patton, Germany. Renamed 71st Constab. Sqdn., 1945-46. USAF Shaw AFB, Sumter, SC, 1950-1951.

Discharged 1947. His awards include two Overseas Bars, Army of Occupation and Germany Victory.

Married Virginia Deweese and they have a son and daughter. Deweese is disabled and enjoys working puzzles, reading, watching TV. His son retired from the Army in 1987, served in Germany and Korea. Son-in-law retired from USN, 1986. Both after 20 years.

EUGENE EMMETT (GENE) DEYONGE, born Dec. 18, 1928, Worthington, MN attended one year of college and entered the Army Nov. 16, 1948. Military locations and stations: Ft. Riley, KS to Weiden Germany, March 1949, 53rd Constab. then 15th Constab., Weiden. Served with HQ & HQ Co., and C Co., 53rd and 15th Constab. Active duty, Nov. 16, 1948-Nov. 20, 1950. Reserve, Nov. 20, 1951-Nov. 20, 1955.

Discharged Nov. 20, 1955. Assigned to the Post Office 114-1. Graduate of Postal School, Frankfurt. His awards include the Army Occupation, Good Conduct and National Defense Service Ribbon.

Married Marilyn L. DeYonge and they have children: Gerald, Linda, Randy and Barbara and grandchildren: Jennifer, Melisa, Jeffery, JoAnna, Renne and David.

Employed with Montgomery Ward for 33 years, mainly in management. He was store manager for 15 years. Retired Aug. 1, 1984.

ROBERT EUGENE DICKEY, born May 7, 1929, Robinson, IL, enlisted RA June 4, 1947 at Ft. Sheridan, IL. Basic training Ft. Ord, CA.

Duties: US Constab., Straubing, Germany, January 1948-May 1950, 6th A/C Regt., Band; Ft. Sill, OK, February-August 1951, 18th FA Bn., Babenhausen, Germany, September 1951-August 1954; Ft. Chaffee, October 1954-May 1955; Corpus Christi NAS, TX, Army Reserve Advisor, June 1955-June 1956; Japan, October 1956-September 1958; Redstone Arsenal, October 1958-December 1963; Augsburg, Germany, 24th Inf. Div., January 1964-December 1966; Ft. Stewart, GA, January 1967-February 1968; Vietnam, March 1968-March 1969; Ft. Hood, TX, April 1969-April 1970.

Retired May 1970. Awarded Army Commendation Medal, Good Conduct Medal w/six clasp and other service medals and campaign ribbons.

Married Lora B. Wallace, Nov. 25, 1995. They have two sons from a previous marriage. First grandchild was born Nov. 27, 1995. When not reading is planning a trip or traveling.

JOHNIE DILLION
photo only, no bio submitted.

DOMENICK DI MARCONTONIO, born Dec. 14, 1923, Philadelphia, PA, entered US Army 1945. Basic training, Aberdeen Proving Grounds, MD. Went to Ord. School at Atlanta, GA.

Duties with US Constab.: 1946, B Trp., 81st Constab. Sqdn. at Bad Merganthine Germany; 1946, B Trp., 81st Sqdn. at Fulda, Germany; 1947, C Trp., 22nd Sqdn. at Bad Hersfeld; 1948, C Trp., 24th Sqdn. Bad Hersfeld.

Returned to states in 1949 and stationed at Ft. Monmouth, NJ.

Discharged 1950 with medical service connected disability with rank of staff sergeant. Received the following medals: WWII Victory Medal, Good Conduct Medal and Army of Occupation (Germany) Medal.

Married Elfriede at the village church in Marbach Germany 1949. They have two daughters and two grandchildren. He is a member in the following organizations: American Legion, VFW, DAV. Served as past commander of VFW Post 6072. Served as Bradford County, PA commander, VFW. Retired from Ingersoll Rand Co., where he was employed as a machinist until retiring in 1985.

EDWARD J. DIXON, born Aug. 17, 1928, New Britian, CT, joined the RA Oct. 5, 1946. Military locations and stations: basic training, Ft. Jackson, SC; US Constab., Germany, Feb. 14, 1947-Feb. 24, 1948. Served with 14th Regt., HQ & HQ Co., Kitzingen; 6th Regt., HQ & HQ Co. Schweinfurt.

Discharged Feb. 24, 1948 as private first class. His awards include the Army of Occupation and WWII Victory Medal.

JOHN T. DONAHUE, born May 19, 1927, Hartford, CT, inducted into service Oct. 30, 1950, Hartford. Military locations and stations: Camp Pickett, VA; Ludwigsburg, Germany; Security Plt., Hersfeld Germany; HQ Trp., 24th Constab. Sqdn., March 1951-December 1952.

Discharged Dec. 24, 1952 and received the Germany Occupation Medal and Marksman Medal.

Married Helen and they have three daughters: Lenora, Patricia and Cathy. Now enjoying retirement.

EDWARD L. DONELSON, born April 4, 1923, Lompoc, CA, inducted into service July 12, 1943, Santa Maria, CA. Military locations and stations: various Air Corp. Fields in states; Orly Field and V-30 in France; 1st Constab. Bde. (HQ) Air Section at Y-80 and Biebrich Germany, 1946-47.

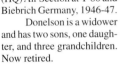

Donelson is a widower and has two sons, one daughter, and three grandchildren. Now retired.

REECE BASCOM DUGGAR, born Oct. 3, 1926, Lake City, TN, inducted into service May 29, 1945, Ft. Oglethorpe, GA. Basic training, Ft. Knox, KY. After basic assigned to Center HQ, Ft. Knox as clerk postal section, then to plans and training section.

Enlisted in regular army March 14, 1946 at Camp Pickett, VA.

Shipped out of Camp Kilmer, NJ, June 1, 1946, arriving in LeHavre, France, June 10, 1946. From Replacement Center at Marburg, Germany, assigned to A Trp., 27th Constab. Sqdn. Schweinfurt, Germany. After Constab. training. Assigned to HQ Sqdn., 27th Constab. and was present July 1, 1946 when Constabulary was activated (charter member).

Detached service Clerical School at Kitzingen, and prior to returning to the US was on detached duty at 22nd Sqdn. at Hammelburg.

Received Army of Occupation and WWII Victory Medals.

Duggar was discharged March 5, 1947, Ft. Dix, NJ. Married Helen Nelson, Nov. 22, 1947. They have one daughter. He has a BS in education from the University of Tennessee.

Retired Oct. 1, 1988, as a journeyman machinist from Martin-Marietta Energy Systems, Inc., with 31 1/2 years company service. He has been a licensed amateur radio operator since November 1955, with the call letters K4GQU.

Duggar belongs to American Legion Post 2, Knoxville, TN; US Contabulary Association and American Radio Relay League, Inc.

FRANK B. DUNGAN JR., born Feb. 15, 1928, Toledo, OH, enlisted in the RA, Sept. 13, 1948; basic training Camp Breckenridge, KY.

Duties: 74th Armd. FA Bn. (US Constab.), Landshut, Germany, January 1949-July 1953 HHC 6th Armd. Cav. Regt., Straubing, Germany, August 1953-May 1954; HHC 504th MP Bn. Camp Gordon, GA June 1954-February 1955; HHC 3rd Armd. Cav. Regt., Ft. Meade, MD, March 1955-July 1955; August 1955-March 1957, Nuremberg, Germany; April 1957-February 1958; Bindlach, Germany; March 1958-August 1958; Ft. Meade, MD. (Operation Gyroscope). HQ XX US Army Corps, Ft. Hayes, OH, September 1958-July 1959. HHC 13th Sig Bn., 1st Cav. Div., Korea August 1959-September 1960. HQ US Army Rec. Sta. Ft. Jackson, SC October 1960-June 1963; HQ 8th Inf. Div., Bad Kreuznach July 1963-May 1965 Germany; HQ 87th Inf., 8th Inf. Div. June 1965-April 1966 Baumholder, Germany; HQ 921st Engr. Gr May 1966-June 1966, Ft. Leonard Wood, MO. HQ 5th Engr. Bn. July 1966-June 1967, Ft. Leonard Wood, MO; HQ 192d Maint. Bn. July 1967-October 1967 Ft. Bragg, NC; 378th Maint. Spt. Co., November 1967, Ft. Bragg, NC; 573rd Pers Sv. Co., December 1967-February 1968, Ft. Bragg, NC; 7th Bn., 9th Arty., attached 54th Arty. Gp. March 1968-March 1969 Vietnam.

Dungan retired April 1, 1969. Awards and medals include the AOCCM (Germany); DNSM; Good Conduct Medal, NDSM w/OLC, Army Commendation Medal, VSM, RVCM w/dev; Bronze Star, Rep of Vietnam Cross of Gallantry w/palm. Member, VFW and US Constabulary Association.

Married Ursula I. Ellwanger, Sept. 6, 1958. They have one son, one daughter, one grandson and two granddaughters. Retired Dec. 31, 1996 from South Texas Blood & Tissue Center, San Antonio, TX after 20 years. He bowls, reads and has traveled the 50 states, all of Canada and a few trips to the UK and Germany with Ursula.

RAYMOND H. DUNKEL, born Lackawanna, NY, attended Silver Creek High School, Silver Creek, NY. Married to Lorraine A. (Kaznowski) Dunkel and they have daughters, Maryann J. and Jean M. and three grandsons.

Enlisted in the US Army March 1947. Retired Aug.

1, 1970 after 23 years of continuous service. Presently resides in Farnham, NY. Active duty assignments were primarily with combat engineers units located stateside and overseas (Germany, Korea and Vietnam). During the period 1949-1951 assigned Co. C, 54th Engr. Bn. (Combat) US Constab. at Boelingen, Germany.

Awards include the Bronze Star Medal w/OLC, Air Medal, Army Commendation Medal w/2 OLC and the Good Conduct Medal (5 awards).

Member of US Constabulary Association, National 4th Infantry (Ivy) Division Association, Army Engineer Association, American Legion, Veterans of Foreign Wars and Loyal Order of Moose.

ROMAN DYBULAK, born Feb. 17, 1929, Newark, NJ, inducted into service Aug. 18, 1948, Newark, NJ.

Military locations and stations: Camp Breckenridge, KY August 1948-September 1948; Hershelt, Germany, December 1948, B Trp., 22nd Constab.; Schweinfurt, Germany, December 1952; Wildflicken, Germany, December 1952; USA, Ft. Dix, May 1954, HQ Co., 365th Regt.; Camp Drum, NY; April 1955-November 1955; Korea DMZ, December 1955; HQ Co., 2nd Bn., 19th Inf.; US Army, Ft. Dix, 1957, Committee Gp., 365th; Germany, Gillhousen, 1958, B Co., 48th Inf., 3rd Armd. Div.; US Army, Ft. Dix, September 1962, Committee Gp.; Vietnam, November 1966, 9th Inf. Div., wounded January 8 and again on Feb. 14, 1967; US Army, Valley Forge Hospital, PA, April 1967-May 1968.

Discharged May 1968. Awarded Bronze Star, Purple Heart w/cluster, Commendation w/cluster, Occupation of Germany, two Defense Medals w/cluster, Good Conduct Medal w/four stars.

Married Marie G. Drozd. They have four daughters and three grandchildren. Marie died Aug. 4, 1991. Member of DAV, VFW and US Constabulary Association.

STEPHEN E. (SPECK) EARLEY, born March 14, 1926, London, KY, joined the Army Dec. 15, 1945. Military locations and stations: Camp Atterbury, IN; Ft. Knox, KY for training; Camp Pickett, VA; Camp Kilmer, NJ; Camp Philip Morris, LeHavre, France onto to Germany. Served with A Trp., 1st Constab., Sqdn., 15th Regt. Graduated from Ordnance School December 1946 as armorer.

Discharged as T-4, September 1948, received Army of Occupation Medal, WWII Victory and Good Conduct.

Memorable experiences: stay at Camp Philip Morris in La Havre, France, riding the box car through France to Germany. They were on the train about three days. Would have to sit long periods waiting for another engine to come help push train up steep grades. Getting everything ready for general inspection for Constabulary.

Earley is widowed. He was married to Edith and they had children: Karen, Connie and Margaret. Karen resides in Spain; Connie in Florida; Margaret lives in Mt. Carmel. Also has eight grandchildren and one great-grandson. Employed as supervisor manager, Martinizing Cleaners. Retired September 1986.

WILLIAM W. ELKINS, born Feb. 1, 1926, St. Petersburg, FL. Served in US Merchant Marine June 1944-September 1945. Joined Regular Army Sept. 7, 1947. Basic training, Ft. Jackson, SC.

Duties: US Constabulary, Villingen, Germany, January 1948-August 1952; 8th Inf. Div., Ft. Jackson, SC, September 1952-January 1954; Special investigator, FMD, January 1964-August 1955; Stuttgart Mil Post, Germany, September 1955-September 1959; Advisor Spec Forces FMD, Orlando, FL, November 1959-May 1961; Advisor CATO MAAG Vietnam, May 1961-April 1962; USA Gar, Stuttgart, Germany, May 1962-March 1965; Advisor USAR, Salem, VA, March 1965-February 1968; Advisor KMAG, Korea, February 1968-December 1968.

Retired Jan. 1, 1969. Received several medals including: AOM, NDSM, GCM w/OLC, ACM w/OLC, AFEM w/Bronze Star, ARVN Campaign Medals, Achievement Award. Member DAV, VFW, US Constabulary Association, American Legion and National Association Realtors.

His education includes BS Columbia College, Columbia, MO, Florida Real Estate Institute.

Married Lore E. Elkins, Sept. 13, 1952. Employed ARAMCO, Saudi Arabia and ARCO, Prudhoe Bay, AK for period ten years. Plays golf, writes short stories and travels.

GERALD S. EPLEE (from an old letter) The 15th Constab. Sqdns. candidate for "Trooper of the Week" a 20 year old T/S Gerald S. Eplee of Battle Creek, MI whose parents Mr. and Mrs. Albert Eplee reside Battle Creek, MI. Before T/Sgt Eplee joined the Army he was a high school student. He received his training in heavy weapons at Camp Blanding, FL for a period of 15 weeks. In March 1945 he was shipped overseas and joined the 17th Cav. Recon. Sqdn. April 11, 1945. September 4, 1945 he was transferred to the 15th Cav. Sqdn. T/Sgt. Eplee has 21 months of service, 16 of which he spent overseas. He participated in many battles in Central Europe and received the Victory Medal, the Occupation Ribbon, Good Conduct Medal, ETO Ribbon and the Battle Star for Central Europe.

T/Sgt. Eplee performed the duties of a personnel sergeant major in the personnel section of the 15th Constab. Sqdn.

T/Sgt. Eplee is a fine example of a soldier and trooper.

EMIL (ZEKE) EVANOVICH, born July 4, 1927, Maynard, OH, attended the Army September 1945. Military locations and stations: Ft. Knox, KY; Schwabish Hall; Stuttgart; Schondorf; Bremerhaven, Germany. Served with 771st Tank Btry., 2nd Constab. Trp. C.

Discharged November 1948 as corporal grade 4. His medals include the WWII Victory Medal, Army of Occupation Medal, Rifle M-1 Medal.

Memorable experiences: patrolling and setting check points at different locations to check vehicles and passports.

Married Doreen Rae and they have children: Bettina, Keith and Leisa and grandchildren: Aimee, Ryan and Nicholas. Employed with N.L. Industries as a millwright. Disabled and retired July 1985.

ALFRED LEO (LEVIN) EVANS, born Aug. 18, 1927, New York City, received a BS of education Oswego. Attended Sunny College at Oswego, NY; MS Indiana University in audio-visual.

ERC, inactive, private, completing high school, December 1944-February 1945; ERC, active, private ASTPR, University of Delaware Engineering, February 1945-August 1945; AUS, active, private infantry basic, 17 1/2 weeks, Ft. McClellan, AL, August 1945-February 1946; AUS, active, private acting corporal of guard, Guard Det., QM Depot, Liege, Belgium, February 1946-March 1946; AUS, active private, Clerk, HQ & HQ Det., 531st QM Graves Bn., Rouen, France; AUS, Active private first class, Interpreter, map clerk, 603rd QM Graves Regt. Co., France; RA.

Re-enlisted March 1947, Heidelberg, Germany), personnel, PFC, Records, payrolls, leave orders, HQ Sp. Trps., TUSA; RA, T/5, Cpl. E-4, Co. clk, supply asst. 85th Constab. Car Plt., Stuttgart, Germany, June 1948-September 1948; RA, Cpl. E-4, EUCOM Ordnance School, Eschwege, Germany, Auto Field Maint. and Rebuild. Whold. Vehicle, 14 1/2 weeks 0965 Motor Pool Admin and Spvn 3 1/2 week 014, September 1948-February 1949; RA, Cpl. E-4, 85th Constab. Car Plt., Unit Supply Sgt., Stuttgart, Germany, February 1949-February 1950; HQ US Constab., Ordnance Sec., Admin. Sec. Librarian, Ord Pub., Stuttgart, Germany, February 1950-May 1950; RA, Cpl. E-4, HQ US Con Ord Sec, Opns Div., Stuttgart, Germany, Topo draftsman, Opns Clerk, Classification: Top Secret, Cosmic, May 1950-November 1950; RA, Sgt. E-5, HQ US 7th Army, Ord Sec Opns Div., Stuttgart, Germany, Asst. Opns NCO, Gen Staff Briefing Asst. Topo draftsman, Classification: Top Secret, Cosmic, November 1950-September 1952; 7th Army Non Commissioned Officers Academy, Munich, Germany, six weeks, Honor Graduate, RA, Sgt. E-5, September 1952-November 1952; HQ 7th Army, Ord. Sec. Opns Div., Stuttgart, Germany.

Returned to duty, see above, November 1952-October 1953; RA, Sgt., E-5, 86th Ord Co., DS, Ft. Totten, NY, Tech Supply Sec., October 1953-March 1954; ER, active, Sgt. E-5, Co. B, 798th Ord. Bn., Syracuse, NY, 1st Sgt., February 1957-June 1958; ER, Active, SFC, E-6, Co. B, 798th Ord Bn. Syracuse, NY, 1st Sgt., June 1958-August 1958; ER, Active, SFC, E-6, 406th CAMG Co., Bloomington, IN, operations training sergeant, September 1958—.

Fred passed away Oct. 17, 1997 and is survived by his wife Georgia; children: David Jeno, Deborah Robin and Daniel Louis Evans; grandchild, Katelin Baker; and daughter-in-law, Cindy Evans.

Employed as teacher at East High School, Rochester, NY, 24 years, operating engineer part-time at several places but the longest at Genessee Brewing Company, Rochester, NY. Retired 1984, enjoyed volunteering at VA Hospitals and trail work.

DALE EVANS, born July 3, 1922, Delaware, OH, served in the military service from April 1, 1939 through Dec. 1, 1967. Retired Dec. 1, 1967. Served in Continental US included the following units: 166th Inf., 37th Div., HQ Southern Defense Command, 728th MP Bn., School Troops, Field Artillery School; 5th Army Military Escort Co., HQ CCB, 3rd Armd. Div., A Co., 83rd Recon. Bn., 3rd Armd. Div., HQ Advisor Gp. Ohio Military District/Duty W/107th Armd. Cav., E Co., 6th Armd. Dav., B Trp., 1st Sqdn., 1st Training Bde., Ft. Knox, A Trp., 5th Cav. Sqdn., 9th Div.

Foreign service: E Co., 2nd Bn., 162nd Inf., 41st Div., WWII South West Pacific area; HQ and B Trp., 24th Cav. Sqdn. (US Constabulary) Austria 1st Recon Co., 1st Inf. Div., Erlangen Germany, 16th Tank Co., 16th Inf., 1st Inf. Div., Nurnberg, Germany, H Trp. and Tank Co., 3rd Bn., 2nd Armd. Cav., Amberg, Germany; HQ Co., 7th Cav., 1st Cav. Div. Korea, B Trp., 3rd Sqdn., 9th Cav. Sqdn., 1st Cav. Div., (DMZ) Korea, G Trp. 2nd Sqdn., 14th Armd. Cav. Regt., Bad Kissingen Germany, C Trp., 1st Sqdn., 7th Cav. (DMZ) Korea.

His awards include the Combat Infantry Badge, Bronze Star, Purple Heart, Army Commendation, Good Conduct, American Defense, American Campaign, Asiatic Pacific Campaign, WWII Victory, WWII Occupation, National Defense, Presidential Unit Citation, Philippine Liberation, and Philippine Presidential Unit Citation.

ANDREW W. (DUKE) EVERETT, born May 25, 1927, assigned to 5th Cav. Regt., and was present at the inauguration of the 5th Constab. Regt., July 1946. Assigned to the Motorcycle Plt., HQ Trp., HQ Sqdn., and rose to rank of sergeant.

Went into the Public Information Office of the 2nd Constab. Regt. after it moved to Augsburg in 1947. Was a staff sergeant by the time he returned to the States and

was discharged December 1948.

Recalled to active duty for the Korean War September 1950. Served in the Camp Stoneman, CA PIO until released from active duty December 1951. Received a BA in education, California State University, Los Angeles, 1956.

Taps May 1988. Survived by daughters, Susan Carol Hamilton of Coos Bay, OR and Ingrid Elaine LeMasters of Norco, CA; son Eric Carl Everettt of Lake Elsinor, CA and five grandchildren.

JOHN T. FAGAN JR., born Jan. 28, 1924, Evansville, IN. Enlisted into the USN 1942 and served on LST #5. They made invasions in Sicily, France, Anzio and went in with 3rd Div. He was wounded in Sicily and blown of ship.

Enlisted in the Army in November 1946. Went to Germany and was until the Constabulary until 1951 C troop, 1st 15th Fox Trp., 2nd of 14th AC. Also served in Africa, Sicily, Italy, Southern France and Korea. Bases: Great Lakes; Little Creek, VA; Aberdeen; Ft. Dix; Camp Kilmer; Ft. Ben Harrison; Magigan Army Hospital; Ft. Leonard Wood; Niki Sites in Illinois; Rhode Island.

Awarded Purple Heart, Combat Infantry Badge, American Defense, UN, ETO, Good Conduct Army and Navy, Korean Occupation.

The best thing to come out of his service time was the fact that he met and married his wife in Germany.

His wife Steffi Horoschiefska (Polish) is deceased. They had children: John, Patricia, Brenda and Nannette and grandchildren: John, Wayne, Steffi, Susan and Dominia; great-grandchild, Domenica Valenti.

HALSTEIN FALCH, born in Oslo, Norway, came to the US 60 years ago and settled in Brooklyn, NY. He became a citizen in 1943. Falch lived in Hopatcong for 19 years.

He was a truck driver at East Coast Laundry Company in Brooklyn, NY for 20 years.

Served two terms in the 3rd Army of the Rainbow Div. He was in the original group of Constabulary in Germany during WWII. After coming home he served two years in the National Guard stationed at West Point. He also served as the original historian for the publication of the Constabulary's Book.

Served three years on the Hopatcong Board of Education and donated his artistic skills to the local schools for a Reading Program called Books and Beyond. He was responsible for the VFW emblems that decorate the local Veteran's Field in town. Member of the local VFW Post 10101 in Hopatcong.

Member of the Masonic Sunset Lodge Free and Accepted Masons of Brooklyn, NY in which he served as secretary for 18 years.

Survivors include his wife Sarah; two sons, Richard of Bensonhurst, NY and Victor of Dingmans Ferry, PA; a daughter, Anita Plantamura of Hopatcong; brother, Victor of Brookville, FL; five grandchildren.

Halstein Falch died July 26, 1997 at the Dover campus of Northwest Convenant Medical Center. He was 71.

BRUCE M. (FARNY) FARNHAM, born Oct. 20, 1931, North Troy, VT. Entered the Army Aug. 4, 1949. Military locations and stations: Ft. Dix, NJ; Ft. Belvoir, VA; Camp Kilmer, NJ; Ft. Devens, MA. Served with 9th Inf. Div., 515th Engr. Petr. District Co.; Co. D, 14th Armd. Cav. US Constab.

During Korean war served in Germany with US Constab., Co. D, 2nd Bn., 14th Armd. Cav.

Discharged Dec. 3, 1952 and received the American Defense and Army of Occupation.

Memorable experiences: patrolling the border was always an experience.

His wife Irene died in 1996. They had children: Keith, Craig and Maureen and grandchildren: Matthew, Amy, Ericka, Amanda, Jarred and Danielle. Employed as compliance officer, Vermont Meat Inspection Service retiring Nov. 1, 1993.

JOHN E. (JOHNNY) FAULK, born Nov. 18, 1927, Ft. Benning, GA, received a BBA and JD degree. Enlisted in the Armor/JAGC Nov. 28, 1945. Commissioned June 1963. Military locations and stations: Augsburg, Germany, served with 42nd Sqdn., 2nd Constab. Regt. and various USAR JAG units. Held commands 154th JAG team and 156th JAG Team-USAR.

Retired as lieutenant colonel, 1980 USAR. Memorable experiences: serving with US Constab. Married Patti and retired as judge 1992.

BERWIN LEROY (BER) FELKER, born June 19, 1928, Oshkosh, WI, attended Oshkosh, WI High School and Diesel Institute, Chicago, IL.

Joined the US Army in 1946. Military locations and stations: Germany in Weiden and Zech border at Vohenstrauss. Served with 11th Regt., 91st Bn., 94th Sqdn., C Troop. Discharged in 1948.

Married Ruth Bernhardt in Germany in 1947 and they were married 13 years. He has been married for 32 years to Saundra. Currently still employed with the San Diego Auto Auction.

EDWARD WILLIAM FERENCE, born Nov. 7, 1927, Central City, PA, enlisted in RA, December 1944; basic training, Ft. McClellan, AL.

Served 4th Armd. Div., Germany. In April 1946, unit became 25th Constab. Sqdn., Regensburg. Attended US Constabulary School, Sonthofen, Germany and Counter Intelligence Corps (CIC) School, Oberammergau, Germany. Intelligence NCO and provost sergeant in Straubing and Landshut. Discharged August 1947.

Graduated from University of Pittsburgh with Civil Engineering degree, structures major, February 1951;

member of Sigma Tau, Phi Theta Kappa and Tau Beta Pi honor fraternities. Graduate work in advanced structures, Columbia University. Structures engineer at North American Aviation, Boeing, Grumman, Martin, General Electric and AVRO for 23 years. Principal engineer at Westinghouse 16 years, nuclear power division; retired 1990.

Married Virginia Dedik, 1960. They have two sons, a daughter and two grandchildren. Hobbies include woodworking, jogging, antique cars and a mountain retreat.

FRED E. FIMBEL JR., born Aug. 27, 1931, Poughkeepsie, NY, entered the Army August 1948. Military locations and stations: Augsburg, Germany 1948-52; Vietnam 1966-67; Ft. Dix, NJ 1948. Served with 73rd Armd. Ord, US Constab.

Discharged Jan. 1, 1969 as staff sergeant. His awards include the Bronze Star Commendation, Army Good Conduct, three Air Force Good Conduct, three Army Occupation, Vietnam Service w/3 Stars and National Defense w/ star.

Married to Dorothy C. Fimbel and they have children, Fred E. Fimbel III and Ann Marie Fimbel.

REV BRAXTON FINCHER, born March 28, 1928, Charlotte, NC, entered military service Dec. 28, 1945. Basic training, Ft. Riley, KS, Horse Cav.

Arrived Europe at LeHavre, France, US Constab. Augsburg, Germany "D" Trp., 74th Sqdn., 5th Regt., 1946-48. Inactive Reserve 1948-51. Reenlisted active service; assigned HQ Commandant Supply, Kraiserslautern, Germany. Volunteered Korea. Arrived Korea at Inchon, assigned 160th Inf. Regt., 40th Inf. Div., 1952-53. Arrived Ft. Bragg, November 1953. Assigned 407th Abn. Quartermaster Co., 82nd Abn. Div. Chaplain's Assistant until discharge July 19, 1954. 263rd Armd. Regt., 118th Inf. Div. June 1961. Discharged physical disability May 1963, USANG.

Medals earned include the Combat Infantryman's Badge, National Defense Service, Sigman Ree, two Overseas Bars, Korean Service w/3BSS, United Nations Service, Army of Occupation (Japan and Europe), WWII Victory, Army Lapel Button.

Life member VFW and US Constabulary Association. Attended Southern Wesleyan Seminary Central, SC 1949-51. Back to school 1954-59. Major theology; minor Bible.

Married Betty Turner Feb. 6, 1954. They have two daughters. Both members of US Constabulary Association. They also have two grandchildren, one great-grandson, three step grandchildren. Betty died in December 1985. He married his second wife, Margie, in April 1988.

Now engaged in gospel mission Ancient of Days Ministry since 1984. Ancient of Days for the present age financed by B.D.Q. Communication Company and other donations, with proceeds from long distance telephone service that interests non-profit organizations to raise funds using prepaid calling cards. Funds raised in this manner are split 50/50. The organization wins - raising funds - and Ancient of Days Ministry wins - doing good in God's Kingdom on earth.

ROBERT A. FISCUS, born May 17, 1930, Brookville, PA, received his masters degree. Joined the Army Nov. 19, 1946. Military locations and stations: US Constab.,

Regensburg, Germany March 1947; Straubing, Germany, July 1948; Ft. George G. Meade April 1951-October 1951; Gettysburg, PA ROTC 1951-54; Panama Canal Zone 1955-58; Ft. Bliss, TX, 1959-60; St. Louis Air Def. 1960-61; Korea, 1961-62; Germany, 1963-67; Vietnam 1967-68.

His commands: Ft. Bliss, TX; Dong Tam, Vietnam. Discharged July 31, 1968 as corporal. Served five campaigns in Vietnam.

Married Joan P. and they have children: Rose Marie, Deborah, Linda and Barbara and grandchildren: John, Jill, Zac, Adam and Madelyn. Employed with Civil Service. Home Improvements (owner); 20 years tax preparation (owner). Retired July 31, 1968.

EDWIN MARTIN FORBES, born Sept. 11, 1931, Monroe, MI, enlisted Army Sig. Corp, Oct. 12, 1948, Seattle, WA. Basic training, Ft. Ord, CA, October-December 1948. Duties: 1949-1952, 97th Sig. Bn., Boeblingen, Germany, US Constab./7th Army; 1952-54, T&T Co. 50th Sig. Bn., XVI Corp., Sendai, Japan.

Discharged Sept. 30, 1954, Ft. Lewis, WA, with the rank of corporal. His awards include the Army of Occupation Medal and Germany National Defense Service Medal.

Married Helen Louise Campbell April 13, 1957 and they have children: Edwin, Toni, Cheri, Ruby, Robert, Peggy; 16 grandchildren and one great-grandson.

Employed with Douglas Aircraft Co., Long Beach, CA, October 1954. Retired Aug. 18, 1989 (branch manager, production control) 34 years, 10 months.

ORLANDO N. FRANCO, born April 11, 1927, Schenectady, NY, received a BS and EE from the University of Missouri, class of 1953. Joined the Army July 6, 1945. Military locations and stations: Camp Blanding, FL and Berlin, Germany. Served with 78th Inf. Div. and 16th Constab.

Discharged Jan. 6, 1946. Married Rose and they have children: Betty Ann, Bruce and Brian and grandchildren: David Alan, Brian and Leigh Ann. Employed with General Electric Co. in engineering. Retired April 1, 1993.

HUBERT FRANKLIN, born Sept. 12, 1928, enlisted RA, August 1948. Attended basic training Ft. Jackson, SC, 5th Div.

Duties: 1948-1951, US Constab. "B" Trp., Schweinfurt and Herford, Germany; 1951-52, 509th Armd.

FA, Ft. Knox, KY; 1952-55, 14th Armd. Cav., I Co., Herford, Germany; 1955-59; Armd. School, Ft. Knox, KY, TDY West Point USMA; 1959-60, 15th Armd. Cav., A Co., Schwabach, Germany; 1960-62, 7th Army Combines Arms Schools, Vilseck, Germany; 1962-64, USATC Co. A, 3rd Bn., 1st Tng. Bde, Ft. Knox, KY; 1964, Walter Reed Hospital, excision of aortic valve and replacement with star. Edwards Valve Prothesis; 1965-70, temp. disabled ret. list.

Retired Jan. 1, 1970 and received the National Defense Medal, Army Good Conduct w/OLC and Army of Occupation, Germany.

Married Anna Ruth Clark, Oct. 9, 1952 and they have one daughter and four grandchildren. His hobbies include gardening, playing the guitar and being a US History buff.

ROBERT L. FRANKLIN, born Feb. 26, 1931, Wilkes-Barre, PA, joined the US Army, March 3, 1949. Military locations and stations: Ft. Jackson, SC; Camp Lee, VA; Landshut, Germany; Ft. Sill, OK; Ft. Bragg, NC; Ft. McClellan, AL; Ft. McCoy, WI; Ft. Meade. Served with 2nd Inf., 74th AFA Bn., 2154 ASU, Arty. OCS, 402nd MP, 358 CA Bde. Discharged October 1987 as CSM (E-9). Recalled to active duty during the Persian Gulf War 1990-91.

His awards and medals include the Legion of Merit, Meritorious Service Medal w/OLC, ARCOM w/3 OLC, AAM, GCM, AOM, MHA, Parachute Badge, NDSM w/ Bronze Star, HSM, NCOPOR, ASR, AFRN, ARCTR, PA COM MDL.

Married Regina R. Storz Franklin and they had children, Robert G. (deceased) and Jeanmarie McCabe; grandchildren: Lindsey McCabe and Erika McCabe. Retired as vice president, Atlantic Carriers, retired Aug. 30, 1990.

EDWARD PAUL FREEDMAN, born March 6, 1928, Torrington, CT, entered West Point, July 1946. Graduated and commissioned June 2, 1950.

Duties: US Constab., Landshut, Germany (D, Tk, E Co., 2nd Bn., 6th Armd. Cav.) 1950-52; CO, E Co./ Regt., S-3 Sec, Straubing, 1953-54; Tk Co CO, Camp Irwin, CA, 1954-55; APMST Hofstra College Long Island, NY, 1956-59; MBA Management, Hofstra College, 1959; G3 Sec, 3rd Armd. Div., Frankfurt, Germany, 1959-61; Exchange Off (S3, Bn XO0, Germany Army Panzer Bde, Nurnburg, Germany, 1961-63; US/Germany Tank Dev. Prog., Washington, DC, 1964-65; MA German, Middlebury College, VT 1966; Asst. Prof., Germany, USMA 1966-68; BCT Bn. Co., Ft. Ord, CA, 1968-69; Spt Cmd SPO, Cam Rahn and Dep Sr. Adv. VNMA Dalat, Vietnam 1969-70; Def/Army Attache, Bern Switzerland 1972-75; Strategic Studies Institute, USAWC, Carlisle Bks, PA 1975-N. Retired 1977. Decorations include Legion of Merit, MSM w/OLC, BS w/OLC, ARCOM, several service medals.

Employed as study center coordinator, University Southern California 1977-78. Full professor of Business Admin., Professor Emeritus, Northern Virginia Community College, 1978-90.

Married Vera Glaetzer, Nov. 18, 1953. They have three sons and two grandchildren. His hobbies include landscaping, history (WWII, Germany, Slovakia, Central Europe), languages (German, Slovak, French and Italian), travel and reading.

WILLIAM JOSEPH FREEMAN JR., born July 10, 1928, Fitzgerald, GA, enlisted in the RA, July 28, 1948; basic training, Ft. Jackson, SC.

Duties: US Constab., 2nd Armd. Cav. Regt., December 1948-July 1952, Augsburg, Glenhausen, Fulda, Kronach, Bamberg (Germany) with lots of maneuvers and border patrol. One year extension Korean conflict. Served in the Georgia ARNG April 1954-January 1982. Commissioned 2nd LT, Armor, in 1956, 190th Tank Bn., (platoon leader); 121st Inf. (Mech) (Platoon Leader); 48th Armd. Div. (108th Armd. (BN Sig Off); 30th Inf. Div. (Mech) (3rd Bde Composite Co. Commander); 48th Inf. Bde (Mech) (Bde Sig); 48th Inf. Bde (Mech) (S-5 Civil Affairs); 111th Sig. Bn. (Corp. Commander); and State HQ (staff duty). January 1982-January 1987 Individual Ready Reserve.

Military education: US Constabulary NCO Academy, Series-10, Command and General Staff College, National Defense University and numerous staff refresher courses at Ft. Benning, GA and Ft. Gordon, GA.

Retired July 10, 1988, as a colonel with more than 30 years total service (Active Army, National Guard and Individual Ready Reserve). Medals received include the Meritorious Service, Army Good Conduct, Army of Occupation (Germany), National Defense, Armed Forces Reserve Medal w/2 Hour Glasses, Army Reserve Achievement Medal w/2 OLC, NCO Professional Development Medal w/numeral one, Army Service Ribbon, Georgia Commendation Medal, Georgia Service Medal w/Boar's Head and Army Lapel Button.

Married Auguste Regina Sippel, April 5, 1952. They have one son, one daughter and four grandchildren. Retired 1990 from Civil Service (USAF) with 35 years service as an electronic systems unit chief. He likes to hunt, fish, read and travel.

DON E. FRENCH, born Dec. 22, 1926, Bristol, CT, attended Wesleyan University.

Joined the Armor April 1, 1949. Military locations and stations: Ft. Riley, KS; Ft. Knox, KY; Bad Hersfeld, Germany; Korea; Pentagon, Washington, DC. Served with 24th Constab. Sqdn., (Germany); 64th Tank Bn., 3rd Div. (Korea), ACSI, Pentagon, DC. Held commands as CO with B Trp., 24th Sqdn; CO, C Co., 64th Tk. Bn., 3rd Div., (Korea).

Achieved the rank of major and discharged March 1, 1959. Served in Korea campaign (Chorwon) 1953 and awarded the Bronze Star.

Memorable experiences: patrolling US/USSR border 1949-52 Germany (Cold War); attached to and supporting Greek Expeditionary Force (UN) Korea (1953) and being designated honorary member, serving with OCS (ACSI) Pentagon, DC.

Married Gladis French and they have children: Christina, Katie and Peter; grandchildren, Beckie and Missy. Employed with CIGNA as agent and registered representative of CIGNA Securities.

CHARLES PURVIS FRINKS, born Sept. 8, 1928, Alexandria, VA, enlisted in RA in 1945; basic training, Ft. Knox, KY.

April 1946-November 1948: E Trp., 15th Cav. Recon. Sqdn.; Light Tk Trp., 15th Constab. Regt.; Horse Plt., 15th Constab. Regt.; D Trp., 1st Sqdn., 15th Constab. Regt.; H&HT 51st Sqdn., 6th Constab. Regt. January, 1949-April 1952: Recon. Plat. 73rd Heavy Tank Bn. and 37th Recon. Co. at Ft. Benning, Korea and Camp Polk. Received direct commission in Armor April 1952 and reported to 1st Armd. Div. as Recon. platoon leader, 1st Medium Tank Bn. (ex-1st Constab. Sqdn.) at Ft. Hood, TX. Returned to

Germany (1953-1955) and assigned to H Co., 6th Armd. Cav. Regt., (ex-6th Constab.) at Regensburg. Attended flight school 1955; became qualified in both fixed and rotary wing aircraft, serving in 4th Armd. Div. 1956-60; commanded C Trp., 3/7 Cav. (Ft. Benning, GA) 1961-62. Flight leader in 22nd Special Warfare Aviation Detachment (Ft. Bragg) 1962-63; Platoon leader, Airlift Plt., 52nd Avn. Bn. (Vietnam) 1963-64; Commander, Avn. Co., 6th Special Forces Gp. (Ft. Bragg) 1964-65; and instructor pilot, flight leader and director Methods of Instruction, US Army Primary Helicopter Training School (Ft. Wolters) 1965-66, retired November 1966.

Awarded WWII Victory Medal, Good Conduct Medal w/OLC, Army Occupation Medal, Korea Service Medal w/5 Campaign Stars, Vietnam Service, Army Expedition Medal, Army Commendation w/V device, Air Medal w/15 OLC and two V Devices and Bronze Star.

Following retirement spent 30 years as manager in defense industry companies providing services to all branches of the Department of Defense in Conus, Korea, Vietnam, Mid-East and Europe.

Married Lesel McCrostie and they have three sons and one grandson.

ARTHUR M. (ARTIE) FROELICH, born May 25, 1928, Lackawanna, NY, joined the Army Inf. Oct. 3, 1946. Military locations and stations: Basic training, Ft. Knox, KY; Feb. 4, 1947 to ETO; Feb. 14, 1947 Freising Germany; Straubing, Germany. Served with D Co., 25th Constab., 11th Regt.

Discharged April 21, 1948 as T/5 radio operator and awarded the Army Occupation, WWII Victory Medal.

Memorable experience: worked on check point on Germany and Czech border in Furstenwalde, Germany, "Russians" on Czech side, US on German side.

Married Florence and employed as crane machinist, Bethlehem Steel, Lackawanna, NY, retired September 1984.

ROBERT WESLEY FRY, born Aug. 6, 1929, Memphis, TN, enlisted in the RA at age 16, March 28, 1946, St. Louis, MO. After only six weeks basic training in Ft. Lee, VA, shipped to the Philippine Islands, returned to the US in 1947 for discharge. After a short time reenlisted, shipped to Keesler Field, MS; Ft. Jackson, SC; Signal Corps Photographic Center, Long Island, NY; to Ft. Dix, NJ, for shipment to Germany in January 1948 and assigned to 6th Constab. Regt. in Schweinfurt, with TDY to the 53rd Constab. Sqdn. in Schwabach and Weiden which was recognized as the 15th Constab. Sqdn. with the mission as the principal keepers of law and order in Germany along the US Zone, Soviet Zone and Czechoslovakia borders. With duties as SIS investigator, official US Army photographer, provost sergeant, NCO in charge of the Special Police Plt., commander of the Honor Guard and first sergeant of HQ Trp.

Commissioned a second lieutenant, January 1952 assigned as recon platoon leader in A&B Trps. and as Trial Counsel on several special court martials. Remained with the 15th Constab. Sqdn. until July 11, 1952 when he returned to the US for Command and Staff assignments in Ft. Leavenworth, KS, Keflavic, Iceland (with the 2nd Bn. Combat Team), Ft. Benning, GA; Ft. Lawton, WA; Munich, Germany (with the 2nd Bn. Combat Team), Ft.

Benning, GA; Ft. Lawton, WA; Munich Germany (what the 21st Inf. of the 24th Inf. Div.). During his Army career he achieved 14 enlisted and commissioned ranks and was selected for promotion to lieutenant colonel prior to his retirement April 30, 1966 as senior officer advisor in the VI US Army Corps General Officer Command, Pontiac, MI.

Married Irma Gebhardt, Jan. 11, 1952; they have one daughter and triplet grandchildren. After retiring from the US Army they moved to Seattle, WA and he has held progressively responsible staff, management and consulting positions as an employee and owner of national and international companies located in the Pacific Northwest.

JOHN FUDALA, born Aug. 19, 1931, Hudson, PA, inducted into service Aug. 26, 1948, Whitehall St., NY. Military locations and stations: Camp Breckenridge, KY, August -December 1948; US Constab., Straubing, Germany, HQ & HQ Co., 6th AC, Security Plt., December 1948-June 1949; Ft. Sill, OK, June 1949-August 1951; Reenlisted in AF; Mitchell AFB, NY, September 1951-November 1953; Francis E. Warren AFB, WY, November 1953-March 1954; Harlingen AFB, TX, March 1954-November 1955; McGuire AFB, NJ, November 1955-July 1956; Keflavik Airport, Iceland, July 1956-June 1957; Dow AFB, ME, August 1957-June 1962; Thule AFB, Greenland, June 1962-June 1972; Olmsted AFB, PA July 1963-May 1967; Elmendorf AFB, AK, July 1967-June 1970; Grand Forks AFB, ND, June 1970-June 1972. Retired June 1, 1972. Retired from Postal Service October 1992.

He crossed the Atlantic on the *Pvt. Joe P. Martinez* arriving in Germany, New Years Day 1949, and processed through Marburg. At Out Post #1 reunion in April 1997 he met two of his shipmates, although they didn't know each other in 1948. Upon arriving in Germany he was puzzled why he only saw dogs and no cats. He was told the Germans had eaten the cats to survive.

Assigned to the Security Plt., 6th A/C, HQ & HQ Co., Straubing. They were required to be six feet or taller. Maintenance of their uniforms had to be done as a group. They provided security for the regimental commander during Command Post Exercises. He once stood Honor Guard for Gen. Lucias D. Clay in Grafenor.

At Straubing there was a Polish DP who cleaned their barracks. He wanted Fudala to visit his house. This would have required going through a hole in the fence. As this would have been fraternization, he never did go.

He remembers standing in the street in Amberg, acting as a combat Mp, waiting to direct convoy traffic. It seemed as if he was the only American in town. Quite a feeling for a 17 year old.

Received Outstanding Unit Award, Occupation Medal, Army of Good Conduct, National Defense Medal and various ribbons.

Married Sally Cunningham Sept. 5, 1959 and they have one son and three grandchildren. Currently enjoys Candle Pin bowling and traveling. Fudala is a member of US Constabulary Association, Air Force Sergeant Association, VFW and Knights of Columbus.

DAVID PAUL FULLER, born Jan. 17, 1933, Linden, PA, entered the Army April 4, 1950. Military locations and stations: Ft. Dix, NJ; Ft. Knox, KY; Fussem and Nurnberg, Germany. Served with C Btry., 70th Armd., FA Bn.

Achieved the rank of E-4 Cpl., discharged April 9, 1953. His awards include the AOM, Germany and Army Good Conduct.

Memorable experiences: While on maneuvers at Fulda Gap. Made a wrong turn while posting guard and ended up in the Russian zone.

Married Gloria E. Fuller March 1, 1958. His children include: Joy, William, Randy, Cathy, Cindy, Robert, Maryann and Tim. Grandchildren: Tony, Kylie, Kelsie, Ashkei, Sharrise, Raquel, Beau, Krystopher, Devyn, Kayleen, Danyelle.

Employed with the Merchant Marine, Bethlehem Trans. Corp. Avco Lycoming, Williamsport, PA as millwright, retired July 13, 1992, Lycoming Textron.

JOHN E. GARRISON, born Sept. 21, 1929, Vineland, NJ, enlisted in RA Sept. 21, 1948. Took basic training at Ft. Dix, NJ. Retired Aug. 25, 1971.

Duties: US Constab. Deggerndorf and Regensburg, Germany, 1949-50, (3rd Bn., 6th Armd. Cav. Regt.); Berlin, Germany 1950-52 (Heavy Mortar 69th Inf. Div.); 1953 (114th Tank Bn., NJ NG), Vineland, NJ; 1954-55 (M Co., 60th Inf. Regt., 9th Inf. Div.) Heilbronn, Germany; 1955-1957 (I Co., 3rd Bn., 6th Armd. Cav.), Regensburg, Germany; 1963-64 (C Co., 4th Bn., 13th Armor) 3rd Army and (2nd Bn., 72nd Armor, 2nd Inf. Div.) Ft. Stewart, GA; April-June 1964 (US Army Chemical School, Ft. McClellan, AL); June 1964-September 1964 (22nd Chemical Co. (DS) Ft. Hood, TX; October 1964-September 1968 (Military Assistance Advisory Gp., Republic of China), Taiwan; September 1968-September 1969, (HQ 1st Bn., 5th Cav., 1st Cav. Div.), Vietnam; October 1969-August 1971 (HQ 1st Bn., 1st Training Bde.), Ft. Knox, KY. Graduated, Advanced Armor Course, Ft. Knox, 1957, Advanced Chemical NCO, Ft. McClellen, AL 1964.

Awards and decorations: Combat Infantry Badge, Bronze Star, Air Medal, Joint Services Commendation Medal, Army Commendation Medal, Good Conduct Medal (7th Award), National Defense Service Medal, Army of Occupation Medal, Vietnam Campaign Medal (three campaign stars), Vietnam Service Medal, Presidential Unit Citation, Vietnam Cross of Gallantry w/palm.

Married to Helen Jo Ann (Combest) Garrison, July 19, 1958 and they have one son and two grandsons. Graduated from University of Louisville 1987. Retired Sept. 30, 1994 from the Cumberland Federal Savings Bank, Louisville, KY as vice president, Property Management and Security.

RICHARD T. GEIST, born Nov. 16, 1927 Philadelphia, PA, inducted into service Feb. 28, 1946, Philadelphia. Discharged May 7, 1947. Military locations: Ft. Knox (basic); Weinheim, Germany (15th Constab. Regt.).

In 1946 and 1947 after Uncle Sam's draft call and basic training at Ft. Knox, he served as an editor of *The Trooper* of the 15th Constab. Regt., in Weinheim, Germany. Their task was to feature news from the squadrons or of a Kinderfest or of an

inspection/visit by Gen. E.N. Harmon. The staff has many trips that provided close contact with troopers and the general public.

Then came 20 years in the Coast Guard Reserve. In his mid-30s, he enrolled in the Coast Guard Auxiliary's "Boat Handling" course. He did well and the instructor suggested joining the Reserve, as he had no boat for them, he applied and qualified for direct commission as LTJG. Assigned to a vessel augmentation unit as military requirements officer. Advancing, he served as training officer, elective office and lastly aboard the sutters active and decisive as Reserve CO.

His awards include the Victory Europe, German Occupation and Good Conduct. Married to Jane and has two sons, one daughter, two stepsons and seven grandchildren. Enjoys church work, travel, monitoring Wall St.

PHILLIP R. GEORGE, born Oct. 4, 1930, Denver, CO, enlisted February 1949, Los Angeles, CA. Attended basic at Ft. Ord, CA. May 1949, reported to Ft. Bliss, TX. Assigned to 35th Bde. Leadership Course. On completion, reported to the 518th AAA Gun Bn. (Coast Arty. Corp.).

Shortly transferred to the 46th RCAT Detach. as a radio repairman. January 1950, requested a EUCOM assignment. Arrived Marburg, Germany and was then assigned to the 16th Constab. Sqdn. (Sep). On its deactivation in November 1950 it was reactivated as the 1st Btry., 6th Inf. Regt. This entire assignment was in Berlin, Germany.

September 1951, returned to the ZI on emergency leave. Due to circumstances, requested and was granted a re-assignment to the ZI. Joined the newly federalized 44th National Guard Div. at Camp Cook, CA as training cadre. This camp is now Vandenberg AB. Took his discharge at this location. Upon discharge, became a police officer with the City of Bell, CA. Left the city of Bell and became a police officer with the city of Pasadena, CA.

Married the former Donna Lindgren in 1956 and has one son and one daughter.

Medically retired from the Police Department in 1976, after 20 years.

JOHN S. GERETY, born Marshfield, MA, July 17, 1913, graduated Norwich University. Commissioned second lieutenant Cav. 1937. Entered active duty 26th Div. Jan. 16, 1941. Commanded 2nd Bn., 111th Inf. Regt., Pacific Theatre, 1943-45. P and O Div. War Dept. Gen. Staff 1946-49. Executive officer 2nd ACR 1949-50. CO 2nd Bn., 2nd ACR 1950-52. Norwich University ROTC Instr. Gp. 1952-53. G-3 Army Field Forces Bd. #5 1953-56; CO Field Training Teams 1 & 3, JUSMAT, Turkey. CO Schl. Regt. The Armd. School 1958-59. G-3 the Armd. Center, Ft. Knox 1959-61. Chief of Staff, 4th Armd. Div., Germany 1961-62. CO 7th Army Tng. Center 1963-64. CO ROTC Instr. Gp. University of Maine 1964-68. Retired Dec. 5, 1968.

Awarded the Combat Infantry Badge, War Department General Staff Medallion, Commendation Medal, Bronze Star Medal, Legion of Merit Medal, Pacific Theater of Operations Ribbon, EUCOM Theater of Operations Ribbon, EUCOM Occupation Ribbon.

Married Marjorie Achorn Gerety, Dec. 9, 1996. He has four children: Patricia, Nina, John and James. Current activities: being thankful for each day.

PAUL K. (KEN) GIGNAC, born Oct. 26, 1925, Everett, MA, graduated from Wentworth Inst. Joined the US Army Dec. 18, 1945. Military locations and stations: Ft. Knox, (basic), 72nd Constab. Sqdn., Boeblingen and 10th Constab. Regt. Mobhringen.

Discharged as sergeant June 18, 1948. Married to Ruth and they have children, Brenda and Joy. Employed with Townsend Company, Division of Tentron, plant superintendent, plant manager, Canadian plant, retired March 1990.

JOHN H. GILLIGAN JR., born Aug. 8, 1928, Wakefield, MA. Joined the Army Feb. 6, 1946. Military locations and stations: Ft. Devens, MA; Ft. McClellan, AL; Camp Kilmer, NJ; Germany; Frankfurt; Nurnberg; Hildeberg; Weisbaden; Marberg; Wetzlar.

Served with HQ & HQ Trp., 3rd Constab. Regt. Discharged July 14, 1947 as T/5. His awards includes WWII Victory Medal, German Occupation Medal, Good Conduct Medal and Marksman Medal.

Memorable experiences: Served with great young men and officers; raids on camps; they were alerted many times to go to war with Russian forces.

Married to Marjorie A. Witter Gilligan and they have one son, Mark, daughter, Donna and granddaughter, Kara. Employed as skilled laborer, retiring in 1986.

PAUL ANDREW GJEVRE, born Oct. 30, 1928, Mitchell, SD, enlisted RA, Ft. Crook, NE, Nov. 18, 1946. December 1946-February 1947, basic training, Ft. McClellan, AL. Shipped overseas to Germany, March 1947 on the *General Stewart*.

April 1947-October 1947, 37th Constab. Sqdn. at Fussen, October 1947-March 1948; 42nd Constab. Sqdn. Augsburg, clerk in Provost Marshal's office at Augsburg.

Discharged as technician fifth grade, Camp Kilmer, NJ, March 30, 1948.

Married Marilyn Johnson, April 2, 1955. They have six children. Employed as telegrapher and train dispatcher, in Enderlin, ND 1949-57. Chief train dispatcher Erie Mining Railroad, Aurora, MN, 1957-90. Retired to boyhood home, Rosholt, SD, 1990. He and his wife Marilyn operate a commercial strawberry operation.

ALAN R. GLADSTONE, born June 11, 1929, Walton, NY, graduated Downsville Central School, NYS, 1947.

Joined the Army Sept. 2, 1948 and discharged Aug. 20, 1954. Military locations and stations: Camp Breckenridge, KY, 1948; HQ US Constab. Finance Section, Vaihingen, Germany, 1949-50; 7824 SCU Robinson Barracks, Stuttgart Military Post Finance Office, 1950-51; 78th Finance Disbursing Section, Vaihingen, Germany, HQ 7th Army, 1951-52; 454th Finance Disbursing Section, Camp Pickett, VA 1952-54.

Memorable experience: September 1949, General I.D. White issued a decree that he wanted the Constabulary to be 100% insured under the National Service Life Insurance Program. He, along with three others, visited every Constabulary unit in the US Zone of Occupation from September-December. They travelled in a silver Volkswagon with the "Circle C" painted on it. Perhaps some of you may recall these vehicles. (About 96% of the Constabulary became insured).

Married to Clara Mae and they have children, Scotty R. Gladstone and Vicki L. Gladstone; grandson, Millard Allan Gladstone.

Employed with the First National Bank of Downsville, NY, board chairman, president and CEO, 1947-48 and 1954-91. Retired Oct. 1, 1991.

JAMES E. (DUKE or MOTHER GODFREY) GODFREY, born June 26, 1921, Stone Harbor, NJ. Joined the Army. Military locations and stations: Co. C, 397th Inf., 100 Div., Ft. Jackson, TN Maneuvers; Ft. Bragg, NC, Combat; European Theater, Stuttgart, Germany; Berlin, Germany, Co. C, 16th Constab. Sqdn.; Ft. Riley, KS, 397th Inf., 100th Div., Co. C, 16th Constab. Sqdn.

Discharged Oct. 21, 1949 as staff sergeant. Fought in the Rhineland Campaign. His awards include the Combat Infantryman's Badge, Bronze Service Star, EAMET Ribbon, Good Conduct Medal, Presidential Unit Citation, Victory Medal, Occupation Medal, American Theater Ribbon.

Memorable experiences: Combat with 100th Div. Constab., patrolling Berlin and Autobahn, between Berlin and English sector, Germany; motor sergeant in Berlin and Graffenwhor, Germany (16th Constab. Sep) Berlin, Germany.

Married Dora C. Block in Berlin, Germany, Feb. 2, 1948. They have two sons, James David and Randy Blake; granddaughter, Michelle and grandson, James Joseph Godfrey. Employed as tractor-trailer driver, construction supervisor. Enjoys playing golf and travel. Retired from civilian employment January 1986.

RICHARD F. GOLDEN, born Nov. 17, 1928, Sacramento, CA, enlisted RA February 1945, San Francisco, CA. Military locations and stations: Camp Beal, CA; Ft. Knox, KY; Germany; Ft. Monmouth, NJ; Korea; Japan; Travis AFB, CA; Mather AFB, CA; Vietnam; Spain; Patrick AFB, FL.

His awards include the Airman's Bronze Star w/2 OLC, Air Medal w/2 OLC, Meritorious Service w/2 OLC and Air Force Commendation w/2 OLCs.

Married and has seven children. USAF retired, Vol. Bureau of Land Management.

ROBERT LEE GONTERMAN, born July 13, 1927, Louisville, KY, inducted into service Jan. 29, 1945, Louisville, KY. Military locations and stations: January 1945-December 1945, Ft. Riley, KS; February 1946, Service Troop, 2nd Cav. Regt.; Freising, Germany, detached duty with 66th Constab. Sqdn. Degendorf, Germany 1947; B Trp., 2nd Constab. Sqdn., Augsburg, Germany 1947-48.

Discharged Sept. 23, 1948, Camp Kilmer, NJ and received a Good Conduct Medal, WWII Victory and Army of Occupation.

Gonterman has never married. SSgt USAF Ret. May 1, 1996, Department of Army Civil Service. Retired July 2, 1988.

JOHN J. GRADY, born Dec. 3, 1932, Central Falls, RI, received AS degree in law enforcement, Bryant College, Smithfield, RI.

Joined the US Army Dec. 7, 1949. Military locations and stations: Ft. Dix, NJ; Weiden, Germany; Nurnberg, Germany; Ft. Meade, MD. Served with M Co.,

39th Inf. Regt., 9th Inf. Div., Trp. C, 15th Constab. Sqdn., HQ & HQ Co., 2nd Armd. Cav. Regt., HQ Co., 1st Bn., 2nd Armd. Cav. Regt.

Memorable experiences: serving as a patrol member patrolling the Czech and East German borders. Then, as border patrol operations non-commissioned officer for Troop C, 15th Constab. Sqdn. and later at 2nd A/C HQ in Nurnberg, Germany. Five years duty in Germany.

Married Elizabeth A. Grady and they have four daughters, eight grandchildren and two great-grandchildren.

Employed as Rhode Island State Trooper from 1956 to 1966; then Federal Law Enforcement as a special agent, Bureau of Alcohol, Tobacco and Firearms, Department of the Treasury, Boston. MA. Retired Nov. 30, 1988.

STEPHEN JR. (ITALIAN STALLION) GRASSETTI, born Dec. 26, 1929, enlisted in US Army July 1948, Ft. Dix, NJ. Overseas October 1948 to I Co., 14 A/C Regt. Tank training and demolition school. Duties: border patrol, giving classes in demolition. Commissioned PFC, 1948; Corporal 1949; Sergeant 1950. Was tank commander and received Occupation Germany.

Honorably discharged October 1951. Worked for McCrory Corp. Retired 1992. Played and coached many sports. He still enjoys hunting and fishing.

Married Faith Robinson, January 1958. They divorced in February 1981. They have six children: Gina, Steve Jr., Lillian, Jolene, Vincent and Beverly; 14 grandchildren: Stevie, Nicholas, Emily, Drew, Lauren, Jessie, Karli, Trista, Jenna, Daniel, Maleria, Eric, Megan and Taylor. Currently the state inspector for the VFW of Pennsylvania and councilman for the Olyphant, PA bureau. Resides with his mother in Olyphant, PA. Engaged to Lil Straka.

ROBERT CHARLES STUART GREENWAY, born April 13, 1928, Loyalhanna, PA, entered military service Oct. 16, 1945; basic training, Ft. Bragg, NC. Discharged March 4, 1947, Ft. Dix, NJ.

Duties: US Constab., Freising, Germany, March 1946-January 1947. Served as a scout car driver and commander with Trp. C, 42nd Constab. Sqdn., 2nd Regt. Stationed at outposts in Pffafenhofen, Ingolstadt and Wasserburg in Bavaria. Attended 3rd Army Ski School near Garmisch. Greenway was involved in an incident in Wasserburg where a DP was wounded while fleeing arrest. Troop C was also part of a combined Constab. operation in Bavaria that was looking for war criminals. His unit also worked in programs for German youth activities. For a period of time Troop C was located next to a woman's prison. The troopers were outside looking in. Trooper Greenway was an honor guard and was inspected by many dignitaries including Gen. Harmon. He remembers riding in a 40 and 8 box car from Le Havre to Bamberg. His father also rode in a 40 and 8 during WWI with the 15th US Engrs. Capt. William Greenway and his French born wife Edith Stuart Greenway are buried at Arlington National Cemetery. His brother Cdr. William Greenway USNR (Ret.) served in the Pacific Theatre during WWII.

His decorations and medals include the Army of Occupation Medal, WWII Victory Medal and M-1 Carbine Marksman.

Education includes BS, University of Virginia; MA Columbia University. Attended the University of Grenoble,

Sorbonne, and Harvard University. He was a Kellogg Fellow at Columbia.

Married Mary Elinor Watts in 1957. They have a daughter, son and granddaughter. As a civilian he worked with the Department of the Army in Paris with MAAG for three years. He is a retired educator and was a director of counseling services. His hobbies include genealogy. An ancestor Gen. Francois Auguste Damas served under Napoleon and married a member of the German nobility named Caroline Catherine Claire von Nell from Trier. Another ancestor Louise Catherine Duval was a cousin of the Empress Josephine Bonaparte. Greenway is still in touch with cousins in England, France and Germany and visited them last year.

ALVA A. GREER, born May 11, 1926, Lima, OH, enlisted in RA, Sept. 1, 1948. Received basic training, 101st Abn., Camp Breckinridge, KY.

Duties: from December 1948 through April 1952, Fritzlar and Fulda Germany, Tank Co., 1st Bn., 14th Armd. Cav. Regt., US Constab. Received Army of Occupation and Good Conduct Medals. Discharged June 15, 1952, Camp Atterbury, IN.

Retired Jan. 1, 1988 from Lima, OH Post Office with a 39 year Civil Service Career. Duties: Tank Plant Security Force and US Postal Clerk.

Married to Ellen Rita Brookman June 19, 1954. They have one daughter, Suzanne, one granddaughter, Jennifer and two grandson, Derek and Erik.

He most enjoys sports, music, reading, photography, gardening and fish pond management. Alva collects stamps, coins, books, photos and all types of weapons.

His special interests are his family, country home and small lake fish management. The least of his interests is traveling.

DR. RUSSELL F. (RUSS) GREER, born Nov. 10, 1919, Suffield, CT, attended Suffield Academy 1938; Dartmouth College AB 1942; Cornell University (DVM) 1945.

Served in the US Army, USAF 1943. Military locations and stations: NYC, NY; Stuttgart, Germany; Ft. Worth, TX; Washington, DC; Puerto Rico; Plattsburg, NY; Georgia; Colorado Springs, CO; Alaska.

Served with Veterinary Corps on Surgeon's Staff. Served as command veterinarian on command surgeon's staff.

Discharged November 1966 as lieutenant colonel. Awarded Good Conduct Medal, American Theater, Army of Occupation in Germany, Air Defense Command and Commendation Medal.

Memorable experiences: serving as veterinarian at 3rd Bde. HQ in Stuttgart, Germany where three horse platoons were on border patrol, i.e. The Calvary.

Married Gloria in 1945 and they have children: Michael, Randy, Melissa and Lance and a grandchild, Tiana. Employed as public health veterinarian two years in California; one year private practitioner in Connecticut. Opened own practice in San Diego, CA in 1971. Practiced limited to companion animals. Retired from USAF Veterinary Corps Nov. 30, 1966.

RAYMOND J. (RAY) GREUNKE, born Jan. 12, 1926, Randolph, NE. Joined the Army Inf. June 15, 1945. Landed at Bremerhaven, Germany, Jan. 1, 1946, then to Bamberg, Germany to the 2nd Cav. Recon Sqdn. (Mech.), then 2nd Cav. Sqdn. Went to Sonthofen Germany, started Radio School there and then 2nd Sqdn. Cav. was sent to Lenggries, Germany and there he finished Radio School and was in HQ and HQ Troop as radio operator until he was made communications chief of 2nd Sqdn. In 1947 2nd Cav. was sent home on paper, then he was sent to D Trp., 66th Constab. Sqdn. as communications chief of D Trp. Left Germany July 1947 to US Camp Kilmer, NJ. Received discharge Aug. 15, 1948.

Awarded the WWII Victory Medal, Army of Occu-

pation Medal, Good Conduct Medal and Radio School US Constab.

Married April 2, 1950 to Marcella N. Honcik and they have children, Michael and Rodney and grandchildren: John, Wendy, Julie and Scout. Employed with Geor. A. Hormel and Co. Retired April 22, 1977.

GERALD SPENCER (JERRY, MR. G or GEE) GRIGSBY, born April 15, 1928, Uniontown, PA, received an AS in education, AA psychology, BS criminal justice. Los Angeles Community College, Alabama University Athens State College, Athens, AL.

Served with the US Army, Dec. 7, 1945. Commissioned Sept. 1, 1966. Military locations and stations: Karlsruhe, Phorsheim, Landshut, Baumholder, Germany; Salzburg, Austria; Verdun, France; Anyang, Seoul, Teajon, Korea: Saigon, Qui Neon, An Khe, Vietnam; Ft. Knox, KY; Ft. Pickett, VA; Ft. Benning, GA; Ft. Campbell, KY; Ft. Myers, VA; Ft. Belvoir, VA; USN EOD School, Indianhead, MD; Indiantown Gap MR, PA Ft. Lee, VA and Ft. Stewart, GA.

Served with 1st Armd. Div., 1st Tank Bn., 1st Constab. Sqdn., 51st Tank Bn., 6th Armd. Cav. (US Constab.), 522nd MP Co., EOD School, Raritan Arsenal, NJ 89th EOD Sqdn., 6th EOD Sqdn., 57th EOD Det., 69th EOD Det. EOD School, Indianhead, MD J4, MACV, VN, LOGEX Committee, Ft. Lee, VA, 7th Ord Co., Project officer, Savanna Depot, IL, 664th Ord Co., 184th Ord. Bn., 205th Ammo Det., 833rd Ord Co.

Held commands as platoon leader, 664th Ord. Co., 7th Ord. Co., 833rd Ord Co., CO, 205th Ammunition Plt. (SEP).

Enlisted as master sergeant, officer: CWO, CW3. Retired March 1, 1974. He received seven Battle Stars, Meritorious Service Medal, two Bronze Star Medals, three Commendation Medals w/V device, Good Conduct Medal 6/knots, WWII Victory Medal, Occupation Medal, National Defense Service Medal w/cluster, Armed Forces Expedition Medal w/star, VN Campaign Medal w/7 stars, VN Service Medal and Meritorious Unit Citation.

Memorable experiences: The Constabulary combined Search and Seizure operation of Amberg, Germany soon after the units were first equipped 1946. The feeling of elation after participating in a standoff of an NVA Regt. with 1 ARVN SF Bn., 1 US "B" team and 1 ARVN EOD team w/2 US Army Advisors at Song Be, VN in 1965.

The capture and arrest of three armed robbers, when he was chief of police in a small town in Florida, 1975.

Married to Mary Catherine and remarried to Song. He has children: Vicki, Gary, Tony, Barry and Mary and grandchildren: Kristi, Jennifer, Kara, Michael, Jacob, Heather, Brandon and great-grandson, Gabriel. Employed with Mulberry Police Department: Chief US Civil Service: DoD Police Officer, Service Manual Writer, Munitions Instructor. Retired Jan. 5, 1995.

JOSEPH E. (BUD) GRONER, born Oct. 7, 1928, Bristol, PA, graduated Bensalem High School in 1946. Enlisted in the Regular Army Philadelphia, PA, Sept. 21, 1946; basic training at Ft. Knox, KY.

Served in Coburg, Schwabach and Bayreuth Germany as part of the 4th Armd. Div. Served in HQ and HQ Trp. of the 6th and 53rd Constab. Sqdns. in Germany.

Received Army of Occupation Medal, WWII Victory Medal and Good Conduct Medal. Discharged at Camp Kilmer, NJ, Feb. 11, 1948. Owned and operated Langhorne Speed Shop, Langhorne, PA, from 1948 to 1978. Retired 1980 to Daytona Beach, FL.

Editor of Motor Sports and High Performance for Motor Age Magazine. Founding Father of the US Constabulary Group, First National Commander of the US Constabulary Association.

Member of Newtown Masonic Lodge #427 F&AM, 32nd Degree Mason, member of Lehigh Consistory, VFW Post 8696, Palm Coast, FL; American Racing Legends, National Old Timers, Auto Racing Club, Society of Automotive Engineers, US Constabulary Association.

Married to Elaine (nee) Gring, Feb. 5, 1955 and they have a son, Jeffrey; daughter, Sandra and granddaughters, Stefani and Kirstin.

Groner passed away Aug. 1, 1996. Military service by the US Constabulary Association.

HOWARD H. GROSS, born April 25, 1927, Baltimore, MD, joined the Army September 1944. Military locations and stations: basic training, Camp Fannin, TX; Parachute School, Ft. Benning, 41st Inf. Div., Mindinao, Philippines. Served Occupation Japan, 41st Div.; Occupation Germany, Constabulary. Held commands as operations sergeant, 72nd Sqdn., Boblingen, Germany.

Discharged April 24, 1947 as sergeant. Served campaigns in Mindinao, Philippines.

Awarded the Good Conduct Medal, Presidential Unit Citation, Philippine Liberation, Asiatic-Pacific Campaign, Victory and Occupation Medals.

Memorable experiences: Having French toast on Mindinao to celebrate wars end; when they hadn't seen an egg in months-go figure.

He and his wife Helene are separated and they have children: Jerry, Susan, Carol, Barbara, Sharon and Dean. Employed 36 years with Bethlehem Steel, Baltimore. Part and full-time tractor-trailer driver. Retired Jan. 1, 1984, Bethlehem Steel, April 30, 1989 truck driving.

JOSEPH GRYKIEWICZ, born Sept. 25, 1927, Steubenville, OH, enlisted in the RA, Oct. 23, 1945. Received basic training at Ft. McClellan, AL.

Major assignments: 1946-48, 11th Constab. Regt., 51st Constab. Sqdn., and 6th Constab. Regt. in Weiden, Regensburg, Passau, Landshut and Straubing, Germany. 1949-50, Rynkyus Army Hospital, Okinawa; 1950-51, 618th Medical Clr. Co. (Sep.), Korea; 1951-53, Fitzsimmons Army Hospital, Denver, CO; 1953-55, 41st AIB, 2nd Armd. Div., Mannheim, Germany; 1956-60, Co. B, 1st Bn., MTC, Ft. Sam Houston, TX; 1960-63, 42nd Amb. Co. (Sep), Munich, Germany; 1963-65, 94th Evac. Hospital, Ft. Lewis, WA. Retired Dec. 1, 1965.

Joe married Shirley Wiseman, Oct. 6, 1949. They have a son, Shirdan; daughter, Joni Ries and grandson, Mickey Ries and granddaughter, Erica Ries.

JAMES W. GUEST, born May 16, 1928, Bridgeport, CT, entered the RA April 1946, Ft. Eustis, VA. Sent to Bamberg, Germany and then reassigned to the 15th Constab. Sqdn., serving with the medical detachment in Schwabish Hall. The medical detachment transferred to Fussen where he reenlisted in April of 1949. There they

made a part of the medical detachment 70th FA Bn. There he attended several medical courses and supply school.

On Aug. 28, 1951 married Gisela Vago. You may remember her, AKA Giselle, as an employee of the PX. The 70th moved to Nurnberg in 1952. Later that year they came home by boat and was assigned to a hospital at Ft. Sheridan, IL. He was discharged during that October in 1952.

Now 46 years later, he and Giselle have four children and 11 grandchildren. Started a local branch of a regional casket company of which he now serves as the branch manager/vice president.

ROGER RAMON GUILLAUME, born Nov. 28, 1930, Sioux City, IA, enlisted RA Aug. 2, 1948; basic training, Ft. Knox.

Duties: HQ 22d and 24th Constab. Sqdn., Bad Hersfeld, Germany, December 1948-December 1952 (EUCOM Intelligence & MP School, Oberammergau, June-July 1952); HQ 14th Armd. Cav. Regt., Fulda, Germany, January 1953-July 1953; HQ 30th Tank Bn., G-1 Section, 3rd Amd. Div., Ft. Knox, July 1953-December 1954.

Army Language School, Presidio of Monterey, CA, December 1954-March 1956; Straubing Sub-Post, Straubing, Germany, March 1956-March 1959; AG Section, III Corps. AG Section, HQ Ft. Hood, March 1959-June 1963; Military Assistance Training Advisor Course, US Army Special Warfare School, Ft. Bragg, June 1963-July 1963; Defense Language Institute, Presidio of Monterey, CA, August 1963-October 1963; AG Section, HQ MAAG-Vietnam, October 1963-May 1964; AG Section, HQ MACV, Vietnam, May 1964-June 1965; US Army Procurement Center, Frankfurt, Germany, June 1965-August 1968.

Retired Sept. 1, 1968. Retiree Mobilization Program 1981-90. Decorations: Bronze Star, Army Commendation (two OLC), Good Conduct (six), Army of Occupation Germany, National Defense Service, Armed Forces Expeditionary, Vietnam and Vietnam Service Medals.

Married Trudy Herzig, March 7, 1953. They have one son, one daughter and three grandsons. National Commander, US Constabulary Association. Evangelism Board, Shepherd of Hills Lutheran Church (WELS). San Diego Gas & Electric Co., September 1968-retired February 1988.

HELEN M. (BLY) GUNDRUM, born Feb. 14, 1924, Fairmont, WVA. Entered WAC DET Sept. 2, 1944. Military locations and stations: Basic training, Ft. Ogelthorpe, GA; Camp Shelby, MS; (HQ Trp.); Bamberg, Germany (G-4 Supply).

Served Heidelberg, Germany (G-4 Supply) HQ Constab.

Achieved the rank of staff sergeant. Discharged Oct. 31, 1947. Awards include the WWII Victory Medal, Army of Occupation Medal, Good Conduct Medal.

Married Cpl. Walter C. Gundrum, St. Agnatius Loyola Cathedral in Heidelberg, Germany. Had first son (Clinton) in Stuttgart Army Hospital.

They have children: Clinton, Judith, Edward, Diane, Walter J., Peter, Garry and Linda and 13 grandchildren. Employed as homemaker or domestic engineer (LOL).

WALTER C. GUNDRUM, born July 15, 1926, Addison, WI, served with Btry. D, 28th Bn., 7th Training Regt., Dec. 13, 1945-Feb. 13, 1946; 10th MP Co., 10th Inf. Div., Feb. 14, 1946-April 1, 1946, Ft. Sill, OK; 820 MP Co., Bamberg and Heidelberg, Germany; Constab. HQ.

Discharged Sept. 13, 1949, Ft. Riley, KS. His awards include the Rifle M-1 Marksman, Occupation Ribbon (Europe) and Good Conduct.

Married to Helen M. Gundrum for 50 years and they have 13 grandchildren. Employed as toolmaker at AOSmith Corps. Retired Jan. 1, 1992.

WILLIAM C. HAGEN, born Aug. 22, 1931, Boston, MA, inducted into service Sept. 6, 1948, Boston, MA. Military locations and stations: Ft. Dix, NJ 9th Inf.; Schweinfurt, Bad Kissengen, Germany, 2nd Bn., 14th AC, 1948-52; 1952-53, Korea-5th RCT; 1953-54, Ft. Devens; 1954-77, IRR; 1977-91, 94 ARCOM, NH.

Discharged Aug. 22, 1991, Ft. Devens, received Meritorious Service Medal, three ARCOM, Good Conduct Medal, Combat Infantry Badge, Army Occupation, Korean Service, UN Service, USAR Service.

Married 43 years, has three sons, one daughter and 10 grandchildren.

NEWTON HAGY JR., born Sept. 22, 1929, Camden, NY. Joined RA Oct. 2, 1946. Military locations and stations: Ft. Dix, basic training. Stationed Germany, Constab. Co. Clerk, Schwabish Hall and Boeblingen, demo and guard troop. D Trp., 15th Sqdn., Clerk School.

Awarded Army of Occupation and WWII Victory Medal. Married Anna M. Taylor June 23, 1951 and they have two sons, one daughter and four grandchildren. Retired construction surveyor, now bank courier.

E.F. HALL, *photo only, no bio submitted.*

KENT WORTH HALL, born Jan. 30, 1929, High Point, NC, inducted into service Nov. 3 , 1944, Ft. Bragg, NC. Military locations and stations: Ft. Bragg, Ft. McClellan, European Theater, 37th, 4th Armd. 1945. June 1946, Constabulary. September 1948 US Zone.

Discharged Sept. 21, 1948 and awarded the Good Conduct, Army of Occupation, Overseas Service Ribbons, Presidential Unit Citation.

Married Ramona Haney Dec. 22, 1951 and they have three sons and five grandchildren. Retired City of High Point (police sergeant) with 30 years service.

JOSEPH L. HAMILTON, born in Los Angeles, CA, enlisted May 7, 1946, as a sergeant first class he spent 20 years in the US Army of which 12 years were overseas in such places as Germany, Africa, Korea, Japan and Vietnam.

He participated in six major campaigns, three in Korea and three in Vietnam. Among this 14 ribbons and decorations are the Air Medal, Bravery Gold Medal of Greece, Parachute and Glider Badge, Korean Presidential Unit Citation, Meritorious Unit Citation, Army and the RVN Gallantry Cross w/Palm Leaf.

Served with a member of airborne, cavalry, armored, ASA, Special Opn duty, which included the 3rd Plt., 7766 Horse Trp., US Constab. with the mission of patrolling the East Germany and Czechoslovakian border.

Upon retirement in 1966, he spent 23 years with US Post Office. He was married for 37 years and has three children and four grandchildren.

ALBERT G. HAMMOND, born June 8, 1932; hometown, Colebrook, NH. Inducted on Oct. 27, 1949 at Ft. Preble, South Portland, ME. He was a member of F Trp., 2nd Bn., 14th Armd. Cav. Regt. stationed at Schweinfurt, Germany and Bad Kissingen, Germany. Military duty assignments included, armored reconnaissance crewman, scout section chief; sought routes for main forces, created maps; qualified for 3/4 ton truck and M24 tanks; earned Good Conduct Medal and Army of Occupation. Honor-

ably discharged Jan. 13, 1953 and settled in Connecticut. Married Anita-Belle Thibodeau in August 1953, they had four daughters, one son (who died in infancy), three granddaughters, and six grandsons. Retired owner/operator of A&B Sport Shop in Vernon, CT; better known as "Duke", was very prominent throughout New England and New York in the sporting goods field. Still lives in Connecticut with his wife and enjoys gardening, summers at his Maine vacation home, and spending lots of time with his nine grandchildren.

CHARLES R. HAND, born Sept. 21, 1928, Talladega, AL. Entered service Feb. 26, 1946, Ft. McClellan, AL. Discharged January 1953, Ft. Knox, KY; Camp Kilmer, NJ; Sonthofen, Germany; US Constabulary, July 1946-June 1949, 11th Sqdn., Rothweston, Germany July 1946-June 1948. Deactivated 1948. Reassigned to 14 A.C. Fritzlar, Germany 1948.

Awarded the Victory Medal and Good Conduct, ETO.

Was in HQ Trp., 11th Sqdn. in Message C&R until deactivated carried messages to troopers at outpost, in most parts of Germany with outpost around Kassel, Germany. He can't remember all village in that area, mostly between Kassel and Berlin when they had the Berlin Airlift. The Autobahn was hot in those days, after being assigned to 14th AC it was mostly combat training at Grafenwohr Germany and he lost contact with everyone he had served with until he found out about the US Constabulary Association.

ROBERT G. (BOB) HANNAH, born March 11, 1927, Westfield, NY, joined the Army, April 1, 1944. Military locations and stations: Camp Blanding, FL, 18 weeks basic. Date of enlistment RA Dec. 10, 1945, Bamburg, Germany. Served with 1st Div., 3rd Army, 15th Constab., HQ Weinheim, Germany.

Discharged July 4, 1947 as private first class. His awards include the Army of Occupation Medal, WWII Victory Medal and Good Conduct Medal.

Memorable experiences: after the war, they shot mines in the English channel on the way to Le Havre, France. Good memories of driving jeeps for the MID for Lt. Politier.

Married Florence Ethel Hannah and they have children: Rebecca, Robin and Robert and grandchildren: Christine, Jennifer, John, Joseph, Katelyn, Mike, Sean, Ryan, Racheal and two great-grandchildren, Briana and Erica.

Employed 43 years with GE as crane operator. Retired from GE April 1, 1987.

WILFRED J. (BILL) HANSMEIER, born May 30, 1928, Spokane, WA. Joined the US Army, Jan. 29, 1946. Military locations and stations: Ft. Knox, KY, basic training; Berlin, Germany; Camp Atterberry, IN; Bismark, ND. Served with 16th Constab., (Sep), Berlin (B&E Troops) July 1946-March 1952.

Discharged Aug. 1, 1952 as sergeant first class. Awarded the WWII Victory Medal, Army Occupation Medal, Good Conduct and w/Clasp.

Memorable experiences: in charge of Helmstedt aid station for two weeks in the Russian Zone during Berlin airlift. Worked 5-3 at Berlin Mile Post. Head recruiter, Bismark, ND and Grand Forks, ND 1952.

Married to LaWana K. and they have children, Robert WS. and Lausanne; grandchildren: Tilee, Tiffany, Scott, Keith and Michael. Employed in various business and sales work. Retired September 1992.

RICHARD JUNIOR HARNE, born Dec. 10, 1928, Hagerstown, MD, entered the US Army, Dec. 11, 1945, age 17 and served from 1945-1948.

Received basic training, Ft. Meade, MD. Stationed at Ft. Sill, OK and Camp Phillip Morris. From 1946-48 drove M-8 Armd. Car, Co. C, 42nd Constab. Sqdn., Augsburg, Germany.

Retired September 1948, as corporal with Good Conduct Medal, European Theatre Badge, and Expert Marksman Medal. Employed by Fairchild Aircraft and retired from Mack Trucks, Inc. 1991.

Married Bryweag Bryan, Nov. 6, 1949 and they have two sons, five grandchildren, two step-grandchildren and two great-granddaughters. One deceased grandson.

He coached Little League, Senior Div. of Baseball. He is an avid sports fan and travels.

ROBERT J. HARRIGAN, born to Daniel J. and Mary Carney Harrigan, Jan. 31, 1928 in Herkimer, NY.

Married Mary A. Townsend, Nov. 25, 1950 and have five daughters and ten grandchildren. Enlisted in the US Army for 18 months upon graduation from Thomas R. Proctor High School in Utica, NY.

Various locations after being inducted into the US Army at Albany, NY, Oct. 1, 1946: Reception Center, Ft. Dix, NJ; RTC Ft. Knox, KY; ORD Camp Kilmer, NJ; Training Det. 2nd Constab. Regt., Freising, Germany; Trp. C, 68th Constab., 2nd Constab. Regt., Augsburg, Germany.

Discharged as a T-4, Feb. 2, 1948 at Camp Kilmer, NJ. Immediately upon being discharged enrolled in college majoring in accounting. He was fortunate in obtaining a position in accounting with General Electric Co. located in Utica, NY. Retired from GE, Jan. 1, 1991 after a rewarding career as a cost accounting manager in defense electronics.

CLOYD D. (C.D.) HARRIS, born July 3, 1923, Altoona, PA, joined the service Army, Aug. 15, 1942. Military locations and stations: Ft. Knox, KY, Warminister, England, Normandy, France to Berlin, Germany. Served with Armd. Div. 21 + 22 24 Constab. Sqdn. Germany.

Discharged Jan. 10, 1952 as corporal. Battles and campaigns: Normandy to Berlin, all five campaigns.

Awarded ETO five stars, Presidential Unit Citation for St. Lo, breakthrough at St. Lo, France, Belgium Fourreguerre, Battle of the Bulge.

Memorable experiences: end of WWII, two weeks in Paris and Mulehasen border check point. When they backed down a Russian officer and six Russian soldiers.

Married Matilda Harris and they have children: Astrid and Ruth; grandchildren and great-grandchildren: Ronnie, John, Jessica, Meredith, Margo and Matthew. Employed elect. steam power PLT, operator, fireman. Retired June 1, 1987.

HARVEY L. HARRIS, born Howell County, MO, 1931. Raised Wayne County, IL. Basic at Camp Breckenridge, KY, 516th 101st Abn. early 1948. Late 1948, 51st Constab. Sqdn. and 2nd Bn., 6th Cav. Regt. at Landshut, Germany through 1951.

His family includes one son, John Wiley Harris, 35 and one granddaughter, Amanda Kay Harris, 16 at this time.

He really enjoyed Germany in those days. Especially remembers, Garmisch, Bertzhgarden, Munich, Landshut, Saltzburg Austria. He also liked the German people and the DPs.

In a way he was lucky as his buddy John could speak German fluently, helped out a lot. Also his buddy Francis Weaver at Gettysburg, PA and they have stayed in touch over the years.

He never went very high in the service, but he had a lot of fun. After all what would they do without the privates.

HAROLD KENNETH HARRISON, born July 29, 1929, Washington County, VA, attended Greendale High School, Abingdon, VA.

Joined the Army Oct. 29, 1946. Military locations and stations: Marburg, Germany; Wetzlar, Germany; Fussen, Germany; Augsburg, Germany; Weilburg, Germany. Served with 35th, 37th, 42nd Constab. Sqdns. Commands held: Patrol leader for 42nd Constab.; chief duty driver (42nd).

Discharged March 29, 1948 and T/5. Awarded Army of Occupation Medal and WWII Victory Medal.

Memorable experience: He landed in Germany March 25, 1947 through the port of Bremerhaven and was sent directly to a replacement depot at Marburg. After approximately one week, he was sent to Wetzlar for training in police patrol and riot control. His unit also took driving courses in M-8 Armored cars, M-20s and jeeps.

From Wetzlar he was sent to Weilburg and served there for three months with the 37th Constab. Sqdn. Job duties with the 37th included black market searches in dislocated persons or DP camps. Next, he served with the 35th Constab. in Fussen. Finally, after one month in Fussen, he was ordered to Augsburg where the 42nd Constab. was stationed. His duties with the 42nd included serving as the chief duty driver and patrol leader while checking roadblocks, controlling speed traps, and general patrolling of small towns and villages. One exciting aspect of his training while in Augsburg involved preparing for the Berlin air-lift. Unfortunately, however, he was discharged from the Army before it took place.

Perhaps the most exciting part of my time in the US Constab. was being fortunate enough to see and tour many of the medieval castles in Bavaria. He also had the opportunity to visit a former Nazi extermination camp. To say the least, he enjoyed his time in the Constabulary. It was a great outfit with a great bunch of guys.

Married for 48 years to Frances Haga Harrison and they have children: Debbie, Donna and Darryl and grandchildren: Stacy, Jessica, Jon Derek. Employed with Smith's Transfer Corp.; Trailways Bus Lines; Foremost Dairies; Yellow Freight Systems (post-retirement Rapid Freight and Bristol, TN Leisure Services). Retired from 1991 Yellow Freight.

EDWARD L. (ED) HART, born Feb. 8, 1927, Ringtown, PA (Schuylkill County), joined the Army May 24, 1945. Military locations and stations: Basic training, Camp Gordon, GA; advanced training, Ft. Eustis, VA; Troop A, 15th Cav. Recon Sqdn. Trp. Served with A 15th Constab., Eberbach, Germany; Stuttgart, Germany. Held commands in Search and Seizure patrols.

Discharged Nov. 2, 1946 as Tech 4 sergeant. Awarded Army of Occupation Medal, WWII Victory Medal, Army Lapel Button and two Overseas Service Ribbons.

Memorable experiences: August 1946, by special order went to Nurnberg war crime trials; also took part in Gen. Patton's funeral.

Married Margaret E. Hart, Dec. 17, 1953 and they have children, Gary L. and Richard E and grandchildren, Neal and Elizabeth. Employed as life time farmer and township supervisor. Attends United Church of Christ. Still farming 400 acres, mostly vegetables.

WILLIAM F. (BILL) HART, born Sept. 12, 1931, Plainville, CT, graduated high school and attended some college and NCO Academy.

Joined the service Jan. 4, 1949, 3rd Bn., 6th AR Cav. Military locations and stations: Degerndorf (By Inn) (May

Barracks) (2) Regensburg. Served with HQ & HQ 3rd Bn., G Co., 3rd Bn. Served as staff sergeant. Discharged June 16, 1952 and awarded the Good Conduct.

Memorable experiences: he is very proud to have served in the US Constab. and fortunate to serve with the many friends there - God bless them all!

Married to Betty S. Hart and they have children: Ruth McGhee, Jennifer Abalan, Robert Hart (William Jr. deceased); grandchildren: Alexander and Ian Bello and Kristin McGhee; Victoria and Nichole Abalan.

Employed as meat cutter-meat manager, 1954-1970, Local 371 (UFCW) (meatcutters) Union (Rep) 1970-96. Retired March 23, 1996.

LEROY (LEE) HARVEY, born May 18, 1929, Denver, CO, attended college for two years. Joined the Army, April 18, 1945. Military locations and stations: Germany, Korea, Okinawa, Ft. Knox, Ft. Carson, Ft. Lewis and Ft. Sill. Served with 2nd Bn., 42nd Sqdn. Constab., 3rd, 4th and 5th Inf. Div., 3rd Armd. Div.

Retired Aug. 30, 1968, MSG E-8. Served in the Korea and Vietnam campaign.

Awarded Parachute Badge, EAME, WWII Victory, Army Occupation, National Defense, Army Commendation w/OLC, other service medals and campaign ribbons.

Memorable experiences: all the time he was in Korea and Vietnam.

Married to Joan A. Harvey and they have children, Dennis and Carol and grandson Ben Lee Barrett. Employed Current Inc., maint. sup. August 1966-May 1986. Retired Aug. 30, 1968.

ALLEN SIDNEY HATCHETT, born July 4, 1928, Kansas City, MO, enlisted Regular Army, Nov. 14, 1946. (Also enlisted USN, 1943, age 14). Basic training, Ft. McClellan, AL, 1946-47.

US Constab., March 1947-April 1948. Discharged May 1948. Constab. basic, Freising, Germany, April-May 1947; 2nd Constab. Sqdn., Lenggries, Germany, May-August 1947; 35th-42nd Sqdn, Augsburg, Germany (2nd Regt.), August 1947-April 1948.

Graduated number one in class and broke code speed record, 2nd Regt., Radio Operator School, Augsburg. (catcher, clean-up hitter on troop softball team).

USAF, 1948-50, radio operator, Nome, AK. Radio-TV newsman; when at KAKE-TV, Wichita, KS, decided to go to college. Entered University of Missouri-Kansas City, June 1974; received BA, Economics, December 1976.

Two semesters of law school, University of Arkansas-Fayetteville, 1977-78. Now attending City College, San Francisco, taking mathematics, physics, astronomy, chemistry.

Plays tennis, tutoring girlfriend, who is Chinese, in English.

RUTLEDGE P. (HAP) HAZZARD, born April 11, 1925, Birmingham, AL. Received a BS from the US Military Academy 1943-46; MS, University of Southern California 1954-56; MBA, American University, 1965.

Joined the Army, Arty. June 1946. Commissioned June 1946.

Military locations and stations: 46-47 Artillery Basic, Ft. Sill; 47-50 16th Constab. Sqdn. (Sep), Berlin, Germany; 1950-53 Instructor USMA; 1953-54 Arty. Ad-

vanced, Ft. Sill; 1956-59 Army Ballistic Missile Command, Redstone Arsenal, AL; 1959-60 Command & General Staff College, Ft. Leavenworth, KS; 1960-63 Army Missile Intelligence, Pentagon; 1963-64 Korea; 1963-64 Industrial College of Armed Forces, Washington, DC; 1965-68 Office of Joints Chief of Staff; 1968-69 Vietnam; 1969-73 Missile Project Manager, Redstone Arsenal, NJ.

Held commands: HQ Trp., 16th Constab., Berlin 1949-50; 7/5 Bn. (HAWK), Korea 1963-64; 52nd Arty. Gp., Vietnam, 1968-69.

Discharged November 1973 as brigadier general. Awarded Medal for Human Action, Berlin, Distinguished Service Medal and Legion of Merit (4).

Memorable experiences: Berlin airlift.

Married to Ann for 46 years and they have children: Ann, Rutledge and Thomas and grandchildren: Elizabeth and Amy. Employed with the Central Intelligence Agency 197-86, Photographic Intelligence. Consultant 1986-93.

RALPH M. HEATH, born Feb. 15, 1924, Jennings County, IN, entered the service twice prior to being fully accepted. Was walking guard duty when Pearl Harbor was bombed. In 1943 arrived in Africa then Italy where he was wounded by bullet and flak. In August 1944 his unit landed in Southern France and was part of Task Force Butler which penetrated deep behind enemy lines. On Sept. 21, 1944 was captured and escaped enroute to Germany near Strasbourg and returned to his unit.

Later Heath received a direct commission, was integrated into the RA and served with the Constabulary from 1946 to 1952.

He served in various command and staff assignments, normal school and education for his army career. He and his wife Polly have four sons and one daughter. Today Ralph and Polly enjoy country living in Texas when not on visits to the doctor or pharmacy.

DAVIS A. HELTON, born March 6, 1928, Ridgedale, MO, attended college two years.

Joined the infantry February 1946. Military locations and stations: 358th, 42nd Constab. Sqdn., Fussen, and Augsburg, 1946-48; SOS AAA OPN, Det., 12th PH AAA Gp., 1950-51; Ft. Bliss, Karlsruhe, Mannheim.

Discharged October 1952 from ERC as staff sergeant.

Married to Susan and they have no children. Employed in 1951 as Missouri State Highway Patrol, Radio Div. at Rolla, Jefferson City, Springfield, Sept. 1, 1988, Communications Field Engineer.

ROY R. HENZLER, born Sept. 17, 1928, Buffalo. Joined the Army Nov. 2, 1950. Military locations and stations: Camp Edwards, MA; Bad Hersfeld, Germany. Served with 398th AAA AW Bn. US Constab.

Discharged Nov. 2, 1952 as corporal. Married Rose Marie Henzler and has children: Judy Ann and Kenneth

Roy and grandchildren: Karen, Kevin, Mitchell and Amelia. Employed with Westinghouse Electric for 36 years.

ALFRED OLIVIER HERO JR., resigned as captain in November 1953. Born, New Orleans, LA, Feb. 7, 1942. BS in military art and engineering, USMA 1945. Company-Grade (Basic) Officer's Course, The Infantry School, Ft. Benning, GA, summer, 1945. Second lieutenant, 309th Inf. Regt., 78th Div., Hof Geismar, Germany. Fall and early winter, 1945-46. Moved to Zellendorf, Berlin, with unit December 1945. Transferred sometime in 1946 to 16th Constab. Sqdn., Berlin, commanded successively by Lt. Col. Samuel McClure Goodwin and Robert C. Works, in Berlin, when 78th Div. was demobilized. Served therein as armored-car platoon leader, horse-platoon, and communications officer.

Reassigned to graduate school, Vanderbilt University, August, 1948, from which received MA degrees in psychology and Political Science, respectively, in 1949 and 1950. Office of Assistant Chief of Staff, Army, the Pentagon, June, 1950-September, 1952. Officers' Advanced Course, The Infantry School, Ft. Benning, GA, September 1952-June 1953. Staff and Faculty, The Infantry School, thereafter until resigned following November.

Executive secretary, 1954-70, and Director, 1970-82, The World Peace Foundation, Boston, MA. PhD, Political Science, The George Washington University, 1957. Visiting Scholar, Harvard University Center for International Affairs, 1982-83. Visiting Claude T. Bissell Professor of Canadian-American Relations, University of Toronto, 1983-83. Author of books and articles on US foreign-policy making, US-Canadian relations and Louisiana history. Active in inherited family business with cousins, Belle Chasse, LA, 1984-96. Due to serious heart ailment, moved near son and his family in Ann Arbor, MI, August 1996.

Married Barbara Ann Ferrell, May 1954. They have two sons, two daughters, two grandsons, and two granddaughters. Divorced 1972. Hobbies: hunting, fishing, serious music from Bach, Wagner, Webern and Glas through modern jazz, serious theater, and books and magazines in English, French and German. Active in Episcopal Church.

JOHN CHRISTAN HETZEL, born July 1, 1929, North Arlington, NJ, enlisted in the RA Sept. 5, 1946. September 1946-March 1947, Basic and Advanced Individual Training, Ft. Belvoir, VA; March 1947-March 1953, 555th Engr. Gp., (US Constab. 1950-51), Russelsheim/M-Kaufbeuren, Ettlingen and Karlsruhe, Germany; March 1953-March 1956, USAR Adv. Gp., NY, NY; March 1956-September 1956, 9th TC Gp., (Trk), Saran, France; September 1956-March 1960, 237th Engr. Bn. Munich-Regensburg, Heilbronn, Germany; March 1960-April 1962, NYNG Adv. Gp., Hudson, NY; May 1962-May 1966, 237th Engr. Bn., Heilbronn, Germany; May 1966-November 1966, Co. A, 1st Bn., TESR, Ft. Belvoir, VA. Retired Dec. 1, 1966 as platoon sergeant. December 7, 1966 to present, Bendix/Allied Signal, materials planner.

Awarded the Good Conduct Medal (Sixth Award), WWII Victory Medal, Army of Occupation Medal (Germany) and National Defense Service Medal w/OLC.

Married Gerda E. Mozer, Sept. 5, 1952. They have three sons, three granddaughters and one grandson. Life member American Legion, life member NCO Association, life member Army Engineer Association, member American Veterans, US Constabulary Association, Army and Air

Force Mutual Aid Association and coordinator, 555th Engr. Gp. reunions.

THOMAS J. (TOM) HICKEY, born Sept. 22, 1927, Olean, NY, received a BBA, St. Bona Venture University, joined the US Army Feb. 25, 1946. Military locations: basic training, 8th Btry., Ft. Knox. Served with 1st Sqdn., 15th Regt., Knielengen, WB.

Retired May 18, 1947 as private first class. His awards include the WWII Victory Medal and Army of Occupation Medal.

Memorable experiences: alerted Mil. Intelligence to KGB Agent leaving AM Zone with 2-way radio hidden in car.

Hickey is divorced and they have children: Paul T., David M., Kevin J., Jeff and Daniel T. and grandchildren: Brian, Jack, Colin, Eve and Lucas. Employed as project engineer, Aurora Pump. Retired March 17, 1986.

CLINTON A. (CLINT or SLIM) HOGG, born Sept. 17, 1931, Baltimore, MD. Joined the US Army, March 31, 1950. Military locations and stations: 16th Constab. Comp. D, Berlin Germany.

Served with 9th Inf. Div., 16th Constab., 6th Inf. Regt. Discharged April 1, 1953 as corporal. He was awarded the Occupation and Good Conduct Medal.

Married to Annamarie P. Hogg and has children: Barbara and Christina and grandchildren: Ron Jr., Michael and Wayne. Employed at Newport News Shipbuilding and Dry Dock Comp., general foreman in electrical department. Retired Dec. 1, 1993.

JOHN P. HOLLERN JR., born July 29, 1930, Covington, KY. Reentered US Army at age 16 Dec. 16, 1946 after having been discharged from Army Air Force at age 15.

Duties: US Constab., 13th and 6th Sqdns. of 6th Regt., and I Co., 14th A/C Regt. at Bamberg, Coburg, Friedburg, and Bad Hersfeld Germany March 1947-June 1954. Trained for and gyroscoped with the 3rd A/C July 1954-October 1959. Retired 1SG 1968. Voluntarily recalled to serve with 3/4 Cav. and 1/10 Cav. in Vietnam and Cambodia. Then to the 3rd Armd. Div. and re-retired as G-3 SGM.

Received several awards including Meritorious Service Medal, Bronze Star w/OLC, Commendation Medal, w/PLC, National Defense Service Medal w/star, WWII Victory Medal, Republic of Vietnam Gallantry Cross w/Palm and other service awards and campaign medals/ribbons.

Attended University of Kentucky and received the state's first ever associate degree in real estate. Retired as a real estate broker in 1995. Married Eleonore G. (Trudy) Volk of Coburg, Germany and raised four sons. Has resided in Vine Grove, KY for 25 years.

JOHN MANT (HILLBILLY) HOLT, born April 6, 1920, Myra, KY, Pike County.

Joined the Army April 8, 1940. Military locations and stations: Brooklyn, NY; Ft. Knox, KY; Italy; France; Germany; Belgium; Rhineland; Colorado Springs, CO; Ft. Ord, CA; Edgewood Arsenal, MD; Camp Edwards, MA. Served with 106th AAA Bn., 45th Div., Thunderbird Div., 4th Inf. Div., HQ & HQ Co., Fairbanks, AK. Held commands as field first sergeant-mess steward, platoon sergeant.

Discharged Sept. 1, 1962 as S.F.C. Fought battles

and campaigns: Rhineland-Central Europe, Battle of the Bulge, Central European Theatre.

Awarded the American Defense Ribbon, American Theatre Ribbon, Good Conduct Medal, European African, Middle Eastern Theatre, w/2 Bronze Stars, WWII Victory Medal, RVP. Duck Lapel Button.

Memorable experiences: It was a snowy, wet and cold Christmas day in 1944 when Sgt. Hammer ordered foxholes to be dug for their four 50s and 37mm anti-aircraft gun and for themselves. After digging all day they were cold, wet, bone tired and lonesome. Holt discovered he only had one dry sock, so he decided to crawl out of his foxhole in search of a dry one. He only crawled a short distance when the Germans lobbed a grenade into his foxhole.

He checked with his buddy, he didn't have any, so he crawled out to go to another foxhole when the Germans blew the hole up he was just in. When he reached the other hole, his friend has received a Christmas gift from home—a pair of purple socks. He offered both, but, needing only one he took it and left, crawling back to his own foxhole. The Germans lobbed another grenade and he lost his second buddy after just leaving his hole. Holt's life was spared three times by crawling from one fox hole to the other looking for a sock. To this day he wears one purple sock in memory of the two buddies he lost that Christmas. The purple sock has created much laughter for others, but in his heart there are tears that time has not erased with years.

Married to Rosemary E. Holt and has stepchildren: Jeanine, Ann, Michelle, Mary, and Kathleen; 11 grandchildren: Dennis, Misty, Jamie, Wendy, Pam, Valerie, Stefanie, Marty and Randy, Stacy and Jeremy, plus six great-grandchildren.

Retired as NOC nurse. Employed with food and liquor management. Franchise management, VFW Aux offices, local and district.

GEORGE E. HOOKER, born Aug. 13, 1928, Hamilton, OH, associate of science (electrical engineering).

Joined the US Army Oct. 5, 1946. Military locations and stations: Ft. Hayes, OH; Camp Atterbury, IN; Ft. Knox, KY; Camp Kilmer, NJ; Rothwestern, Germany; Sonthofen, Germany; Fritzlar, Germany.

Served with US Constab., C Trp., 11th Sqdn., 7801st SCU.

Discharged Feb. 11, 1948 as private first class. Awarded the Army of Occupation Medal and WWII Victory Medal.

Married Hazel L. Hooker (Lakes) married Rosana, George Jr., Anita, Homer, Richard and grandchildren: Kelli Macky, Will Stang, Lanell Stang, Matthew Kupehunas. Employed as pattern maker, engineering assist., tinner, instrument tech., pre-startup inspector, automatic controls engineer. Retired June 30, 1989.

CHARLIE F. HUGHES, born Jan. 14, 1925, Selma, AL, joined the Army Nov. 6, 1944; basic training, Ft. Bragg, NC. From there he went overseas on the Marine Robin after 13 days in a large convoy they landed in LeHavre, France. Went through Belgium, Luxembourg and southern Germany was in C Btry., 630th FA. In Durlock, Germany when several of them were sent to Sonthofen to open the school, and get it ready for the first Constabulary class. He was in training aids and film

library. Worked with a great bunch of people. Some of their names: Gilbert Zibacous, Brooklyn; Domonick P. Tricado, NJ; Charles Mier, Chicago; and Olgar a D.P. from Russia. He met Gen. Harmon one night when he was CO. He remembers just before the first class arrived they had to paint the decals on all the helmet liners; they made it in time. The school was for Hitler youth training, it had a tunnel going to all the buildings to keep them out of the snow.

Awarded ETO Ribbon, Army of Occupation, Good Conduct and Victory Medal.

VANCE HUTTON JR.,
photo only, no bio submitted.

CLAYTON WARREN (RED) INGHAM, born May 1, 1930, Essex, CT, enlisted in RA, September 1949. Basic training, Ft. Dix, NJ, joined US Constab. 1950-51 in Coburg and Friedburg, Germany. 1951-55 I Co., 3rd Bn., 14th AC Bad Hersfeld, Germany patrolling the East-West border; 1955-56, Ft. Meade, MD; 1956 recruiter at Ft. Hood, TX; August 1957-58 Reserve Recruiter, Ashland, KY; December 1958-September 1961, 9th AC Augsburg, Germany; 1961-1969 recruiter in Connecticut.

Retired December 31, 1969. Received the National Defense Service Medal w/OLC, Army Occupation Medal for Germany, Good Conduct Medal 5th award and Army Commendation Medal.

Was adjutant, Out Post 1 US Constabulary Association 1996-1996. Clayton passed away April 20, 1996 and is survived by his wife, Rose Mike Ingham, three daughters, Carlena Myatt, Rosanne Lagasse, Chris Cormier, six grandchildren. A son Clayton Jr. passed away Dec. 10, 1969.

ALFRED DAY INLOW, born Aug. 20, 1931, Woodlake, CA, joined the RA October 1948 in Medford, OR. Basic training with 4th Inf. Div. at Ft. Ord, CA. First duty assignment with the elite US Constab., 519th FA Bn. Sonthofen/Babenhausen, Germany 1949-52; US Marines 1953-56; Oregon National Guard HQ Btry., 732nd AAA Bn., 1956-58; US Marines 1958-62 (CPL); US 8th Army 1962 Korea; 1964, Ft. Riley 5th Army; 1965 Mannheim Germany, 81st Maint. Bn., 7th Army; 1968 Dalat Vietnam (forward support) 557th Light Equipment Maintenance Co., 1st Logistical Command; 1969 Stuttgart Germany, 7th Corps; 1971 Dalat Vietnam (forward support) 557th Light Maintenance Co., 1st Logistical Command; 1972 Advisory Duty Advisor to National Guard San Bernardino, CA. Changed over to US Army Readiness Region IX stationed at Ft. MacArthur, CA, 6th Army; 1974 Korea Camp Carroll Army Depot, 8th Army.

1976 Ft. Ord, CA, 7th Maint. Bn., 7th Inf. Div. retired. May 1, 1977 (master/sergeant). Received several medals during his career, including Bronze Star w/2 OLCs, Army Commendation Medal w/OLC, Army Good Conduct w/6 knots, Occupation of Germany, Marine Good Conduct w/star various other medals.

1978 Civil Service for federal government, with assignments in Germany, Italy and Korea and Sharpe Army Depot Stockton, CA. Retired September 1993, GS-11. Some of his most elite assignments, while working with Civil Service. Quality assurance; 1984-87 instructor on the M1 Abrams Tank at Vilseck Germany. Member of Constabulary Association, Camp White Historical Association, and DAV.

Married Swanee B. (KIEL) Inlom and they have sons, Fred and Charles Inlow; stepson, David Frick and five grandchildren. Resides in Eagle Point, OR.

ALBIN F. IRZYK, born Jan. 2, 1917, Salem, MA, graduated Mass. State College (UMASS), commissioned second lieutenant Cav. ROTC. Career Army officer (31 years). Commanded 8th Tank Bn., 4th Armd. Div., which spearheaded Patton's 3rd Army. Wounded twice. Stayed in occupation of Germany with 4th Armd., then with US Constab. Was S-3, and XO of the 1st Constab. Bde. in Wiesbaden. Later, commanded the famed 14th Armd. Cav. Regt. along the Iron Curtain during the Berlin Crisis of 1961. For two years headed the US Army Armor School, Ft. Knox. Served two years (seven campaigns) in Vietnam (Asst. Div. Comdr., 4th Inf. Div.). Was deputy C.G., Ft. Dix, NJ and C.G. Ft. Devens, MA.

Awarded the Distinguished Service Cross, Distinguished Service Medal, Silver Star w/OLC, Bronze Star w/3 OLC and Purple Heart w/OLC.

Graduate National War College. Holds master's degree in International Relations. His book, *He Rode Up Front for Patton* was recently published. Married to Evelyn for 51 years. They have three children: Jane, Albin F. Jr. and Laura and five grandchildren. Retired as brigadier general.

RAYMOND D. (RAY) IVERSON, born March 1, 1927. Joined the service Jan. 4, 1946. Military locations and stations: Ft. Sill, OK; Darmstadt, Germany; Constabulary School, Sonthofen, Germany.

Served with 14th Sqdn., C Trp., Discharged as T/5 May 6, 1947. Awarded Army of Occupation Medal, WWII Victory and Marksman.

Married to Rose and they have children: Darlene, Douglas, Denise and Steven and grandchildren: Eric, Andy, Zachery, Ben and Amber. Enjoys dairy farming. Retired November 1994.

IRVING DENNIS JACK, born Nov. 30, 1927, Nickleville, PA, joined the US Army Dec. 17, 1945 and commissioned Dec. 17, 1945. Military locations and stations: Camp Lee, VA; Boeblingen, Germany.

Served with Trp. A, 72nd Constab. Sqdn. as technician fifth grade. Discharged May 24, 1947 as T/5. His awards include the WWII Victory Medal.

Jack is a widower and has children: Don, Ron and Denise and grandchildren: Chad, Cassie, Christopher and Christine. He is self-employed.

WILLIAM K. JACKSON, born May 4, 1926, Utila Bay Island, Honduras. Inducted Ft. Riley, KS, January 1945. Trained in M5A and M24 Lt. Tanks. Served as inductee from January 1945-October 1945. Reenlisted in Regular Army from October 1945-October 1946. Discharged Tech 4 Sgt. at Ft. Dix, NJ.

Duties: served in Philippines from August 1945 to October 1945, Lt Tank Trp., 14th Constab. Regt., from March 1946-October 1946 in Kitzingen and Schweinfurt, Germany, search and seizure. Awarded the Asiatic-Pacific Ribbon, European Theater Ribbon and Army Commendation Ribbon. Hobbies: free lance writer. Member of WWII Reenactment. Co. A, 70th Tank Bn., Big Rock, IL. Takes part in parades and military displays, dressed in exact replica of Constabulary uniform. Retired, married and living in Geneva, IL.

ROBERT J. JARRETT, born March 4, 1928, Queens County, NYC, attended Bushwick High School, Brooklyn, NY. Served as a messenger Civil Defense 1942-43. Enlisted New York State Guard, Co. G, 13th Inf. Regt. October 1943-February 1946. Enlisted Regular Army February 1946-October 1947. Service with Co. B, 10th AIB, redesignated 10th Sqdn., 14th Regt., US Constab. Served in Kitzingen, Elsenfeldt, Aschaeffensburg, Lohr, Wurzburg, Germany.

Married Virginia McAndrews May 1948-1973. Divorced. Marriage produced four children: Robert S., Janet V., Lillian F, William E.; three granddaughters and three great-grandsons. Married Therese Puccino nee (Grotheer) July 5, 1979-1991 Divorced. Employed with New York City Board of Education, Bureau of Maintenance retired 1985.

Past Association Offices Jr. Vice Commander OP #2, National Recruitment Officer, National Senior Vice Commander, National Commander 1993-95, National Trustee 1995-97. American Legion Deputy District Commander 13th District PA 1995-97.

JOHN D. (JEFF) JEFFREY, born Oct. 12, 1929, Somerville, MA, joined the US Army in 1946. Military locations and stations: Ft. Dix, USA; Germany, Kitzingen, at Kitzingen Constabulary training; Hammelburg and Schweinfurt. Served with 14th AC Kitzingen, HQ Co., 22nd Sqdn., Hammelburg and A Co., 28th Inf. Sqdn. Schweinfurt.

Discharged 1948 as private first class. Battles and campaigns: EM Clubs (only kidding!)

Memorable experiences: did check points and road blocks, parades, etc. But one thing does stand out. When stationed at Kitzingen he was put on a special guard post with a young man (trooper like Jeffrey) by the name of Robb. Trooper Robb was from Pittsburg, PA. Big Ralph Kiner fan. They had this special detail on the outside of the rear gate. Seems that had a block of storage garages that were sort of built into the hillside. Well it seems on inspection one day, approx. 1/4 of the bricks in the rear were missing. Trooper Robb and Jeffrey got this special detail to catch the thief. Well it was double day light saving time and it didn't get dark until around 11 p.m. So they showed up at 8 p.m. and hid in the brush and sat in their jeep and nothing until about 11:30-12 p.m. Then they heard this hammer chipping away at the rear of the building. They looked down and saw a bicycle with a wire basket on the front and two more slung over the rear wheels. So they made a deal. They let this poor guy break his back all night and after he was just about ready to pack up they would then swoop down and arrest him. They did just that at 5:30 a.m. He was pooped and he wouldn't run because of the bike. At that time the bike was worth a million, approx. 2-3 hours after they had him locked up, his mother and two sisters came to try to get the bike back. Now this was really fun (to him anyway) and its always popping up in his head when he needs a laugh. No kidding he killed himself all night and then Jeffrey and Trooper Robb stuck a pin in his bubble. Enjoyed his Constabulary service and it sure was one sharp outfit.

Married 45 years to Shirley A. Jeffrey and they have children: John, Andrew, Richard and Steven and granddaughter, Rachel L. Jeffrey. Member of Teamsters for 48 years. Employed with Adley Express Co., Yellow Freight, Eastern Freightways, Boss-Lined Lines and Star Market Company. Retired Jan. 1, 1993 and loving it.

WILLARD A. (SUG) JENKINS, born July 7, 1929, Ettan, VA, Madison County, joined the Army June 28, 1948. Military locations and stations: Ft. Jackson, SC; Ft. Eustis, VA; Constabulary NCO Academy, Jensen Barrack, Munich, Germany. Served with A Co., 54th Combat Engr. Btry., Panzer Kaserne, Berb, Germany, near Stuttgart.

Achieved the rank of sergeant first class and discharged Aug. 30, 1951. Awards include the Army of Occupation, Army Good Conduct and Overseas Service.

His wife Betty Jane Jenkins is deceased. They had children: Kelly Faye Jenkins and a son, Billy Joe Jenkins and grandchild, Amy Jenkins. Employed with the Virginia Department of Highways, supt. 16 years; senior building inspector, 21 years, Fairfax County, VA. Retired July 3, 1987.

FREDERICK E. JEWELL, born Oct. 8, 1929, Newark, NJ. Joined the Army Aug. 16, 1948. Military locations and stations: Camp Kilmer, NJ; Ft. Dix, NJ. Took basic training, 2nd Armd. Div., Ft. Hood, TX. Served with 24th Constab. Sqdn., D Trp., Fulda, Germany.

Achieved the rank of staff sergeant and discharged Aug. 2, 1952. Member of VFW Post 5383 Newark, NJ American Legion Post 58 AZ US Constabulary 8 Outpost. Awarded the Germany Occupation and Good Conduct Medal.

Memorable experiences: going to Germany and being in the 24th Sqdn., D Trp., with the best troopers and they have their reunions in September.

Married to Antonie M.E. Jewell. His wife is from Fulda, Germany. They were married Dec. 13, 1951. Employed with A McDermott Trucking and Ricking for 33 years; Apollo Trucking and Rigging six years. Retired Oct. 8, 1992.

DAVID A. (DAVE) JOHNSON, born Jan. 9, 1927, East Orange, NJ, received a BS in agriculture, Rutgers University, New Brunswick, NJ, June 1950. Joined the service Feb. 10, 1945. Military locations and stations: Camp Gordon, GA, March 1945-May 1945; Aberdeen Proving Grounds, MD May 1945-September 1945, various forts and camps for reassignment, Darmstadt and Sonthofen, Germany. Served with 14th AIB, 1st Armd. Div, 14th Constab. Sqdn. April 1946-September 1946.

Discharged Nov. 6, 1946 as private first class. Attended Aberdeen Proving Grounds School; Small Arms Weapons Constabulary School, Sonthofen, Germany.

Awarded the Army of Occupation Medal and Victory Medals.

Married May 23, 1953, Dorothy Eadie Johnson and they have children: Donald Andrew, Douglas Alan and Daniel Albori; grandchildren: Trevor Douglas and Cassidy Traylor Johnson. In 1954 joined Bloomfield Lodge #40, F&AM (Masons) and elected worshipful master December 1970, served in this office in 1971.

Member of the Episcopal Church of the Advent, Bloomfield, NJ until the church closed in 1996. During the years there, he served as vestryperson and delegate to the Diocesan Convention. He is now a member of Christ Church, where he serves as alternate delegate to the Diocesan Convention and also as an Acolyte.

Post commander of Miles Suarez Post #711, Bloomfield, NJ in 1996-97 and now currently one of the trustees.

He and his wife travels some. They have made four trips to the United Kingdom, two trips to Germany and one to Italy, as well as in this country and Canada.

DONALD JOHNSON, born March 19, 1926, Easton, PA. Entered military service June 26, 1944 and received his basic training at Camp Stewart, GA with the 66th AAA Bn. the transferred to Camp Gordon, GA for infantry training.

Shipped overseas and joined 771st Tank Bn., Co. B. From June to October they were in seven different towns and wound up in Schwaebisch Hall where they moved into civilian homes. They changed from the 771st Tk. Bn. to 71st Constab. Sqdn.

Memorable experience was going to Paris, France to draw vehicles and on the return trip on the Autobahn, it was like the Indianapolis Speedway with racing, speeding and anything you could imagine taking place. The MPs got wind of the antics and stopped them at a checkpoint. When they returned to HQ, four jeeps were totally wrecked and at least 12 jeeps had the front ends pushed in, but still runable.

Returned to the States in June 1946 and received his discharge on July 22, 1946. Awards include the Good Con-

duct Medal, American Campaign, EAME Campaign, WWII Victory Medal and Army of Occupation.

He returned home to his wife Rita and two sons. Over the years they added three daughters, eight grandchildren and eight great-grandchildren to the family. He is a life-time member of the VFW, American Legion and 771st Tank Bn. Assoc. and member of 71st Constabulary B Troop.

LEE F. JOHNSON, born Feb. 2, 1922, McKeesport, PA, graduated high school and received two years college credits. Joined the US Army Dec. 1, 1942. Military locations and stations: Ft. George G. Meade, MD; Camp Van Dorn, MS; Camp Maxey, TX; European Theater Operations; Germany (Augsburg, Nurnberg, Ansbach and Erlangen). Served with 395th Inf. Regt., 99th Div., WWII; 5th and 2nd Constab. Regts. (1946-48); 2nd Armd. Cav. (1948-50), Mil Pol (1950-52), MPCID (1952-66).

Assigned to Trp. C, 74th Sqdn., 5th Constab. Regt. 1946. In 1947 his above unit was re-designated as Troop C, 2nd Sqdn., 2nd Constab. Regt. In 1948, this unit was again redesignated as Co. C, 1st Bn., 2nd Armd. Cav. Regt. in which he served until August 1950 when he was redeployed to stateside.

Retired Nov. 30, 1966 as chief warrant officer-2. Fought battles and campaigns: Ardennes (Battle of Bulge), Rhineland Campaign and Central Europe Campaign, WWII.

Awarded Purple Heart, Bronze Star, Army Commendation, Good Conduct, American Theater Medal, European Theater Medal w/3 Battle Stars, Victory Medal, Occupation Medal (Germany), National Defense Medal, Belgian Fourresguerre, and Distinguished Unit Citation.

Memorable experiences: WWII, US Constabulary Operations and Military Police Criminal Investigations, Veteran Orgs. (Mil. Order Purple Heart, VFW, 2nd Cavalry Association, US Constabulary Association, Retired Officers Association, National Association Uniformed Services, CCC Alumni.

Married Susanna K. Johnson and they have children: Elizabeth Sue Rolls and granddaughter, Suzanna Lee Rolls. Employed with the US Government (General Services Administration) Criminal Investigator (1967-80), GS-13. Retire Dec. 30, 1980.

RONALD BEDELL JOHNSON, born Sept. 4, 1929, enlisted December 1945, age 16 years. Basic training, Mechanized Cav., Ft. Knox.

Assigned to 2nd Cav. Regt., Freising, Germany June 1946; was present at the inauguration of the 2nd Constab. Regt., July 1946. Assigned to the Motorcycle Plt., HQ Trp., HQ Sqdn. Graduated from the Regimental NCO School.

Moved to Augsburg August 1947 and was in the Motorcycle Plt. of the 5th Regt. for a short period until it became the 2nd Regt. again. Graduated from the Constabulary School in Sonthofen.

Returned to US and discharged October 1948. Recalled to active duty for the Korean War September 1950. Attended Advanced Military Police School, Ft. Gordon, GA. Released from active duty December 1951.

BA, history and Political Science, UCLA 1957. Public administrator, city of Los Angeles for 30 years, retired November 1989.

Married to Olga (nee Olga Danzer of Augsburg); two daughters, two sons, and seven grandchildren.

CHARLES A. JOHNSTON, born Aug. 1, 1925, Wellston, MO, received a master of vocational education (Practical Arts Vocational and Technical).

Joined the US Navy September 1943 and US Army May 1946. Military locations and stations: WWII Pacific Theater (Navy) Post War Ft. Lee, VA; Camp Kilmer, NJ; ETO Stuttgart/Schwabish Hall Germany).

Served with Navy two years; Army US Constab., 7th Army Cml. Corp. Discharged from the Navy September 1945 as EM Striker and from the Army as corporal. Campaigns include Navy Support Saipan/Philippine Liberation.

His awards include the usual service ribbons, Pacific Theater, WWII Victory, European Theater, Occupation Germany.

Memorable experiences: opening first CBR School in 7th Army in Unterturkheim, Germany as operations NCO and transient hotel manager. Serving special services entertaining airlift personnel during Berlin airlift.

Married Jeannine in 1954 and they have children: Steven, Christopher and Jeffrey and grandchildren: Abby, Martha, Andrew, Kelly, Danae, David and Denise. Employed at McDonnell Aircraft for 18 years, aircraft E&E mechanic to cost estimator. US Army Troop and Air Support Commands, St. Louis, European Command, contract administration. Retired Jan. 1, 1992.

WILLIAM L. (BEN) KABLACH, born Jan. 30, 1928, Troy Hill, Pittsburgh, PA, received a BS in Business Administration from Duquesne University.

Joined the Army Jan. 25, 1946. His military locations and stations: Ft. McClellan, AL, infantry training, three months; Bad Neustadt, Fulda CAP, 9 months border patrol; one month Wildflicken, Polish DP Camp; two months Hammelburg; prisoner of war camp.

Discharged July 10, 1947. Awarded WWII Victory Medal and Germany Occupation Medal-Army.

Memorable experiences: encounter with Russians on border last prisoner of war guard duty. Last camp closed in June 1947.

Married to Eleanor. She is now deceased. He has children: William, JoAnn, John and Janette; grandchildren: Sara, Daniel and Laura. Employed as fire captain, Pittsburgh Bureau of Fire for 33 years. Retired May 29, 1991.

FRANK KACZMAR, born Oct. 15, 1929, Jersey City, NJ. Joined Ra, Aug. 15, 1949. Basic training, Ft. Dix, NJ. Stationed in Fussen, Germany; Nurnberg, Germany. Joined US Constab. January 1950.

He was in Germany for five years. Went to Ft. Benning, GA when he came back to stateside where he was discharged Aug. 13, 1955. His awards and medals include the Good Conduct and National Defense Occupation.

Married Gloria Edsall in 1956 and they have three daughters. Also have six grandsons, one granddaughter and two great-granddaughters.

Belongs to VFW Post and American Legion. He enjoys stock car and Nascar racing.

MICHAEL KANE
photo only, no bio submitted.

WILLIAM JAMES KASBOHM, born July 31, 1931, Manitowoc, WI, entered the military August 1948 at age 17. Retired from the military April 30, 1969, Ft. Sheridan, IL, 5th Army.

Service history: 1948-1952, Straubing, Germany, US Constab., 6th Armd. Cav. HHC; 1952-55, Ft. Sam Houston, TX, 62nd MP Plt., supply sergeant; 1955-60, Ft. Sam Houston, TX, 52nd MP Co., supply sergeant; 1960-63, Erlangen, Germany, HQ Co., CCB, 44th Armd. supply sergeant; 1963-64, Ft. Sill, OK, A Co., 2nd 32nd Gun Bn., supply sergeant; 1964-67, Ft. Sill, OK, Post Chaplin Supply S-4; 1967-68, Vietnam, S-4 sergeant; 191st Ord. Bn.; 1968-69, Ft. Sheridan, IL, HQ 5th Army DCSLOG S-4, supply sergeant; 1969-69, Ft. Sheridan, IL, S-4 113 MI DET (Ret.) as MSGT E-8.

His awards and medals include the Army Commendation Medal w/OLC, Good Conduct Medal (5th Award), National Defense Service Medal, Vietnam Service Medal, Vietnam Campaign Medal, Army of Occupation (Germany), numerous letters of commendation.

Education: NCO Academy 7th Army; US Army Adjutant General School, Unit Supply QM School.

Married to Judith Ann Summers and has four sons and three daughters and 11 grandchildren. Retired from the US Army after 21 years service.

HENRY S. (HANK) KECKI, born May 17, 1931, Ludlow, MA, attended Parochial School for eight years and trade school for three years.

Joined the US Army Sept. 26, 1949. Military locations and stations: Ft. Dix, NJ, basic training; overseas to Marburg Port of Embarcation; to Coburg.

Served with I Co., 14th Armd. Cav. Div. Bad Hersfeld, Germany. Squad leader 81mm mortar.

Discharged Aug. 5, 1952 as corporal. Awards include the Army Occupation Medal (Germany), Good Conduct, NATO Ribbon, Sharp Shooter Medal.

Memorable experiences: the most memorable experience was while hauling high octane gasoline with his truck not realizing they had a flat tire, the truck was hard to drive, so they pulled over and the tire began to really burn. They ran away to a distant and watched it explode. Also the 50 cal. ammo in the truck let go it was like 4th of July. Everything burned to the ground.

Married Victoria Kecki and they have children: Susan Marie Kecki and Paul Kecki. Employed as accoustical partition for offices; also worked as cabinet maker at Hampden Engineers, MA. Retired May 22, 1993, Long term disability, bad knee, arthritis.

CHARLES E. KEITH, born in Worcester, MA, Aug. 18, 1927, graduated from Commerce High in 1945. While still in school, joined the ASTRP (Army Specialized Training Reserve Program). Served three months at Mass State University and then went to Norwich University Military School in Northfield, VT. Completed six months of training there. November 9, 1945 reported to Ft. Devens, MA for active duty in the army. Went to Ft. McClellan, Anniston, AL for basic training. Completed basic training in February 1946. In March of 1946 went to ETO (European Theater of Operations) via a liberty troop ship, arriving in LeHavre, France. In April, went to Friesing, Germany for duty in the US Constab. for the Army of Occupation, 3rd Army, 2nd Regt., 42nd Sqdn., Co. A. Went to Frankfurt, Germany to attend an I&E (Information and Education School. Also attended radio school for eight weeks. Was given the job of company clerk, keeping all the Co. A personnel records for 190 men. On Jan. 30, 1947

left Bremerhaven, Germany for the states aboard the ship *Adm. Hugh S. Rodney.*

Was discharged March 8, 1947 from Ft. Dix, NJ with the rank of technician fifth grade. Awarded the Army of Occupation and WWII Victory Medal.

FORD C. KEMERY, born Jan. 4, 1933, Brady Bend, PA, joined the Army Feb. 23, 1950. Military locations and stations: Augsburg and Amberg, Germany. Served with Constab. Co. H, 3rd Bn., 2nd Armd. Cav.

Discharged October 1952. Awarded the Good Conduct and Expert Rifleman.

Memorable experiences: he was in a musical show with about 65 other troopers and two lovely ladies from the USO. They put on their musical show at almost all the military posts in Germany and Austria.

They were scheduled to go to England and back to the States and to Japan. But President Truman called a national emergency and that ended their show. Their show was called Sing Brothers Sing.

Returned to his wife as a cook for the remainder of his tour of duty. Their unit also patrolled the Russian border.

Married to Hildegard Kemery for 42 years and they have no children. Employed as millwright at Ford Motor Co., Buffalo, NY. Retired in 1985.

RUSSELL VANCE KENNEDY, born Feb. 19, 1928, Philadelphia, PA, enlisted in Naval Reserve, Aug. 12, 1947-Nov. 8, 1950. Drafted into US Army Nov. 8, 1950. Basic training, Ft. Belvoir, November 1950-February 1951.

Served with US Constab., Babenhausen, Germany; 519th GA Bn., HQ Btry., February 1951-October 1952, 7th Army, Non-commissioned Officer's Academy, Munich, Germany 1952. US Army enlisted Reserve Oct. 18, 1952-Oct. 2, 1956.

Married Sandra Littleton, Sept. 24, 1960. They have three daughtes, one son, four grandsons and one granddaughter. Retired from Boeing Helicopter Corp. 1994.

Member of Philadelphia Continental Chapter Sons of the American Revolution; board member Society of the War of 1812 Pennsylvania, American Legion, Red Cross volunteer. Board of Deacon's Olivet Presbyterian Church, gardening.

RAY D. (POSSUM) KERNS, born Sept. 19, 1924, Mason County, WV, joined the Army, Horse Cav., Nov. 11, 1945. Commissioned Dec. 5, 1945. Military locations and stations: training Ft. Riley, KS served in Freising, Germany to Heidelberg to Stuttgart to Villingen.

Served with 42nd Sqdn. (1946) transferred to 2nd Constab. Horse Plt., later known as 7766th Horse Trp. Held

command as sergeant in charge of the Horse Plt. trucks and trailers, 1946-48. Discharged as sergeant September 1948. Served during peacetime.

Awarded WWII Victory Medal, Army of Occupation Medal, a letter of commendation from major general.

Memorable experiences: participating in the Constab. Horse Show in Vaihingen and building lasting friendships with the troopers.

Married Claradell and they have children: Cynthia, Cheryl and James and grandchildren: Chelsea, Mechelle, Melany, Allen, Matthew, Seth and Brandon. Employed in farming (46 years) and school bus driver (31 years). Retired January 1995.

RICHARD A. (KILROY) KIDWELL, born Feb. 19, 1927, Columbus, OH, joined the 6th Cav. October 1944. Military locations and stations: Ft. Knox, KY; Bayreuth, Germany. Served with 6th Constab. HQ.

GERALD KIFFEL, born Aug. 28, 1928, Chicago, enlisted August 1945 on 17th birthday. Assigned to ASTRP Program at Houghton, MI. Enlisted RA Jan. 5, 1946. After basic training in Little Rock, AR, shipped overseas, arriving Camp Twenty Grand, LeHavre April 13, 1946. Rode 40x8 box cars to Germany. Assigned to Co. K, 30th Inf., 3rd Div. at Bad Sooden. Later served with 30th Inf. HQ Message Center at Kassel and German night fighter base, Rothwesten.

July 26, 1946 assigned to 11th Constab. Sqdn., 1st Regt., later 12th Sqdn. October 1947 selected to return stateside to attend West Point Prep School at Stewart Field, NY, May 1948. Passed entrance exams but deceived appointment.

Reassigned to 1802nd Sp. Regt., working with cadets at Camp Buckner, August 1948. Sent to HQ Det. 1, Ft. Riley, eventually discharged Dec. 13, 1948. Recalled briefly to active duty in March 1951.

Earned BA and MA in history from DePaul University. Retired in 1990 as assistant superintendent of schools for Wheeling-Buffalo Grove, IL.

ANDREW F. KING, born Oct. 21, 1932, in New York City. Entered military service at age 16 on March 17, 1949, NYANG with the famous Fighting 69th Inf. Regt. Enlisted in the Regular Army March 17, 1950; basic training at Ft. Dix, NJ. August 1950 assigned to Co. I, 3rd Bn., 14th Armd. Cav. Regt. US Constabulary in Coberg, Germany. Duties: police patrol, downtown Coberg and base security. September 1950 chosen through regiment competition to drive Gen. I.D. White, Commanding General Constabulary Forces, but because of not being qualified for passenger car on military license was denied the appointment at last moment. October 1950, 3rd Bn. relocated to Friedberg, Germany. Duties: Armed Border Patrol between the Russian and US Zones of occupation. 1952, 3rd Bn. moved to Hersfeld, Germany continuing their border duty. April 1953 Honorably discharged from military service.

February 1955, entered the New York City Police Dept. Served in a variety of capacities including as a motorcycle officer and before retirement in 1975, a public relations officer in the South Bronx. Received several medals for excellent police duty and nominated for the mayor's award for program innovation within the police department 1975, became director of safety and security and worked in two major hospitals until retirement in 1993. June 1977, graduated college with a degree in police science and administration.

Held three appointed offices in the "Association." Was the first national historian on Constabulary history. The first national recruiting officer contributing to the growth from 300 to 1,000 members and was the public information officer answering inquiries about the organization. 1993, was appointed chairman and planned the first national reunion of the "Association" held in Ft. Mitchell, KY.

Married Kathleen Fagan Sept. 22, 1956, and they have three sons, one daughter and eight grandchildren. Past post commander of the VFW. Awarded the Outstanding Commander's Award and Life Membership in 1983. Twenty years with the Boy Scouts of America retiring in 1976 as district commissioner. Awarded the Bronze Pelican by the Catholic Church and the Silver Beaver, the highest BSA award for voluntary service to scouting. Editor of the Trooper, the newsletter of the Constabulary Veterans of America, a social club of Constabulary veterans and wives meeting once each year.

WILLIAM F. KIRCHMAYER, would be willing to bet that he was one of the few troopers in the US Constab. who grew up in Occupied Europe, emigrated to the US in 1949, and returned as a US soldier to help occupy Germany, enlisted in Milwaukee, WI, February 1950, and took his basic training at Ft. Knox, KY. Their troopship arrived in Bremerhaven in July of the same year.

He lived in the US less than a year prior to enlisting in the Army. His family lived in what is now Slovak Republic and they were living in Lower Austria when the Second World War ended. They experienced first hand what life under Soviet occupation was like. He was assigned to Dog Co., 2nd Bn., 2nd Armd. Cav. Regt., (US Constab.) in the Sheridan "Kaserne" Augsburg.

Their company, minus the tank sections, was given the mission of clearing a bridge over the Neckar River during the NATO maneuver, "Operation Rainbow," September 1950. The 2nd AC acted as aggressor forces. They were issued green wool uniforms, red overseas caps, and sported yellow collar tabs, indicating cavalry. Rank insignia was worn upside down.

The German civilians usually distrusted Aggressor Troops due to the strange uniforms, sometimes thinking them to be French or maybe Russian in origin. Once he was asked, "Are you really Amis?" This bridge was in small town in the US Forces securing the far end with a sandbagged bunker. As he was the only trooper fluent in German, their Company CO, 1st Lt. Warren Gossett, had him talk with an old man who owned a rowboat down by the river's edge, but using the boat to cross with didn't work out.

Later they flagged down a farmer driving a small truck with high wooden sideboards on the bed. He asked the man if he would be willing to give a few of them a ride across the bride to the outskirts of the town. Although reluctant, he did consent. They loaded 15 troopers into the back of the truck. The sergeant and he got to ride in the dab with the farmer. They made use of extra coats and caps for the ride across, looking like a pair of local farmhands. It was dark by the time they drove across the bridge and they were stopped at the checkpoint. A couple of soldiers approached the truck, looked in the cab, and waved them through. As agreed, the farmer stopped and they all unloaded quickly at the edge of town. He was rewarded with cigarettes and was glad to be on his way.

Quietly, the squad moved out through the darkened streets and gardens back toward the bridge site and the unsuspecting GIs guarding it. The road intersection at the bridge was well lit by street lights. They charged out of the shadows toward the bunker, firing their weapons as they ran. Their MG-jeeps were driving across the bridge, giving us supporting fire. So effective and quick was their attack that the defenders didn't even have time to get the

cover off of their 90mm Recoiless Rifle. They captured eight men. The smoke from the many blanks fired hung like fog at the intersection for awhile.

His most memorable "adventure" as an aggressor happened at the start of the NATO exercise when their Plt. Leader Lt. Charles Lehner masterminded a bold plan to capture a train. It was in the training area of Vilseck. They took off late at night, driving with blackout lights on the muddy, rutted tank trails into the pine forest. They arrived at an assembly area and parked some distance from a large tent. The lieutenant disappeared in the pitch dark. After quite some time, he came back and said, "Let's get the hell out of here before we get captured!" By the time they got back to their platoon campsite, it was 0400 hours. Short night! The lieutenant had the driver and Kirchmayer "saddle up" again early in the morning for a quick trip to the Tank Training Center Vilseck.

After they reached the main gate, he told the German Industrial Policeman that the lieutenant was a courier to see Col. Brown (Base CO). They drove directly to the railroad station. There they found out the loading schedules, departure and arrival times of the transport that was to move the medium tanks of the 1st Inf. Div. after rejoining the rest of their 3rd Plt. They changed uniforms and were then ready to start their mission as aggressor forces. Their column of jeeps and 1 1/2-ton trucks wound itself down the country road until the platoon leader signaled to pull off the road and proceed across a rolling pasture into a small stand of trees. From there, the troops moved down the hill on foot. The combined Recon and Inf. sections, supported by the 81mm mortar section, got ready to set up for an ambush. Below the slope the rail line cut through a rocky embankment on a curve. They waited about an hour before they could hear a train approaching in the distance. The Rocket Launcher Team moved down along the tracks with the lieutenant and Psg. The Mg. Squads got ready on top of the bluff. Needless to say, the freight trains, made up of boxcars and flatcars, came to an unscheduled halt below the embankment. The German train crew was very nervous, but not as upset and angry as Col. Creighton Abrahms, the CO of the medium tank battalion. He threatened to run his M-26 tanks sideways of the flatcars, but didn't after being told by the umpire, who was a Major, that he would be reported to EUCOM HQ. The unit was judged as knocked out and had to wait a prescribed period of time at their destination before rejoining the maneuver. Colonel Abrahms became their regimental commander while they were at Augsburg and he mentioned his first address to the assembled troops that he never forgot what the 2nd A/C did on "Operation Rainbow."

DONALD LEMOINE KJOS, born Nov. 6, 1928, Mott, ND, enlisted in Regular Army Dec. 4, 1946, Ft. Snelling, MN. Basic training, Ft. Bragg, NC. Arrived in Germany April 1947 from May 1947 Constabulary School Sonthofen, Germany. July and August Budingen to Augsburg, Germany. Stayed with C Trp., 68 Comstap Sqdn., 2nd Regt. until April 1948. Returned to Camp Kilmer, NJ for discharge. Received WWII Victory Medal and Army of Occupation Medal.

Married Viola Friez, May 15, 1956. They have one son and one daughter. Retired July 15, 1992. Returned to part-time work at Spearman, TX.

LEONARD J. (LENNY) KLUCAR SR., born Nov. 4, 1926, born Cleveland, OH, attended some college as police officer Merchant Marine Upgrade School. Adj. General School in Germany. Much schooling as police officer including FBI, Photo School, Eastman Kodak and Lorain, OH Community College.

Served in the US Army, 1946-48 and US Merchant Marine 1944-46. Military locations and stations: served in MM North Atlantic in enemy action 1945. Joined Army 1946, Camp Lee, VA and then ETO. Served with US Constab. HQ and HQ Trp., Heidelburg, Germany; HQ Trp. Finance Officer Clerk, also HQ Visitors Bureau.

Discharged Jan. 12, 1948 as private first class. Battles and Campaigns: US Merchant Marine, Jan. 21, 1945, North Atlantic; their ship was torpedoed and abandoned.

Received several medals as M. Seaman Leatter of Appreciation from President Truman Re MM Service, Army Medal, Occupation, Victory, Good Conduct and Meritorious Service.

Most memorable experience: accidentally broke up a large black market ring while on assignment in Germany. Enjoyed riding and teaching riding (horseback) at Patton Barracks (Heidelburg). Took leave to Slovakia and visited his father's home and relatives there.

Married to Charlotte for 50 years and they have children: Leonard Jr.; daughter-in-law Shelda and Karen Klucar Harvey, son-in-law, Mark; grandchildren: Jeanette Klucar, Ryan and Erin Harvey.

Employed with many positions, deputy county treasurer; 26 police veteran. Presently township trustee in Turon County, OH. Retired from Lakewood Ohio Police April 1979 with 26 years service.

NEIL J. KNOPP, born Aug. 8, 1929, Oswego, NY, inducted into service Sept. 22, 1948. Military locations and stations: basic training, Ft. Dix, NJ; US Constab., I Co., 3rd Bn., 6th AC, Deggendorf; Germany and Regensburg, Germany. Medical evacuation in Valley Forge Army Hospital, PA (tuberculosis) January 1952-April 1953.

Discharged April 1953 and received the Army of Occupation Medal (Germany), National Defense Service Medal and the Good Conduct Medal.

Met future wife, Sgt. Marlene Denbrock, while he was a patient at Valley Forge Army Hospital. Married Aug. 6, 1953 in Chapel at Valley Forge Army Hospital. Married Aug. 6, 1953, in Chapel at Valley Forge. They have three children: Dr. Michael Knopp, Karen Knopp, RN and Police Sgt. Mark D. Knopp and five grandchildren.

Refrigeration, heating and air conditioning technician, Oswego Hospital, retired April 1995, due to disability.

Volunteer, Oswego Hospital, Usher, St. Paul's Church. Reading, traveling and planning for construction of his retirement home.

JOSEPH KOLNIAK, born Aug. 12, 1929, Ecorse, MI, graduated Allen Park High School and Mechanic School 1947, Bayreuth, Germany.

Joined the Army Jan. 31, 1946. Military locations and stations: February 1946, Ft. Bragg (eight weeks); Basic Field Arty., April 1946-47; Coburg, Germany, 6th Constab. Sqdn., A Trp., 1947-48; Erlangen, Schwabisch Hall Germany; 5th FA Bn., 1st Inf. Div., 1949-50, Ft. Bliss.

Discharged Jan. 30, 1950 as T/5. His awards include the Occupational Medal and WWII Victory Medal.

Memorable experiences: he was in the Honor Guard when Gen. Harmon arrived in Coburg on the Constabulary Train. They escorted the general to the 6th Const. Sqdn. Kaserne.

Married Margaret and they have children: Joseph Jr., Donna, Steven and Susan and grandchildren: Christopher, Michelle, Joseph III, Mandy, Katie, Brandy, Alicia, Margaret, Chelsey and Hunter.

Employed with Great Lakes Steel Div. of National Steel. laborer, apprentice brick layer, electrician, crane operator, electrical foreman, locomotive repair ship foreman. Retired April 1, 1989, 39 years service.

WALTER T. KOSIC, born Nov. 27, 1915, Center Twp., PA, served in the US Army December 1934 through March 1937. Military locations: Panama Canal Zone, June 1942 through May 31, 1960; Ft. Bragg; Ft. Meade on cadre 1942 to 1944.

Joined 4th Armd. Div. which became the Constab. January 1946, A Trp., 66th Constab. Sqdn., September 1947. Served in ETO and WWII.

Received all the awards given for peace time; war time; five campaigns, ETO, plus Presidential Unit Citation and and French Fourrageure.

Memorable experiences: breaking up a black market ring and solving three murders; able to visit all countries in Europe and escorting war dead after WWII.

Married Henrietta and they have children, Diana and Denise and grandchildren: Jesse, Eve and Trevor. Employed with Pennsylvania State Government as investigator. Retired US Army 1960 and from civilian employment November 1980.

WILLARD R. KRUPSKY, born Aug. 28, 1929 in Butte, ND, entered military Dec. 4, 1946 at Ft. Snelling, MN. Basic training, Ft. Bragg, NC.

From 1947-49 Germany, US Constab. 6th, attended Constabulary School at Sonthofen in Bavaria.

Korea Nov. 1, 1950-Nov. 1, 1951, 1st Cav., 70th Tank B Co. 1952 Ft. Hood, TX non-commissioned officer academy. 1952-53 returned to Germany, 2nd Armd. Div. 1953-54 stationed at Ft. Carson, CO; Camp Irvine, CA and Ft. Knox, KY. Discharged at Ft. Knox, Sept. 19, 1954.

Medals include the WWII Victory, Army of Occupation, Good Conduct, Korean Service, two Purple Hearts, four Battle Stars and other service medals and campaigns and ribbons.

He is a member of DAV, VFW, AMVETS, American Legion, US Constabulary Association and Korean Veterans (The Graybears). Worked on railroad 38 years, retired June 1, 1993 at Minot, ND.

LOUIS W. (DOCK) KUBILUS, born June 4, 1929, Dickson City, PA, joined the Army Aug. 9, 1948. Military locations and stations: basic training, Ft. Bragg, NC; 1948-1951, H Co., 2nd Bn., Augsburg, Germany; Ft. Eustis, VA; Korea, 1951-52; 73rd Tank Bn., (Korea) Co. C.

Discharged Aug. 9, 1952 as corporal. Served with the 7767 Tank Tng. CTR, Tank Crewman, AOM (Germany), KSM, w/2 BSS, UNSM.

Memorable experiences: crossing both oceans, found his Fräulein and married her.

Married Rose Bettio and they have children: Max, Walter, Thomas, Anthony, Louis Jr. and Maria and 11 grandchildren. Employed over the road as truck driver. Retired August 1992 and enjoys traveling.

ELROY T. KUCHTA SR., born Aug. 11, 1927, Milwaukee County, WI. Drafted Aug. 21, 1945. Received cavalry training at CRTC Ft. Riley, KS. Attended and graduated from radio operators school. Sent to Europe in February 1945 via Le Havre, France and sent to 3rd Army Radio School at Seckenheim, Germany. Upon graduation sent to 2nd Cav. Regt. at Freising, Germany and from there to the 66th AFA at Degerndorf. Unit was later changed to 66th Constab. Sqdn. Assigned to the radio section of H/H Trp. 1946 changed status to three year regular Army enlistment.

1948 attended German language school at Oberammergau and then transferred to the 7827/20 MIS (Military Intelligence Section). Was stationed in the Bad Rechenhall area and later in Munich.

1949 extended enlistment for one year. Sent home for discharge in May 1950. Joined (voluntarily) USAR in June 1950. In August was notified of "recall" and in September was recalled to duty. Sent to Camp Rucker, AL to train new troops. In February 1951 sent back to Europe at Karlsruhe. Served there until September 1951, sent home and was discharged October 1951. Stayed in Army Reserve until 1959.

Attained the rank of Regular Army permanent staff sergeant. Reserve master sergeant E-7 (prior to E-8 and E-9 ranks).

Those who served with him would well remember the escapades of Col. Rocky Stone and also Buck Jones.

MELVIN L. (MEL) KUHN, born June 8, 1927, New Orleans, LA, attended 7th Army NCO Academy, Munich, Gremany (circa 1951); Quartermaster School, Lengries, Germany January 1953.

Joined the US Army Aug. 11, 1948. Military locations and stations: Ft. Jackson, SC (basic); Bad Hersfeld, Germany; Schweinfurt, Germany; Bad Kissingen, Germany; Leipheim, Germany; Illesheim, Germany; Ft. Hood, TX (three times); McAllen, TX; (C Trp., 22nd Constab. and C Trp., 24th Constab. Sqdn.

Served with Constabulary, 4th Armd. Div., 2nd Armd. Div., USAR Advisory Gp. Held commands as 1st Sgt., Co. C, 508th Tk. Bn., 1SG HQ Co., 3rd Bn., 14th Cav., Co. C, 3/14th Cav.

Retired Sept. 1, 1968 as first sergeant. Awarded the Army Commendation Medal, Good Conduct Medal, six awards; Army of Occupation (Germany) and National Defense Service Medal.

Memorable experiences: nine total years in US-USSR Zone border patrol assignments. Seven total years serving as tank battalion operation sergeant. (508th Tank Bn.; 2nd MTB, 66th Armor; 1st MTB, 6th Armor; HQ Trp., 3rd Recon, Sqdn., 14th A/C.

Married to Getrud for 41 years, she died July 11, 1964. They have children: Corey Kuhn and Cindy McManus; grandchildren: Shane Tyler, Matthew Kuhn, Michael Kuhn, and Cassandra Kuhn. Employed as terminal manager for SMT Freight Lines, 21 years (Sept. 1, 1968-July 1, 1989. Retired from the Army Sept. 1, 1968 and retired from civilian employment July 1, 1989.

ELLIS R. KUNKEL, born Feb. 3, 1926 in the farm house, son lives in now. Being the last of seven boys had to stay home to do the farming as his father was working on the railroad.

In April of 1945 he got his greetings letter from the President of the US and left for the service on May 3, 1945, going through New Cumberland and on to Camp Gordon, GA. He had infantry training for the Pacific, but with President Truman using the A bomb and giving Japan other ideas, he was in the first group to go to Europe as replacement for those that were there through the war.

They left Newport News, VA, Nov. 8, 1945 on an Italian troop ship going to LeHavre, France, and then on a troop train to Bamberg, Germany, arriving there on Nov. 21, 1945. After being processed he was sent to Munich, Germany to Co. A, 97th Signal Bn., with HQ Co. being in Bamberg. Their duty was maintaining communication for 3rd Army, and at the time they were stringing wire at what had been a German ammunition depot.

They were in Munich until Feb. 14, 1946 when they were recalled to Bamberg and went to C Trp., to begin organizing the US Constab.

Among the first order of business was three truck loads of troopers going to Paris to bring back Jeeps, which was some experience by it self. Next, they went with 15 6 by 6s to Frankfurt for trailers for the Jeeps.

He was in charge of a VHF radio group setting up radio communcations, except the last two months or so he was put on repairs, repairing the carrier bays and radios.

They left Bamberg Sept. 18, 1946 for Bremerhaven for the trip home. They left Bremerhaven on September 25 for New York on the USS *Stevens* Victory Ship, arriving in New York on October 4. After going through Camp Kilmer it was on to Ft. Dix with separation date of Oct. 26, 1946.

March 22, 1947 he married Verna E. Remp and they started farming. They have a daughter, Karen and son, Terry and five grandchildren.

From 1959-1961 he served on the Farmer's Home Board and in 1962 he was nominated for directorship in the Farm Credit System, which he's still serving to date. In 1964 two positions for rural mail carrier became available. After taking and passing the test he was appointed carrier to Route #1, Kempton, PA, Jan. 16, 1965.

In 1981 his son decided he wanted to take over the farm, which meant he had to build a house and move out of the one he was born in. After being rural carrier for 28 years, he retired Jan. 2, 1993 and went back to helping on the farm. Kunkel died March 29, 1997.

CALVIN J. LANDAU, born May 2, 1927, Hazleton, PA, enlisted into Army November 1944. Commissioned Cornell University ROTC June 1947. Entered active duty October 1948 and retired March 1978.

Duties: Rutgers University, New Brunswick, NJ, ASTRP 1944-45; Cornell University, 1945-48 (ROTC); 101st Abn. Camp Breckenridge, KY 1948-49; 70th FABN Fussen & Nurenberg, Germany, 1949-52 (US Constab.); Ft. Hood, TX, 1st Armd. Div., 1952; Ft. Sill, OK, Btry. Off. Course 1953; Korea, 7th Inf. Div. Arty. 1953-54; Hong Kong Mil Attache 1953; Japan, 1st Cav. Div., 82nd FA Bn. 1954-56; Ft. Sill and Ft. Bliss, Arty. Adv. Course 1956-57; Ft. Bliss AAA Gun. Bn. and Air Defense School instructor 1957-60; Ft. Leavenworth C&GSC 1960-61; University of Miami Degree 1961-63; Oberammergau Germany, USAEUR School, ParaMilitary Action instructor 1963-64; Heidelberg, Germany, USAEUR DCSOPS DA, International and Political Affairs (Staff for Army Aviation, Psychological OPN, Special Forces and Vietnam) 1968-70; Carlisle, PA, Army War College 1970-1971; Ft. Sill, OK, CO Arty. Training Bde and Deputy Asst. Cmdt. for training and education. The Artillery School, 1971-74; Ft. Meade, MD, asst. Chief and Chief of Staff First Army 1974-78.

Awards included: Distinguished Service Medal, Legion of Merit, Soldiers Medal, Bronze Star, Air Medal w/OLC, Presidential Citation, WWII, Korean and Vietnam Service and Army Occupation Forces, Germany.

Landau married Barbara Cohen 1953 producing two daughters, and son Jeffrey (LTC Army Artillery). Following Barbara's death 1983, married Ann Honig 1985, was VP General Development Corp., Miami, FL 1978-88 and since 1988 Southeast Regional director for Cornell University with office in Miami, FL. Golf, tennis and skiing are regular sports activities.

LEO E. LANGLOIS, born March 1, 1932, Pawtucket, RI, joined the Army Sept. 14, 1949. Military locations and stations: Augsburg, Villseek and Beirut. Served with Tk. Co., 1st Bn., 2nd A/C. Held position as commander.

Retired as sergeant Dec. 19, 1952. Awarded the Germany Occupation Medal.

Married Mary Langlois and they have children: Diane Araujo, Janet Hayden and Leo Langlois; grandchildren: Matthew Hayden, Dana Hayden, Jason Langlois, Jennifer Langlois and Christopher Araujo. Employed as foreman, American Insulated wire; assistant Atlantic Ten Pin Lanes as supervisor L.G. Balfour, retired March 1, 1997.

WALTER P. LAUTE, May 15, 1928, St. Louis, MO, inducted into the US Army 1946-1948 Jefferson Barracks; USAF 1949-52. Discharged from the US Army November 1948; USAF November 1952. Military locations and stations: Ft. McClellan, AL; Wetzlar, Germany; Weilburg, Germany; Limburg, Beidenkopf, Bad Schwabach, Kastel, Augsburg, Germany; Lowry AFB, CO; Spokane, WA; Yokota AFB, Japan; Lakes Charles AFB, Lake Charles, LA.

Served with the US Constab. from 1946 until 1948. He was with D Trp., 37th Constab. Sqdn. He was stationed at Wetzlar, Weilburg, Germany. They also had duties at outposts such as Limburg, Biedenkopf, Kastel, Bad Schwabach. Duties included patrols, black market operations, working with the German police. Later he was transferred to C Trp., 42nd Constab. Sqdn. at Augsburg, Germany. He was an M-8 armor car driver, also involved in raids on suspected black market operations at DP camps. He also attended Constab. School at Sonthofen (twice). Returned to the US in November 1948. Discharged at Camp Kilmer, NJ. Joined the USAF in 1949, was involved in the Korean War 1950-51. He was tail gunner on a B-29 bomber. Flew 56 combat missions and was discharged at Lake Charles, LA November 1952. He was proud to serve in the Constabulary as well as USAF.

Awards include the WWII Victory, Army of Occupation, Air Medal w/4 OLC, Korean Service Medal w/3 Bronze Service Stars, UN Service Medal. Married and has two children. Now retired.

WILIAM J. LAWSON JR., born Dec. 8, 1926, Baton Rouge, LA, joined the USNR Dec. 5, 1944. Boot camp, San Diego, CA. Electricians School, Gulf Port, MS. Served on ammunition dump, Samar Island, Philippines. Discharged July 1946. Received commission LSU USAR (FA)

June, 1948. Assigned to 70 FABN Constab., Fussen, Germany, February 1949. Ft. Sill, OK April 1952, CO HQ Btry., FARTC. Discharged June 1, 1953. Past Post Commander VFW.

Owned and operated Jackson IGA Supermarket, Jackson, LA until Jan. 1, 1976. Owned and operated Lawson's Antiques and Lawson's Crystal by Rae. Retired January 1993. Married Rae Dawson Nov. 2, 1948 and they have three children, seven grandchildren and four great-grandchildren.

Past president (20 years), Silliman Private School Corporation; past master (five times) St. Albans #28 F&AM; Past Worthy Patron St. Albans #80 OES, 32 degree Mason Scottish Rite and York Rite, Past President Jackson Lions Club.

JAMES H. (JIM) LENKER, born Dec. 17, 1927, Millersburg, PA, attended Constabulary School, Sonthofen, Germany.

Enlisted in the Army March 13, 1946. Military locations and stations: Ft. Bragg, NC, Hersfield, Germany. Served with B Trp., 91st Constab. Sqdn. as operations clerk. Discharged Aug. 17, 1947 as corporal at Ft. Dix, NJ, Aug. 17, 1947.

Awarded the Army of Occupation Ribbon, WWII Victory, Good Conduct and Overseas Service.

Married to Anna (Leitzel) Lenker Sept. 5, 1948 and they have two sons and three grandchildren, Brian, Ashley and Erin. Retired carpenter and now has a Blue Bird trail.

WILLIAM KENNETH LEONARD, born Jan. 30, 1927, Chambersburg, PA, inducted into service July 17, 1945, Harrisburg, PA. Military locations and stations: Germany and Austria.

Awarded the Army of Occupation Medal, WWII Victory Medal. Married Betty L. Shatzer, March 15, 1947. They have three children: William Jr., David and Alison. Currently enjoys woodworking, gardening and mallwalking.

G. PHILIP (PHIL) LEVEQUE, born Feb. 21, 1928, Fredericksburg, VA. Earned BA degree in political science, Brown University.

Joined the Army July 3, 1945 and was stationed at Virginia Military Institute, Lexington, VA; Fort Bragg, NC; and 68th Constabulary Sqdn., Büdingen, Germany. He served with ASTRP Unit at VMI and 68th Constabulary Sqdn.

Discharged Aug. 20, 1947 with the rank of corporal. Awards include the WWII Victory Medal and Army Occupation Medal (Germany).

He had quite a few memorable experiences, the re-

counting of which would now be considered "politically incorrect."

Phil is married to Maxine and they have two children, George Lawrence and Sarah Anne, and grandchildren: Rachel, Stephanie, Patrick and Amanda.

Employed 21 years with the city of Richmond, VA in personnel and budgeting and 15 years with the Commonwealth of Virginia. He retired May 31, 1990.

ALFRED LEO LEVIN (See ALFRED LEO EVANS)

DAILEY F. (REBEL) LEWIS, born July 12, 1927, Turner Douglas, WV. Took basic training at Ft. Knox and then transferred to the Transportation Corp. He arrived at LeHavre, France on April 8, 1946 and was then transported to Marburg aboard the 40 & 8 train. He was then assigned to various QM Transportation Cos. and sent to Belgium, Leige and Antwerp. He was in the 3594th Trucking Co., the 76th GM car platoon among others. They wound up at the 508th Engrs. in Paris, France, where these units were deactivated.

Early in 1947 he transferred to the 13th Constab. at Bamberg. He was in HQ Co. and also C Trp. His next move was to Coburg and B Trp., 6th Sqdn. He attended Sonthofen School three times and ran border patrols and train checks.

One of the most memorable experiences he had was upon returning from a train check one night while stationed at Ludwigstat outpost. After they cleared their weapons outside and was going down to the basement to turn in their weapons, the trooper who was in charge of the arms room and had went with them on the train check for the first time, fired his 45 cal. pistol and the bullet hit him on the left heel. He had evidently pulled the slide back before removing the clip. He would like to hear from any trooper remembering this incident. Also at this same outpost, he was given a tablespoon full of pure scabie lotion that was marked cough syrup.

Incidently they were given several lessons by the lieutenant in charge on clearing weapons.

Lewis is divorced and has children: Diana, Dailey, Jr., David, Sharon, Phyllis, Gloria, Daniel; 33 grandchildren and 12 great-grandchildren. Employed as sergeant, security and maintenance with Sears.

EDWARD R. LEWIS, born July 26, 1927, Philadelphia, PA, joined the Army Sept. 19, 1945; basic training Ft. McClellan, AL. From 1946 to May 1947 US Constab., Budingen, Germany; 68th Constab. Sqdn., A Trp., September 1946 European Intelligence School. December 1946, NCO, Operations, May 1947. Discharged July 4, 1947.

Married Catherine Fonder, Nov. 21, 1953. They have two daughters and one son.

Education in Architecture Association. Partner in Architecture Office; manager of Philadelphia office July 1973-1984. May 30, 1984-May 30, 1994, architect with USN (NAVFAC).

DOMINIC P. LICASTRO, born Feb. 16, 1925, Southbridge, MA. Inducted into service Feb. 1, 1946, Worcester, MA.

Duties: US Constab. 1946-48, 820th MP Co. Military and locations: Bamberg, Heidelberg, Vainingen, Stuttgart Discharged November 1948 with the rank of T/5.

Active Reserve 1948-50 military intelligence.

Recalled to service 1950 as sergeant. Served at Ft. Holibird, MD and Ft. Bragg, NC. Discharged April 10, 1952. Appointed police officer Aug. 2, 1953. Retired February 1976 after 22 1/2 years of service.

Appointed chief of security at Harrington Memorial Hospital, Southbridge, MA 1980. Retired February 1995. Served USN Feb. 22, 1942-April 3, 1942 (medical discharge).

US Maritime service and Merchant Marine August 1943-45. (Navy medical discharge changed to regular discharge August 1945.) Enlisted US Army February 1946.

Awarded the Army Commendation Medal, Good Conduct, Army Occupation, Victory Medal and National Defense. North Atlantic War Zone - Combat Ribbon, Victory Medal (Merchant Marine). Appointed Justice of the Peace 1980 to present time.

Married Dorothy Jean Radford July 24, 1948 at Plymouth, England; daughter, Nancy (Licastro) Benoit. He has grandchildren: Justin F. Benoit and Sarah M. and Karen E. Licastro. Jr. Vice commander, VFW; Historian American Legion; past senior vice commander, Italian American War Veterans.

Hobbies include building model WWII airplanes, ceramics and traveling.

DONALD A. LIEDKE, born Sept. 13, 1927, Maywood, IL, joined Army 1945. Basic Ft. Sill, OK and Ft. Knox, KY. Duties 1945-46: France and Germany; 191st Tank Bn., 774th Tk Bn., and 778th Tk Bn. Units deactivated then 37th Constab. Sqdn. Sent to Constabulary School at Sonthofen, Germany; 94th Constab. Sqdn. Trp. C, 42nd Constab. Sqdn.

Served in various cities in France, Belgium and Germany. Bad Aibling (German Army PW Camp); Rudesheim, Weiden, Limburg, Waldsassen, etc. Returned to US in September 1948.

Reenlisted early 1949. Sent to 712th Engr. Co. at Granite City, IL until Korean War. To Japan August 1950 then to Inchon, S. Korea September 1950. Then North Korea and back to Pusan, South Korea. To Japan February 1952; US and Atlanta Army Depot, GA. Discharged September 1952.

Earned National Defense Medal, WWII Victory Medal, German Occupation Medal, Korean Service Medal w/6 Battle Stars, UN Service Medal and Distinguished Unit Emblem.

Member of Vets Groups, 191st Tank Battalion Association, 778th Tank Battalion Association, US Constabulary Association, Korean War Vets, VFW and American Legion.

Retired from International Harvestor/NAVISTAR

International after 34 years. Lives in community of Brookridge, outside of Brooksville, FL with wife, Henrietta (42 years). Has three sons, three daughters and five grandchildren.

FRANCIS V. LINARDO, discharged from the Army in June of 1947. He then proceeded to school under the GI Bill of Right. He was taking up a mechanical and electrical course in engineering, as he was attending school he took his first job with Hazeltine Electronics out in Little Neck, LI helping to design mobile radar equipment, until the Korean War in 1951. He then applied for a job at Gibbs & Co. Inc., Marine Engineers & Naval Architects and was accepted into the Electrical Div. where he worked himself up to head of lighting section. Gibbs & Co. Inc. was responsible for the design of many Navy destroyers, guided missile destroyers and auxiliary ships.

The last design he worked on was the guided missile destroyer *Arleigh Burke* (DDG-51) when "Desert Storm" came along and funds were curtailed to Gibbs & Cox Inc. He was asked to retire, just 20 days short of 40 years of service. So he retired Jan. 19, 1991 at 63 years of age.

DONALD G. LINGAFELTER *photo only, no bio submitted.*

BILLY R. LINGO, born Jan. 7, 1930, Houston, TX, raised in Sweeny, TX, joined the US Army, Sept. 7, 1948. Basic training, Ft. Jackson, SC. Arrived Weiden, Germany Dec. 24, 1948. Assigned to D Trp., 53rd Constab. Sqdn. (became 15th June 1949). Army Clerk School, Darmstadt, March-May 1949. Pers. Clk. for D Trp., at Weiden May 1949-August 1952. Pers. Sgt. Maj., August 1951-January 1952. Promoted to sergeant first class Dec. 1, 1951. Transferred to Ft. Hood, TX, March 1952. Discharged as sergeant first class, June 19, 1952. Returned to Sweeny, TN.

Employed at Phillips 66 Refinery, Old Ocean, TX, July 1952-November 1959.

Enlisted in USAFR as staff sergeant, March 12, 1955. Employed as Air Reserve technician (ART), Pers. sergeant major, November 1959-June 1966. Direct commission as captain from CMSgt (E9), June 20, 1966. Served in personnel at every level of command except HQ USAF. Promoted to colonel, July 1, 1980. Served two four year tours on active duty: Colorado, March 1977-March 1981, and at DoD, Pentagon, December 1985-January 1990. Retired Jan. 7, 1990. Total service, 38/07/07.

Married Rosemarie Gerda Szengel, Dec. 10, 1951, in Weiden. She was the cashier at the Service Club Snack Bar in the Weiden Kaserne. They have two sons, four grandchildren and one great-grandchild.

Awards include the Defense Superior Service Medal, Legion of Merit, Meritorious Service Medal w/2 OLC,

USAF Commendation Medal, USA Good Conduct Medal, USAF Outstanding Unit Award w/OLC, Army of Occupation Medal, National Defense Medal, USAF Longevity Service Award w/8 OLC, Armed Forces Reserve Medal w/2 Hour glasses and more.

President/co-owner with wife of BRALCO, Inc., dealing in commercial computer equipment.

Resides in Marietta, GA. They enjoy retirement, travel and power boating at Lake Alatoona, north of Atlanta, GA.

FRANCIS H. (FRANK) LIVERS, born Feb. 2, 1927, Owensboro, KY, Attended two years Community College, 1972-73.

Served in the Army June 8, 1945-June 6, 1954; USAF, January 1957-February 1968.

Military locations and stations: basic training Troop K, 1st Training Regt., CRTC, Ft. Riley, KS. December 1945, 78th Inf. Div., Horse Plt., Berlin, Germany; 16th Constab. Horse Plt., 1946-50; Berlin Military Post, Horse Plt. 1950-51; Ft. Custer, MI January 1952-September 1952; Korea, October 1952-February 1954; Ft. Gordan, GA, April 1954-June 1954. Wurtsmith AFB, MI, January 1957-May 1962; Sondrestrom, Greenland, June 1962-June 1963; 64th Radar Sqdn., Lewistown, MT, July 1963-January 1968.

Achieved the rank of staff sergeant and retired Feb. 1, 1968. Fought in the Korean campaign October 1952-February 1954.

Awarded the WWII Victory Medal, Army of Occupation, Berlin Airlift Device, Medal for Humane Action, Army Good Conduct, National Defense Service Medal w/ Bronze Star, Korean Service Medal w/3 Bronze Stars, United Nations Service Medal, Army Commendation Medal, Meritorious Unit Citation, AF Good Conduct w/4 Loops, AF Longevity Service Award Ribbon w/4 Bronze OLC; Air Force Small Arms Expert Marksmanship Ribbon.

Memorable experiences: Berlin Blockade; participating in horse shows between the British and French occupying forces in Berlin; Korean Prisoner Exchange (his company performed escort duty and communication.)

Married Janet M. King, March 2, 1957 and they have three daughters, six grandchildren and two great-grandchildren.

Employed in customer service, production scheduler, purchasing, shipping and receiving, inventory, machinist, molder for plastic prototype and production parts.

He holds memberships in American Legion, American Military Society, Constabulary Association, Retired Enlisted Association, American Association of Retired Persons, Fort Custer National Cemetery Honor Guard.

DONALD WILLIAM LIVINGSTON, born Dec. 10, 1928, Universal, IN, joined the Army, Oct. 19, 1945. Military locations and stations: basic training, Camp J.T. Robinson, AR, A Btry., 465 AAA Bn., Sonthofen, Germany; D&G Trp. Constabulary School, Sonthofen, Germany.

Discharged in 1948 and achieved the rank of T/5. His awards include the Army of Occupation Medal and WWII Victory Medal.

Married to Patricia Ann (Harris) Livingston and they have children: Norman, Dale, Brenda, Catherine, Gail;

grandchildren: Sherry, Heather, Robin, Trisha, Allison, Donald and Shawn.

Employed with MFG Packing Company, Long Beach, CA for 18 years; 12 years as plant foreman; Sycamore Vending, 11 years, one year as foreman. Retired 1990.

JOSEPH C. (JOE) LONDON, born March 27, 1929, Jersey Shore, PA, joined the service Sept. 18, 1946. Commissioned April 16, 1948. Military locations and stations: Aberdeen Proving Grounds, Bamberg and Coburg, Germany.

Served with Trp. A, 6th Constab. Sqdn. Discharged July 16, 1948 as T/5.

Awarded WWII Victory Medal and Army of Occupation Medal.

Memorable experiences: small arms weapons mach. 8 week.

Married Dorothy Shafer and they have children: Joseph Harold London and Jack Allen London; grandchildren: Jack Jr., Jason, Melissa, Debra and John London. Employed as electrical and electronic instructor.

RICHARD A. LOUGEE, born Oct. 22, 1928, Pittsfield, NH, enlisted April 1946, Ft. Devens, MA. Basic training, Ft. Eustis, VA. Arrived in Germany August 1946. Assigned to B Trp., 71st Constab. Sqdn., Schwabisch Hall. June 1947 71st was deactivated. It was now the 15th Constab. He was still in B Trp. 1948 transferred to 2nd ACR in Augsburg. 1949 home for discharged. Reenlisted 1952 and was assigned to 12th Ord. Bn. (SW) (1952-58); Fire Control Maintenance School, Ft. Bliss, TX, 1958-59; 43rd Missile Bn., Ft. Richardson, AK, 1959-62; 5th Missile Bn., Franklin Lakes, NJ, 1962-65; 51st Missile Bn., Ft. Hancock, NJ, 1965-67; 506th Field Depot, Vietnam, 1967-68; 19th Arty. Gp. Highlands, NJ, 1968-69. Retired in 1969.

Awarded the Bronze Star, Commendation Medal, Good Conduct Medal w/5th Award, WWII Victory, OAM, Germany, NDSM, w/OLC, RVNCM, RVNSM.

Married Ruth Hodges in 1950 and they have four sons, four granddaughter, three grandsons.

GEORGE M. LUDYNY
photo only, no bio submitted.

JAMES V. (JIM) LULLIO, born Sept. 22, 1926, New Rochelle, inducted into service Aug. 10, 1944. Military locations and stations: basic training, Camp Blanding, FL. Served in Germany, Augsburg, Bamberg, Mannheim. Early 1945-late 1946, 51st Inf., 4th Armd. Div. Returned 1947 and assigned to 42nd Constab. Sqdn., 2nd Regt. Later changed to D Co. 2nd Bn., 240 ACR. Left early 1952 for Korea; ASG to 5th RCT then transferred to 223rd Inf., 40th Div., Co. E as 1Sgt. Returned to Ft. Dix until 1960. Returned to Germany, 51st Inf., Co. D. Returned home 1963.

Retired Sept. 1, 1965 at Ft. Dix, NJ. Awards and medals include: Combat Infantry Badge, Army Commendation, Wharang Distinguished Service Medal (Korean) Army Good Conduct Europe and Korean Service Medal.

Married Erma and they have daughter, JoAnne and son, Vincent, grandson, John and granddaughters, Rebecca, Julanne and Jamie.

Semi-retired working with inmates in New Jersey's prisons teaching them to operate heavy equipment (bulldozer, loaders, backhoes and motor graders. Hobbies include playing golf and bowling.

KIT. R. LUOMA, born Nov. 4, 1930, Burton Station, OH, attended Kent State University. Joined the US Army October 1951. Military locations and stations: Ft. Sill, OK. Basic training, (Constabulary-7th Army) Budingen, Germany. Served with 517th AFA at Budingen, Germany, 1953-53; Stand-by Reserves, 1953-59.

Battles and campaigns: Army of Occupation-West Germany (1952-53).

Discharged as private first class in 1959. Awarded Army of Occupation, Good Conduct and carbine-qualifications medal.

Memorable experiences: training times at Wildflecken, Grafenwohr, and Baumholder in West Germany. The alerts of the "Fulda Pass"; patrolling near the Russian sector of West Germany; The German Beer, Schnitzel, and being a Constabulary Trooper.

Married Evelyn A. and they have children, Tracy and Kevin and grandchildren: Casey and Chelsey.

Employed at a rubber company as lab tech; landscaper; assembler; metal fabricator; township trustee. Involved in his community. Retired December 1991.

JOHN M. (JO JO) LUONGO, born Sept. 15, 1931, Brooklyn, NY, received a BS major accounting, June 1962. Joined the Army, Oct. 1, 1948. Military locations and stations: Fritzlar and Fulda Germany.

Served with 14th Armd. Cav., HQ & HQ Co., (RCT) as MSG Center Chief. Discharged June 21, 1952 as Corporal.

Luongo is single and employed as chief internal auditor ITT Rayonier. Retired Nov. 24, 1974, disability.

DONALD P. (DYNK) LYNK, born June 5, 1926 Hudson, NY. Attended Morrisville Ag & Tech, Gen'l Electricity.

Joined the Army Nov. 4, 1944. Military locations and stations: Camp Blanding, FL; Inf., basic 1944-45; 106th Inf. Div. Spec. Forces, 106th Recon. Sqdn., France-Belgium 1945. Served 3rd Armd. Div., 83rd Armd. Recon., 1st Armd. Div. Command held: 81st Armd. Recon. Trp., 141st Signal Co.

Discharged Aug. 31, 1946 as tech. fourth grade. Battle and campaigns: Battle of Bulge, European Theatre of Operations.

Memorable experiences: after WWII, the 106th Inf. Div. engaged in the largest operation ever assigned to a unit its size. Headquartered at Bad Ems, Germany, the screening of 950,000 German POWs were handled and 9,000 prisoners a day discharged. Transported by truck and rail to all parts of the American Occupation Zone. Also redeployed thousands of displaced persons back to their communist 1st countries, which they had fled.

In charge of the motor pool and message center at Bad Mergentheim, one of his drivers in Frankfurt reported to him, he had been struck in a safety zone at an intersection by Gen. Patton's chauffer, which resulted in Patton's death. The chauffer was speeding in a safety zone and struck the 6x6 in the side. Gen. Patton suffered a broken mech. Patton's white bulldog and the chauffer were unharmed.

Awarded the Purple Heart, Army Good Conduct, American Campaign, European Theatre of Operations, WWII Victory, Occupation Medal, WWII Battle of Bulge, Commemorative Victory in Europe, Commemorative WWII Commendation Unit Citation, 106th Inf., Liberation of France Medal.

Married to Elizabeth Lynk and has children: Donna Sue Campion; Scott Preston, Gary and Gregg (twins). Grandchildren: Katie Jones, Courtney, Moriah, Morgan, and Colin Lynk. Employed in construction 1950-61; Self-employed, 1961-88, Lynk Construction Co., company owner. Lynk Gravel Pit, 1988-98. Retired December 1988, but still working.

LOUIS ALLISON LYNN, born July 1, 1931 in Brookport, IL, enlisted in regular army July 11, 1948. Basic training, Ft. Knox, KY. Duties include 16th Constab., Berlin Germany, Korea 38th Inf., 2nd Inf. Div., Ft. Campbell, KY, 2048 ASU, Ft. Riley, KS and Bamberg, Germany, 10th MP Co., 10th MT Div., Bamberg, Germany, 7th Army, 42nd Inf. Scout Dog. Plt., Ft. Campbell, KY, 502nd A/B Regt. (101st A/B Div., Ft. Bragg, NC; 10th Special Forces Gp., Anchorage, AK; A Co., A/B 6th Inf. Regt., Vietnam 8th Cav. (A/B) 1st Cav. Div., Ft. Campbell, KY drill instructor 2038th Tk. Bn., Korea Korean Military Advisory Gp. Capital Rock Div.

Lynn retired March 1, 1969, received several medals during his career, including Bronze Star, Good Conduct w/OLC, Purple Heart, Master Parachute Badge Infantry Badge w/star and various other awards.

Married Lenora M. Bennett March 1970; they have two sons, two daughters and six grandchildren. He is National vice-commander (west) US Constabulary Association; member VFW Lynn likes to garden and read.

HILSON L. MACDONALD, born May 10, 1924, Thornton, NH joined US Army Dec. 14, 1945, basic training, Ft. Knox, KY.

Duties: US Constab. May 18, 1946 to May 1951 at 35th Constab., Fussen, Germany later renamed 2nd Armd. Cav., Bamburg, Germany then to 1st Armd. Div., Ft. Hood, TX, then back to Germany Frescaty AF; Mannheim, Germany then to Infantry School, Ft. Benning, GA; 3rd Inf. Div.,

Kitzingen, Germany back to infantry school, Ft. Benning; 7th Army Training Center, Grafenwohr, Germany; Ft. Hamilton, NY retirement June 1, 1966.

Married to Hoko Weikle, Oct. 18, 1980. Belongs to VFW, American Legion and US Constabulary Association. Presently retired.

JULIUS W. MAGASICH, born Philadelphia, was the son of the late Joseph J. Magasich and Mary P. Klobcar. A graduate of Ridley Township High School, he was employed as a bus driver by the Greyhound Bus Co. for 28 years before his retirement in 1984.

A US Army veteran of WWII, he was a member of the Herbert Best Post 928, Veterans of Foreign Wars of Folsom, and Our Lady of Perpetual Help Catholic Church, Morton.

He died July 3, 1996 and is survived by a brother, Emerick Magasich; two sisters, Dolores M. Sprohar; Mary A. Collins; an aunt, Milka Yuric and several neices and nephews.

FIELDING R. MAGNESS, born Nov. 17, 1925, Plainfield, OH. Discharged Oct. 31, 1965 as SFC E-7.

Military locations and stations: 63rd Inf. Div., ETO 1944-45; B Trp., 12th Constab. Sqdn, 1946-47; 24th Inf. Div., Korea 1950-51; France 1953-54; Eniwetok Proving Grounds, 1957; Heidelburg Germany 1961-63 various stateside posts.

Awarded ETO Ribbon w/3 Battle Stars and Korean w/6 Battle Stars, Combat Infantry Badge two awards, Bronze Star, Purple Heart, three awards, Presidential Unit Citation w/3 awards, Korean Presidential Unit Citation, Army Commendation, Good Conduct, Army Occupation, Victory, National Defense, American Campaign and UN Medal.

Married to Elizabeth J. Jan. 18, 1953 and they have a son, William J. and grandchildren, Alicia and Lindsay.

REV. JOSEPH MALONEY JR., born Nov. 5, 1931, Wilkes-Barre, PA. Entered military service Aug. 15, 1946, age 14 and served in the USAAC, 1946-48.

From 1949-51, Straubing, Germany, US Constab., 6th Armd. Cav., HHC; Ft. Polk, LA, 1952-53; 7th Inf. Div. in Korea, 1953-54; 526th AAA Msl. Bn., Ft. Hancock, NJ, 1954-56, 11th Armd. Cav., Landshut, Germ, 1956-57; Ft. Jackson, SC and Ft. Knox, KY, 1957-62; Korea DMZ, 1st Cav., 1962-63; Ft. Belvoir, VA, 1963-65; advisor, 10th Vietnamese Inf. in Vietnam, 1965-66, Ft. Dix, NJ, 1966-67.

Retired Dec. 31, 1967, as sergeant first class and holds two Combat Infantry Division Badges, Bronze Star, Commendation Medal and other service medals and campaigns and ribbons. Member, DAV, VFW, US Constabulary Association and Korean Veterans.

Education includes Licentiate in Theology, 1979; M Div., 1983; Episcopal Theological Seminary, Lexington, KY; BS in public administration (cum laude), Upper Iowa University, 1983. He was a rector, Holy Cross Episcopal Church, Wilkes-Barre, PA, when he retired due to disability in April 1989.

The Rev. Maloney passed away in 1995 and is survived by his wife Joan Dolores, two sons, two stepsons, two daughters, 10 grandchildren, and one great-granddaughter.

ANTHONY (TONY) MALVASO, born July 24, 1927, Rochester, NY, served in the US Army 1945-46 at Ft. Dix, NJ; Ft. Knox, KY and Camp Stoneman, CA. Re-entered the US Army in 1949 and sent to Japan. In November 1950 was sent to Korea and assigned to the 9th Inf. Regt., 2nd Inf. Div. Wounded in December 1950 and again in January 1951. Returned to the front lines both times. Participated in the major campaigns of Chinese Intervention 1950. Operation Killer, Chinese spring offensive 1951, Bloody Ridge and Heartbreak Ridge.

During Operation Killer his patrol was cut off and surrounded, for two weeks they lived on rice found at a small village and water melted from snow. A tank column broke through to retrieve them. Returned to the US in December 1951. Sent to Ft. Hood, TX serving with the 1st Armd. Div. In 1952 was sent to Germany and assigned to the US Constab., 2nd Armd. Cav. Regt., H Co., 2nd Bn., at Amberg, West Germany. Did border patrol duty on the Czechoslovakian/West Germany border at Weiden, West Germany.

Awarded the WWII Victory Medal, two Purple Hearts, Commendation Medal, Presidential Unit Citation twice, Korean Presidential Citation, Korean Service Medal, United Nations Medal, Army of Occupation Japan and Germany, Good Conduct Medal, Combat Infantry Badge and National Defense Medal. Discharged in 1954. Married Jo Ann Dalia and has one son and one daughter. Is retired from Eastman Kodak Company and resides in Rochester, NY.

PAT MANCINELLI, born March 25, 1928 NYC, military locations and stations: February 1946, Ft. Monmouth. Military locations and stations: Ft. Knox, 1st Constab., Rothwestern Germany, Service Trps.

Awarded Sharpshooter Medal, ETO Medal and Good Conduct.

Married and has five children and eight grandchildren. Retired as owner of printing business.

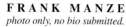

FRANK MANZE
photo only, no bio submitted.

EDWARD F. MARCHESI, born June 16, 1927, East Boston, MA, joined the US Army Aug. 2, 1945. Military locations and stations: Ft. Knox, KY; Rothweston, Germany; numerous other German cities: Kassel, Eichenberg, Witzenhausen.

Served with US Constab. C Trp., 11th Sqdn., 1946-47. Discharged Feb. 22, 1947 as private first class and received the WWII Victory Medal.

Memorable experiences: great education, especially at Eichenberg Railway Station.

Married June Marchesi and they have children: Edward Jr., John, Michael and Marianne; grandchildren: David, JoAnna, Matthew, Mickey, Jordan, Michelle and John. Employed as mechanic and retired Dec. 31, 1989.

JAMES A. (JIM) MARINELLI, born Nov. 1, 1927 in Laurium. Joined the USN Nov. 1, 1944. Military locations and stations: USS *AE Anderson,* Berlin.

Awarded the American Campaign, Asiatic-Pacific Campaign, EAME, WWII Victory Medal, Army of Occupation, Berlin, Humane Action, Good Conduct, Philippine Liberation Ribbon and Presidential Unit Emblem.

He is divorced and is carpenter. Retired July 5, 1974.

MARVIN E. (MARTY) MARTIN, born May 5, 1927, Bedford County, VA, received an associate of science degree, two years college.

Basic training: Aberdeen Proving Grounds, MD, September 1945-December 1945; Advanced training, Atlanta Ord. Depot, January 1946-February 1946; 81st Constab. Sqdn., Fulda, Germany March 1946-October 1947; 2104 ASU A.P. Hill Military Reservation, Fredericksburg, VA; October 1950-December 1951; Conarc HQ, Ft. Monroe, VA, May 1958-November 1961; Armish/MAAG Teheran, Iran November 1961-January 1961; Ft. Bliss, TX, June 1965-March 1966; 55th Avn. Yongson, Korea March 1966-April 1967; Instructor Avn. School, Ft. Rucker, AL, April 1967-April 1968; warrant officer, Co. A, Hunter Field, GA, July 1968-August 1969; supply officer, 610 Trans. Co. RVN September 1969-August 1970; supply officer, 1st Maint. Bn., Hunter Field, GA, October 1970-November 1971; Maintenance officer, Components Repair Chief, Co. A, 1st USATC Corpus Christi, TX and RVN November 1971-December 1972; supply officer, DMMC Ft. Bragg, NC, January 1973-May 1977; May 31, 1977-retirement as chief warrant officer 3.

Awarded the Bronze Star Medal, Meritorious Service Medal, Army Commendation Medal, Army Good Conduct Medal w/2 loops, WWII Victory Medal, WWII Occupation Medal, National Defense Service Medal, Armed Forces Expeditionary Medal, Vietnam Service Medal w/Silver Service Star, Vietnam Campaign Ribbon, RVN Gallantry Cross w/Palm, Army Presidential Unit Citation, Army Meritorious Unit Citation, Republic of Vietnam Gallantry Cross w/Palm Unit Citation, Senior Aircraft Crewman Badge.

Married to Daniele and they have children: Michael, Dayna, Terrie and Lance and grandchildren: Chelsea, Hannah, Curtis and Shane. Employed as assistant professor, Emory Riddle Aeronautical University. Retired May 1990.

MAURICE (PAT) MARTIN, born March 30, 1931, Boston, MA, joined the Massachusetts National Guard, 101st Inf. Div., Yankee Div., 1947-49; joined the Army Nov. 23, 1949, attended basic training, Ft. Dix, NJ, 39th Inf. Div. Military locations and stations: Schweinfurt, Bad Kissingen, Germany. Served with E Co., 2nd BLT, 14th Armd. Cav. Regt., 7th Army, tank commander. Discharged March 5, 1953 as sergeant. Awarded the Good Conduct Medal, Army of Occupation, Germany.

Memorable experiences: to be stationed and serve with a good group of men, during his military service. He still thinks of them, bless them all.

Married to Dorothy L. Martin and they have children: Bruce, David, Martin, Susan Carrol Valleary and grandchildren: Jennifer Martin, Eric and Edward Valleary, Joseph Spatafore. Employed with Cambridge YMCA, Cambridge, MA, building and property manager. Retired Nov. 4, 1994.

JULIUS TAFT (J.T.) MASSEY, born Oct. 25, 1908, Tyler, TX, joined the US Army January 1944. Military locations and stations: 716th Railway Operation Bn.; 6981st Inf. Rifle Co; 42nd Constab. Sqdn. D Trp.

Served all duty in the ET of operations. Discharged January 1947 as sergeant. While in the 6981st Inf. Rifle

Co., the unit received three Bronze Stars, Good Conduct Medal, Marksman Rifleman.

He had seven children: Frances, Charles, Jerry, John, Eleanore, Vickey and Nickey; grandchildren: Glenn, Melissa, Linda, Larry, Lucy, Lydia, Mark, Ben, Phillip, John, Jr., Kenneth, Sharon, Steve and Jeff. Employed as Merchant Marine, truck driver and taxi driver. Massey was killed Jan. 4, 1960 by unknown assailant.

WILLIAM F. MASSEY, born Oct. 3, 1927, Hartsville, TN, attended University of Tennessee in 1951. Joined the Infantry Sept. 18, 1946. Military locations and stations: Ft. Oglethorpe, GA, October 1946-January 1947; HQ Trp., 28th Constab. Sqdn., Schweinfurt, Germany, February 1947-December 1947. Served with HQ Trp., 28th Constab. Sqdn.

Discharged Jan. 20, 1948 as private first class. Awarded the Army of Occupation Medal and WWII Victory Medal. Memorable experiences: 100 mile march.

Massey is widowed and has daughters, Sheila and Lita and grandchildren: Lauren, Lindsey, Thomas and Candice. Employed as postmaster, Hartsville, TN from 1966-1988. Retired Jan. 2, 1988.

A.J. MASTRIANNI, inducted in 1945. Basic training FA, Ft. Bragg, NC. Arrived LeHavre, France, in 1946. Immediately assigned 2nd Constab. Regt. in Freising, Germany. Reported to Service Trp., Transportation Plt. Became a special transient driver with most of his duties on TDY. Traveled extensively all over Allied Zones, transporting materials, and personnel in Jeeps and trucks. Was discharged in 1947 and joined the 309th Transportation Bn. Ready Reserve during the Korean War. Separated in 1953 with the rank of master sergeant, battalion supply sergeant.

He's a former general aviation pilot. Was the only fixed wing pilot in the Reserve Battalion. Turned down rotary wing training offered him. Became a member of the Civil Air Patrol flying many missions on search and rescue over land and sea. Became a squadron commander and retired with the rank of major.

He's a retired chairman of the Conservation Commission, Town of Plainville, CT, having served 25 years. Also was a conservation officer for 35 years. Member of the American Legion and life member of the VFW. Former commander of Outpost I, US Constabulary Association.

JAMES ORLANDO MATHIS, born June 23, 1931, Tuckerton, NJ; received his wings as an Aircraft Spotter 1945, enlisted in the RA, US Constab., Sept. 27, 1948; basic training, Ft. Dix, NJ.

Assignments: US Constab.: HH&Svc. Trp., 53rd and 15th Sqdns., US Constab. NCO Academy Munich, HQ & HQ, 6th Armd. Cav. Border Patrol, Weiden, Regensburg, Cham, and Regen, Germany; January 1954, Ft. Bragg, NC, Special investigator, PM Sect., December 1955, Ft. Dix, NJ, 716th MP Bn.; August 1956 First Army HQ, Governors Island, NY, NY, CID; July 1957 The USAADS, Ft.

Bliss, TX; October 1960, D Btry., 3rd Msl. Bn., 71st Arty., Germany; September 1963, A Btry., and HQ, 2nd Bn. (HERC), 52nd Arty., HAFB, FL; February 1968, C Btry., 5th Bn., (HERC), 56th Arty., IN; March 1970, A Btry., 4th Bn., (HERC), 1st Arty., MD.

Retired March 1, 1971. Received three Army Commendation Medals, Army of Occupation Medal, National Defense Service Medal w/BSS, and other medals, ribbons, badges etc.

Married Hedy K.F. Feilner, Aug. 17, 1954 in Weiden, Germany. They have two sons and two grandchildren. He is also a retired computer analyst/programmer.

JAMES A. MCCABE, born Aug. 21, 1928, Brockton, MA, attended University of Maryland and West Virginia University, accounting courses and Dept. of State Foreign Service Institute (Czech Language - one year course).

Served US Army, February 1946-December 1948 (17 years old); US Air Force, October 1949-December 1966 (retired).

Military locations and stations: 51st Constab. Sqdn., Passau and Landshut (Germany) (1946-48); MATS Haneda AB, Tokyo, Japan (1950); DO #8 USAF OSI, Seoul, Korea (1951); MAAG Italy, US Embassy, Rome, Italy (1953-57); Asst. Air Attache, US Embassy, Prague, Czech (1960-62); HQ USAFE, Wiesbaden, Germany (1963-65); AFROTC Det., West Virginia University (1966).

Battles and Campaigns: United Nations Summer-Fall Offensive and Second Korean Winter.

Awards and Medals: several medals to include WWII Victory Medal, Army of Occupation Medal for Germany and Japan, UN Service, Korean Service Medal w/2 Bronze Service Stars and the Rep of Korea Presidential Unit Citation.

Memorable experiences: 1. 51st Sqdn. S-2 monthly liaison visits to US Military Govt. offices located in Southern Bavaria to receive information regarding intelligence and blackmarketing activities in area of jurisdiction; MAAG Italy duties for the training of Italian AF pilots in the US; Asst. Air Attache, Prague, Czech.

Married Patricia Marshall, May 8, 1954 in St. Peter's Basilica, Rome, Italy.

Employed with the US Navy Air Systems Command, Washington, DC as inventory manager for the Air-to-Air Sparrow Missile and Surf-to-Air BPDMS missile for period 1967-83. Retired as GS-12 on Aug. 21, 1983.

TOM PORTER MCCLENAHAN, born June 23, 1930, Quinton, OK. Enlisted Regular Army July 22, 1948. Served in Constab. with I Co., 3rd Bn., 14th A/C (1948-52). Discharged as SFC. Entered Navy 1954 and commissioned ensign and designated a naval aviator at Corpus

Christi, TX, 1956. Involved in eight operational deployments to the Western Pacific, Southeast Asia and Mediterranean areas between 1957 and 1972. Served as CO of Carrier Airborne Early Warning Sqdns. 120 and 125, as well as commander, Carrier Airborne Early Warning Wing Twelve.

Awarded bachelor of science degree from the Naval Postgraduate School and master of science in International Affairs from George Washington University. Graduate of the Naval War College and the Industrial College of the Armed Forces. Retired from Navy at NAS Norfolk, VA, Aug. 1, 1980. Currently resides in Virginia Beach with his wife, Zara. They have two sons and three grandchildren.

JIMMIE R. MCGAUGH, born March 10, 1929, Drew, MS, joined the Army Nov. 7, 1945. Military locations and stations: Ft. Knox, 25th Mech. Cav. Sqdn., 11th Armd. Cav. Regt., Regensburg, Germany; Ft. Hood, TX; 72nd Tk. Bn., 2nd Inf. Div., Korea. Served with MP Co., Ft. Meade, MD; C Co., 722 MP Bn., Korea. Held commands as squad leader, platoon sergant, CO oper. sergeant, security sergeant, France.

Battles and campaigns: Bronze Medal, Korea, Good Conduct Medal w/4 Loops, Occupation Ribbon, Germany and Korean Service Medal, Bronze Star, Exp. Marksman Badge.

Memorable experiences: being on Czech border when Czech changed to Communist.

Married to Wladislawa and they have children: Jim Jr., John R. and Jill R.; grandchildren: Jennifer, Stephie, Jaime, Johna, Jillian, Johnnie, Jake Robert. Employed as Sr. guard inst. (in charge of) for all commissioned and non-commissioned officers of University of Texas, Police Houston. Retired March 1, 1996 (Army); Sept. 1, 1987 (University of Texas).

EARL F. MCGILL, born Oct. 16, 1927, Louisville, KY, joined the Army Jan. 23, 1946. Military locations and stations: Wetzlar, Germany. Served with Med. Det. 3rd Constab. Regt.

Discharged July 17, 1947 as T/5. Awarded Army of Occupation Medal and WWII Victory Medal.

Memorable experiences: playing football and baseball. Visits to Frankfort, Heidelburg and Bad Neuheim in Germany. Reunion with five buddies in Louisville, KY in 1994 having not seen each other since 1947.

Married 48 years September 1977 to Doris M. McGill and they have sons, Gary L. McGill and John C. McGill; grandchildren: Kristen, Brian, Jennifer and Madalene. Self-employed, had a bakery distributorship. Served the commissary at Ft. Knox, KY. Retired January 1986.

ROBERT L. (BOB) MCGRAW, born Oct. 15, 1924, Grant County, IN, joined the Army December 1945. Military locations and stations: Ft. Knox, KY; Bamberg, Heidelberg, Germany. Served with 820 MP Co., as desk sergeant.

Discharged April 1948 as sergeant. Awarded the WWII Victory Medal, Germany Occupation and European Medal.

Married to Arlene and they have a son, James and daughter, Sherry; granddaughter, Natalie; grandson, Kevin. Employed with General Motors Corp., assistant supt., production control. Retired August 1983.

GERARD E. (JERRY) MCKENNA, born Nov. 27, 1927, Providence, RI, received BS Providence College 1951; Extension Courses RIC. Joined US Army Jan. 28, 1946. Military locations and stations: Ft. Devens, MA; Ft. Bragg, NC; Ft. Dix, NJ; Camp May, Degerndorf, Germany. Served with 66th Constab. Unit.

Discharged April 26, 1947 as T4 and received the WWII Victory Medal and ETO Medal.

Married to Mary E. and they have children: Gerard E. II, William M., James J., Maureen A., Kathleen T., Kevin P., John L. Employed with United Aircraft as tabulator tech, Gilbane Building, accountant. JJ Gregory NE district salesman. Retired Jan. 30, 1990.

MARVIN EARL MCKINNEY, born June 8, 1927, Cincinnati (Hamilton County) OH, enlisted in the Regu-

lar Army June 26, 1949; basic training, Ft. Jackson, SC.

Attended Potential Leadership School (PLS) at Ft. Jackson, SC 1948. Assigned as cadreman with Svc. Btry 19th FA Bn. for one cycle of basic training. Departed for Camp Kilmer, NJ in November 1948. Left for Germany aboard the USAT *General Darby.* After processing at Marburg, Germany was assigned to 2nd Constab. Bde. (2d Dragoons) at Augsburg, Germany. Left Augsburg and joined what was then the 91st FA Bn., at Sonthofen, Germany (later redesignated as 519th FA Bn.). Upon returning The Burg at Sonthofen to the German control, the 519th moved to Babenhausen Germany where they lived in tents until the Kaserne was completed. Departed Germany aboard the USAT *Rose* in December 1952 and was assigned to 31st Inf. Div. (Dixie) at Camp Atterbury, IN. Moved to HQ, 5th Army on departure of 31st Div. for Ft. Carson, CO. Discharged at Camp Atterbury, IN in March 1954.

Reentered service Jan. 21, 1955, Ft. Jackson, SC and assigned 516th Abn. Bde, 101st Abn. Div., Ft. Jackson. Transferred to 757th FA Bn., 18th Abn. Bde., Ft. Bragg, NC in October 1955. Assigned to Civilian Component Duty in Raleigh, NC with North Carolina Military District in March 1956. Departed Raleigh, NC and assigned to HQ Btry., 50th AAA Bn. (AW) (SP), Inchon, Korea. Returning to CONUS in December 1957 assigned to 9135 SU at Ft. Lee, VA which was later consolidated with Ft. Lee Post and redesignated the 5435 SU. Departed Ft. Lee, VA in August 1959 and sailed for Germany aboard the SS *Atlantic* and assigned to HQ Co., 68th Armor Bn. (Later redesignated 64th Armor Bn.). After four years with the 68th/64th was assigned to the Adjutant General School at Ft. Benjamin Harrison, IN as an MOS test developer in NRTD.

Levied from Ft. Benjamin he was assigned to Enlisted Personnel Directorate at the Pentagon where his responsibilities was with the build up of forces in Vietnam. Departing the Pentagon was assigned to the 9th Medical Center as personnel sergeant major at Heidelberg Germany later transferred to HQ, USAREUR and 7th Army at NCOIC Personnel Actions Div. Left Heidelburg in 1970 and was assigned 6th Army HQ at Presideo of San Francisco in the Operations Div. Left 6th Army in 1971 and was assigned to Vietnam arriving in Long Binh. Returning to CONUS was assigned to Brooke Army Medical Center at Ft. Sam Houston, TX. Left Ft. Sam Houston and assigned to Enlisted Personnel Directorate, Washington, DC where he became sergeant major of the directorate. Retired as CSM in April 1975.

Received four awards of the Army Commendation Medal, two Awards of Meritorious Service Medal and the Bronze Star; Occupation Medal Germany; National Defense Service Medal w/OLC; Vietnam Campaign Medal w/3 Combat Stars; Good Conduct Medal w/7 loops, three Overseas Hash Marks.

Married the beautiful Marianne Heidl (deceased) in Babenhausen Germany, Aug. 8, 1952. They have one son, Kenneth and two grandchildren, Jeremy and Jessamy.

Life member of VFW; member of US Constabulary Association; member of 50th AAA Bn. Association; member of American Legion.

JOHN C. MCLAUGHLIN, born March 2, 1930, Pittsburgh, PA, entered military service March 3, 1947; basic training, Ft. Bragg, NC.

Duties: assigned to Ft. Mason, San Francisco, CA in 1947, where he served aboard USAT *General E.T. Collins, General Eltinge* and the hospital ship *Hope* as a

medical technician; transported troops and dependents to Guam, Okinawa, Philippines, China, Japan and Korea. From 1948-52, Augsburg and Amberg, Germany, US Constab., 2nd Armd. Cav. 1953-54; Ft. Knox, KY; Ft. Benning, GA (jump school) later assigned to 11th Abn. Div., Ft. Campbell, KY. 1955-64 enlisted in USAF as pararescue technician and survival instructor. Assignments included Guam, Newfoundland, Azores and United Kingdom. Medically retired from USAF 1964 due to injuries sustained from a parachute jump.

1964-86: employed by City of Pittsburgh Police Department. 1964-69 patrol officer. 1970-86 assigned to Investigations Branch and promoted to detective. Assignments: Organized Crime Section, Federal Strike Force and Homicide Section. Retired April 4, 1986.

1986-present: Does volunteer work, travels, reads, is a private pilot, uses computer and searches for former service friends.

JOEL A. (MAC) MCLEAN, born June 17, 1927, Dunedin, FL. Received master's degree plus postgrad, psychology. University of Florida.

Joined the Army Sept. 22, 1945 and again Sept. 31, 1951. Commissioned Oct. 12, 1951. Military locations and stations: Passau, Germany (Constab.) Rank T-4 (2) Camp (now fort or vice versa) Rucker, Dothan, AL. Served with 51st Constab. Sqdn.; 47th Inf. (Viking) Div.; heavy weapons platoon. Discharged March 13, 1947 and Dec. 11, 1957 as first lieutenant.

Memorable experiences: duties as MP unit in Passau-patrols, traffic control, desk sergeant; instructing recruits in 4.2 mm mortar operation.

Married to Jacqueline and they have children: David Bruce McLean, Eric Joseph King and granddaughter, Erin Gayle King. Employed as director, Psychology Department, Sunland Center at Ft. Myers, FL. Retired April 30, 1982.

ROBERT A. (MAC) MCLELLAN, born Sept. 29, 1929, Boston, MA, educated as architectural designer. Joined the US Army Oct. 15, 1946; Sept. 27, 1940. Military locations and stations: Ft. Knox; Ft. Campbell; Ft. Dix; Budigen, Germany; Augsberg, Germany; Ft. Kobbe, Canal Zone. Served with 68th Constab., Germany 33rd Inf. Regt.. Canal Zone.

Discharged Aug. 20, 1948 and Sept. 19, 1951. His awards include the WWII Victory Medal, Army Occupation Medal, Good Conduct Medal, Marksman Badge w/ Rifle Bar and Korean War.

Memorable experiences: baseball, 68th Constab. Sqdn., two years short stop, travel Ansbach Radio School basketball team, Ft. Kobbe (ET Company) baseball (champs).

Married Joan M. McClellan and they have children: Robert M., Thomas J., Paul R. and Stephen and grandchildren: Nathan, Jared, Robert, Stephen and Amy. Employed as self-employed.

GEORGE H. MCNEW, born Sept. 17, 1931, Fayetteville, PA. Joined the service Feb. 1, 1950, Armored. Military locations and stations: Ft. Dix, NJ; Augsburg, Germany; Bamberg, Germany; Baumholder, Germany. Served with 9th Inf. Div., 2nd A/C Constab.; 29th Heavy Tk. Held command as Bat. 2nd Armd. Div.

Discharged September 1952 as staff sergeant. Memorable experiences: Fulda Gap (TK 33); M/Sgt. Ryder, Sgt. Morgan, Cpl. Malpica and Pvt. Rollins.

Married to Dot J. McNew and they have children, Sharon Shipp, Keith and Kevin and grandchildren: Ryan Shipp, Seth, Ethan and Garreth McNew. Employed with United Telephone Company of Pennsylvania, US Sprint, cable splicer and cable supervisor for 40 years. Retired March 1993.

JOHN J. MEGYESI, born Aug. 23, 1932, Toledo, OH. Joined the Army, September 1949.

His military locations and stations: 1948, Camp Lejeune, NC, basic training; 1949, Ft. Knox, KY, basic training; 1950, Ft. Benning, GA, 703rd Ord Co., 1950 Sonthofen, Germany, 519th FA Bn., 1951 Kaufburn, Germany, 18th Engr. Bn., SP 24th Constab., 1951, Fulda, Germany, 18th Engr. Bn. SP, 24th Constab., 1951, Bad Hersfeld, Germany, 18th Engr. Bn. SP, 24th Constab.; 1953 Hurst, Germany, 317th Engr. Bn., A Co., 1953 Frankfurt, Germany, HQ Co V Corps; 1955, Ft. Knox, KY, 341st Trans. Co.; 1955, Ft. Knox, KY, 522nd Armd. Eng. Co., 1956, Ft. Knox, KY, HQ & HQ Co. School Troops; 1957 Keflavik, Iceland, HQ Icelandic Defense Force NATO; 1958, Ft. Myer, VA, HQ Btry., 19th Arty. Gp. (AD); 1959, Selfridge AFB, MI; HQ Btry., 28th Arty. Gp. (AD); 1960, Ladd AFB, AK, 18th Engr. Co., (CONST); 1960, Ft. Wainwright, AK; UAS Spt. COMD Supply Det. 1870-1; 1960, Ft. Wainwright, AK, HQ & HQ Yukon Command; 1963, Ft. Hood, TX, A Co., 501st S & T Bn., 1st Armd Div.; 1963, Ft. Hood, TX, HQ & HQ Co., and Band 1st Spt. Command 1st AD; 1965, Ft. Monroe, VA, HQ Co., USCONARC Spt Element; 1966 Phu Loi, Vietnam, HQ Trp 1st Sqd 4th Cav. 1st Div.; 1967, Ft. Monroe, VA, HQ Co. USCONAR Spt Element; 1969, Mannhiem, Germany, HHC 1st Support Bde; 1972, Ft. Hood, TX, Ret.

His awards include the Bronze Star, Army Commendation w/3OLCs, Army of Occupation, Germany, Good Conduct w/7 knots, three Vietnam Medals.

Memorable experiences: assigned to Icelandic Defense Force NATO Base Keflavik, Iceland where the wind never stops blowing.

Employed as computer operator Fairbanks MUS, state of Alaska Department of Public Safety, Fairbanks; Bechtel Inc., field buyer, purchasing agent, senior field buyer; Alyeska PSC, Camp Warehouse supervisor; ITT/ASI inventory spec. Barrow, AK; Frontier Flying, cargo manager; Jackovich, IN, inside sales, Fairbanks, AK; materials manager, wholesale supervisor; Samson Hardware, inside sales, manager Samson Mini Store, Jackovich, IN, materials manager.

Married Nina and they have children: Lesleyann, Helena and John B and grandchildren: Tyler, Conner, Duane Joseph and Emma.

EDWARD H. MIDDLEKAUFF, born Nov. 16, 1929, Pt. Pleasant, NJ, entered military service Oct. 18, 1948, age 19. Basic training and Leadership School with 17th Abn. Div., Cadre, Camp Pickett, VA.

Arrived overseas at Bremerhaven March 1949 and assigned to HQ Trp., 2nd Constab. Bde., Munich, Germany, as a staff car driver for Brig. Gen. Bruce C. Clarke. This assignment took him to most of the cities and units assigned to 2nd Bde. Since Gen. Clarke was a skilled armor tactician he was a combat ready general given to training his troops and "being there" for tank operations. This kept him moving all over Bavaria trying to be where his staff wanted me next.

Later reassigned by request to the Brigade S-1 Section and later assumed the role of personnel sergeant. Remained in this position thoroughout the existence of the 2nd Bde, USC.

Was in on setting up the initial personnel work for the NCO Academy attended by so many troopers. Played a role on support for boards called for all types of proceedings.

Returned stateside and joined the Inspector Generals Staff, Army Transportation Corps, Ft. Eustis, VA.

Discharged July 15, 1952, Indiantown Gap, PA. Service medals include the Army Good Conduct and Army of Occupation (Germany). Member VFW and US Constabulary Association.

Married Shirley Marie Schmidt, July 25, 1953 and they have two daughters, four grandsons and one granddaughter.

Chaplain, Outpost Two and former National Recruiting Officer, US Constabulary Association.

Studied electronics, Devry Institute and entered the electronics field in sales, management and later managed industrial/commerical corporate branches. Finally resigned general manager position went back to sales and then retired.

Hobbies include: creative art painting, sculpture, writing social/political critiques, and collecting pictures which depict horse-drawn vehicles of typical or unusual purpose.

FORD LEROY MILKS, born Aug. 16, 1928, Traverse City, MI. Joined the Army Jan. 30, 1946. Military locations and stations: Ft. Sheridan, Ft. McClellan, Karlsruhe, Schitzingen, Mosbach, Goppingen, Stuttgart, Bremerhaven to Bremen.

Served with the 15th Constab. Sqdn., Trp. B, 1st Sqdn. Awarded WWII Victory Medal and Occupation Medal Germany.

Memorable experience: when 15th Regt. prepared for Gen. Eisenhower which didn't show up send Gen. Montabert. After exchange of medals at third Army parade grounds in which B Trp., 1st Sqdn. a battalion of infantry from the 47th Inf., a detachment of WACS and the 60th 61st bands were received by Gen. Keyes.

Married Doris V and they have children: Vennetta, Steven, Teresa and April and grandchildren: Pam, Jason, Ben, Paul, Damien, Chauncy and Nicole.

Employed carpenter sup. Retired June 1970.

GEORGE A. MILLARD, born Oct. 3, 1927, Providence, RI. Inducted into the US Army, Oct. 18, 1945, Ft. Banks, MA. Discharged Aug. 24, 1948.

Military locations and stations: Ft. Riley, KS; Berlin Germany; April 1946-February 1947; Feb. 1947-Aug. 24, 1948; Horse Plt., Trp. D, 16th Constab. Sqdn. Sep

Awarded WWII Victory Medal and Army of Occupation, Germany.

He is single and currently enjoys military history, dogs, theatre, reading and TV.

DONALD D. (BUD or LITTLE) MILLER, born Aug. 29, 1930, Morgan County, IN, joined the US Army October 1948. Military locations and stations: Basic training, Camp Breckinridge, KY; Weiden and Hof Germany; Ft. Hood, TX. Served with US Constab. 15th and 53rd A Trp.

Discharged August 1955 as corporal. Memorable experiences: couple of skirmishes on Czech border with patrolling border outside Augsberg.

He was married to Donna Dee and she is deceased. They had children: Dennis, Daniel, Donny, DeAnna; 9 grandchildren and eight great-grandchildren. Employed at aircraft and rocket welder for 22 years; tooling coordinator final 3 1/2 years. Disabled May 1987.

HARRY F. MILLER, 740th Tk. Bn., Europe, WWII, 9th Inf. Div., Bad Tolz, Germany 1946. 2nd Constab. Regt., 35th and 42nd Constab. Sqdn. 1946-48. 71st and 11th Signal Bn. Far East 1948-51. 116th Signal Co./8608 AAU (ASA) Scheyern, Germany 1952-53. Entered USAF HQ Eastern Air Defense Force 1953-55, 1956-57. 720th AC&W Sqdn., Alaska 1955-56. HQ USAFE and 17th AF, Ramstein, Germany 1957-62. HQ SAC 1962-66. Retired January 1966.

Received Army Glider Wings, USAF and Army Good Conduct Medals, ATO, ETO, WWII Victory, National Defense, Occupation Germany/Japan medals, various USAF ribbons and awards.

Married Helen Carreon Fabian 1975. Have five children. Worked as private investigator, Director of hospital security/safety and for University of Texas Arlington. Retired again January 1989. Reside Seattle, WA. Active as secretary, 740th Tank Battalion Association. He enjoys reading, ballroom dancing and travel.

WILLIAM LEE (BILL) MILTON, born Manlius, NY, joined the US Army May 1946. Sent overseas August 1946. Served with Trp. E and HQ Trp., 28th Constab. Sqdn. at Hof, Germany. 28th Sqdn. deactivated 1947. Reassigned to 94th Constab. Sqdn. at Weiden. 94th Sqdn. deactivated and merged into the 91st FA Bn., 1948. 91st FA Bn. stationed at Weiden and Grafenwhor for most of 1948, then assigned to 7732 FA Gp. at Sonthofen.

Attained the rank of sergeant and discharged February 1949 with honorable discharge. Received WWII Victory Medal and Army of Occupation Medal.

Attended the US Constabulary Trooper School at Sonthofen October 1946.

Memorable experiences: A Sgt. Neff (or Reff) and Milton skied the first ski patrol on part of the Russian border zone from their post at Hof, covering approx. 20 miles. He believes this was written up in the Lightening Bolt or Stars and Stripes in November or December 1946.

Married to Barbara and they have children: Barbara, Karen, Janice, Wendy and Cynthia; grandchildren: Adam, Shawn, Reston, Christine, Elizabeth Michael, Monica, Kelly, Christopher, Garret Julie, William.

Retired February 1991, 23 years service with county government.

FRANK L. MISITI, born Aug. 9, 1927, Harrisburg, PA. Drafted into the US Army, Oct. 10, 1945. Military locations and stations: Gottingen, near Augsburg and Fussen; basic training at Ft. Knox, KY; the Armored School at Ft. Knox. Served with HQ Trp., 5th Constab. Regt. Commands held: radio operator. Discharged March 4, 1947 as T/4.

Awarded Army of Occupation Medal and WWII Victory Medal.

Misiti is single and they have children: Frank Jr., Joseph, Gary, Mary, Monica. grandchildren: Larina, Elaine, Alberto, Jessica, Rachelle, Stephanie, Genevieve, Gary Jr., Heather and Nicholas.

Cumberland Electronics, co. owner of electronics parts distributor. Retired June 1991.

WAYNE J. MOE, born April 20, 1920, Dawson, MN, received a BS degree; attended Command and General Staff College; Infantry Advance Course.

Joined the infantry Feb. 10, 1941. Commissioned June 12, 1942. Military locations and stations: Germany three times; Finland; Korea; Vietnam; Pentagon twice; Ft. Sam Houston; Ft. Riley; Ft. Benning; Ft. Polk.

Served with the Army Staff, 1st, 4th, 7th Armies; US Constabulary; 423rd, 50th, 9th Inf.; Co. I, 423rd Inf. Troops E&D, 14th Sqdn. and Trp. B, 22nd Sqdn., US Constab.; 3rd Armd. Rifle Bn.; 50th Inf., 1st USAAG, Vietnam.

Retired July 1, 1973 as colonel. Battles and campaigns: served in combat in ETO (three Battle Stars); Korea (two Battle Stars) and Vietnam (two Battle Stars).

Awarded Combat Infantry Badge w/star, two Legions of Merit, three Bronze Stars w/V Device for valor, Purple Heart, Vietnamese Distinguished Service Cross and Honor Medal; Finnish White Rose.

Memorable experiences: Serving in US Constab. 1946-49; commanding 3rd Bn., 50th Inf. and Wildflecken training area, Germany 1958-60; serving as US Attache to Finland 1965-68.

Married Jean Soblom in 1945. They have four daughters: Judy, Barbara, Mary and Laurie and grandchildren, Laura and Matthew. Employed in real estate since 1974. Owns Cardinal Realty. Not yet retired.

WILLIAM H. MOFIELD, born July 20, 1930, Pointer, KY, entered the military service in March of 1946 at the age of 15 years.

Serviced in Germany in military government in Erlingen, Germany until April 1948, was sent home for being to young.

Went back to Germany, September 1948 to 10 Constab. Sqdn., then it was changed to 1st Bn. A/C. Moved from Fritzlar to Fulda. Came home in 1953. Went to 4th AD until December 1955. Then he served from December 1955 until December 1960 in USAF at Garrison AFB, Peru, IN.

Awarded the Presidential Commendation ETO, German Occupation and Good Conduct Medal.

SAMUEL MONASTERSKY, born Oct. 21, 1928 in Newark, NJ. Sammy as known to his friends enlisted in the Regular Army, October 1946. He received his basic training at Ft. Dix, NJ. Medals include the Army of Occupation, WWII Victory Medal. Duties: 14th Constab. Regt., Fritzlar, Germany 1947-48.

He retired June 30, 1990, after 20 years as a fourth grade teacher. He received his bachelor of arts in 1970 and master of arts in 1973 from Newark State College. He was one of the original founders of Temple Sha'arey Shalom. He sang in the choir for 28 years.

Sammy passed away Feb. 16, 1996 and is survived by his wife, Danise, and his two sons, Glenn and Bruce and four grandchildren: Daniel, Alexander, Emily and Rebecca.

WILLIAM E. (BILL) MONTGOMERY, born Oct. 10, 1931, Porterville, CA. Joined the service US Army December 1948. Military locations and stations: December 1948-April 1949, basic, Ft. Ord, CA. April 1949 to Swienfurt to Germany 1951 to May 1952 Sixth Regt., Berlin Germany.

Served with 14th Regt., 2 Btry., HQ & HQ US Constab., 14th Armd. Cav.; May 1, 1949-May 1, 1951.

Discharged June 1952 as staff sergeant. Awarded the Good Conduct Medal, German Occupation, Berlin Air Life, WWII Victory Medal.

Memorable experiences: making staff sergeant after rank was unfrozen. Being in US Cav. 5 1/2 months before disbanded and sold horses transferred into Armd. Div. transferred back to US.

Married Barbara Lewis July 28, 1953 and they have children: Roger Montgomery and daughters, Lynda Gail and Susan Lynn. Employed with the State of Oregon and retired February 1992.

EDWARD MOORE, born Sept. 4, 1931, New York City, NY, entered service Sept. 16, 1948. Military locations and stations: HQ Co., 70th FA Bn., Fussen, Nurnberg, Germany 3 1/4 years; 1949-52, 41st AAA FA Bn., Ft. Totten, NY, 1952-54. Received basic awards.

Married to Kathleen Cullen and they have seven children and 10 grandchildren. Now a beach bum and retired.

EUGENE (EMERY or GENE) MOORE, born Sept. 25, 1927, Hylton, KY, Pike County, attended one year college, criminal justice.

Joined the US Army in 1945. Military locations and stations: Germany; Vietnam; Ft. Benning, GA; Ft. Jackson, SC; Thailand; Ft. Knox, KY.

Served with E Trp., 94th Constab. Sqdn., 11th Regt., 26th Inf. Regt., 1st Div., 12th Inf. Regt., 4th Div., 19th and 25th MI Gp.; B Co., 33rd Armd. Heavy Tk. Bn.

Discharged Sept. 1, 1974 as E-7. Memorable experiences: life member, VFW, Post #641, Columbia, SC.

Married Kathleen and they have children: Eugene Jr., Eugenia and Doris Ann; grandchildren: Donnie and Jason Laymon, Dessiree A. Moore. Employed as Wells Fargo and Anderson Armd. Car Service; driver and messenger. Retired Sept. 1, 1974 from the US Army.

GEORGE W. MOORE, born Jan. 22, 1927, Gastonia, NC, entered military service June 28, 1945. Basic training at Camp Wheeler, GA. Joined 4th Armd. Div., Landshut, Germany December 1945.

Attended 1st Constab. School, March 30, 1946; Sonthofen January 1947 Investigators Course Sonthofen; February 1947 Co. Administration School, Sonthofen. Stationed Gablingen, Fussen, Kempten, Oberstdorf and Augsburg.

Returned to US 1950 School Trp., Ft. Knox, KY. Assigned to 1st Cav. in Korea July 1950. Returned to US July 1950, operations sergeant with (Med) Tank Co., 30th Inf. Ft. Benning, GA.

Discharged May 24, 1952. Attended business school for two years. Spent 20 years in life insurance business. Retired after 10 years in security with filter company.

Presently retired and having fun selling craft and floral supplies at local flea market. 1950 married Jean Henson and they have two sons, a daughter and seven grandchildren, one great-granddaughter in Saarbrücken, Germany. They have traveled back to Germany four times to visit daughter and grandchildren. Presently married to Shirley Alderman Moore.

ADAM H. MORA, born Dec. 8, 1926, Corpus Christi, TX. Joined the Army March 1945. Retired March 1975 as SGM E-9.

Battles and campaigns: Korea and Vietnam.

Awards and medals: Combat Infantry Badge, Bronze Star w/2 OLC, Meritorious Service w/three awards, Commendation Medal w/4th Award, Good Conduct Medal w/ 9 awards, plus service medal.

Memorable experience: In the spring of 1947, E Trp., 53rd Constab. Sqdn. was formed for a squadron review. There were five platoons in formation, the 1st Sgt. joined the formation, but Capt. Heatherly Troop Commander noticed a pant leg of the first sergeant was out of his boot and advised him of it. The 1st Sgt. being a large person, had to return to the orderly room to fix the problem.

He was a T/5 asst. sqd. leader, 3rd Sqd., 3rd Plt., notice the time was approaching IP time. He broke forma-

tion and assumed the position of the 1st Sgt., called the troop to attention, made an about face and informed the troop commander, the troop is formed, Capt. Heatherly gave the command take your post Sgt. Mora. He then started to return to his original position, when Capt. Heatherly ordered Mora to take the position of the 1st Sgt. addressing him as Sgt. Mora and he complied.

The troop reached the IP on time and everything went well. On returning to the troop area the troop commander called out the command first sergeant. No one moved he had assumed that the first sergeant had some how rejoined the troop, so the troop commander then again order Sgt. Mora front and center. He assumed the first sergeants position and saluted the troop commander. His next order was take charge of the troop and dismiss them and report to me in the orderly.

Saluted and made an about face and gave the command platoon sergeants take charge of your platoons and dismiss then. All platoon sergeants salute and he returned their salutes and went to the orderly room as ordered.

The first sergeant was waiting with a big smile on his face and told him to report to Capt. Heatherly in his office. Only then did he Mora find out that because of his actions he had been promted to buck sergeant.

He was awarded Army of Occupation, Germany, American Campaign, WWII Victory Medal, National Defense two awards, Army Expeditionary Medal, two awards, Korean Service Medal, United Nations Medal, Vietnam Service Medal, Vietnam Campaign and Meritorious Unit Citation, two awards.

His wife Katy is deceased and they had children: Dennis, Diane, Dean, Debbie, Dave and Dan (Gary deceased); seven granddaughters and four grandsons. Retired March 31, 1975, Ft. Sam Houston, TX.

JOHN MORANO, born Aug. 21, 1926, New York City, joined the US Army, Oct. 23, 1944. Arrived in Kassel, Germany November 1945. His assignment was with Troop B, 17th Cav. Recon Sqdn. This outfits' duties were with the District Constab. They were told to find any SS men that escaped from the Russian zone. Their duty was to take into custody any SS troops escaped from the Russian zone, while allowing regular Wehrmacht soldiers to pass.

The set out on the Autobahn for their first assignment. They took a wrong turn. Tried to make a U-turn and wound up stuck in the snow. Two of them walked to a small town that they were to give an envelope to the Buergermeister and with hand gestures tried to explain their predicament with their M8 car.

They went back to their stuck vehicle and an hour later, here comes the Buergermeister with four men, a horse and a cow! They attached a line from the animals to their tow-hook. The horse kept falling down and the cow kept tripping. The horse and cow didn't help. Finally the Buergermeister put a stop to this and decided to go back to town to get a machine. A few hours later he came back with a wood burning farm tractor. This finally pulled them out and they gave each man two cigarettes.

Sixteen years later while he was working for TWA, in walks a new painter. A former SS man. Morano found out he has two apartment houses on Ocean Pkwy., Brooklyn. Drives a Cadillac and a Mercedes for his wife, and put his son into business. There were to "Phils" working in the TWA hangar with them. But the "SS Phil" was nicknamed PHIL THE OVEN. He didn't care as long as he was treated fairly.

With all the work the district did in trying to catch the SS men. They have thousands working in the states. But all the SS soldiers fought on the Eastern front, when they questioned them, they never say they fought on the Western front. What a crock that was!

Discharged May 13, 1946 and received Occupation Medal, American Campaign, ETO, Good Conduct and Victory Medal.

Married Josephine and they have children, Janice

and Ken and grandchildren, Chriss and Kevin. Employed with Trans World Airlines as crew chief (motorized equipment). Retired Feb. 1, 1991 after 26 years service.

KENNETH J. MORELLS, born Oct. 26, 1930, Rochester, NY, inducted into service Nov. 2, 1950, Rochester, NY. Military locations and stations: Camp Edwards, MA (basic training); 459th AAA AW Smbl. Bn., C Trp., 24th Constab. Sqdn., April 1951-Sept. 30, 1953, Bad Kissingen, Germany.

Discharged Oct. 9, 1953 and received the German Occupation.

Married Judith Ann Osborne April 11, 1959. They have two sons, three daughters and 13 grandchildren. Serves as VFW post commander is member of American Legion, Constabulary Association. Enjoys model railroads, model building and air shows.

AL MORRIS *photo only, no bio submitted.*

DAVID ROBERT (DOC) MORROW, born Nov. 30, 1927, Glenolden, PA, educated as aircraft designer. Joined the US Army Feb. 14, 1946. Military locations and stations: Ft. Bragg, NC; Schweinfurt/Main Germany; Weiden Germany; Sonthofen. Served with 27th Constab. Sqdn., A Trp., HQ Trp. Command held: 94th FA and HQ & HQ Trp.

Discharged Dec. 29, 1948 as private first class.

Married Virginia M. and they have children: David, Dolores, Steve, Debbie, Virginia and grandchildren: Jennifer, Julie, Robbie, Stephanie, Joeie, Nick and Jason. Retired as senior electrical engineer from Boeing Co., January 1996.

CLARENCE MORSE, born April 22, 1927, Devils Lake, ND, inducted into the US Army, July 17, 1945. Received his basic training at Ft. Hood, TX. After basic training he was assigned to Camp Pickett, VA. While at Camp Pickett he was discharged from the Army and re-enlisted into the Regular Army, Jan. 21, 1946.

The departed by ship from New York Harbor March 1946 for LeHavre, France. From LeHavre they were transported by train to the concentration camp at Dachau, Germany. At Dachau they changed from the 2nd Armd. Div. to the 35th Constab. Sqdn. From Dachau they went by convoy to Augsburg AFB. From Augsburg he was transferred to Landshut where they formed Trp. E. Assigned to check point headquarters which was in Obersdorf, Germany. While there he was assigned as vehicle dispatcher for Trp. E. After completion of his duties there, he was transferred back to main headquarters in Fussen and Trp. D replaced them. He was discharged from Ft. Sheridan, IL, Feb. 16, 1947.

VIRGIL IRVIN MOSS, born Jan. 12, 1926, St. Louis, MO, inducted into service June 25, 1943, St. Louis. Military locations and stations: ASTP University of Missouri, Columbia, MO, Camp Robertson, AR; Ft. Jackson, SC; Europe; Bamberg; Budingen; Camp Carson.

Awarded seven ribbons, Unit Citation, Fleur de Leis, Fleur de Guerre, Radio Patch, Hash Marks.

Moss is married and has four children and seven grandchildren. Currently involved in YMCA, Constabulary Association, Missouri Wine Society, Masonic Lodge, Jefferson County Genealogical Society.

RAYMOND L. (MULE) MUELLER, born Feb. 1, 1927, Pacific, MO, joined the Army June 18, 1945. Military locations and stations: Ft. Bliss, TX; Camp Funston, KS; Ft. Ord, CA; Ft. Leavenworth, KS; Camp Pickett, VA; Camp Kilmer, NJ; LeHavre, France; all stations in Germany; last station, Hoff, Germany.

Served with 28th Constab, D Trp., 6th Regt., Hoff, Germany. Discharged Dec. 31, 1946 as sergeant.

Memorable experiences: War criminal trials.

Married Evelyn and they have children, Patricia Mueller and Michael Mueller; grandchildren, Jaclyn and Jill Mueller. Employed as superintendent of construction. Retired Jan. 1, 1990.

JAMES ALVA MUNSON, born Dec. 11, 1922, Long Pine, NE. Duties: 68th Armd. FA Bn. and 68th Constab. Sqdn., Germany, 1946-48; faculty, US Military Academy, 1950-53; HQ, 8th Army, Korea (1953-54) and Japan (1954-55); Army Staff, Pentagon, 1956-59, 1966-67, 1970-71; Assistant Attache, Argentina, 1960-63; Commander, 36th Armd. FA Bn., Ft. Sill, OK, 1964-66; Mil Asst to Sec Army, 1967-68; Cmdr., 1st Cav. Div. Arty. (1968-69) and Sr. Advisor, ARVN Arty. (1969); Vietnam; Defense Attache, Mexico, 1971-73; Asst. Cmdr., 1st Armd. Div. and Cmdr. US Mil Community, Bamberg, Germany, 1973-75.

BS, USMA, 1945; Master of International Affairs, Columbia University 1950; Command and Staff College, 1956; Army War College, 1964; Adv. Management Program, Harvard University, 1968.

Retired April 1, 1975. Married Nancy Brewer, Sept. 7, 1945 and they have six sons, one daughter and nine grandchildren. Resides in Falmouth, MA.

JAMES K. (IRISH) MURPHY, born April 30, 1927, Chicago, IL, joined the Army 1948-50. Military locations and stations: Will Kaserne; Munich, Germany; HQ Co., 73 Armd. Ord. Maint. Bn., US Constab. Served with 1st Cav., 1950-52, Korean Inf. F Co.

Discharged Jan. 1, 1952 as corporal. Served in three major battles; Korea and received three Bronze Battle Stars, Combat Infantry Badge/Korean Service Medal, UN Service Medal, European Occupation Medal, Munich Germany.

His wife Mary Lou is deceased and they had children: Judith Lynn Murphy and Kathlyn Ann Kraus; grandchildren: Matt Murphy, Sara Kraus and Alicia Kraus. Employed as welding instructor, Southwest WI Tech College. Retired August 1989.

WILLIAM L. MURPHY, born Oct. 4, 1928, England, CO, entered the Army Jan. 31, 1946 at Ft. Crook, NE. Had basic training at Ft. Lee, VA.

He became a member of HQ Constab. when three Army HQ rotated to the states and Constab. HQ moved to Heidelberg. HQ Constab. moved from Heidelberg to Villigen, Germany and he remained with the unit until June of 1950. Has served other tours at Bamberg and K town; also one tour at Korea.

Served as a cook and mess sergeant. Attendant Cook & Baker School and Mess Sergeant School at Darmstadt in 1947-48.

Served in the Constabulary as a private first class T/5-T/4, buck sergeant and made staff sergeant E-5 on the first Army written test in 1950.

His medals include WWII Victory Medal, Occupation Medal, Good Conduct, Commendation Medal (others unknown).

Married and has a son, Charles and daughters, Kathy and Barbara. Currently enjoys fishing and woodworking.

CHARLES L. MURRAY, born 1927, Indianapolis, IN, entered military service 1945; Military Police School, Buckley Field, CO 1945; 979th MP Co., Wiesbaden, Germany 1945-46, 1st Constab. Bde. HQ Communications, Message Center Courier and Clerk, Wiesbaden-Biebrich, Germany 1946-48. Discharged 1948.

Received ETO, American Theater, WWII Victory Medal, Army of Occupation Medal and Good Conduct Medal.

Education includes doctorate in Podiatric medicine. Practiced Podiatry for 35 years.

Married Patricia Fairchild 1948 and they have one daughter, one son and two grandchildren.

Member of the US Constabulary Veterans Association, American Legion, Veterans of Foreign Wars and American Podiatric Medical Association.

Presently retired, gardening, playing golf and traveling.

NOEL E. (MOE) NEEFE, born Dec. 23, 1930, Rochester, NY, joined the Army Oct. 11, 1948. Attended basic training, Camp Pickett, VA. Served with A Trp., 24th Constab. Sqdn., as corporal.

Discharged June 11, 1952 as corporal and received ETO Ribbon.

Memorable experiences: he first arrived in Bad Hersfeld in January of 1949 and was put on patrol duty. One morning on returning from the border he was unloading a 30 cal. machine gun mounted in an M8 when it fired a round across the yard and out over the Autobahn. It really shook him up and he thought for sure he was going to catch hell, but to his pleasant surprise all he got was a good chewing out. After that all patrols locked and loaded outside the main gate.

Neefe is divorced and has five children: Patricia, Linda, Edward, Lori and Lisa and 10 grandchildren.

Employed as bus operator for city of Rochester. Retired Sept. 30, 1996.

AUGUSTINE C. (GUS) NELSON, born Aug. 28, 1930, Detroit. Received Associates, Communication Arts, University of Detroit; Advanced Management Michigan State, Credit, Union Executive Society.

Joined the Army, December 1949. Military locations and stations: Basic, 101st Abn., Breckenridge, KY; all the rest HQ Spec. Trps.; Villingen, Germany, 1949-1952.

Served with HQ Special Trps, US Constabulary and 7th Army.

Memorable experiences: In 1950 the US Constab. HQ decided it should develop a skeet team and have competition throughout the command. When they were building the range they needed shooters to set the traps, so they asked Nelson (Cpl. Nelson at the time) to try them out. Well he shot the lights out for them. They were going to have an open competition to choose a team and he was then asked to compete. He won the competition and was put on the team. Anytime they had a competition he was put on TDY and traveled all over Europe to represent them. In 1951 they decided to have an enlisted men's team separate from officer. He was one of five to represent the 7th Army in competition. So there was time for recreation and entertainment during the stressful times.

Discharged October 1952 as staff sergeant. Awarded Good Conduct, Occupation, Commendation, Shooting Champion, Top Secret Clearance July 17, 1950.

Married to Pat and they have sons, Alfred and Anthony and grandchildren: Aisilina, Samantha and Alec. Employed HFC manager, 1954-64; manager, credit counseling, 1964-65; press comprehensive invest, 1965-69; CEO Berkley Credit Union, 1969-87. Retired January 1987 because of poor health.

WILLIAM A. NESTOR, born March 20, 1927, Huntington, WV, enlisted RA October 1945, Camp Atterbury, IN. Basic training, Armored, Ft. Knox, KY.

Assigned to Motorcycle Plt., HQ & HQ Sv. Trp., 2nd Constab. Regt., Freising, Germany, July 1946. Attended Clerk Typist School, 2nd Bde. HQ, Munich, Germany, September-December 1946.

Regiment moved to Augsburg September 1947. Assigned to Provost Marshalls office as operations sergeant.

Returned to US and discharged August 1948. Married Janis and they have three daughters, seven grandchildren, and one great-granddaughter. Retired from INCO Alloys International, Inc. April 1, 1986, Huntington, WV.

RICHARD H. NEUMANN, born May 1, 1926, Cheboygan, MI, inducted July 12, 1944. Enlisted in RA June 10, 1946. Discharged Oct. 13, 1947. Army Reserves Oct. 13, 1947-Oct. 10, 1951. US Constab. Fulda, Germany, 81st Constab. Sqdn.

Special assignment: Baltimore, MD February-April 1945. Landed in Le Havre, France April 1945. Basic training CRTC Ft. Riley, KS. Stayed in many towns in Germany and was motor sergeant of Trp. B, 81st Constab. Sqdn. for 30 months. Also taught mechanic school in Fulda, Germany.

Married Carol Oct. 12, 1950 and they have a son. Retired from post office in 1983 with 34 years of federal service. Member of Hope Lutheran Church, Plainwell, MI. Enjoys travel, woodworking and spends winters in Avon Park, FL.

PADRAIG M. (PADDY) O'DEA, born May 13, 1914 in New York City, attended college 2 1/2 years.

Joined the NYNG April 1935 and the US Army Jan. 6, 1941. Commissioned June 6, 1942. Military locations and stations: Ft. Jackson, SC; Ft. Riley, KS; England; North Africa; Italy; Germany; France; Poland; Korea; Ft. Knox, KY.

Retired Aug. 31, 1963 as LTC AUS. Battles and campaigns: Montrevel, S. Fr; Tunisia; Rome Arno, S. France.

Awarded the Distinguished Service Cross, Commendation Medal, POW Medal, Army of Occupation (Germany), WWII Victory, EAME, three Campaign Stars and Arrowhead, American Defense and American Campaign.

Memorable experiences: held POW in Stalag XII A, Limburg, Germany; Offz-Lager 64, Szubin, Poland and Stalag III A, Lukenwalde, Germany. Russian troops captured Stalag II A but held inmates hostage for several weeks. June 1945 freed to return to the US.

His wife Lorraine M. DeMott is deceased and they had daughters, Kathleen and Ann; grandchildren: Ashley Ann, Shannon Marie Merrigan. Employed with USAR, supervisory staff technician, GS-11. Retired May 1, 1989.

JOSEPH G. O'DONNELL, born Jan. 14, 1926, Jersey City, NJ, inducted into the US Army Apr. 12, 1944; basic training Camp Blanding, FL, then to the 2nd Inf. Div. in Europe participating in campaigns in France, Belgium and Germany. Returned to CONUS August 1945 and after a leave, served at Camp Swift, TX until discharged April 15, 1946 as a private first class.

Reenlisted as a private first class in the Regular Army in 1947 at Ft. Dix, NJ. Joined Trp. D, 16th Constab. Sqdn. (Sep) in January 1948 and served until discharged in 1950 as an SFC. Enlisted in the USAF and assigned to Rhein Main AB, Germany until 1951, then assigned to Langley AFB, VA. During the next 24 years served at the following locations: Langley AFB, VA (four times), RAF Station Sealand, N. Wales; RAF Station Alconbury, England, Sembach AB, Germany and Beale AFB, CA.

Retired as a chief master sergeant Aug. 31, 1975. During his career he was awarded the Bronze Star Medal, Combat Infantry Badge, Meritorious Service Medal, AF Commendation Medal w/3 OLC, Army Good Conduct Medal w/ 1 SL LP, AF Good Conduct Medal w/4 OLC, American Campaign Medal, EAME Campaign Medal, WWII Victory Medal, Army of Occupation Medal (Germany), Berlin Airlift Device, Medal for Humane Action and the National Defense Medal.

Married Ursula I. Dettman from Berlin, Germany. They have two daughters, one son and four grandsons. Member of the US Constabulary Association, AF Sergeants Association and National Association for the Uniform Services. Currently spends most of his time visiting with Ursula who is confined to a nursing home.

WILLIAM M. (BILL) OLIVE JR., born June 28, 1920, Cambridge, MA, attended two years college, University of Maryland. Joined the US Army Dec. 1, 1941. Commissioned April 15, 1943.

Military locations and stations: Ft. Lee, VA; Lincoln AB, NE; North Africa, Sicily, France and Germany; Ft. Monmouth, NJ; Vietnam (1957-58); Ft. Ord, CA. Served with 723rd Railway Operating Bn., B Trp., 1st Constab. Bn., Karlsruhe. Served as platoon leader, company commander, assistant logistics chief, MAAS advisor, Log. G-4, Ft. Ord, CA.

Retired Feb. 28, 1962 as major. Battles and campaigns: Northern France, Rhineland, Central Europe, EAME. Awarded Cert. of Achievement, Good Conduct and citations.

Memorable experiences: over the side of a sinking ship in Bari, Italy, July 1943; being Outpost #7 commander, US Constab. 1993-94 and 1996-98; being part of the "elite" meeting Gen. Harmon and the friends renewed and gained of those in his outpost.

Married Beatrice J. Olive and they have children: Wm. M. III, Gary L., Debra, Vicki, Nancy and Susie; grandchildren: Raina, Jeffrey, Leah, Bryan, Kim, Kyle, Linsey, Jennifer, John and Tony.

Employed as material control manager, Sylvania Elec. Mountain View, CA and Materials and warehouse manager, Hamilton/AVNET Electronics, Houston, TX. Retired June 30, 1984.

CARL OLSEN, born Dec. 31, 1926, Staten Island, N inducted into service Jan. 31, 1945, Kilmer. Military loc tions and stations: Ft. Riley, KS; Horse Cav. Ft. Ord, C/ Camp Pickett, VA; Hof, Germany, Constabulary Schoc Bavarian Alps.

Discharged Dec. 3, 1946. Married to Lucille Costel and they have five children. Olsen is now retired.

RICHARD A. (OLE) OLSEN, born Dec. 23, 192? Jersey City, NJ. Joined the US Army Nov. 9, 1945. Mil tary locations and stations: Ft. Hancock, NJ; Ft. McClella AL; Camp Kilmer, NJ; Freising, Germany; Deggendor Laufen, Bad Rieckenhall, Germany. Served with 66t Constab. Sqdn., 2nd Regt.

Discharged Feb. 9, 1947 as T/5. Awarded WWI Victory Medal, Occupation Medal.

Memorable experiences: played baseball for 2nc Cav. Regt., 1946; being inspected and received Octobe 1946 by General of the Army, Dwight D. Eisenhower Serving in the US Constabulary.

Married for 49 years to June and they have children Richard, Thomas, John and Patricia and grandchildren MaryBeth, Richard, John and Jennifer.

Employed as route salesman for S.B. Thomas Inc. 34 years in New Jersey. Western Reserve LIfe, Largo, FL Retired August 1993.

HENRY ONTIVEROS, born July 15, 1927, Ocean Park, CA, entered US Army, Sept. 20, 1945, Los Angeles, CA. Basic training, Camp Roberts, CA.

Duties: US Constab., Trp. B, 91st/22d/24th Sqdns., McPheeters Barracks, Bad Hersfeld, Germany (Hessen), March 1946-October 1952; Constabulary School, Sonthofen, 1947, NCO Academy, Munich, 1949; Demolition (Engineer) School, Murnau, 1951; 194th Tank Bn., 47th Inf. Div., Camp Rucker, AL, January 1953-January 1954; attended Desert Rock V Exercise in Nevada, May 1953; 194th/317th/710th Tank Bns., Camp Stewart, GA, January 1954-January 1955; 57th Tank Bn., 2nd AD, Sandhofen, Germany, March 1955-December 1957; NCO Combat Intelligence Course, Oberammergau, Germany, 1957; 2d Tk. Bn., 37th Armor, 2d AD, Ft. Hood, TX, December 1957-April 1958; 15th Cav, 2d AD, Ft. Hood, TX, April 1958-September 1959; 10th Cav., 7th Inf. Div., Korea, September 1959-August 1960; 37th Armor, 2d AD, Ft. Hood, TX, September 1960-April 1963; 32d Armor, 3d AD, Germany, August 1963-June 1966; advisor group (ARNG), Long Beach, CA, August 1966-June 1969; 38th Inf. Bn., 2d Inf. Div. (DMZ) Korea, June 1969-June 1970; Experimentation Bn., (Inf.), Ft. Ord, CA, June 1970-September 1971.

Retired Sept. 30, 1971. Decorations: Meritorious Service, Army Commendation w/OLC, Good Conduct (eight), WWII Victory, Army of Occupation Germany, National Defense w/OLC and Armed Forces Expeditionary Medal.

Married Annamarie Hofmann, June 17, 1952. They have one son, Robert and three grandchildren: Jennifer, Kristen and Eric. Employed with County Sanitation Districts of Los Angeles County, October 1971-retired September 1987.

HENRY R. (CISCO) ORTIZ, born Feb. 16, 1930, Blythe, CA, joined the US Army July 8, 1948 and was stationed in Coburg, Germany. Served with 3d Btry., 14th A/C. Truck driver, Gas and ammo for tanks.

Discharged June 8, 1952 as corporal and assistant platoon sergeant.

Memorable experiences: border patrol East and West; Berlin Airlift; one of their border patrol got ambushed by the Russian patrol. He believes it was in 1950, winter time.

Ortiz is divorced and has children: Manuel Ortiz Jr., Henry Ortiz Jr., Maria Ortiz Jr., and Eloina Ortiz; grandchildren: Manuel Ortiz Jr., Annyssa and Nathalia. Employed as general building contractor.

WILLIAM A. OSTROWSKI, born June 21, 1930, Chicago, IL, inducted into service December 1946. Military locations and stations: Heidelberg, Germany, 820th HQ MP Co. Discharged June 1948.

September 1948 joined USN and was discharged September 1952. His awards include the Army Occupation, Navy Good Conduct, WWII Victory, Navy Occupation, Korean Service, UN Service and National Defense Service.

Married to Debbie and they have one son, two daughters and three grandsons. Currently enjoys amateur radio K7T11, hunting, fishing and RVing.

JOSEPH A. PALERMO, born Nov. 13, 1926, Staten Island, NY, joined the service Jan. 29, 1945 as cavalry trooper. Military locations and stations: Ft. Riley, KS; Ft. Ord, CA; LeHavre, France; Marburg, Germany; Fulda, Germany. Trained 1st Regt. Horse; 2nd Regt., Mechanized-Ft. Riley, 81 RCM 1st Armd; 81st Constab. Troop D, Entertainer.

Discharged Nov. 1, 1946 and received the Army of Occupation, WWII Victory Medal and the Good Conduct.

Married Frances in 1948 and they have children, Joseph Jr., Julia and Margaret and grandchildren: Christina, Dana, Michael, Jesse, Casey and Chelsea. Employed as General Forest Park Department, Forestry Div., retiring in 1994.

ANTONIO (CHIEF) PALOMAEEZ, born May 10, 1926 at Hachita, NM, drafted into the US Army, July 13, 1944 and had basic at Ft. Riley, KS. Departed to Germany, Jan. 1, 1945 and joined the 4th Cav. until May 1945. Assigned to 24th District Constab. in Darmstadt, Germany, Sept. 28, 1945. Assigned to A Btry., 1st Sqdn., Knielingen, Germany 1948-50, 48th AAA Aw Bn. Knielingen, Germany. 1950, Ft. Monmouth, NJ, Radio Repair School. 1951-52, 2nd Sig. Co., 2nd Inf. Div. In Korea as a radio repairman. 1952-52 Sig. Relay Co. In Yokohoma, Japan. 1952-57, Ft. Bliss, TX, training for SAM FC crewman. 1957-62, Kaiserslautern, Germany, as fire control mechanic. 1962-67, South McGregor Range, Ft. Bliss, TX, chief fire control mechanic.

Retired Feb. 28, 1968 as sergeant first class and holds the following campaigns: Ardennes, Rhineland, Central Europe, ETO, CCF Spring Offensive (Korea) UN Summer Fall Offensive (Korea) and 2nd Korean Winter, Ameri-

can Campaign Medal, EAME Campaign Meal w/3 Loops, and the following awards: Korean Service, United Nations Service, Honorable Service Lapel Button WWII and WWII Victory, Army Commendation, Good Conduct w/5 Loops, American Campaign, Army of Occupation w/Germany Clasp, National Defense Service w/Loop and Republic of Korea Presidential Unit Citation Badge.

Married Luise K. Palomarez June 8, 1947 and they had two sons, Raymond and Hans Jugen (deceased); two daughters, Shirley Bauer, and Beverly Hale. They also have six grandchildren: Tony, Hans, David, Travis, Kiska and Nichole.

Worked with Beech Aircraft for 16 years and retired in May 1991.

ALVARO (AL) PANIAGUA, born Sept. 22, 1930, Del Rio, TX, joined the US Army Aug. 11, 1948. Military locations and stations: Ft. Ord, CA; Ft. Hood, TX; Ft. Polk, LA; Hersfeld, Schweinfurt, Bad Kissingen, Schabach Germany; Korea. Served with 1st Armd. Div., 2nd Armd. Div., 4th Armd. Div., 1st Cav. Div., 35th Engr. Gp., 46th Engr. Bn., CTRP 22d and 24th Constab. Sqdn.

Discharged Aug. 31, 1968 as MSGT E-8 and his awards include the first OLC to National Defense Service Medal, Army Commendation w/OLC, Good Conduct Medal, 4th Award, Army Occupation w/OLC (Germany).

His wife Maria Theresia died and they had children: Amanda Payne and Anita Paniagua; grandchildren: Anna and Amy Payne. Employed as mail carrier, US Postal Service for 17 years (1968-85). Retired from service Sept. 1, 1968.

JOHN PAUN, born Jan. 13, 1917, Ely, MN, inducted into service at Ft. Sheridan, IL, April 1945. Military locations and stations: Camp Fannin, TX, May 1945, 17 weeks basic training; Ft. Riley, KS, September 1945-advanced training; Camp Pickett, VA to New York and on the boat to France, Camp Pall Mall, Etretat, France; train to Ulm, Germany, 1st Armd. Div., 13th Tank Bn., US Constab. formed in Germany 1946; Ulm, Bayreuth, Stuttgart, Bamberg, Pegnitz and Burgebruck. (All in Germany).

Awarded the German Occupation Medal, WWII Victory Medal and the Good Conduct Medal.

Married Marge Wrede, Sept. 16, 1950. Enjoys retirement, traveling and reading.

JOSEPH W. (PELCH) PELCHER, born April 13, 1927, Troy, NY, received a BBA in accounting from Siena College, NY, Loudonville.

Joined the Army July 6, 1945. Military locations and stations: Berlin, Germany, served with 7th Inf. Div., Trp. D, 16th Constab. December 1945-March 1946. Discharged Dec. 20, 1946 as T-5 car commander.

His battles and campaigns: Army of Occupation (Germany), Good Conduct, WWII Victory and Army of Occupation, Germany.

Memorable experiences: patrolling the Autobahn between Berlin and Helmstadt and playing on the 16th Constab. Sqdn. Bulldogs for football team in 1946.

Married Trudy and they have children: Suzanne, Christine, Pam, Joe, Marty, Dan, Jean, Trudy, Mike and Coleen; 21 grandchildren: Jeff, Wes, Joy, Shannon, Laura, Joey, Keith, Tara, Steve, Kate, David P., Russ, Danielle, Brecka, Sarah, Mike, Cressa, Rhiannon, Tom, David W. and Jeremy.

Employed as tax manager, NYS Department of Taxation and Finance. Married 50 years Oct. 9, 1997.

DONALD RODERICK PERKINS, born April 15, 1927, Peabody, MA, raised in Las Cruses, NM. Drafted into the Army at Ft. Bliss, TX, July 25, 1945. Basic training at Camp Robinson, AR.

Duties: 27th Armd. FA Bn., 27th Constab. Sqdn., Eberbach, Fulda and Schweinfurt, Germany, 1946. 3rd Army OCS, December 1946, Seckenheim, Germany. 5th FA Bn., 1st Inf. Div., 1947. Joined 716th AAA Gun Bn., NMARNG, 1948-50. Recalled in August 1950 for Korean War. Served at Ft. Bliss and in 50th AAA AW Bn. and 933 AAA AW Bn. in Korea, 1951-52. Joined 102nd FA Bn., MAARNG, 1953-54. Rejoined NMARNG in 200th AAA Gp., 1954-59. Joined WIARNG, 32d Inf. Div. Arty., 1959-62. Active duty for Berlin Buildup, 1961-62. Remained on active duty, 1962-75 in HQ, National Guard Bureau and DCSOPS in the Pentagon, and Office Chief of Staff, CONARC and TRADOC at Ft. Monroe. Retired at Ft. Monroe, May 31, 1975.

Awarded the Legion of Merit, Meritorious Service Medal, Commendation Medal, WWII Victory Medal, German Occupation, National Defense Service, Korea Service, UN Service and Reserve Service Medals, Department of the Army General Staff Badge.

BA in History, NM State University. Employed 11 years as Army Affairs Director, National Guard Association of the US, defense consultant for BMY Corp for seven years, all in Washington, DC. Divorced and has four children.

Currently Washington representative for the Military and Hospitaller Order of St. Lazarus of Jerusalem, a volunteer job for an ancient, chivalric, charitable Christian Order.

HENRY PETERSEN, born Jan. 7, 1929, Brooklyn, NY, enlisted in 82nd Abn., Oct. 17, 1946, age 17. Basic training Ft. Bragg, NC, Co. B, 42nd Bn., 4th Regt., RTC. Completed training Dec. 7, 1946.

Sent to Germany February 1947. Attended US Constabulary School, Sonthofen, Bavaria, Class #13, May 1947. Assigned to A Trp., 11th Constab. Sqdn., and 27th A Trp. Constab. Sqdn. stationed in Limburg, Darmstat, Weisbaden, border patrol. Transferred to HQ & HQ Co., 14th Armd. Cav. (S-3 schools and training) December 1947, Fritzlar, Germany and served there until September 1950. Held in service for convenience of government for the Korean Conflict. Returned to the states on the USNS Henry Gibbins October 1950. Was assigned to Ft. Riley, KS, HQ Det. #1, 5021 ASU Publications. Honorably discharge October 1951. Awarded WWII Victory Medal and Army of Occupation Medal (Germany).

Married Olga Hruschkova, and they have one daughter. Upon discharge worked for 20th Century Fox, New

York City. Attended school under GI Bill. Graduate Heffley Brown and New York University with AAS degree. Was court reporter in the district attorney's office, Staten Island, NY. Joined the New York Central Railroad in January 1956 in sales-marketing. Retired as manager with Conrail in 1989 after 33 years RR service. Relocated from New York City to North Carolina.

Vice President ASF-Western Carolinas Association, Masonic Temple #387, Hendersonville, Oasis Temple, Charlotte, NC, 32nd degree Master Mason, Scottish Rite Asheville, NC, life membership VFW Post #5206, American Legion #77, Hendersonville, NC, life membership US Constabulary Association, National Treasurer US Constabulary Association, travels.

DOYLE E. (PETE) PETERSON, born Nov. 21, 1926, Healdton, OK, joined the US Army June 6, 1944. Military locations and stations: Camp Hood, TX; Germany: Darmstadt, Karlsruhe; Mannheim; Bamberg.

Served with 84th Inf. Div., Co. K, 334th Regt., 14th Constab. Sqdn.

Discharged Nov. 19, 1945 and Nov. 14, 1946 as corporal.

His awards include the Expert Infantry Badge, EAME, Army of Occupation, Victory and Overseas Service Bar.

Memorable experiences: traveling in Germany and France; startup of Constabulary in Darmstadt, Germany.

Married Letha L. Peterson and they have children: Brenda K. Chaplinsky and Glen Edward Peterson. Their grandchildren: Sonya, Tonya, Laura and Erin Chaplinsky. Employed as machinist and project assist. with E.I. DuPont. Retired Dec. 31, 1984.

ROY PFANDER JR., born March 28, 1929, Ocean City, NJ, received a BA, St. Leo College; MPA Golden Gate University.

Joined the US Army September 1948. Military locations and stations: Germany, Korea, Vietnam, USA. Served with US Constab., 2nd, 3rd Armd. Div., 45th Div., 8th Army, Parachute Rigger School, 7th Army and Transportation Units overseas and USA.

Achieved the rank of command sergeant major and retired December 1978. Fought battles and campaigns in Korea and Vietnam. His awards include the Master Parachute Badge, Parachute Rigger Badge, Legion of Merit, Bronze Star, Army Commendation, Korean and Vietnam Campaign and service, other US and Allied awards.

Memorable experiences: serving with medical section and B Trp., 24th Constab. Sqdn., then reunion with troopers 40 years later.

Pfander is married to Elaine and they have children: Wanda, Gail and Lisa and grandchildren: Brett, Ryan and Skylar. Employed second career in civil service, Ft. Eustis, VA. Retired 1994.

OMER S. (BILL) PINCKSTEN, born June 5, 1932, Pocahontas, MO, enlisted in the RA, April 18, 1950, basic training, Ft. Riley, KS, G 6, 8th Inf., 10th Inf. Div.

Assigned HQ Trp., 15th Constab. Sqdn., Weiden, Germany, September 1950 (10 days), reassigned B Co., 1st Bn., 2nd ACR (Armd Cav. Regt.), Augsburg. As a Jeep operator other duty stations: Mainz, Grafenwohr and Bayreuth. Transferred to service company, 1st Bn., 2nd ACR as a truck driver.

Rotated to Ft. Riley, KS September 1953 to Ft. Polk, LA; Ft. Bragg, NC. Back to Ft. Riley, KS, May 1954. 10th Recon Co. Discharged April 1955 as a staff sergeant (T).

Enlisted USAF May 4, 1955 as a air policeman at Scott AFB, IL. Anderson AFB, Guam October 1955-September 1957, Little Rock AFB, AR, September 1957-June 1959; Chateauroux AB, France, June 1959-March 1963; FE Warren AFB, WY, March 1963-September 1967, McCoy AFB, FL, September 1967, w/TDY to Okinawa, Taiwan, October 1968-March 1969; Cam Rahn AB, Vietnam June 1969-June 1970; KI Sawyer, AFB, MI, June 1970-November 1972. Retired Nov. 30, 1972.

Married Anneliese Schroder, Weiden, Germany, Feb. 5, 1955 and have been married for 43 years. They have two children and two grandchildren.

Life members: VFW, 2nd Cavalry Association, USAF Security Police Association. Member, US Constabulary, 306th Bomb Wing, and 1881 Communication Squadron. Life member Air Force Sergeant Association.

ROBERT F. PLATH, born Jan. 12, 1932, St. Martins, WI, joined MIARNG June 1948. Enlisted regular army June 1950 and discharged May 25, 1953.

Military locations and stations: Basic training, Ft. Ord, CA; Signal School, Camp Gordon, GA, November 1950-July 1951; July 1951 disenfranchised, 24th Constab. Sqdn., Hersfeld, Germany. Late 1952 to May 1953, 14th Armd. Cav. in Fulda, Germany. Discharged May 25, 1953.

Married Norma Amidon July 3,1955. They have two children and five grandchildren. Current activities include fishing, hunting and travel.

THE REV. GLENN K. POLAN, born Jan. 13, 1927, Nixon, TX, enlisted in the RA, Oct. 6, 1946 after serving in the US Merchant Marines 1945-46 in the Pacific and Atlantic. He received his basic and clerk technical school training at Camp Lee, VA. Duties in Europe: detached service to HQ, 14th Constab. Regt., Fritzlar, Germany from Trp. D, 22nd Constab. Sqdn., Hersfeld. Discharged 1948, Camp Kilmer, NJ. Medals: Army of Occupation and WWII Victory.

Received his bachelor of arts degree from Texas A&I University, master of arts, Sam Houston State University and master of theology, Southern Methodist University. He was ordained an elder in the Texas Conference of the United Methodist Church and served as pastor to several Methodist churches in Texas and campus minister to Sam Houston Sate University, Rice University and the Texas Medical Center.

He married Ruth Walker, July 6, 1946 and they have two sons, Kraege and Ted and five grandsons.

ERNEST WILLIAM (BILL) POPP, born Nov. 16, 1931, Brooklyn, NY, joined the US Army, Sept. 7, 1949. Military locations and stations: Schweinfurt, Bad Kissingen, Germany, Ft. Lewis, WA and University of Nevada, Reno, NV, Saigon, VN.

Served with 9th Inf. Div., US Army Europe, US Constab., MAGV Vietnam; 4th Inf. Div., 2nd Inf. Div., 14th Armd. Cav., 2nd Bn.

Discharged as first sergeant E8, May 19, 1972.

Battles and campaigns: VN Counteroffensive Phase II, VN Counteroffensive Phase III, TET Counteroffensive; VN Counteroffensive IV; VN Counteroffensive VI, TET 69/ Counteroffensive VII, VN Summer-Fall 1969.

Awards and medals include BSM, PH, JSCM, AGM, GCM w/Silver Bar and three knots, NDSM w/OLC, AOM, Germany, VSM, VN Medal of Honor, VN Staff Service Medal, VN Staff Training Medal, VN Air Service Medal, VN Campaign Medal, VN Presidential Citation w/Bronze Palm.

Memorable experience: TET 1968 Offensive, was wounded during street fighting in Saigon.

Married Lieselotte Lina Popp and they have children, William John (37) and Robert Ernest (33); grandson, Marc Robert (8). He retired in 1993 from King County Public Works as storekeeper. Retired Dec. 1, 1993.

Member of VFW, DAV, American Legion, Auburn, WA, Elks, MOPH, NCOA, NAUS.

JOHN F. (PRICEY) PRICE, born March 26, 1926, Queens, NY City (Forest Hills), attended Constabulary RadioTelegraph School in Freising, plus high school and two year equivalency Medical School in Degerndorf.

Drafted into service Jan. 23, 1946. RA July 23, 1946. Military locations and stations: Ft. McClellan, AL; Ft. Hancock, NJ; Bamberg; Freising; Degerndorf; Bremerhaven; Ft. Hamilton, NY; (later, Ft. Benning, GA and Ft. Eustis, VA).

Served with IRTC, USZC, 66th Constab. Sqdn., 15th Inf. Regt., HQ 3rd Inf. Div., 724th ROB.

Discharged Nov. 23, 1950 as sergeant. Awarded WWII Victory, Occupation-Germany; Gold Cross Medal, stolen by military scoundrels who summary court martialed him for perfect obedience of a direct order, resulting in his serving as message center chief for two years as a private when he should have been promoted to SFC. He also served as squadron chaplain's assistant to help Chaplain Charles B. Whitman process a mountain of GI marriage applications. He was advised against a "hazing" issue because he still had two years to serve in the 66th Sqdn.

Married 51 years to Irma (formerly Irmgard nee Huschka). They have children: Lita, Joan, John and Veronica; grandchildren: Chris, Richard, Thomas, Timothy, Michael, Curtis, John, Matthew, Kevin, Brian and Jennifer; stepgrandchildren: Jennifer, Nicole; stepgreatgrandson, David.

Employed as switchman April 23, 1943; Carman Jan. 1, 1943), Long Island Railroad Company. Conductor of "Degnon Freight" with two furloughs to serve in Army WWII and Korea until July 1, 1977 by company under contract with United Transporation Union.

JIMMIE F. (PRITCH) PRITCHETT, born June 28, 1930, Yale, OK, joined the US Army Dec. 16, 1948. Attended basic at Camp Chaffee, AR. Served with HQ & HQ Co., 6th Armd. Cav. Security Plt.

Discharged July 14, 1952 as sergeant and his awards include the Occupation Medal (Germany) and the Good Conduct Medal.

Married Dec. 24, 1952 to Albert Hacker Pritchett and they have children: Teresa, Randy, Ronnie and Roger and grandchildren: Kyle, Caleb, Jimmie, Adam, Brian and Shawnee. Worked most of his life as a timber faller in Oregon until injuries forced him to quit. Later worked as clerk in Ace Hardware until retirement, May 1, 1992.

JOHN MICHAEL PROCHAK, born Feb. 26, 1923, Campbell, OH, volunteered for induction and entered service, March 4, 1941, Ft. Hays, Columbus, OH. Discharged Aug. 29, 1945, Camp Atterbury, IN. Reenlisted Aug. 6, 1946. Retired from active military service, Dec. 31, 1965.

Took basic training with Co. B, 6th QM Trng. Regt. at Camp Lee, VA, March-June 1941. Assigned to Co. B, 94th QM Baking Bn., June 1941-September 1943. Served at various posts in the US and overseas. Co. E, 3rd Ranger Bn. September 1943-January 1944, Italy. He was captured on Anzio, Jan. 30, 1944 and liberated at Hagenow, Germany, May 2, 1945. Discharged Aug. 29, 1945, Camp Atterbury, IN. Reenlisted, Aug. 6, 1946. Served at Camp Lee, VA August 1946-January 1947. Troop D, 24th Constab. Sqdn. in Linz, Austria January 1947-March 1948. Co. D, 796th MP Bn., Vienna, Austria, March 1948-June 1948. 541st Signal Depot Co. Wels Austria, June 1948-November 1949. 52nd Replacement Co., Ft. Riley, KS, November 1949-May 1950. 541st Signal Depot Co., Wels Austria, May 1950-March 1952. Heavy Mortar Co., 350th Inf. Regt., Salzburg, Austria, March 1952-September 1953. Infantry School, Ft. Benning, GA, September 1953-February 1954. ROTC Instructor Gp., Youngstown College, Youngstown, OH, February 1954-June 1955. 503rd Abn. Inf. Regt., 11th Abn. Div., Ft. Campbell, KY, June 1955-December 1955. Tank Co., 503rd Abn. Inf. Regt., December 1955-December 1959. ROTC instructor group, Youngstown University, Youngstown, OH, December 1959-May 1962. Co. C, 1st Bn., 27th Inf. Regt., 25th Inf. Div. Schofield Barracks, HI, May 1962-May 1965. ROTC instructor group, Kent State University, Kent, OH, May 1965-December 1965. Retired Dec. 31, 1965, Kent, OH.

During WWII he served at various posts in the US. Landed in Morocco, Nov. 18, 9142. Served in North Africa, Sicily, Italy, Germany. January 30, 1944, he was captured at Cisterna, Anzio Beachhead and was liberated May 2, 1945 at Hagenow, Germany. Other overseas service, Thailand, Vietnam and Okinawa.

Awards include the Combat Infantry Badge, Senior Parachutist Badge, Bronze Star, POW Medal, Good Conduct Medal w/6 OLC, Army of Occupation, Germany, American Defense Service Medal, American Campaign Medal, AEME Campaign Medal w/4 Battle Stars, WWII Victory Medal, National Defense Service Medal.

Married Theresia Muhlbacher of Vienna, Austria, July 3, 1950 at Camp McCauley Linz Austria. He have two daughters, three granddaughters and one grandson.

After retiring from the Army he worked in management of a food and vending company. In 1972 along with four other investors they began their own vending company. He retired Nov. 11, 1980 and enjoys reading, gardening, fishing, hunting and spending time with his family.

DAVID GLENN PRUITT, born June 29, 1929, Hoopeston, IL, enlisted RA, Dec. 2, 1946, Ft. Knox, KY. Retired Dec. 31, 1966.

Military locations and stations: basic training, Ft. Knox, KY; Germany (91st Constab., Bad Hersfeld); Ft. Dix, NJ; Camp Kilmer, NJ; Pine Camp, NY; Orleans, France; Ft. Lee, VA; Korea; Ft. Myer, VA; Alaska; Ft. Stewart, GA; Germany (Berchtesgaten); Ft. Hamilton, NY.

His awards and medals include the WWII Victory Medal, Good Conduct Medal and Army Commendation Medal.

Married to Maxideen, a former WAC and they have two daughters who are school teachers and two granddaughters. Currently a funeral home employee and antiquing pursuits.

DONALD EUGENE PURRINGTON, born Sept. 19, 1929, Windom, MN, joined the MNARNG Nov. 13,

1947, enlisted in the Regular Army, Nov. 16, 1948; basic training, Ft. Riley, KS.

Other duties: US Constab., Straubing, Germany, March 1949-December 1951; Ft. Sill, OK, Arty. OCS, February-July 1952; Ft. Lewis, WA, July 1952-February 1953; Korea (2nd Inf. Div.) February 1953-April 1954; Ft. Carson, CO, April 1954-January 1958; Germany (Schwabisch Hall) January 1958-June 1961; East Lansing, MI, advisor to MIARNG June 1961-June 1964; University of Omaha (Bootstrap) July 1964-February 1965; Korea (Eighth Army HQ, Inspector General's Office) February 1965-April 1966; Ft. Riley, KS, April 1966-June 1967, where he attended Assoc. Command and General Staff School, University of Chattanooga (military science professor) June 1967-May 1970.

LTC Purrington retired June 1, 1970 and Bronze Star Medal (Meritorious Service), Meritorious Service Medal, Army Commendation Medal w/OLC, Army Achievement Medal, Good Conduct Medal, Army of Occupation Medal, National Defense Service Medal, 3rd Award, Korean Service Medal, United Nations Service Medal w/OLC.

Married Roselyn Sellers, Feb. 14, 1953 and they have two sons and one granddaughter.

National commander, US Constabulary Association, lay reader, parish administrator, St. Elizabeth Episcopal Parish, Burien, WA. He plays handball, reads and travels a great deal.

ORVIN J. QUALE, born Aug. 5, 1922, Chippewa Falls, WI, enlisted in RA March 6, 1946. Basic training, Ft. Knox, KY. Duties: US Constab., 15th Sqdn., 15th Regt., Schwetzingen, Germany 1946-47, 1st Sqdn., 15th Regt, Karlsruhe, 1947; Contabulary Flight, Stuttgart, 1948-52.

Disk and records clerk, radio operator, airplane mechanic, line chief. Retired at Camp Irvin, CA, October 1953.

KENNETH W. QUIGLEY, previous to joining 16th Constab. in Berlin, Germany, worked as electrician for Kaiser Shipbuilders, Inc., Vancouver, WA on outfitting dock, 1942-44.

Joined Merchant Marine and shipped to Pacific warzone on ammunition ship 1944-45. Awarded Pacific Warzone Bar Liberation of Philippines, Victory and Chinese medals.

Went to Berlin to 16th Constab. Sqdn., Separate B Troop, Oliver Barracks, 1946-48. Took part in raids, road patrol, road blocks, zone patrol, dress parades and other types of guard duties.

Awarded Army Occupation Bar, WWII and Victory Medal. Worked for US Post Office in Portland, OR 30 years, 25 years on same route. Now retired in SE Portland, OR. Hobbies are photography, gardening, and singing in Men's Chorus.

Married Evelyn M. and they have children: Patricia, William and (Mary Ann, now deceased); grandchildren: Bill, Brian, Jeff, Noel, Angela, Brenna and Brooke. Employed as letter carrier, US Post Office, for 32 years retired in 1983.

ALFRED D. (AL) RAMIREZ, born May 25, 1929, San Bernardino, CA. Joined the US Army May 29, 1948, commissioned NCO. Military locations and stations: Ft. Ord, CA; Ft. Benning, GA; Ft. Bragg, NC; Ft. Jackson, SC; US Forces, Austria, 1948-52; Camp Roberts, CA; Ft. Hood, TX; Korea, 1953-53; Ft. Lewis, WA; Yakima Firing Center, WA; Camp Irwin, CA.

Served with 4th Div., 82nd Abn., Constab. 88th Div., 1st Armd., 25th Inf. Div., 44th Inf. Div. Held commands as squad leader, tank commander, section leader (Korea), platoon sergeant.

Retired June 11, 1954 as sergeant 1/c, platoon sergeant. Awarded Korean Service Medal w/3 stars, UN Service Medal, Good Conduct, Occupation (Germany) Medal and National Defense.

Memorable experiences: being under the gun and holding the Russians at bay in Europe; ground combat in Korea as tank commander and hitting a land mine on an assault mission; coming under intense mortar and artillery fire while disabled.

Married to Eleanor and they have children: Arnold, Patty, Liz, Helen and Chris; 11 grandchildren and six great-grandchildren. Employed USBR operator, Imperial Irrigation Dist. (operator) at present, 44 years total for both agencies. Plans to retired May 25, 1999.

CHARLES E. (CHARLIE) RANSOM, born May 18, 1928, Brandon, OH, joined the US Army, March 20, 1946. Military locations and stations: Ft. Knox, KY, 13th Sqdn., Bayreuth; 28th Sqdn., HOF; 94th Sqdn., Weiden; 529 MP Svc. Co., Giessen-Wetzler.

Discharged March 1, 1949 as private first class. Awarded the Occupation Medal, WWII Victory Medal, European Theater and the Good Conduct.

Memorable experiences: meeting his wife Ingeborg in September 1946 and their wedding Dec. 22, 1948, Giessen, which was a military wedding, by buddies of the 529th MP Service Co., and being snowed in at Post 10 from just after X-Mas 1946 until March 1947 nothing moved.

Married Ingeborg Thamm Ransom and they have children: Charles E. Ransom, Jr. and Rebecca M. Ransom Hart; grandchildren, Brad Hart and Jeremey Hart. Employed PPG Industries for 39 years; laborer, time study/industrial engineering, plant safety and security supv. Retired Jan. 31, 1984.

MERLIN WILLIAM RAU, joined the service Feb. 27, 1945, Ft. Snelling, MN. Commissioned Feb. 14, 1946. Military locations and stations: Basic training, Camp Joseph T. Robinson, AR OCS, Ft. Benning, GA; B Trp., 74th Constab. Sqdn., April 18, 1946-Nov. 2, 1946, Augsburg and Donaworth, Germany; Korea, July 1950-July 1951, 21st Inf. Regt. of the 24th Inf. Div., and 7th Cav. Regt., platoon leader, 2nd Plt., L Co.; Ft. Leonardwood, MO, 1951-54, 25th Armd. Engr., Bn., Germany 1954-1957, Augsburg, Oberammergau, Bayreuth; Monterrey, CA, 1958, Army Language School, Germany, 1959-61, 318th US Army Security Agency; Ft. George G. Meade 1961-63, National Security Agency, Berlin, Germany, 1963-66, Army Security Agency, Vint Hill Farms, VA, 1966-68, US Army Security Agency.

Held commands as executive officer of B Trp., 74th Constab., Germany; 60mm mortar squad leader, 24th Inf. Div., infantry platoon leader, 7th Cav. Regt.

Battles and campaigns: Korea July 1950-July 1951, five major campaigns.

Retired Dec. 31, 1968 as captain. Awarded Expert Infantryman's Badge, Combat Infantryman's Badge, Bronze Star, two Presidential Unit Citations (US and Korea), Korean Service Medal w/Silver Star, Army Commendation Medal and several other service ribbons.

ENEO S. REBOLI, born and raised in Newark, NJ, and educated in Newark Schools and attended Rutgers University. Enlisted in the RA Sept. 9, 1948. Basic training, Ft. Dix, NJ. Assigned to the 15th Constab. Sqdn., in Weiden, Germany 1948-52 where he performed border patrol duties, then assigned to the special police unit under the command of then 1st Sgt. Robert W. Fry. Reboli participated in all sports while in the service.

Joined the Newark Police Department in April 1955, after completing four years with the 15th Constab. Sqdn. It wasn't very long before he realized that his life long pursuit was to be the defender and enforcement of the law. While serving as a detective with the Newark Police Bureau of Investigations, he was instrumental in solving numerous crimes and made multiple arrests. Reboli was injured many times during his police career, and was the recipient of many decorations. His list of achievements are numerous but here mentioned are a few: The Highest Police Award, The Medal of Honor and the New Jersey State PBA Valor Award. In December 1982 Reboli received the John I Crecco Foundation Award for his years in public service. For the past 20 years he spent his time in government with the Essex County Adjusters Department in New Jersey. Rising to the rank of chief in 1988, Eneo continued to service in government and soon was elected to the Office of Councilman of Fairfield, NJ, where he worked as a liaison to the TBSA rules and regulations committee. He is currently elected to the Board of Directors of the Essex County Federal Credit Union and is pursuing his interest in philanthropy. Eneo has two sons, Larry and John, one daughter, Joan Reboli Bonadeo and one grandson, Lawrence John. Larry is presently a member of the New Jersey State Police and is publisher of Reboli Newspapers, a group of township newspapers circulating throughout Northern New Jersey and Joan and account executive with CIO Communications, magazine publishers.

LEROY KIRKPATRICK REED, born March 10, 1924, Amberson, PA, joined the Army, Nov. 6, 1944. Military locations and stations: New Cumberland Induction Center, PA; Camp Blanding, FL; Ft. Meade, MD; Camp Shank, ETO, Ft. Dix, NJ. Served with 771st Tank Destroyer Bn., 4th Armd. Div., 2nd Cal Gp., 66th Constab. Sqdn. Fought campaigns in Central Europe

Discharged as SSG E-6 Aug. 30, 1946. His awards include the Army Good Conduct, European Theater w/ Campaign Star, Victory and Army of Occupation.

Reed is widowed and has children: Philomena, Geraldine, Monica and Kirk; grandchildren: Anderson, Keith and Reed. Employed Letter Kenny Army Depot, missile mechanic and inspector. Retired Oct. 20, 1980.

ALBERT RICHARD REINKE, born Sept. 28, 1926, Bakersfield, CA, drafted Nov. 11, 1944. Basic infantry training, Camp Roberts, CA. Infantry OCS, Ft. Benning, GA, March 16, 1945, commissioned second lieutenant, July 19, 1945. Assigned Camp Hood, TX, July 24, 1945. Transferred to Europe Dec. 10, 1945, 771st Tank Bn. Assigned US Constabulary School, Sonthofen, Germany, June 1, 1946. Transferred to Camp Beale, CA, March 5, 1947 for separation from the service, April 13, 1947, the rank of first lieutenant armor.

GI Bill student at Pacific University, August 1947 to May 30, 1952 awarded degree Doctor of Optometry.

Returned to active duty, US Army, as captain, MSC on Aug. 30, 1962. Served at Walter Reed Army Medical Center; Schofield Barracks, HI; US Army, Vietnam; US Army Combat Developments Command; 7th Medical Command, Heidelberg West Germany and Brooke Army Medical Center, Ft. Sam Houston, TX.

Awards include the Legion of Merit, Bronze Star, Meritorious Service Medal, Army Commendation Medal, Army Good Conduct Medal, Service Medals include American Campaign, EAME Campaign WWII Victory Medal, Army of Occupation Medal, National Defense Service, Vietnam Service w/4 Battle Stars, Republic of Vietnam Campaign, Republic of Vietnam Gallantry Cross Unit Citation.

JAMES H. (JIM) RESH, born Nov. 6, 1927, Christiana, PA, received a BS in business administration from Temple University. Joined the US Army, Sept. 15, 1945. Military locations and stations: Ft. Lee, VA; Heidelburg, Germany. Served with HQ, 3rd Army, US Constab. SHAEF. Held commands as chief clerk, Finance Section.

Discharged Sept. 30, 1948 as staff sergeant. Memorable experiences: serving with some of the finest young men he's ever known.

Married Irma B. Resh and they have children: James Jr., William, Suzanne and Diana; grandchildren: Brent, Adam, James, Alec, Samuel, Blake, Ashley and McKenzie. Employed as regional director, National Association of Securities Dealers, Inc. Retired March 1976.

ALBERT REVIELLO, departed Camp Shanks, May 13, 1946 as part of the 9222 TSU-TC POW Escort Guard

Det. #2 returning German prisoners of war back to Germany. Arrived May 26, after a stopover in England, at Bremerhaven, Germany. From Bremerhaven was transferred to Neustadt, Germany where the 12th Constab. Sqdn. was stationed. After a few months of raiding DP camps was assigned as Enlisted Club manager until hi tour was up. Departed Germany on May 23, 1947. Enlisted in the USN in 1948 for four years. After being discharged was in the USNR for four more years and in the Pennsylvania National Guard for 12 1/2 years for a tota of 23 years total.

ABRAHAM LINCOLN (LINK) RHEA, born June 22, 1921, Altamont, TN, entered military service Octobe 1942, basic training, Camp Atterbury, IN.

Service history: WWI Campaigns in Normandy, Northern France, Rhineland and Central Europe, Co. M 3rd Btry., 331st Inf., Regt., 83rd Inf., Div. October 1943-October 1945; Germany (Kassel), 11th Constab. Sqdn., January 1946-July 1947; Germany (Bad Hersfeld, Boeblingen, Fulda) 91st Constab. Sqdn., September 1947-May 1950; Germany (Schweinfurt, Bad Kissingen) 24th Constab. Sqdn., May 1950-December 1952; Germany (Bad Kissingen) 2nd Btry., 14th Armd. Cav., December 1952-May 1953; Ft. Knox, KY 131st Tank Bat. and 509th Tank Bat., May 1953-April 1955; Korea, Tank Co., 19th Inf., Regt., 24th Inf Div., May 1955-November 1956; Ft. Knox, KY, 3rd Medium Tank Bat., 33rd Armor, November 1956-August 1959; Germany (Baumholder) 2nd Bat. 68th Armor, August 1959-June 1961; Germany (Schweinfurt) 3rd Bat., 37th Armor, June 1961-April 1964; Bakersfield, CA Advisor Gp., California National Guard, May 1964-April 1967; Germany (Schweinfurt) 3rd Bat. 64th Armor, April 1976-July 1969.

Rhea retired August 1969. He is the recipient of the Purple Heart, WWII Victory Medal, Combat Infantry Badge, Occupation Medal, EAME Campaign Ribbon w/5 Bronze Stars, Silver Star Medal, Good Conduct Medal (5th Award), National Defense Service Medal and numerous letters of commendations.

Link Rhea resides with his wife Lydia in Bakersfield, CA where he was a sales rep for a local supply company until December 1988. They have one son, two daughters, one granddaughter and one grandson. He loves traveling, bowling, gardening, and rug making.

HAROLD LEE RICHARDSON, born Aug. 27, 1932 Etowah County, AL, enlisted RA Sept. 7, 1949; 14 weeks basic, Co. E, 11th Inf. Regt., 5th Inf. Div., Ft. Jackson, SC; 5th Signal Co., Ft. Jackson; Ft. Dix, NJ May 1950; Weiden, Germany June 10, 1950, 15th Constab. Sqdn.; Ft. Rucker, AL, April 20, 1952 (mail clerk). Discharged Feb. 17, 1953.

Patrol and outpost leader (Germany), highest rank, staff sergeant. His awards include the Army Occupation of Germany. Married Anna Childress and they have 10 children, and 21 grandchildren. Loves all sports.

BENJAMIN LEE RICHMOND, born Dec. 20, 1930, Modesto, CA. Enlisted in the RA, Oct. 25, 1950, Sacramento, CA. Basic training served in Ft. Knox, KY.

Duties: US Constab., based in Regensburg, Germany, December 1950-September 1953. Experiences in Germany were varied. They traveled about with the 6th AC and worked border patrol. Cold days, long cold nights. Germany is a beautiful country. It was a wonderful experience serving his country there.

Honorably discharged Oct. 7, 1953. Received Army Occupation Medal, Germany and National Defense Service Medal, Co. G, 6th Armd. Cav.

Married to Mildred Jan. 29, 1970 until her death 1997. Through combined families he has eight wonderful children: Sabrina, Ben Jr., Dennis, Laura, Lilea, Dorrie, Dan and Ed. Ten energetic grandchildren: Casey, Kim, Tina, Aubrey, Chardi, Brett, Ian, Joseph, Lilea Jr. and Wayne. No great-grandchildren to date. One little dog, Belle.

Retired Dec. 30, 1992 from 19 1/2 years as a maintenance mechanic with the State of California, San Luis Reservoir, Merced County.

Hobbies include: genealogy, computer games, reading, Constabulary reunions and occasional traveling to visit friends and family.

WILLIAM H. (RICK) RICHTER, born Jan. 11, 1927, Connellsville, PA, joined the US Army, September 1945. Military locations and stations: basic training, Camp Robison, AR; Germany, two tours; Japan; Korea two tours; Okinawa, two tours.

Served with 15th Cav. Regt., 15th Constab. Horse Plt., 4th Inf. Div., 3rd Inf. Div., 24th Inf. Div., 1 Msl. Bn., 3 Mls. Bn. Fought the Spring Offense campaign in Korea.

Retired Jan. 31, 1972 and received the Good Conduct w/2 Silver Knots, Commendation Medal and German Occupation.

Memorable experiences: formed the 15th Constab. Horse Plt., Karlsruhe Germany. Assigned to the Ajax missile sight that blew up in Middletown, NJ, May 22, 1958. Btry. 526th AAA Nike Bn.

Married Betty and they have daughter, Georgeanna Kay Wilson and grandchildren: Bobby Richter Wilson and Billy Joe Wilson. Retired from civilian employment January 1989.

MARVIN E. RINEER, born May 31, 1930, Quarryville, PA, served Delaware National Guard January 1947-February 1948. Joined service Feb. 18, 1948. Military locations and stations: Ft. Dix, Ft. Monmouth. Re-up Ft. Dix, Marburg, Germany; Boeblingen, Germany; Paris, Fontainbleu and Orleans France. Served with 9th Inf., Signal School, 97th Signal Bn., 7784 Sig. Co., 805 Station Hospital USAR.

Discharged April 23, 1953, SFC and received the Occupation of Germany Medal.

Memorable experiences: was only in 97 Sig. for six months, (July-December 1950) then assigned to France (January 1951-April 1953). Enlisted in Army Reserve January 1955, discharged May 1962, 805 Sta. Hospital.

Married Eva and they have no children. Employed as construction painter foreman and retired July 1, 1990.

JOHN H. RIVERS, born July 20, 1925, Rochester, NY. Joined the Army Signal Corp, July 20, 1945. Commissioned 1947. Military locations and stations: Heidelberg, Germany and Bamburg, Germany.

Served with the 97th and discharged as T-4 Dec. 24, 1948.

Rivers is a widower and has children: John M., Lynda M. and Karen A.; grandchildren: Carl, Denis, Michael and Stacey. Employed with Eastman Kodak Co., as lab technician, 40 years, two weeks, two days, retiring Jan. 3, 1983.

DALE A. (ROCKY) ROCKFORD, born Feb. 8, 1927, Battle Creek, MI, joined the US Army, February 1947. Military locations and stations: Ft. Lewis, WA; Ft. Lawton, WA; 1947-51; Berlin-Germany, 1952-53; Korea, 1953-56; Ft. Bliss, TX; Ft. Lawton, OK; Korea; Vietnam; Germany. Served with Constab. D Trp., Horse Plt., Berlin Germany.

Retired February 1967 as SSG E-6. Held command as platoon sergeant. Fought battles and campaigns in Korea and Vietnam. His awards include the Good Conduct Medal, Silver Stars and Battle Stars.

Memorable experiences: airlift Berlin at Spandau Prison; control Autobahn; checkpoint patrol, Helmstedt, Germany.

Rockford married Edith, 1951 Berlin Germany and they have a daughter, Pamela Lynn. Employed with armored car in El Paso, Federal Reserve Bank, Houston, TX. Retired April 1989.

GILES RONNEBAUM, born July 22, 1928, Montezuma, OH, joined the US Army, Jan. 22, 1951. Military locations and stations: Straubing, Germany. Served with 6th AC, Air Section. Discharged as private first class, December 1952.

He married Eileen and retired from farming in 1995.

BRUCE H. ROSS, born Dec. 9, 1927, Atlanta, GA, enlisted in the RA, Nov. 28, 1945. Basic training at Ft. McClellan, AL. March 1946-July 1946: Co. I, 7th Regt., 3rd Inf. Div., Tann Lenggries, Germany. October 1947-August 1948: C Trp., 66th Constab. Sqdn., Degerndorf, Germany. January 1949-November 1950: HQ Co., 1st Bn, 18th Inf. Regt., 1st Div. Lenggries, Germany. November 1950-May 1951: RHQ Co. 22nd Inf. Regt., Ft. Benning, GA. May 1951-February 1954: RHQ Co. 22nd Inf. Regt., Schweinfurt, Kirch-Gons, Germany. February 1954-August 1956: 29th Inf. Regt., 30th Inf. Regt., and the Infantry Center Advanced Leaders School, Ft. Benning, GA November 1956 to February 1959: Attached to USN Amphib. Gp. 2, Little Creek, Norfolk, VA and the Mediterranean. March 1959-March 1963: HQ USARPAC, Ft. Shafter, HI. March 1963-February 1966: 4th Inf. Div., Ft. Lewis, WA.

Retired February 28, 1966 and received the Expert Infantry Badge, Good Conduct, WWII Victory, Army of Occupation and National Defense.

Life member of TREA, VFW, American Legion and Amvets. Married Joanne Hout April 28, 1951. They have four daughters, one son and 10 grandchildren.

ROBERT ROUSSEL *photo only, no bio submitted.*

CLARENCE A. ROWE, of HQ Trp., 16th Constab. Sqdn., (separate), Berlin, Germany holds a Thompson Submachine gun during the Russian-East German 1950 May Day Celebration in the city.

Clarence was from Iowa and he and Solosky had become friends when they first met on the troop ship *General Alexander M. Patch* and stayed best friends throughout their three plus year tour of military service in Berlin.

He married a Berliner, Helga Willberg, and after a military career of 22 years, retired in 1971 with the rank of sergeant first class with his wife Helga in Tampa, FL.

Clarence died in 1983 and is buried in Arlington National Cemetery, Virginia. Solosky and his wife are still good friends of Helga, whom they visit and correspond with often.

Clarence felt serving in the Berlin Occupation was a highlight in their Constabulary adventures of which they are justly proud.

Posthumously submitted in memory of Clarence A. Rowe, friend and comrade by Al Solosky.

ROBERT G. RULE, born Dec. 27, 1927, Plymouth, OH, enlisted in the RA, Oct. 3, 1946 in New York City. He was sent to Camp Kilmer, NJ and then to Ft. Jackson, SC.

Before he enlisted, he had just returned from the South Pacific, where he was in the Merchant Marines. He had been in the Atlantic and Pacific War Zones. After army basic training, shipped to Bremerhaven, Germany. From there, he went by railroad to Austria. Stationed with A Trp., 24th Contab. and then was stationed at Eblsburg for a year and half. Lastly he was assigned to Inns on the Danube where he worked border patrol. Discharged April 9, 1948.

JOSEPH G. RUSSO, born Dec. 3, 1927, Buffalo, NY, enlisted in the Army Reserves Jan. 29, 1945-Feb. 21, 1946. Inducted into service Feb. 22, 1946, Buffalo, NY. Discharged May 6, 1947.

Military locations and stations: Ft. Knox, KY; US Constab. European Theater of Occupation, Trp. A, attached to HQ, Regensburg, Germany.

Awarded Lapel Button, Inactive Reserve ERC no days lost; Army of Occupation; WWII Victory Medal and Good Conduct Medal.

Married to Carol and they have one daughter and three grandchildren.

Retired member US Constabulary Association; life member Catholic War Veterans, DAV, VFW, AMVETS and American Legion.

RICHARD (RIPPER) RYPMA, born 1928, Gates, NY. Joined the service Dec. 22, 1945. Served with 2nd Constab. in Germany. Discharged in 1947 as T/5 and received Good Conduct Medal, Occupation, Victory Medal and ETO Medal.

Married Jacqueline and they have children: Debra, Walter and Charles; grandchildren: Nathan and Madeline Sheffield, Lexi Rypma and Tori Rypma. Employed as a carpenter and retired in 1986.

REMO P. SABETTI JR., born Mable, AL, June 11, 1928, enlisted US Army, Feb. 12, 1946, Washington, DC, sent to Ft. Meade, MD, then to basic training at Ft. McClellan, AL, Co. D, 24th Bn., 7th Regt., 1 RTC.

Other duty stations: C Trp., 72nd Constab. Sqdn., 10th Constab. Regt., July 1946 Boblingen, Germany. Rotated with other 72nd Sqdn. troops to Ulm, Germany to patrol border and set up road blocks on the Autobahn, 30 days at a time.

1948 sent to Graffenwohr, Germany to train with the 1st Inf. Div., changed to 1st Recon Trp., 1st Inf. Div. early 1948 and sent to Erlangen, Germany. Also served at various times overseas and in the US with the 14th, 15th, Const. Regt. at Fulda, Germany and the 6th and 11th A/C, HQ Co., 509th Tank Bn. Recon Plt., Ft. Knox, B Trp., 1st Recon Sqdn., 9th Cav., 1st Cav. Div., Korea November 1960 to 1961 then to Ft. Knox to USATC pushing recruits and one year Walter Reed Hospital as a patient and back to Ft. Knox. G-3 range as a range NCO. Went to Valley Forge Hospital, January 1964 for physical evolution board. Was retired March 18, 1964, 30% disability, 18 years, one month, 18 days as SFC E-6.

Married Mary L. July 13, 1968 and they have two children and six grandchildren. Retired General Electric Co. December 1990 after 26 years.

ENRIQUE H. SAÉNZ,

born May 25, 1928, served 1944-1946, Brownsville, TX. Military locations and staions: Germany, Korea, Alaska and Vietnam.

Retired Sept. 1, 1972 and his awards include the Purple Heart, Combat Infantry Badge, WWII Victory Medal, Korean Service Medal, Vietnam Campaign Medal, other medals and campaign ribbons.

Married Lilo, Dec. 26, 1950 in Zurich Switzerland and they have four sons and one daughter. He enjoys traveling, hunting and fishing.

KENNETH L. (KENNY) SAGER,

born March 15, 1929, Olney, IL, is life member of Lutheran Church. Inducted into military service January 1951. Basic training, 14 weeks, 101st Abn., Breckinridge, KY.

Duties: shipped to Hersfeld, Germany, July 1951. Assigned to 24th Constab. HQ Co.; border guard and worked in motor pool. Shipped back to states December 1952. Discharged from Ft. Custer, MI, January 1953.

Married Delores Hearring Nov. 20, 1953. Went to Mechanic School on GI Bill 1954-56. Had three children: Dave, Julie and Tim. His wife Delores passed away Feb. 28, 1995 with liver cancer. He worked at Pure Oil Co. and Cooper Oil Co. until 1968. 1968-1994 mechanic for UPS, 26 years. Retired March 1994. He has a motor home and loves to travel. When not traveling he resides in Olney, IL.

ALBERT SALLUSTIO,

born July 18, 1928, Brooklyn, NY, enlisted in the RA, Dec. 16, 1946; basic training, Ft. Dix, NJ.

Duties: US Constab., Germany, 35th Sqdn., Fussen, April 1947-September 1947, D Trp., 42nd Sqdn., 2nd ACR, Augsburg, October 1947-May 1948. In addition to regular troopers duties he played on the 35th Sqdn. baseball team and 42nd Sqdn. basketball team (Regimental Champions).

Medals include the WWII Victory Medal and Army of Occupation Medal, Army Lapel Button.

Education: Mondell Institute, Academy of Aeronautics, NYC, NY; BS Aeronautical Design, 1952 (under GI Bill).

Engineering career in aerospace industry spanned 42 years. Worked on many military and commercial aircraft programs including major USAF and Space programs. Retired as senior project engineer, Sept. 30, 1993.

Married Roberta Rogers, May 29, 1982. One stepdaughter and two grandchildren. Member: VFW Post 67, US Constabulary Association, 2D Cavalry Association, Sacramento Golden Seniors Softball Club. In addition to playing softball he enjoys travel and gardening.

ELBERT H. (HERKY) SAMPSON,

born Feb. 27, 1931, Weymouth, MA, joined the US Army May 1949. Military locations and stations: Ft. Dix, NJ; Augsburg, Bamberg, Munich, Germany.

Served with 39th Inf. Regt., Ft. Dix, 2 AC Regt., Germany as squad leader. Discharged September 1952 as sergeant.

Memorable experiences: border patrol out of Kronach and the thousands of people fleeing the east zone.

Married Charlotte Ann Sampson and they have children: Wayne, Gary and Charlene; grandchildren: Amy, Walter and Sterling. Employed in firefighting, retiring as captain, shift commander, 1981.

WILKIN SAUNDER

photo only, no bio submitted.

DAVID J. (DAVE) SCHARDT,

born Aug. 26, 1926, East Saint Louis, IL, received a BS from the University of Illinois.

Joined the AUS, Nov. 4, 1944. Military locations and stations: Camp Robinson, Little Rock, AR; ETO; France; Belgium; Austria; Hungary.

Served with 940th FA, 15th Army, 68 AFA, 1st Armd., 68th Constab. as section leader. Achieved the rank of sergeant and discharged Aug. 26, 1946. Received one Battle Star for ET O and the Good Conduct Medal.

Memorable experiences: sad and glorious: as a member of the third class at Sonthofen he was fully aware of the greatness of the Constabulary.

Married Joyce Pitman Schardt and they have children: Dianne S. Lowry and David P. Schardt and grandchildren: Aislinn E. Lowry, David York Schardt. Employed as supervisor safety and training, retired Jan. 1, 1986.

MARTIN B. SCHENCK,

born Sept. 7, 1922, Perth Amboy, NJ, joined the US Army, Dec. 8, 1938. Military locations and stations: Germany, Australia, Japan, Hawaii, South America.

Served with USN, Pearl Harbor Dec. 7, 1941. Fought the war in Pacific. 14 AC, US Constab., Ft. Knox, Ft. Polk, Ft. Rucker, Ft. Hood.

Discharged Sept. 1, 1970 as first sergeant. November 12-13, 1942, Pearl Harbor attack, three battles in Pacific, went on submarine made seven patrols, Army, Constabulary, started and finished 11th A/C Vietnam, Korea.

His awards include Silver Star, Bronze Star, Purple Heart and Vietnam Gallantry Cross.

Married Yvonne Schenck and they have children: Mushie Schenck, Patty Schenck and Pete Schenck. Retired Sept. 1, 1970.

MAX SCHLOSSBERG,

born Aug. 26, 1905, Riga, Russia, attended two years college and received an AA degree from the University of Maryland; two years language, one year Russian; one year Bulgarian at ALS Monterey.

Joined the Army November 1941. Commissioned February 1942. Military locations and stations: Ft. Sill, OK; Camp Ritchie, MD; Ft Slocum, NJ; Yeoville and London, England; Linz; Steyes; Salzburg; Austria; Berlin; Heidelberg; Frankfurt; Ft. Ord, CA; Ft. Riley, TX; Monterrey, CA.

Served with 502 M1 Gp., 526 M1 Co., 1st Div. HQ Command Berlin, 4th Cav. Gp., 4th Cav. Regt., B Trp., 4th Constab., HQ Command Australia, Salzburg and others.

Retired the fall of 1964 as major. Battles and campaigns: Normandy, Germany, France, Battle of the Bulge, Occupation of Austria.

Awarded the National Defense Medal, EAME Campaign, American Campaign, Armed Forces Reserve, Army of Occupation, WWII.

Memorable experiences: French Liberty, Normandy landing, Bronze Star, Presidential Unit Citation, Rifle Marksmanship Medal.

Married 51 years to Theresa and they have children: Leon, Deborah, Mona, (twins 1st Americans born in Berlin); grandchildren: Sondra, Lindsey, Michael and Matthew. Retired from civilian employment November 1964.

HAROLD G. SCHOLL,

born July 30, 1927, Salfordville, PA. Drafted in the Army August 1945. Military locations and stations: Ft. Sill, OK; basic training FA 105 Cannon, Weisbaden, Germany; Camp Pickett, VA (prior to Germany); HQ 4th Armd. Div. and HQ 1st Constab. Bde. were in Weisbaden, Germany December 1945-February 1947.

Discharged March 9, 1947 as technician fourth grade. Awarded the Army of Occupation, WWII Victory Medal, European Theater Campaign and Good Conduct.

Memorable experiences: Divisional HQ and APO333 Postal Sergeant, 105 Cannon Combat Team Sergeant; member VFW, US Constabulary Association (Outpost #2); friendships are his memories; 4th Armored Division Association.

Married June (Shafer) in 1951 and they have children, David and Heather Frantz and grandchildren: Amy and Andrew Frantz, Jeffery Scholl. Employed for Ford dealer as parts manager for 42 years, retiring September 1989.

DANIEL JOHN SCHULTE, born Sept. 16, 1927, Astoria, NY, left New York in 1941 to Catonsville, MD. Attended Mt. St. Joseph HS in Irvington, MD and graduated from St. Anns Academy, NYC in 1945. While in Maryland, joined the State Guard.

Entered US Army from Montclair, NJ in November 1945. Basic and AIT in Camp Crowder, MO and at Ft. Monmouth, NJ. 3196th Sig Svc. Co. in Leghorn, Italy, December 1946-December 1947 when Med. Theater of Opns. closed. 82nd AB Div. in Ft. Bragg, NC, January-July 1948. Joined A/16th Constab. Sqdn. (Sep) in Berlin in July 1948. Deactivated 16th Constab. and activated 6th Inf. Regt. in Berlin 1950. 16th Inf. Regt. in Nurnberg, Furth in 1951. Promoted to MSGT August 1953. Joined the 25th Signal Co. in Ft. Devens, MA in 1953. Army Language School in Monterey, CA to study Russian. Field Arty. OCS in July 1955 and commissioned 2nd Lt. Arty. in February 1956. 4th Armd. Div. in Ft. Hood, TX and gyroscoped to Nurnberg/Furth in January 1958 as Bn. Recon/S Off. Assigned to 4th AD Arty. Staff as adjutant departing in 1961 to Ft. Bliss, TX for advanced training in Air Def. Arty. Instructor in Command and Staff Dept. until 1963 when assigned to MACV in Ban Me Thuot, Vietnam. Earned the CIB before returning to Ft. Bliss in 1964 and promotion to major. COMZ in Mannheim, GY in 1968 as assist IG for 3 1/2 years. Promoted to LTC and returned to CONARC HQ in AIT Branch. Retired after 27 years in 1972 and returned to El Paso, TX.

Entered El Paso City Personnel Dept. for two years. Received bachelors degree from University of MD in Heidelberg in 1970. Completed masters degree in Educational Counseling and Guidance and in School Administration from University of Texas at El Paso in 1972 and moved over to the YSLETA Independent School District as a vocational educator and counselor. Retired from the schools in 1992. Now engaged in rotary work full time as district governor of RI DiSt 5520 for 1997-98.

Dan is married to Kathleen M. Ralphs and they have three children and four grandchildren.

He is past president of The Retired Officers Association, member of the 4th Armored Division Association and the US Constabulary Association. He is a woodworker and enjoys flying.

FRANK J. (CHICKIE) SCIRICA, born June 28, 1925, Norristown, PA, drafted into the US Army on June 29, 1945. Received basic training in Ft. Knox, KY, in 1925. Qualified as medium tank operator.

Duties: January 1945 stationed at Freising, Germany, assigned to 6981st Inf. Rifle Co., 42nd Cav. Recon Sqdn. which later became Trp. D, 42nd Constab. Sqdn.

During his time in the 42nd Constab., he was assigned to a squad that traveled throughout Germany to many cavalry squadrons providing demonstrations on the functions of the new Constabulary. All the Cavalry squadrons later became permanent Constabularies. They performed raids in various cities throughout Germany. In 1946, he became a T/5 squadron leader. In addition, he became the athletic non-com of the squadron and played football for the 2nd Bde. They practiced in Freising and their home field was in Munich.

Received several medals including Army of Occupation, WWII Victory Medal, Army Good Conduct and two Overseas Service Ribbon.

Attended Ursinus College in Collegeville, PA and received his BA in economics in 1951. He later married Pauline White, April 30, 1960 and had three daughters: Antonia, Lia and Cina and one son, Frank J. Scirica, II and nine grandchildren. He is a member of the US Constabulary Association and the VFW.

Retired Jan. 1, 1989 after 33 years with Steel Heddle Manufacturing Co., as vice president of Materials Management and currently resides in Norristown, PA with his wife of 38 wonderful years.

He enjoys playing golf, fishing for trout and bass and spend much time reading.

CHESTER SEDWICK, born July 25, 1927, Erie, PA, joined the US Army, Aug. 30, 1946. Military locations and stations: Fussen, Germany; Constab, Basic Augsburg, Germany; Bayreuth, Gemany.

Served with 74th Constab. Sqdn. Reorganized as the SFC-ACT Plt. Leader, 2nd Armd. Cav.

Discharged December 1953 as SFC. Schools, NCO Academy, Munich, Germany and Tank School. Awarded the usual, Occupation and Good Conduct.

Employed as motor pool supervisor for AF Rescue, retired June 1981.

WILLIAM J. SEELY, born April 5, 1921, Velma, OK, entered service June 1943 at Lubbock, TX. Basic training at Camp Wallace, TX. Joined 1st Div. (Red One) in ETO (Germany) December 1944.

Returned to states after end of WWII (October 1945). Discharged from service. Reenlisted May 1946 and was sent to Regensburg, Germany and joined US Constab. May 1946.

Assigned to the 25th Constab. Sqdn. D, Troop at Straubing, Germany 1946 to 1949. Returned to States to Ft. Hood, TX 1949. 2nd Armd. Div. in 1950, returned to Mainz, Germany with the 2nd Armd. Div was first sergeant of C Co., 42nd AIB.

Married Ruby Holt Sept. 3, 1949 and have children, Thomas and Barbara Seely; grandchildren, Allen, Lowrie, Kellie Jackie. Employed at Southwest Lab. In charge of structural steel inspection Ft. Worth, TX.

MYRON J. SEESE, born Oct. 15, 1927, Center Point, WV. Drafted December 1946 and sworn in at Ft. Hayes, OH, January 1946. Basic training, Ft. Bliss, TX to Coburg, Germany June 1946. Assigned to the new 6th US Constab. Sqdn. in the old German Army Barracks. They were stationed in part of the camp and displaced persons occupied the remainder.

Their duties were patrolling the border between the US and Russian zone of the divided Germany. They were stationed off base most of the time is houses along the border. In winter as well as summer, patrols consisted of one non-com, driver "open jeep" and an ex-Germany soldier; soldier who fluent in English. They were also under the command of Gen. Harman. Winters are very cold in Germany. After ten months and having been drafted with many young men enlisting because lack of work, he was discharged April 30, 1947 at Ft. Dix, NJ. Awarded the Victory Medal, European Ribbon and Occupation Ribbon.

Married Rhea Scott and they have two children, Myron II and Myradean Stewart and four grandchildren. He and his wife enjoy church activities and visiting their grandchildren.

JAMES WOODROW SELLSTROM, born March 30, 1927, Round Rock, TX, inducted into service June 21, 1945, Ft. Sam Houston, TX. Military locations and stations: IRTC, Camp Fannin, Tyler, TX; Ft. Riley, KS; HQ Trp., 2nd Constab. Regt., Freising and Munich, Germany.

Awarded the Army of Occupation Ribbon (Germany), Victory Ribbon, one Overseas Bar, Lapel Button.

Married Jean Quist July 14, 1949 and they have two sons, one daughter and six grandchildren. Elder in Presbyterian Church. Retired after 39 years Southwestern Bell Telephone Co.

Sellstrom collects antique cars, restores old farm tractors. Travels and enjoys his family. Go to car show and tractor shows.

GORDON CLIFFORD SEVERUD, born May 4, 1924, Minneapolis, MN, enlisted June 20, 1942 in the USAAF at Ft. Snelling, MN. Took basic training at Jefferson Barracks, MO. Graduated Airplane Mechanics School, Lincoln, NE in December 1942. Attended B-25 Maintenance Course at North American Aviation Inc., Inglewood, CA in December 1942-January 1943. Assigned to Tyndall Field, FL. Attended aerial (gunners flexible) AAF Gunnery School February and March 1943. Promoted to "Buck" sergeant upon graduation. Reassigned to 309th BG, Columbia Army AB, Columbia, SC. Trained as a B-25 combat crew member (engineer gunner) for six months and sent overseas October 1943. Joined the 340th BG in Italy. Participated in 55 combat missions over Italy and Southern France. Reassigned stateside October 1944. Received 30 day leave at home in Minneapolis, MN, and sent to Santa Ana, CA for rest camp. Reassigned to Chanute Field, IL to attend helicopter-maintenance. Completed in June 1945. Sent to Morrison Field, FL to help in the recovery of their aircraft returning from Europe. Discharged Sept. 16, 1945 at Camp McCoy, WI.

Reenlisted May 3, 1946 at Ft. Snelling, MN in RA as a staff sergeant with assignment to Germany. Went overseas from Camp Kilmer, NJ to Bremerhaven, Germany and on to Rosenheim, Bavaria and assignment to the 9th Inf. Div. in Augsburg. Assigned to the 60th FA Bn. and to the Air Section (10 L-5s). Transferred to the 5th Constab. Regt. in Jan. 1947 when the 9th Div. was sent back to the States. The 2nd Constab. replaced the 5th at a later date. Married Theresia Kagerer, Dec. 2, 1948 in Augsburg, Germany and they were rotated stateside. Discharged in Mar. 1949.

Enlisted in the USAF Reserve in June 1949 in Minneapolis. Stayed in Reserve until March 1, 1950 and was put on active duty. Transferred to Fairchild AFB, Spokane, WA in May 1951. In December 1952 he was put on orders for the Far East. He ended up in Korea at K-14. Assigned to the 4th Fighter Interceptor Wing who were flying the F-86 Saberjet. This was one Hot fighter outfit. He was assigned to base flight and was in charge of the alert crew for maintenance and service for Transient Aircraft that found their way to Kimpo. They caught the Army, Navy, Marine Corps, Australians, English Aircraft as they came through, from B-29s to Helicopters. Got orders assigning him to a Reserve Flying Center at O'Hare Airport, Chicago, IL, in December 1953. Started his duty with the 2471st AR Flying Center in January 1952. They trained Reserve Officers and Men in C-46 and C-47, C-119 Cargo Aircraft. He pulled duty there from January 1952 until October 1958 and really enjoyed being part of this important Reserve Program. Promoted to technical sergeant in 1956. New orders transferred him to Schilling AFB, Salina, KS in October 1958, assigning him to the 310th BW, 381st BS that was flying B-47 Stratojet, six engine Medium Bombers capable with In-Flight Refueling of bombing anyplace in the world. He held a variety of jobs in this wing. B-47 Crew Chief, duty sergeant, Maintenance Training Control, Maintenance Quality Control. Promoted to master sergeant May 1, 1963. He retired Feb. 1, 1964.

Awarded the Air Crew Member Badge, Aerial Gunners Wings, Air Medal w/4 OLCs, Distinguished Unit Citation, Italy, Sept. 23, 1944, Air Force Outstanding Unit Award, Army Good Conduct w/5 Loops, American Campaign, EAME w/6 Battle Stars, WWII Victory Occupation Army, National Defense, Korea Service w/3 Battle Stars, AF Longevity w/4 OLCs, Korean Presidential Citation, UN Medal.

GERALD R. (WHITEY) SHALLBERG, born July 10, 1927, Wausa, NE, joined the Army August 1945. Military locations and stations: Ft. Leavenworth, KS; Ft. Sill, OK; Ft. Ord, CA; Camp Kilmer, NJ; Ft. Sheridan, IL. Served with CCA, 1st Armd. Div., 3rd Constab. Regt.

Discharged March 1947 as T/4. Attended second class of US Constab. School, Sonthofen.

Memorable experiences: near ditching in North Atlantic in January 1947.

Married JoAnn and they have children: David, an engineer in Johnson County, KS. Employed with the Nebraska Department of Agriculture and US Postal Service. Retired August 1987.

EDWARD C. SHOBER, born Sept. 6, 1930, Summit Hill, PA, joined the US Army Sept. 20, 1948. Military locations and stations: Camp Breckinridge, KY; Germany; Fritzlar, Fulda and Schweinfurt. Served with Co. A, 1st Bn., 14th AC.

Discharged June 17, 1952 as sergeant. Awarded Good Conduct Medal and Occupational Ribbon.

Memorable experiences: border patrol in all kinds of weather; being a member of the 14th Armd. Regimental Football Team, 49-50-51, playing in the Vittles Bowl 1949.

Shober is a widower and has children: Edward Jr., Mary Jean, David, Anne, Joan and Patricia; grandchildren: Christe, Stephony, Laren, Kaitlyn, Patrick, Zachary, Marie, Lara Elizabeth, Anthony and Mary. Employed as construction inspector, construction supervisor, construction manager, Pennsylvania Dept. Environmental Resources. Retired December 1992.

ROBERT J. (BOB) SILER, born April 14, 1929, Hastings, NE. Joined the RA June 6, 1946. Military locations and stations: Basic and tech, Ft. Eustis, VA; 16th Constab. (Sep), Berlin. Served with Trp. A, 16th Constab. Sqdn. (Sep). Discharged June 17, 1949.

Memorable experiences: Arrived Berlin February 1947; flew out on coal plane June 1949.

Married Phyllis A. and they have children: Russell, Susan, Brian and Rosalind; grandchildren: Steve, Alex, David, Rachel and Kiersten. Employed as plumber for 40+ years, retiring Dec. 2, 1991.

WALTER T. SINNER, born June 18, 1928, Woubay, SD, inducted into service Oct. 5, 1946, Sioux Falls, SD. Discharged February 1948. Military locations and stations:

Ft. Riley, KS; Ft. Jackson, SC; Kitzingen, Germany, 27th Sqdn., 14th Regt.

Awards include the WWII Victory Medal, Army of Occupation and Good Conduct.

Married Marlene Goebel Dec. 26, 1953 and they have one son, one daughter, three grandsons and one granddaughter. Retired and member of American Legion, VFW, DAV and Constabulary.

KENNETH L. SKAGGS, born Oct. 31, 1927, Miami, Oklahoma, moved with parents to Phoenix, AZ, December 1944. Joined the RA Nov. 7, 1945 with his best friend, at that time you could enlist under the buddy system and served the first three years together. They were sent to Ft. McArthur, CA where his buddy went AWOL. Hasn't seen him since.

Took basic training at Ft. Knox, KY. Went to Germany March 21, 1946 with 2nd Constab. Regt. Light Tank Trp. Served at Karlsruhe until March 1947 and was then assigned to the 7776 HQ & HQ Trp. Horse Plt., served in Heidelberg and Vahingon. Highest grade held was T/4.

Departed Europe for USA Sept. 16, 1948. Discharged November 1948. Joined the Phoenix Fire Department September 1950 and served 25 years. Retired as captain January 1976.

BERNARD H. SKOLD, born April 1, 1915, on a farm near Haxtun, CO. After graduating from high school he enlisted in the RA Medical Department at Ft. Logan, CO and was stationed at Fitzsimmons Army Hospital, Denver, CO for two enlistments.

While at Fitzsimmons he attended the University of Denver, part-time, and completed the requirements for admission to the College of the Veterinary Medicine, Colorado State University. He purchased a Class III discharge when he received his letter of acceptance to the college.

During the four years at the veterinary college he enlisted in the Colorado National Guard and was discharged prior to graduation. After graduation from Colorado State University he was drafted and assigned to the Army Ordnance Department at Ft. Ord, CA. He applied for a direct commission in the Veterinary Corps Reserve and was commissioned a first lieutenant Nov. 1, 1942.

Stationed at Camp Lockett, the assigned post for the 10th and 28th Horse Cav. Regts. and HQ, 4th Bde., 2nd Horse Cav. Div. as assistant station veterinarian until 1944. After the Horse Cavalry was disbanded he was stationed at HQ, 9th Svc. Command at Presidio of San Francisco and Ft. Douglas, UT.

Sent to the ETO in 1946 and assigned to HQ, 2nd Constab. Bde., Saar Kaserne, Munich as brigade veterinarian to care for the mounts of the horse patrols in the three regiments of the 2nd Bde. While there he attended the war crimes trials in Nuremburg.

After leaving the US Constab. he was stationed in Paris, France with the American Graves Registration Command where his duties were to inspect the food supplies and the food factories that furnished food to the Army. While stationed in France he was commissioned major in the RA.

Upon returning to the US he was stationed in Chicago at the QM Depot to teach in the Meat and Dairy Hygiene School and QM Subsistence School. In 1953 he was assigned to ROTC duty at Colorado State University as assistant professor of veterinary ROTC. During that

three year assignment he obtained an advanced degree in veterinary pathology.

His last Army duty was the Armed Forces Institute of Pathology at Walter Reed Army Hospital in Washington, DC. While there he was offered a position of professor at the College of Veterinary Medicine, Iowa State University, if he would retire from the RA. By 1960 he had completed 26 years of Army service and had reached the rank of lieutenant colonel. He elected to retire Nov. 1, 1960 and moved to Ames, IA. Taught veterinary medicine for 20 years at Iowa State until 65 years of age and eligible for full Social Security and CREF benefits.

Skold and his college sweetheart, Ellen Marlatt have been married for 53 years. They have a married daughter and two married grandchildren. They currently live in the university retirement community, which has a health care center, in Ames, IA.

ROBERT F. (BOB) SLOATE, born Nov. 25, 1929, Queens, NY, NY. Joined the Army Nov. 25, 1946. Military locations and stations: Basic, Ft. Dix, Constab. 1947-50; 11th Abn. Div., 1950-51; Ft. Campbell, KY, 73rd Tk. Bn., 7th Inf. Div., Korea, 1952-53; Ft. Knox, KY, 1953-55; 2nd Armd. Div. 1955-58; Ft. Bliss, TX, 1958-64; JTF2, 1964-68; Tk Co., 1st Bn., 14th ACR. Served with 12th Constab. Sqdn. Served as platoon leader, Korea 1952-53.

Retired August 1968 as MSG E-8. Awards include the Purple Heart, two BS, JCS Commendation Medal, NDS w/OC, UN Service Medal, Korean Campaign Medal, Occupation Medal, Good Conduct and Korean Presidential Unit Citation.

Memorable experiences: playing ice hockey for the Constab. 1947-48. Constabulary was runner up in Europe Championship. Tank driver instructor, Constabulary Tank School, Vilseck, Germany 1949-50.

Married Charlene and they have children: Robert Jr., Vivian, Micaela, Charles, Steve and Regina; grandchildren: Jerrod, Kellie, Bryant, April, Lauren, BJ, Ronnie, Candi, Christi and Traci. Employed with El Paso Ind School District, senior Army instructor, JROTC retired 1991.

GEORGE W. SMALL, born Nov. 27, 1926, inducted into Army March 20, 1945 at Jefferson Barracks, MO. Basic training, Camp J.T. Robinson; Little Rock, AR, Co. A, 126th Bn., 80th Regt. Sent to Camp Maxey, TX. Went to Ft. Ord, CA to board ship USS *Marine Tiger* Aug. 13, 1945 to Pearl Harbor; Philippine Island, Rep. Depot, Northern Luzon. Temporarily assigned to AFWES Pac HQ at Manila. Reenlisted RA for one year. Returned to the US on the USS *John Pope.*

Sailed on the USS *Coaldale* to Europe, LeHavre, France. March 30, 1946, Bamburg, Germany, Dachau, Augsburg. Assigned to Light Tank Trp., 5th Constab. Regt. as a company clerk in Regt. HQ as sergeant. Left Bremerhaven Germany, Oct. 15, 1946 on *Adm. Rodman* for discharged, Nov. 9, 1946, Ft. Mead, MD.

Married Dorothy Brown, April 12, 1947. They have one son and two grandchildren.

Farmed and worked as a postal clerk and is now retired. Traveled to Elderhostels their main interest now.

BUELL B. SMITH, born Oct. 21, 1926 and was drafted into the Army in September 1947. After his discharge he went to the FBI in Washington, DC.

He worked at the FBI in during the day and attended night school at Strayer College of Accountancy in Washington, DC. He received his bachelor of commercial science degree in 1954 and a master of commercial science degree in 1955.

Resigned from the FBI and worked 10 years for a CPA firm as auditor and tax accountant. He then worked 32 years for the US Government.

While working at the FBI, he met a charming young lady and married her in 1952. They have one son and two grandchildren, Callie Elizabeth and Aaron Handley Smith. His wife has become quite a prolific artist using oil paints; his son has a degree in engineering and is employed by the Dept. of Defense and their daughter-in-law is a computer programmer.

CULLEN B. (C.B.) SMITH, born Aug. 2, 1929, Martin, KY. Joined RA August 1948. Military locations and stations: Ft. Knox, KY; Coburg, Germany; Friedburg, Germany; Bad Hersfeld, Germany.

Served with I Co., 3rd Bn., 14th ACR, US Constab. (full 40 months). Discharged June 1951 as sergeant. Awarded the Good Conduct Medal.

Memorable experiences: made a lot of friends, saw a lot of historical places. In 1996 he met his company commander he had in 1949. (Ret). Maj. Gen. James C. Smith.

Married Marie and they have a daughter, Elaine. Employed for 32 years with IBM, model maker, tool and die maker. Retired April 1987, but he failed at retirement. He still does same work.

EARL F. (SMITTY) SMITH, born Nov. 11, 1931, Worthington, PA, joined the Army June 16, 1949. Military locations and stations: Basic, Ft. Dix, NJ; Surgical Tech. School, Ft. Sam Houston, TX; 6th A/C. Regt. Straubing, Germany. Served with 9th Inf. Div., Ft. Dix, 6th A/C Regt. from February 1950 to December 1952.

Discharged Dec. 5, 1952 as sergeant. Awarded Good Conduct, Army of Occupation, Germany and National Defense.

Married Shirley A. Smith and they have children: Sherry and Shawnee; grandchildren, Jessica, Amanda, Ryan and Jamie. Employed with International Mill Service, Philadelphia, PA, retired Jan. 29, 1993.

GLENN DONALD SMITH, born Sept. 11, 1930, Damascus, VA, enlisted in the RA Sept. 13, 1948 for assignment to US Constab., European Command, basic training, 9th Inf. Div., Ft. Dix, NJ.

Assignments include: A Trp., 22nd Constab. Sqdn., 1948; A Trp., 24th Constab. Sqdn., 1949-1951, Bad Hersfeld, Germany; C Trp., 24th Constab. Sqdn. 1951-

1953, Schweinfurt, Germany and Bad Kissingen, Germany; 7th Army NCO Academy, 1953-54 Munich, Germany; 30th Tank Bn., School Trps., Ft. Knox, KY 1954; E Co., 2d Bn., 3rd Armd. Cav. Regt., Ft. George G. Meade, MD and Bamberg, Germany, 1955; Tank Co., 3rd Armd. Cav. Regt., 1956-57, Bamberg, Germany; HQ Trp., 2nd Sqdn., 3d Armd. Cav. Regt., Ft. George G. Made, MD 1958-60; HQ & HQ Trop, 3rd Armd. Cav. Regt., Ft. George G. Meade, MD and Baumholder, Germany 1961-66; 9th Military Intelligence Detachment, 9th Inf. Div., Ft. Riley, KS and Vietnam, 1966-67; HQ & HQ Co., 2d Armd. Div., Ft. Hood, TX, 1967-68; HQ & HQ Co., 68th Armd. Bn., 8th Inf. Div., Mannheim, Germany, 1968-71; Air Cav. Trp., 3d Armd. Cav. Regt., Ft. Bliss, TX, 1972-74.

Retired 1974 as first sergeant. He received several medals during his career, including the Bronze Star, Army Commendation Medal (3 OLC), Good Conduct Medal (3 OLC), National Defense Service Medal w/OLC, Army of Occupation Germany, Vietnamese Service Medal, VCM (w/60 device) two Overseas Service Bars.

Member of VFW, Association United States Army, US Constabulary Association. Education includes the 7th Army NCO Academy, Association Intel Analy Course, Air Observer Course, Tank Commander Course. During his 26 years of service, he has served in every leadership position from scout leader, tank commander, platoon sergeant and first sergeant. He has also held positions as S2/G2 NCO at battalion, regimental and division level.

Married Ruth Elinore Jacobs, Dec. 30, 1953, 7th Army NCO Academy Chapel, Munich, Germany; they have two sons and six grandchildren.

HERBERT SMITH, born Sept. 10, 1928, Harrison, NJ, enlisted in the US Army Nov. 9, 1945, sent to Ft. Knox, KY for basic and armor training. Left US in March 1946, for Germany and was assigned to the 17th Cav. Recon Sqdn. (15th Constab. Regt.). This unit was a District Constabulary (DC), unit performing all the same duties as the Zone Constabulary did but done prior to their activation. Once US Constabulary became fully operational the 17th Cav. became Palace Guard for General Keyes and the Third US Army in Heidelberg.

January 1947, assigned to HQ Trp., 15th Constab. Sqdn. in Schweizingen. July 1947, assigned to HQ Trp., 15th Constab. Regt., then transferred in September 1947 to B Trp., 72nd Constab. Sqdn. This unit inactivated in one week after his arrival and they became B Trp., 14th Constab. Sqdn. in Boblingen. January 1948 he was assigned to C Trp., 14 Constab. and their troop was picked to be the demonstration troop for the students at the Constabulary School in Sonthofen. They demonstrated the proper ways to conduct searches, raids, riot control and other duties performed by the Constabulary.

April 1948, the 14th Constab. Sqdn., along with many other Constabulary units were sent to Grafenwohr, Germany for maneuvers and combat training exercises. During this period the Constabulary was downsizing and although still under the command of the 15th Constab. Regt., the 14th Constab. Sqdn. was assigned to the 1st US Inf. Div, as their recon company In July 1948 he was assigned to HQ and Svc. Trp., 14th Constab. Sqdn. where he was awaiting rotation home. In August 1948, returned to US and was discharged, Sept. 1, 1948, Camp Kilmer, NJ. Awarded the Good Conduct Medal, American Campaign Medal, WWII Victory Medal and Army of Occupation Medal.

Enlisted in inactive reserves and called back to duty for Korea in 1950 and stationed at Ft. Hood, TX. Awarded National Defense Medal for that service. He is semi-retired, living in New Jersey with his wife Nancy. Has a son, Allen; daughter-in-law, JoAnn and three grandsons: Charlie, Allen-Michael and Danny.

SHERMAN L. SMITH, born July 3, 1930, Diamond, MO, entered military services Oct. 1, 1948; basic training, Ft. Jackson, SC.

From January 1949 to April 1954, assigned F Co., 2nd Bn., 14th Armd. Cav., Schweinfurt and Bad Kissingen, Germany; 131st Tank Bn., Ft. Knox, KY, 1954-55; B Trp., 11th Armd. Cav., Ft. Knox, Ky, 1955-56; 826th Tank Bn., Hammelburg, and Schweinfurt, Germany, 1958-58; 826th Tank Bn., Ft. Benning, GA, 1958-59; 3rd Med Tank Bn., 37th Armd., Conn Barracks, Schweinfurt, Germany, 1960-62; C Trp., 7th Cav., Ft. Benning, GA, 1963-64; A Trp., 7th Cav., Ft. Benning, GA, 1964-65; B Co., 2nd Bn., 1st Training Bde, Ft. Benning, GA, 1965-66; K Trp., 11th Armd. Cav., Ft. Meade, MD, May 1966-July 1966; K Trp., 11th Armd. Cav., Republic of Vietnam, August 1966-August 1967; US Army Advisor Gp., Austin, TX with duty station, Dallas and Terrell, TX, September 1997-December 1970; retired from US Army. Decorations: BS, ARCOM w/ OLC, GCMOL (five awards) AOM EUROPE, NDSM w/OLC, VSM w/60 Dev., CIB, Vietnam Counteroffensive Ph II, Vietnam Counteroffensive Ph III, Meritorious Service Medal, December 1970; flight instructor, Brown and Brown Flying School, Rockwall, TX, December 1970-October 1971; Mechanical foreman, Cargill Fertilizer plant, Gibsonton, FL, November 1971-October 1986; purchasing agent, Clifton Consolidated, Wimauma, FL, November 1986-October 1987; flight instructor, Sherman's Flight Training, Wimauma Air Park, Wimauma, FL, November 1987-present.

LEROY SOLICE, born April 17, 1927, Robeline, LA. Drafted July 30, 1945, basic training, Camp Crowder, MO.

April 1946-47; 53rd QM Base Depot, duties at Wurzburg, Germany; August 1947-October 1948; European QM Base Depot Frankfurt and Giessen, Germany (during Operation Vittles-Berlin Airlift).

January 1949-February 1952, US Constab., Straubing, Germany, Svc. Co., 6A/C, alternate driver for regimental commander, Col. Rehm.

1952-54, Ft. Bliss, TX; 1954-56, Ft. Lee, VA; 1956-57, Bad Kreuznach, Germany, 2nd Armd. Div. HQ Co., tank commander and section leader for division commander, Maj. Gen. Babock.

1957-2nd Armd. Div., returned to Ft. Hood, TX; 1957-60, 15th Cav., 2nd Armd. Div., Ft. Hood, TX, basic trainee instructor; 1960-61, Korea, 1st Cav. Div.; 1961-62, Ft. Riley, Kansas 69th Armd.; 1962-65, Budingen, Germany, 12th Cav., 3rd Armd. Div.; 1965-67, Ft. Lee, VA, 228th Ordnance Data Processing.

Retired May 1, 1967. Awards include the Army Commendation Medal, WWII Victory Medal, European Army of Occupation Medal, National Defense and Good Conduct.

Education: high school, Non-Commissioned Officers Command Course, Ft. Lee, VA 1955; M-41 Advanced Armor Course, Vilseck, Germany 1956; 2nd Armored Division Academy, Baumholder, Germany 1957; US Army Armor School, Ft. Knox, KY (13 weeks) 1959; M-60A1 Tank Commander Course, Vilseck, Germany 1964. Served as interpreter during maneuver damage claims in Germany. Attended German Language Courses, (14 credit hours equiv).

Married Annelise Piehler, Dec. 22, 1951. They have two daughters, five grandchildren and one great-granddaughter.

Member of Louisiana Retired Teacher's Association (Junior ROTC Instructor Retired). United States Constabulary Association.

Vice Chairman of the Caddo/Adais Indian Tribe of North Louisiana. He is fully aware that his youth has been spent. That his get up and go has got up and went. But he really doesn't mind, when he thinks with a grin of all the grand places his get up has been.

ALBERT SOLOSKY, born July 9, 1931, Bethlehem, PA, joined the US Army, Sept. 1, 1949. Basic training and leadership school, Ft. Dix, NJ. From March 1950-March 1953 he was stationed in Berlin, Germany assigned to Operations (S-3) in the following units: 16th Constab. Sqdn. (Separate), 6th Inf. Regt., 7781 SCU and 7780 Composite Service Bn. From March 1953 he was the hand grenade range NCO at Aberdeen Proving Grounds, MD until his discharge, Aug. 31, 1953.

Medals received Good Conduct, Army of Occupation Germany and National Defense.

Married Dorothy M. Wingert. They have five children, ten grandchildren and one great-grandchild. He retired from Sears, Roebuck and Co. July 9, 1993. Organizations: US Constabulary Association, VFW, American Legion, 40 et 8, AMVETS, Berlin US Military Veterans Association, NRA and several other local organizations.

LEONARD B. SOSSAMON, born March 22, 1927, Concord, NC, joined the service Aug. 27, 1945. Inducted Ft. Bragg, NC. Basic training, Camp Robinson, AR. Enlisted for three years Dec. 10, 1945. Served with 68th Constab. Sqdn. C Trps., May 1946-October 1948. Took care of company arms room. Discharged February 1952 as staff sergeant.

Memorable experiences: doing patrol work in Germany; also training men at Ft. Jackson, SC. From September 1950-September 1951.

Married Jerline A. Sossamon. They have four sons: Leonard Jr., Joel, Randy, Robin and daughter, Terry; grandchildren: Josh, Tyler, Barry, Jessie, Paul, Alana, Megean and Jennifer.

Employed 17 years truck driving long distance; 30 years electrician (electrician foreman). Retired May 1992. Still works part time as a electrician.

MARVIN GLEN SPITLER, born Sept. 22, 1930, Versailles, OH. USMC 1948-49; US Army 1950-56, Dayton, OH. Arrived in Marburg, Germany May 1950. Assigned to the Constabulary, A Btry., 70th AFA Bn., stationed in Fussen and Nuremburg until May 1952. Camp Rucker, AL June 1952-March 1953; Camp Atterbury, IN, April 1953-January 1954. January 1954 moved with 31st Div. to Ft. Carson, CO. Discharged March 1956.

Received the National Defense Service, Good Conduct and Army of Occupation awards.

Married Shirley Adkins April 7, 1953 and they have one son and one daughter. Volunteers at USAF Museum at Wright Patterson AFB. Retired from General Motors Plant Protection in 1992 and loves to travel.

WILLIAM E. SPRINKLE, born June 18, 1929 at Edwards County, KS, enlisted Smoky Hill AAB, Salina, KS Dec. 1, 1945. Basic training, Ft. Knox, KY.

Served with the 86th Inf. Div. in the Philippines until deactivated December 1946, Okinawa 1946 with

AFWESPAC, 1947 AFMIDPAC in the Mariannas and Admiralty Island, 1947-48.

51st Constab. Sqdn., Trp D, Landshut, Germany 1948. Trp. 2nd Bn., 6th Armd. Cav. Landshut, Germany 1949.

Attended tank school in summer of 1949. Commanded by Capt. George S. Patton III, son of Lt. Gen. Patton of 3rd Army fame in WWII.

Awarded the Good Conduct Medal, Pacific Theater, WWII Victory, Occupation Medal w/Japan and Germany clasp, Philippine Independence Ribbon.

STEWART E. (STEW) STAHL JR., born Feb. 19, 1927, Somerset County, Somerset, PA, inducted into the US Army June 1945, then sent to Camp Blanding, FL where he was trained as an infantryman and passed the tests to drive different Army vehicles.

Later he was sent to Ft. Meade, MD and worked in x-ray section discharging veterans from overseas. He as sent to Bamberg, Germany where he was assigned to Special Services, attached to Constabulary HQ Co., then started driving special services bus.

After having enough points he was discharged at Ft. Dix, NJ, March 6, 1947. During his army duty he received the European Army of Occupation Medal, WWII Victory Medal and Good Conduct Medal.

Received private pilots license in 1947 and a drafting certificate. He worked in construction as a bricklayer until retired in 1989.

WAYNE B. STAMPER, born Dec. 27, 1927, Newberry, MI, enlisted in RA Jan. 21, 1946. Basic training, Ft. Knox, KY with B Trp., 13th Mechanized Cav. Recon MOS 733. Served in 14th Constab. Sqdn., Darmstadt, Germany June 1946-September 1948. Transferred to 10th Constab. Sqdn., Fritzlar Germany September 1948-November 1948. Enlisted in ERC Nov. 19, 1948. Called to active duty Sept. 12, 1950. Korea Feb. 2, 1951-July 22, 1951.

Cpl. Stamper's awards include the WWII Victory Medal, Army of Occupation Medal, National Defense Medal, Korean Service Medal w/2 Bronze Stars, United Nations Medal, Army Good Conduct Medal, Honorable Service Lapel Button, M-1 Rifle Expert Badge.

Battles and campaigns: Pusan Perimeter, Chinese Offensive in Korea.

Stamper is divorced and has children: Wayne A., Russell L., Theresa L.; grandchildren: April, Crystal; great-grandchildren, Justin and Erick.

Employed as sawmill worker, lumber jack, tool & die machine department supervisor. Retired Dec. 27, 1990.

Memories: the satisfaction of capturing an Armed German SS trooper while making a routine house search. He remembers the pride of belonging and close friendship with fellow troopers. The pride of knowing they were the best, the pride of doing the job handed to US. Europe especially Germany is a better place this day because someone drew the line in the sand and guarded it and defended it with courage and devotion to duty. The US Constabulary, the one, the only, the best-fellow troopers well done Stamper salutes you.

HERBERT L. (BILL) STANFORD, born Nov. 1, 1924, Tucson, AZ, joined the service July 1940. Military locations and stations: Monterey, CA (Presidio of Monterey); Ft. Knox, KY, Landshut, Germany, Fulda,

Germany. Served with 11th Cav., 10th Engrs., 6th Armd. Cav., 11th Armd. Cav. Held commands as: Tank Co., 6th A/C, 1st Sgt., 14th Armd. Cav. (SGM).

Discharged Nov. 31, 1965 as command sergeant Major. Fought battles and campaigns: North Africa, Sicily, Italy, France and Germany.

His awards include the Bronze Star Medal w/V Device and Army Commendation Ribbon.

Memorable experiences: Long service with 6th Armd. Cav.; D Trp., 51st Constab. Sqdn., then 6th Cav. (US Constab. Tank Co., Bn. S-3, Sgt., Regt., Sgt. Major).

He is married to Hedwig and they have children: Bill, Eric, Brian and Susan and grandchildren: Gregory and JuliAnn. Employed at Great Western Bank, as assistant vice president; senior bank examinder, State of Arizona Aug. 8, 1986.

FRANCIS J. STANIWITZ *photo only, no bio submitted.*

FRANK L. STEPHENSON, born June 1, 1927, Rock Falls, IL, joined Merchant Marine June 19, 1944-August 1945, Pacific War Zone. Enlisted RA November 1945. Basic training Aberdeen Proving Grounds, Baltimore, MD. Arrived Germany February 1946. Assigned 81st Cav. Recon. Sqdn., Bad Mergentheim. Unit moved to Fulda April 1946. 81st Cav. Recon Sqdn. was changed to Constabulary June 1946. Mid 1947, the 81st Constab. Sqdn. was deactivated and all troopers were assigned to other units. The Provost Marshal section was assigned to HQ 14th Constab. Regt.-Fritzlar, Germany.

Stephenson graduated from Basic Constabulary and Investigators School Sonthofen and Counter Intelligence School - Obberammergau, Germany. Worked as special investigator (MOS 301) for Provost Marshal office May 1946-November 1948. Appointed RA S/Sgt April 28, 1947. Discharged 1951.

His awards include the Philippine Awards, Chinese Medal, three Merchant Marine Medals, while serving in Pacific War Zone (1944-45), US Army Medals: WWII Victory, Occupation Medals and National Defense Service Medal (Korea).

Married Helga Flachshaar Sept. 10, 1948. They have two daughters and nine grandchildren.

Retired from graphic arts business in 1982. Member of Calvary Lutheran Church, Portland, OR.

GLENN F. STEPHENSON, born July 7, 1926, Madison County, IA, joined the US Army March 25, 1946. Military locations and stations: basic training, Ft. Knox, KY March 1946-May 1946; ETO May 1946, 72nd Constab. in Germany, June 1946-August 1948. 1st Div., Germany August 1948-November 1948. Inactive Reserves December 1948-September 1950. Recalled to Ft. Riley,

KS for Cadre Intelligence School September 1950-October 1951.

Married Betty Mae Libby Stephenson and they have children: Tony, Nov. 29, 1948; Patty, Nov. 13, 1950 and Danny, March 11, 1960; grandchildren: Brad, Brandy, Brina-Reese, Cole, Lance, Dustin, Chad, Travis, Josh; great-grandchildren: Cassandra and McKenzie.

Employed as livestock and grain farmer 1952 until retirement in 1993. Spends the winter in Casa Grande, AZ at SKP Coop Campgrounds.

JAMES MELVILLE STEWART, born Sept. 8, 1929, Detroit, MI, enlisted in the US Army Oct. 13, 1948; basic training Camp Breckinridge, KY.

March 1949-November 1950, HQ Trop, 16th Sqdn., (Sep), Berlin, Germany; November 1950-July 1951; HQ, 1st Bn., 6th Inf. Regt., Berlin; July 1951-February 1952, Ag Office, HQ Berlin Military Post; February 1951-September 1953, USA Signal School, Ansbach, Germany; November 1953-February 1957; Det 11, University of Detroit ROTC, Detroit, MI; February 1957-June 1957; Engineer School, Ft. Belvoir, VA; June 1957-June 1958; 20th Engr. Bn., (C) Ft. Devens, MA; June 1958-May 1959, Air Defense School, Ft. Bliss, TX; June 1959-July 1960, 1st GM Bn., 1st GM Gp., Ft. Bliss, TX; July 1960-April 1962, HQ 4th Missile Bn., 44th Arty. Korea; April 1962-November 1962, ECCM Branch, Air Defense School, Ft. Bliss, TX; November 1962-February 1965, 1st AD GM Gp. (Tng), Ft. Bliss, TX; February 1965-September 1965, USA Intelligence Command, Ft. Holabird, MD, September 1965-May 1967, 526th MI Det, Okinawa; May 1967-November 1970, Springfield Office, 113th MI Gp., Springfield, IL; S2, November 1970-November 1971, S2, 525th MI Gp., Vietnam; November 1971-October 1972; Springfield Office, 113th MI Gp., Springfield, IL; October 1972-December 1975, Springfield Office, Defense Investigative Service.

Stewart retired Jan. 1, 1976. He is the recipient of the Bronze Star and Meritorious Service Medals.

Married Koma E. Skinner, Dec. 28, 1951 and they have three sons, six grandchildren and one great-grandson. He reads and travels extensively.

ROY E. STONE, born Aug. 15, 1927, Ft. Worth, TX, joined the US Army January 1946. Military locations and stations: Ft. Benning, GA; Germany; Korea; Ft. Hood, TX.

Served with 94th Constab., 91st FA, 26th FA, 703rd Ord., 3rd Inf. Div., 8th Dav., 1st Armd. Fought battles and campaigns in Korea.

Discharged June 1952 as staff sergeant. Awarded the Combat Infantry Badge.

HARRY T. STOUT, born Sept. 18, 1927, Cartwe County, TN, joined the US Army Oct. 1, 1945. Military locations and stations: Ft. Lee, VA; Kassel, Germany; Ft. Bragg, NC; I Corp. Arty., Korea.

Served with A Trp., 11th Constab. Varies Res. Units, HQ Btry. I Corp. Arty. Battles in campaigns: Army of Occupation, Germany, CCI Korea.

Discharged March 1953 as corporal. His awards include the WWII Victory, UN, Korea Service, Army of Occupation, Good Conduct and National Defense.

Married to Pauline and they have children: Patsy, Cheryl, Tommy and Sam; grandchildren: April, Shaun,

Whitney; great-grandson, Dustin. Employed as truck driver, and locksmith for 30 years.

DOMENICO (NICK) STRANGIO, of Oxnard, CA, was born in San Luca, Reggio Calabria, Italy, April 28, 1928. In 1934 he and his mother joined his father in Buenos Aires, Argentina. September 1940 the family migrated to Sacramento, CA where Nick completed secondary education and on July 5, 1946 joined the US Army. Five months later he was shipped to Germany and assigned as a member of the newly formed D Trp., 16th Constab. Sqdn. (Sept) in Berlin until its deactivation in November 1950. While with the 16th he won two Trooper of the Week awards and was its first member to graduate from the US Constabulary NCO Academy.

Nick served briefly at HQ, 6th ARC, Straubing, Germany, before assignment to the NCO Academy as an instructor/public affairs officer in December 1950; and continued in that capacity when the Academy was re-designated as the Seventh Army NCO Academy Nov. 1, 1951. He returned to the States May 1953 as an SFC and shortly thereafter resigned from the Army. He later joined the USAF and served at Mather AFB, CA; USAFE NCO Academy at Freising; HQ, USAFE, Wiesbaden; Mitchell Field, NY; Selfridge Field, MI and Ramstein AB. His last active duty assignment was at Tempelhof Central Airport in Berlin.

Following retirement in December 1966, he worked as director, public relations/publications, Sacramento Metropolitan Chamber of Commerce. In September 1967 he became the Public Affairs Officer and Head, Presentations Div., Naval Ship Weapons Systems Engineering Station, Port Hueneme, CA. Retired with 40 years of combined federal service in January 1987.

His decorations include both the Army and Air Force Commendation Medals and the Navy Civilian Meritorious Service Medal and other awards/commendations including two California State Assembly and a Ventura County Board of Supervisors resolutions. He served as president of the Port Hueneme Chamber of Commerce, US Navy League, Public Information Communicators Association and the Nemesis Alumni Association; Grand Knight of the Oxnard Knights of Columbus; and is a member of the Berlin Airlift, US Constabulary and the Air Force Public Affairs Officers Associations. He has a BA degree in history and political science from La Verne College and has studied for an MA in mass communication at UC-Northridge.

Married in February 1953 to Ernestine M. (Jean) Brogner in Munich, they have two daughters and seven grandchildren. The oldest lives with her family in Germany; the other, a former professional ballet dancer with the Bavarian National Theater for ten years, lives in Oxnard, CA.

CARROLL D. STRIDER SR., born in Asheville, NC, Feb. 6, 1923, enlisted USMC July 14, 1942. After Parris Island, SC, Quantico, VA and Camp Elliott, CA joined Co. A, 1st Bn., 18th Regt., 2nd Marine Div. in New Zealand February 1943. Took part in combat at Tarawa, Saipan, Tinian, Okinawa, then occupation of Nagasaki, Japan. Discharged as corporal, Dec. 15, 1945.

BS Engr., NC State Regt. Comm. 2nd Lt. in the USA Corps of Engineers, 1950. Assigned platoon leader, Co.

A, 54th Engr. (C) Bn., US Constab., 7th Army, Boblingen, Germany 1950-53, 1st Lt., Kansas City District, KS, Garrison, Dam, ND 1953-54, MIT & Harvard U., MS Civil Engr. 1954-55, Engr. Officer Adv. Class, Ft. Belvoir, VA 1955-56; Captain, CO, Co. A, 76th Engr. Bn., Korea 1956-57; Gen Staff, HQ USASA, VA 1957-58; Major, Comd-Gen-Staff College, KS 1958-59; Assoc-Prof Mil-Sci, State U of Iowa, Iowa City 1959-63; LTC Engr. Sec., HQ USARPAC, 1963-64, CO, 65th Engr. Bn. and Div. Engr., 25th Inf. Div. Hawaii and Vietnam, 1964-67, GS, Plans and Policy Div. DCSOPS, DA 1967-68; Colonel, Industrial College of the Armed Forces, 1968-69, GS, OSD Wpns Sys Eval. Gp., 1969-71, CO & DE, Philadelphia District, OCE 1971-73; Project manager, OSD Mobile Electric Power, 1973-74. July 1974 retired.

Made several trips to Indonesia as an engineer consultant to, and teacher of, top and middle management Indonesian Engineers making bids on construction projects in Saudi Arabia.

Received the LM w/2 OLC, ACM, AM w/2 OLC, ARCOM w/2 OLC, PUC and GCMDL (Marine), GS and OSD IDENT BAD, and other overseas combat and service medals.

Involved in many church and community activities. Col. Strider and Sybil reside in Tyron, NC. They have three children and five grandchildren.

WILLIAM CHARLES STRUB, born April 9, 1927, Brooklyn, NY, entered military service July 10, 1945. Basic training, Camp Wheeler, GA.

Assignments-duties: 309th Regt., 78th Div., December 1945-February 1946; C Trp., 16th Constab. Sqdn (separate) Berlin, Germany, Plat Sgt. & Police Operations NCOIC, February 1946-September 1948; Unit Advisor's Office Armored-Cav., February-November 1949; 325th Tank Bn. S2-S3 NCOIC and first operations NCOIC (ACTA) Armored Combat Training Area, Camp Irwin (now Fort Irwin), initiated programs to train all armored units, September 1950-January 1952; Ft. Devens, MA, 197th USASA Co., 1st Sergeant, October 1961-August 1962; Active USAR service with 77th Inf. Div. as NCOIC G-3 and 411th Engr. Bde NCOIC G-3 retiring from active reserve duty May 1967.

Medals and awards: Army Commendation Medal, Good Conduct, American Service, WWII, Army of Occupation, National Defense and Armed Forces Reserve Medal.

Married Marie J. Borgia Feb. 21, 1959. Civilian occupation: Print advertising production manager. Served on several national task force committees in the printing industry. Semi-retired but continues to work on developing a program for digital communications between advertising agencies and publications.

HERBERT JOSEPH STUTZBACH, born Oct. 20, 1931, Richmond Hill, NY, joined the NYNG March 14, 1940 as a medic with the 104th FA, enlisted in the RA Feb. 20, 1950; basic training, Ft. Dix, NJ.

Duties: 24th Constab. D Trp., Fulda, Germany, June 195-December 1951; Assigned HQ Co., 1st Bn., 14th A/ C, 7th Army, Fulda, Germany, December 1952-March 1953; HD Camp Kilmer, NJ, March 1953; Reenlisted Med Det 42d Div-Arty. NYNG April 1956-Trfd Btry. B, 258th FA Bn., January 1957-redesignated Btry. B., 2nd Howitzer Bn. (155-8") March 1959. Redesignated Btry. A, 4th Rkt/How Bn. 258th FA NYARNG (Honest John Rkt, 8" How) April 1959; Trfd Btry. A, 1st Msl Bn., Nike/Ajax 245th ADA, June 1959; Trfd Btry. B, 4th Rkt/How Bn. June 1961; Trfd Btry. A, 1st Msl Bn. (Nike/Ajax) 245th ADA, November 1962. Redesignated Btry. A, 1st Msl Bn., 244th ADA (Nike/Herc), April 1963; Trfd Co. E (TAM) 42d Maint. Bn., 42d Div., September 1964; Trfd HHD 42nd Avn. Bn. (Fixed Wing) February 1968-Redesignated HHC 42d Avn. Bn. (Helicopter) June 1972-Redesignated HHC 42d Avn. Bde., October 1986. Trfd Retired Reserve December 1987-October 1991, served as Fed Tech 32 years as administrative specialist, NYARNG.

Stutzbach retired from the Retired Reserve as 1SG after serving 39 years, six months, 18 days. He received several medals during his career, including: Aircraft Crewmans Badge, Meritorious Service, Army Achievement, Good Conduct, Army Reserve Component Achievement (four awards), Army of Occupation (Germany), National Defense Service, Armed Forces Reserve, Army Service Ribbon, NYS Military Commendation, NYS Long & Faithful Service (35 years), NYS Professional Development Ribbon #4, NYS Recruiting Medal and Badge, NYS Aid to Civil Authority, NYS Humanitarian Service, 258th Arty 100% duty and attendance.

Married Muriel "Mikki" Lippa, March 14, 1959. They have one son, two daughters and nine grandchildren. Retired life includes gardening, darts and woodworking at home. Life member NCOA, member of the American Legion (27 years), member OP2 Constabulary.

GLEN HOUSTON SUMMITT, born July 15, 1926, Vonore, TN in Monroe County.

Drafted March 23, 1945 at Madisonville, TN and transported to Ft. Oglethorpe, GA where he was inducted into US Army, March 24, 1945. Began basic training for intelligence and recon on April 1, 1945 at Camp Blanding, FL. Completed the course Aug. 13, 1945. Enlisted in the US Army at Ft. Benning, GA, Nov. 17, 1945. Arrived Ft. McPherson, GA, Dec. 31, 1945. Shipped out to Camp Pickett, VA, March 13, 1946 and to Camp Kilmer, NJ, March 25, 1946 for European Theater on the J.W. McAndews, April 1, 1946, arriving Camp Phillip Morris, Le Havre, France April 1946. Left for Austria on 40&8 (cattle car) on April 11, 1946, with stops in Amberg and Munich, Germany. Arrived Hoershing AB (42nd Inf.) May 1, 1946, then to 4th Cav. HQ in Eblesberg (near Linz), to LT TK Trp. in Tollett, troop moved to Gallspach on May 14, 1946. Entire unit moved to Lenzing, June 22, 1946. Troop was disbanded March 1947. Colors returned to the States. Extended enlistment to three years Sept. 18, 1946. Transferred to A Trp., 4th Constab. Sqdn. in Wels, Austria, March 24, 1947. Attended NCO School July 19, 1947-Aug. 2, 1947. Moved to MP Section, Sept. 6, 1947. A Trp. was transferred to Viennia April 22, 1948 and he was transferred to B Trp., July 8, 1948. HQ & HQ and Svc. Trp., 4th Constab. Sqdn. Remained in MPS. Started home (US) Aug. 16, 1948 by way of Frankfurt, Germany (7705 Air Return Center). Had 30 days furlough and Ft. Knox, KY, Oct. 1, 1948. Discharged Nov. 26, 1948. Joined Tennessee National Guard July 16, 1957-July 1983. Reenlisted Dec. 7, 1984 to July 14, 1986.

He was never award any awards or medals.

Memorable experiences: most of the time in Austria-one was the best another soldier and Summitt Christmas 1946, delivered fruit and nuts to a school (one room) in the mountains. First oranges and bananas the children had ever seen.

Married Irmgard Maria Schachinger and they have children: Jo-Ann Marrs and Ricky Lynn Summitt; grandchildren: Eric and Ashley (adopted by Jo-Ann). Worked in Oakridge, TN for nine years 50 weeks. Worked as letter carrier for 32 years. Retired from Tennessee National Guard July 1986. Full retirement Nov. 1, 1991.

JOSEPH S. SWATT *photo only, no bio submitted.*

ALBERT (AB) TAGLIERI JR., born May 31, 1927, Trevorton, PA, joined the US Army September 1945. Military locations and stations: Ft. Knox, KY and Fussen, Germany.

Served with 35th Constab. later name changed 42nd Sqdn. Discharged September 1948 as sergeant.

Memorable experiences: working with German youth.

Married June (Jennis) Taglieri and they have children: Albert III and Jeanne; grandchildren: Jennifer, Marybeth, Albert IV, Adam, Abby-Michelle. Employed as consolidated freight truck driver and self-employed. Retired December 1989.

GEORGE R. TALBOT, born Oct. 24, 1927, Worcester, MA, joined the service October 1945, Mec. Cav. Med. AAAGM Hawk, Ord. Military locations and stations: Germany, Korea, Okinawa, Ft. Devens, MA; Ft. Bliss, TX; White Sands, NM.

Served with 81st Constab., 27th Constab., 11th Evac Host., 24th Div. Med. Bn., 5th Field Hospital, Ft. Devens, F Trp., Ft. Bliss, Msl Ord., Okinawa, Co. A, White Sands, NM.

Retired June 1, 1968 SFC E-7. Memorable experiences: Platoon sergeant gave him artillery 104 for being out of uniform when picture was taken (no brass).

Married Norma Zeringue Talbot and they have children: Edward J., Paula Ann and David W.; grandchildren: Deirdre, Christy, Edward, Jamie and Tiffany. Employed with comp. office, retired May 31, 1968 at White Sands, NM.

ROBERT (TAG) TARTAGLIONE, born June 26, 1931, Yonkers, NY. Joined the US Army, Sept. 16, 1948. Military locations and stations: Stuttgart, Schweinfurt, Degerndorf, Kassel, (US Zone, Soviet Zone Border), Regensburg, Altefeld, Wildflecken, Hammelburg.

Served with 3rd Plt., 7766 US Constab. Horse Plt. Trp., 1st Plt., Tank Co., 3rd Bat., 6th Cav. Regt. Held commands as tank commander, platoon sergeant, B Co., 322 Tank Bat., V Corps, 7th Army.

Achieved the rank of sergeant first class, September 1954. Awarded the Good Conduct Medal, National Defense Service and Army of Occupation Medal.

Memorable experiences: His service in the 7766th Horse Trp. will always be an experience not to be forgotten. Also the friendship and camraderie, he's experienced while a trooper in the US Constab.

Presently single. His wife Harriet died in 1992. They have children: Steven, 41; Michael, 38; grandchildren: Robert, 14; Erin, 11; Kevin 6.

Employed as sheet metal worker, Local Union #38, Sheet Metal Workers Int. Association, retired July 1, 1993.

CHARLES W. (CHUCK) TATE, born Jan. 4, 1927, Pocatalico, WV, joined the US Army May 29, 1945. Military locations and stations: Camp Livingston, LA; Bayreuth, Germany; Bamberg, Germany. Served with 102nd Inf. Div., US Constab. Held commands: Army of Occupation G-4 Section HQ. Discharged Nov. 29, 1946 as technician fourth grade.

Awarded the ETO, Victory, Good Conduct and Expert Rifleman Badge.

Memorable experiences: modeled uniforms for Constabulary for Gen. Harmon to select what they were to wear.

Tate married Lo Vada and they have children: Stephen and Rebecca and a granddaughter, Lauren. Employed with Union Carbide Corp. as senior clerk. Retired Dec. 31, 1988.

SIDNEY CLEMENS TEGNER, enlisted in the US Army in 1929 and served in the FA at Ft. Des Moines until his organization moved to Ft. Riley, KS, October 1933, where it subsequently was redesignated in 1940 as the 3rd FA, an historic regiment whose battery was organized in 1784.

He was respected and admired by his juniors and seniors alike, as evidenced by his selection for enlisted aide to the Chief of FA, and honor reserved for the regiments outstanding soldier. He remained with HQ Btry. of the 3rd, first as a Horse Arty. Btry. and then from 1942 as an Armd. Arty. Unit with the 9th Armd. Div., initially going into action in Luxembourg in October 1944.

He was assigned as first sergeant of HQ Trp., 68th Constab. Sqdn. in Augsburg, Germany during "Army of Occupation." Later he served in the Korean War and retired in 1960 as a command sergeant major with over 30 years service.

Command Sergeant Maj. Signey Tegner (Sid) served in the US Army over 30 years. He died August 1997.

GEORGE TELLMANN, born Aug. 8, 1928, entered the Army Specialized Training Reserve Program in 1945, joined the RA Dec. 21, 1945, assigned to A Co., 301st Signal Operations Bn. manning C Carrier at the Heidelburg Reichpost. In 1946 the 301st merged with the 97th Constab. Signal Sqdn. in Seckenheim; after training in Bamberg he was appointed A Trp. Information and Education NCO in Boblingen Kaserne near Stuttgart. He went stateside and left the Army in November 1948.

Tellmann's work experience included five years as an announcer engineer at WMLT in Dublin, GA; 15 years with AT&T conducting overseas operations and negotiations related to the first transatlantic telephone cables; and 20 years with Comsat Corp. managing operations and negotiations for communications satellites, representing the US in the International Telecommunications Satellite organization "Intelsat" and the International Maritime Satellite organizaton "Inmarsat". In 1988 he retired as vice president Mobile Satellite Communications to become the president and chief executive officer of the American Mobile Satellite Corporation.

Education includes technical training in Advanced Technology at RCA Institutes completed in 1950; BA in International Studies, Syracuse University 1972; MA in International Law and Organization, American University 1975.

He married Mia Penth in Saarland, Germany, Sept. 29, 1948. They have three sons and four grandchildren. He is now fully retired.

RICHARD A. TEMPLETON, born Dec. 15, 1924, Maquoketa, IA, entered US Army, June 10, 1944. Basic training, Ft. Knox, KY.

Served in ETO, November 1944-December 1945. Recon Co., CCA, 2d Armd. Div. Returned to Germany May 1946 assigned to 35th (later 42nd) Constab. Sqdn. in Landshut, Fussen and Augsburg. Left 42nd Sqdn. for CONUS October 1948. Ft. Belvoir, VA, December 1948-May 1951; Ft. Hood, TX, 1951-52; Okla Mil. Dist. 1951-54. 887th and 775th FA Bn., Schwabisch-Hall, Germany 1954-55; MAAG Netherlands 1955-58; AAA&GM Cen. Ft. Bliss, TX, 1958-61; MAAG Laos 1961-62; USAACOM and Engr. Element Frankfurt Germany 1963-66; MACV (J2) 1966-67; USEUCOM Stuttgart Germany (1967-68); 12th Avn. Gp. and MACCORDS VN 1968-69; Allied Mobile Force (Land) Mannheim, Germany (1969-72; STRATCOM-EUR 1972-73. Retired at Ft. Lewis, WA (9th Inf. Div.) June 30, 1974.

Awards include the MSM, JSCM, ACM (2), Belgian Fouragguere and various others. Worked for VA five years; then worked for US Army as DAC-QASAS (ammo inspector) in Zweibrucken and Miesau, Germany for 15 years until retirement again October 1944.

Married Irmgard Esser July 31, 1948. They have one daughter in Texas. They reside in Puyallup, WA.

WILLIAM MICHAEL TEVINGTON, born Sept. 25, 1927, New York, NY, enlisted RA at 17. After numerous stations in US sent to Germany and the US Constab. at Fritzlar with the 14th Constab. Regts. Communications Plt. as a wireman. Moved to Friedburg, Gelnhausen and finally Fulda. Went from wireman to regimental communications chief. Upon return to the US, September 1952, attended 54 weeks of electronics training at Ft. Bliss and assigned to the first corporal missile battalion formed.

Assignment to Germany and the 8th AAA Gp. at Wiesbaden. Unit deactivated, transferred to 1/38 Arty. Assigned NCOIC of the nuclear weapons section. Rotated to the US and assigned as student and instructor at Sandia Base's Defense Atomic Support Agency's Nuclear Weapons School in electronics. Tour in Thule, retired from Army at Killeen base and became a district scout executive. Had positions as a HEW health planner and finally retired as administrator and CEO, Catholic Housing Services for the Archdiocese of Kansas.

Married Dita Sabedot and they have seven children and 13 grandchildren. Former national commander, presently National Historian and commander Constabulary's Outpost 6.

RICHARD A. (DICK) THERRIO, born July 9, 926, Chicago, IL, joined the US Army, Nov. 3, 1949. Military locations and stations: Infantry basic at Camp Croft, SC; F Co., 90th Cav., 10th AD, April-July 1945; Recon Co., C Co., 636 Bn. July-September 1945; A Co.,

774th Tk Bn., September-October 1945. Enlisted in RA Ret. To Europe 1946. Assigned A Btry., 465 AAA Bn., name was changed to D&G Trp., US Zone Constab., middle of 1947 was switched to a SCU to service military community. Returned to US in April 1948 OSS to F Co., 91st Cal. Sqdn. Mech at Ft. Riley. Battle and campaigns: Central European Campaign.

Discharged Oct. 8, 1948 as private first class. Awards and medals include the European Theater Ribbon, WWII Victory Ribbon, Occupation of Germany.

Memorable experiences: the whole experience of four years was memorable, not in combat, but have shelled and bombed. Full-time training with 774th, 1st Bomb, 1/2 day training, 2nd bomb no training.

Therrio married Nina May 19, 1956 and they have a son, Richard Edward Therrio. Therrio retired from Montgomery Ward July 1991.

BARNEY THOMAS
photo only, no bio submitted.

CHARLES LEE THOMPSON, born May 25, 1928, Hardin, MT. Entered military service Nov. 7, 1945 age 17 at Ft. Douglas, UT; basic training Camp Roberts, CA.

May 1946-September 1946 HQ Co., 39th Inf. Regt., 9th Div., October 1946-June 1947, B Trp., 81st US Constab. Sqdn; July-September 1947, B Trp., 91st US Constab. Sqdn.; December 1948-June 1949 USAR inactive; July 1949-March 1951, Ft. Belvoir, VA; April 1951-June 1951 Ft. Knox, KY, Field cadre; July 1951-September 1951, 388th Engrs., Ft. Belvoir; October 1951-September 1592, Korea 388th Engr. Co. with D/S too 12th Marine Air Gp., 409th Engr. Bde. and 82nd Engrs. USAR 1952-68.

Awarded WWII Victory Medal, WWII Occupation Medal, Korean Service Medal w/Star and UN Service Medal.

Married Agnes Phyllis Usselman Feb 1951 and they have one son, one granddaughter and one great-grandson.

Member of US Constabulary Association, Veterans of Foreign Wars, American Legion, Knights of Columbus and Loyal Order of Moose.

GEORGE BRYAN THOMPSON, born Aug. 31, 1927, Philadelphia, PA, drafted 1945 at age 18. Served at Camp Indiantown Gap, PA as cadre. Infantry trained at Camp Robinson, AR; shipped to LeHavre, France, served in Germany as patrol commander, Color Guard and supply sergeant in 42nd Constab. Sqdn., Trp. B.

Graduated 2nd Constab. Regt., Non-commissioned Officers School, Freising, Germany, 1946.

Attended Nuremberg Trials and guarded Nazi SS Troopers at Dachau Concentration Camp.

Expert Infantry Badge, WWII Victory Medal, Occupation of Germany Medal, Good Conduct Medal, American Defense Medal and European Theatre Medal.

Insurance company of North America, Philadelphia, 1947-1980, Underwriting and Product Management positions. Royal Insurance Company, NY 1980-84, product manager GRE, Princeton, NJ, 1984-1991, director of Commercial Insurance, retired after 44 years.

32nd degree master mason, Olivet Oriental Lodge #385, Philadelphia, 49 years; Boy Scouts of America, 57 years; Scoutmaster in three troops; Honorary Executive Board Member, Bucks County Council, BSA, Silver Beaver, Distinguished Service, Bucks County Council, BSA, Scouting Wood Badge, 1992, National VFW Scholarship; life member Unami Lodge No. 1, Ajupeu Lodge No. 33,

Order of the Arrow, BSA; Scouters Key Medal, Scouters Training Medal and Arrowhead Award; District Award of Merit Medals by Philadelphia and Bucks County Councils, BSA.

Honor guard, Veterans of Foreign Wars, Post 6493, Bucks County, PA. Service Officer/Historian, Outpost #2, Life member US Constabulary Association.

Collector of Scouting Memorabilia. Family genealogy, Military History, Americana, Native American Indian and Norman Rockwell. Married Ellen Mae Eggert, Oct. 10, 1953 and they have two sons, two daughters and five grandchildren.

JAMES C. THOMPSON, born Aug. 23, 1926, Haleyville, AL, entered service in May 1945 at Ft. McClellan. Basic training at Camp Wheeler, GA, served briefly with 33rd Div. in Japan immediately after the war. Enlisted in RA in Japan, Dec. 3, 1945, re-assigned to 14th AIB in Darmstadt, Germany. Shortly the 14th AIB became

the 14th Constab. Sqdn. Served the entire enlistment with the 14th Constab. Sqdn. Upon separation, enlisted in the Alabama National Guard which was activated Aug. 30, 1950. Served in Korea from December 1950 to February 1952. Entered a printing apprentice job in 1952. Employed with Birmingham News Co. for 30 years, retiring as a foreman. Married Dorothy Hulsey in 1950, one daughter and two grandsons. Enjoy woodworking, fishing and working with VFW. Was All-American commander, 1991-92. Sec. Treasurer of a reunion committee from Korean War. Also a master mason for 40 years, a long time member of Zamora Shrine Temple in Birmingham.

DONALD OTTO TIMM, born Aug. 8, 1929, Chicago, inducted July 23, 1948, Chicago. Discharged May 7, 1952. Military locations and stations: Ft. Knox, Ft Hood, 2nd Armor, Augsburg, Germany; Ft. Bliss, Ft. Lewis, 2nd Inf. Div., Korea 1950-51 back to Ft. Lewis for discharge in 1952.

Awarded the Combat Infantry Badge, Bronze Star Medal, Korean Service Medal, w/5 Bronze Service Stars, ROK Presidential Unit Citation, German Occupation Ribbon, Distinguished Unit Citation and Good Conduct.

With the US Constab. he pulled a lot of front gate duty. They also were on a lot of road marches getting ready for WWII. He was there for only one year, 1948. He then went to Korea, 1950-51. It was sure rough. They didn't have the right equipment and there were a lot of Chinese to take care of. The Chinese came after the Americans wave after wave; the Americans couldn't kill them fast enough. And to top it all off was the extreme cold - 40 below.

Married to Joan and they have daughter, Mary Kay. Currently retired and trying to do nothing.

GERALD GILBERT (TIZ) TISDALE, born Nov. 4, 1920, Fredericksburg, IA, joined the US Army Aug. 23, 1939, Ft. Des Moines, IA, F Trp., 14th Cav.

Station moved to Ft. Riley, KS. Assigned Cavalry School 1941-44; Ft. Meade, MD, 1944; Ft. Carson, CO, 1944; Camp Stoneman, CA, 1944; New Guinea, (WWII), 1944; Luzon, 1944-45, L Co., 103 Inf. Regt., 43rd Div. (promoted to sergeant); Ft. Riley, KS, Weapons Dept., Army Ground School, 1945-46; US Constab., 1946-July 1949; 14th ACR Regt., Kitzingen, Germany Horse Plt., Border duty (Russian) Sandherm South to Upper Fladugen, North 1946-47; B Trp., 22nd Sqdn., 1947 Hammelberg, Germany; B Trp., 28th Sqdn., 1947 Schweinfurt, Germany; 6th ACR, Coburg, Horse Plt., Nuendorf, Boblingen, 7766 Horse Trp., Munich, 1947-48; Schwienfurt, 1949; Ft. Riley, KS, June 1949-August 1951; Korea, August 1951-September 1942, HQ Co., (fwd), 7th Inf. Div. (1st sergeant); Ft. Smith, AR,

1952; Ft. Polk, LA, 1952; Provisional Co., 37th Inf. Div., Camp Irwin, CA, 1952; Making tank and infantry training films; Ft. Polk, LA, Rifle Team, 6th ACR, 1st Armd. Div.; Ft. Riley, KS, Army Ground School AOC Div. 1953-54; Operations Intelligence Div. Ground School, 5th Army Rifle Team; Intelligence School, Ft. Holabird, MD, 1955-56; Korea, 2nd Tour (21st Inf. Regt., 24th Inf. Div., 1956-57.

Assigned Far East Rifle Team 1957. Home base, Ft. Bullis, TX; Army Rifle matches Ft. Benning, GA; National Rifle Matches Camp Perry, OH. Both competitor and small arms instructor; Ft. Polk, LA, September 1957-1958; Ft. Riley, KS, 1959-62, Army Ground School; AOC Div. Assigned to 5th Army Rifle Team as instructor and competitor. Retired at Ft. Riley, KS May 31, 1962.

Awarded Philippine Invasion, Liberation Medal, Unit Citation w/5 Battle Stars, Korean Occupation Medal, Korean Liberation Medal, Unit Citation, 2nd Bronze Star, Syngman Rhee Award and Far East Rifle Team Award, Good Conduct Medal, five Knots, Army Marksman Medal.

Married 56 years to Carole Evelyn Tisdale and they have four sons who served in service: Larry Eugene, Navy, seven years; Gerald Jr., AF, seven years; Joseph William (deceased), served in Vietnam and Germany seven years service; John Timothy AF, served 20 years. Their grandchildren: Larry Michael and Stephen Daniel Tisdale, Teresa Dawn, Mark Allen, Gerald Scott, Sean Eric, Joel Alexander, Elizabeth Carol, Joseph Christopher, Wendy Christine, Teresa Renée, Christopher Adam, Timothy Aaron, Daniel Scott, Christine Julianne, Tiffany Jeanne, Angel Janette, Matthew Allen, Sara Joanne, Candice Nichole Boyer; four great-grandchildren: Sarah Elizabeth, Ashley Elizabeth Justin Robinson and Zachary Obrien.

JAMES (JIMMIE) TOBIAS, born May 18, 1926, Akron, OH. Joined US Army, Sept. 10, 1944. Commissioned Sept. 10, 1954. Military locations and stations: Joseph Robinson, Camp Swift, Ft. Lewis, Camp Atterbury.

Served with 7th Armd. Div., 23rd Armd. Inf. Commands held: Europe. Discharged Sept. 10, 1954 as sergeant. Battles and campaigns: BB, Rhineland Baltic Sea, Rhor River Pocket, Ardennes.

Memorable experiences: Texas 100th Anniversary.

Married to Miriam and they have several children and grandchildren. Employed from 1955-1993 at Wilburt Ind. as spray painter.

CHARLES TOMASEK, born Feb. 4, 1926, enlisted RA Aug. 23, 1948, basic training at Camp Breckinridge, KY with 101st Abn. Div.

Attended European Command Intelligence School in Oberammergau, Germany.

Received Army of Occupation Medal. Fluent in Russian and Czechoslovakian. He was attached to military intelligence in the 53rd Constab. Sqdn. based in Weiden, Germany.

His function was to accompany a different company patrol each week along the Czech, German and Austrian border where they had contact with the Russian Armed Forces.

"Genuine sacrifices were made in the fight against communism, and they should be remembered."

Member DAV, VFW, US Constabulary Association. Married Evelyn Pospisil, Nov. 18, 1950 and have two daughters, Linda and Marilyn Jo and grandchildren, Sarah and Jeremy.

Retired September 1990 from the US Department of Labor (OSHA) and a Sr. Compliance Officer. Presently residing in Nanuet, NY.

HOWARD (TOMMY) TOMLINSON, born Feb. 14, 1928, Philadelphia, PA. Joined the Army October 1946. Military locations and stations: basic, Ft. Knox, KY; stations: Stuttgart, Heidelberg and Boblingen, Germany.

Served with HQ Trp., 15th Constab. Sqdn. Held commands: orderly/room clerk; clerk typist for CIC office.

Discharged February 1948 as T/5. Awarded the Army of Occupation Medal and WWII Victory Medal.

Memorable experiences: doing patrols, roadblocks, working in CIC office, four visits to Switzerland.

Married 1953 to Charlotte and they have children: Thomas, Gary and Charles; grandchildren: Kelly, Jason, Andrew, Nicole and James. Employed as radio, TV repairman 1949-53. Joined Rohm & HAAS Co. 1953-89, research lab technician. Retired May 1, 1989.

ESTANISLAO S. TORRES born in Knippa, TX. He was drafted in the service May 30, 1945 and enlisted in the Regular Army September 1945 with basic training at Camp Fanning, TX.

Duties: Co. I 7th Inf. 3rd Inf. Div., Tahn Ron, Germany 1946; Trp. C, 2nd/66th Constab. Sqdns., Lenggries and Dergerndorf, Germany, 1946-47; Co. H 60th Inf. 9th Ind. Div. Fort Dix, NJ, 1947-48; Co. G 16th Inf. 1st Inf. Div. Zirndorf and Schwienfurt, Germany, 1948-54; Co. B 38th Inf. 2nd Inf. Div., Fort Lewis, WA, 1954-55; Co. I 61st Inf. 8th Inf. Div., Fort Carson, CO, 1955-56; Co. I, 5th Inf. 8th Inf. Div., Fort Carson, CO; 1955-56; Co. I 5th Inf. 8th Inf. Div., Furth and Zirndorf, Germany, 1956; Co. D, 2nd BG 8th Inf., 8th Inf. Div., Zirndorf and Mainz, Germany, 1956-58; Co. D 2nd BG 8th Inf. 1st Inf. Div., Fort Riley, KS, 1958-60; Co. D 17th Inf., 7th Inf. Div., Korea; Co. D 1st BG 17th Inf. 7th Inf. Div., Korea, 1960-61; C/S Co. 2nd BG 8th Inf., 1st Inf. Div., Fort Riley, KS, 1961-63; HHC 1/16th Inf., 1st Inf. Div., Fort Riley, KS, 1963-65; HHC 1/16 Inf. 1st Inf. Div., Vietnam, 1965-66; Co. B 3rd Bn. 3rd Trng. Bde, Fort Ord, CA, 1966-69; Co. A 2nd/327 Inf. 101st AB Div., Vietnam, 1969-70; HQ Co. 3rd Bn. 3rd Trng. Bde., Fort Ord, CA, 1970-72.

Retired Dec. 31, 1972 as SGM (Ret.). Awards and decorations include the WWII VM, CCMDL (9th awd.), AOM (Germany), NDSM, CIB, VSM w/device, four BSM (two w/V Device), four ARCOM (two w/V Device), Unit Citation, RVN Cross of Gallantry w/palm, two RVN Civ. Hon. MDL1/c and six Vietnam Campaigns.

Married Larissa Bier-Jobzyk and they have two sons, three grandsons, one granddaughter and two wonderful daughters-in-law, Lydia and Linda.

RALPH C. TORRES, born Oct. 16, 1926, Brooklyn, NY, joined USAAC, US Army, Sept. 2, 1945. Military locations and stations: Orly Field France, Frankfurt, Germany; Boblingen, Germany; Saarfelden; Salsburg Austria; Mannheim, Germany. Served with 54th Engr., 70th Engr., 1408 AAF Base Unit; 595 Engr. (Vietnam), 168th Engr., 512th Dump Truck Co., HQ 5th Corp. Senior Engr. OP NCO.

Discharged Sept. 1, 1973 as first sergeant, E-8. Battles and campaigns: two tours duty in Vietnam. As platoon sergeant in combat engr. 168th Engr., 1st Sgt. 595th LE Co.

Memorable experiences: achieving the rank of first sergeant despite height 5'2".

He is married to Bettina Torres and they have children: Clair, Richard, Geraldine and Michael; grandchildren: Prudence, Alice, Mary Beth, Beau, Tammy; one great-grandchild.

Employed supply warehouse; part-time gardener. Worked from 1980-88. Retired 1988. Still working summer hire as gardener. Retired Sept. 1, 1973.

JAMES TERENCE TRACY, born May 25, 1928, Glendale, CA, enlisted in RA at Green Bay, WI, Sept. 15, 48, age 20; basic training with 65th FA Bn., Ft. Knox, KY.

Duties: US Constab., Security Plt., HQ and HQ Trp., 6th Armd. Cav. Regt., Straubing, Germany, December 1948-September 1952. 3rd Armd. Div., Reserve Command, 18th Training Co., Ft. Hood, TX. First Sergeant, October 1952-April 1953.

Participated in US Atmospheric Nuclear Tests-Upshot-Knothole (Encore), Camp Desert Rock, NV, May 8, 1953. 701st Armd. Inf. Bn. HQ, Ft. Hood, TX, Sgt. Major, May 1953-September 1954.

Honorably discharge, Sept. 14, 1954. He coached the 6th Armd. Cav. Regt. Unicorns Football Team to the Southern Conference Championship 1950-51. Jim Tracy played on the 6th Armd. Cav. Regt. Unicorns Basketball Team that won the Southern Conference Championships in 1951 and 1952.

Married Edeltraud Scheitzach, April 5, 1952. They have six daughters and four sons, and seven grandchildren. A member of the US Constabulary Association, and after retirement as lieutenant of police, Milwaukee Railroad Company, enjoys fishing, reading, hunting and traveling.

STEPHEN TRAYNOR, born Jan. 1, 1922, Stephen, MN, drafted US Army August 1944. Trained at Camp Hood, then shipped out to Europe in February, 1945. Joined 63rd Inf. Div. in the same month. Detached from 63rd Div. in July 1945 to be sent to the states. Returned to Germany August 1945 to the Signal Corps.

Enlisted in the RA Nov. 9, 1945. Went stateside for furlough, returned to Germany, February 1946. Volunteered for the Constabulary in February 1946. Sent to Sonthofen Constabulary School Sqdn. as member of the Horse Sqdn. Helped in activating Constabulary School and patroling the border.

Transferred to Special Services School October 1946. Served in Department until March 1947 and was returned to states for discharge. Highest rank of corporal.

His medals include Infantry Badge, Good Conduct Medal, European Theatre Ribbon and Bronze Star. Discharged April 1947. Married to Lorena L. Kindermann May 20, 1950. They have two children, Patricia Louise and Terrance O. and five grandchildren. Worked for Soo Line Railroad for 33 years, retiring January 1982 to Enderlin, ND.

JAMES WILLIS TRAYLOR, born Sept. 29, 1931, Carrollton, GA, enlisted US Army June 24, 1948. Basic training, Ft. Jackson, SC, 7th Inf. Div. October 1948 assigned to Constabulary "Circle C" Cowboys - Combat Engineering until March 1952. 54th Engineering, Boblingen, Germany.

Assigned to HQ 4th Army, Ft. Sam Houston, TX from 1952 to 1959 as personnel sergeant. Volunteered to go back to Germany in 1959. Assigned to 11th Army Cav., Regensburg, Germany. Duties were training sergeant, and career counselor for 26 units, three border camps on the Czechoslovakian border and three stations: Regensburg, Landshut and Straubing, Germany. Went as SGT (E-5) and returned in December 1963 as SFC (E-7).

1963 returned to Ft. Sam Houston, to the 4th Recruiting as assistant operations sergeant. Promoted to MSGT on assignment.

May 1969 assigned to Quinnhon, Vietnam to Reactionary Forces and Career Counselor for eight units. Medivac to the states in 1970 to appear before the physical exam (PE) Board for Retirement with over 22 years active duty. Retired on July 10, 1970.

Awarded the Army of Occupation Medal, Germany, National Defense Medal w/OLC, Army Commendation Medal, two Awards, Good Conduct Medal, six Awards, Vietnam Service Medal w/Bronze Service Stars, Vietnam Campaign Medal, Distinguished Service Medal, five Letters of Commendation and two Letters of Appreciation.

Married Jessie Lee Beck, June 14, 1953 and they have three children and five grandchildren. James enjoys hunting, fishing and working in the garden. Member Disabled Veterans Association, serving as senior vice commander.

GUY KENT TROY, born March 15, 1923, Washington, DC, enlisted AAC 1942; primary flight school, 1943. Entered US Mil Academy, West Point 1943. Graduated Armor Branch 1946. US Constabulary 1947-50; 1971 Constab. Sqdn. later changed to 15 Sqdn. Schwabish Hall 1947-48, 25th Sqdn. Straubing 1948; HQ Trp., 2nd Constab. Brig. Munich, 1948-50; US Modern Pentathlon Team 1950-52; Pan American Games 1951; Gold Medal Olympic Team 1952; 2nd Armd. Div. Baumholder Germany, 1953-56; ROTC instructor New Mexico Military Institute 1956-59; Maag Iran, 1959-60; C&GS Leavenworth Student and Faculty 1960-64; CO 3rd Sqdn., 4th Cav., 25th Div. Hawaii, 1964-66; HQ CINCPAC 1966-67; G-2, 2nd Div., Vietnam 1967-68; Chief DIA Section ANMCC, Ft. Ritchee, 1968-71; Defense Attache, Vienna, Austria 1972-75; Ft. Bragg, NC, 1975-76. Retired 1976.

Married Winifred Charles Dec. 20, 1952. They have two sons, one US Army, one US State Department and four grandchildren. Employed as farmer, small logging equipment distributor.

ROBERT E. TRUAX, born Feb. 21, 1930, Lockport, NY, joined the US Army, Oct. 1948. and went to Augsburg, Germany with HQ & HQ Co., 2nd A.C. Regt., US Constab. until 1951, then to Nurnberg, Germany until 1952.

He was company armorer for 3 1/2 years, was discharged as a staff sergeant in June of 1952.

Married Cindy in 1956 and they have three children: Lance, Wayne and Lisa and five grandchildren: Shane, Tara, Jennifer, Jay and Joel who live in Sebring, FL, Kannapolis, NC and New York. Retired in 1962 after 39 years with the Plumbers and Steamfitters Local #129 of Niagara Falls, NY.

JOHN F. TRUE JR., born Jan. 21, 1928, Tampa, FL, joined the service Feb. 19, 1946, Ft. Banks, MA.

Enlisted RA 1946. Infantry basic training, Ft. McClellan, AL. US Constab. at Bamberg and Heidelberg, Germany. HQ 820th Constab. MP Co.

Discharged July 14, 1947 at Camp Kilmer, NJ. Awarded the M1 Rifle Sharpshooter Badge, Army of Occupation Medal (Germany), WWII Victory Medal, two Cloth Overseas Bars.

Married Eleanor Fantoni, Nov. 7, 1948 and they have one daughter, Nancy; one son, John and three grandchildren: Jonathan, Penelope and Brooke.

Retired after 42 years with the Raytheon Co. Enjoys reading.

GEORGE W. TRUNTICH, born May 19, 1931, Bobtown, PA, a small coal mining community, located in Southwestern, PA, enlisted in the US Army, May 19, 1948 (his 17th birthday). Received basic training at Ft. Dix, NJ. After basic training assigned to A Co., 54th Combat Engrs. (US Constab. Unit) at Boblingen, Germany. Returned to US in summer of 1949. Assigned to 527 QM Sv. Co., Ft. Lewis, WA. Participated in large scale, joint services maneuvers unit was assigned to a USN cargo vessel, USS *Washburn*. Sailed to Honolulu, HI and conducted combat support to 2nd Inf. Div. landings on the Hawaiian beaches.

August 1950, unit was ordered to Japan for additional combat training for 45 days. Deployed aboard USN (APA) personnel carrier landed at Inchon Korea, Sept. 17, 1950. His unit moved north to Yong Dong Po and established a food ration supply support warehouse in an abandoned (but still supplied with beer) brewery. Remained there providing continuous support to US Marines, and numerous US Army units, 5th RCT, 7th Inf. Div. and 2nd Inf. Div.

The beer ration issues were much appreciated by all of the combat units. Seconds were also allowed.

Returned to US February 1952. Discharged April 10, 1952. Returned to civilian status. Awarded the Army Good Conduct, National Defense Service Medal, Army of Occupation, Germany and Korea, Korean Service Medal, w/5 Bronze Stars, United Nations Service Medal and Korean Presidential Unit Citation.

Married Eve Plishka Aug. 16, 1961. They have two sons, Stephen and Jeffery. Answered an inward call and enlisted in another branch of service (USCG) served 20 years. Retired August 1974. Employed with McDonnell Douglas Space and Defense Systems at Kennedy Space Center, FL. His company participated in loading every space shuttle flight with a complex electronic equipment, satellites and many experimental devices.

After his very interesting, exciting, and short career he has again joined the ranks of the retired.

SILAS P. TUPPER, born Aug. 16, 1930, Stockholm, NY, inducted into service Sept. 9, 1948, Watertown, NY. Military locations and stations: basic, Ft. Dix, 1st Constab. Weiden, Germany; Ft. Devens, MA, 510th Tank, Mannheim, Germany; Ft Bragg, NC.

Discharged Jan. 1, 1971 and his awards include the Occupation of Germany, two Loops, Good Conduct, Vietnam Service Medal w/6 Stars.

Tupper is now retired.

EARL R. ULRICH, born June 6, 1927, Bowling Green, MO, joined the US Army, Dec. 1, 1945-Jan. 22, 1946. Reenlisted Jan. 22, 1946. Military locations and stations: Basic training, Ft. Sill, Radio School and US Constab. School at Sonthofen, May 1946. Served with 2nd Constab. Brig., HQ, Munich Germany.

Discharged July 13, 1947 as T/3. Awarded the Army of Occupation Medal and WWII Victory Medal.

Memorable experiences: meeting a German boy he had worked with for two years at Stark Brothers Nursery while he was a POW. They boy saw Ulrich in their mess hall at the Brig HQs and still remembered him.

Married Shirley Ulrich and they have children: James F., David (died at birth), Carl A.; grandchildren: Michelle, Dianna, and Charles Scott, Richard, Mitch. Employed with Hercules Co. "A operator", retired Dec. 31, 1989.

CARL ALLEN (VAN) VAN BUSKIRK, born Dec. 20, 1925, San Jose, CA, drafted into the US Army November 1944; joined RA September 1945. Military locations and stations: Ft. Sill, OK, 1944 to August 1945; Ft. Ord, CA, September 1945-December 1945; Camp Kilmer, NJ, January 1946, LeHavre, France; Amburg, Germany; Munich, Germany. Served with 4th Armd. Div., Munich Germany; HQ (2nd Constab. Brig. HQ).

Discharged March 1947 as T/5. Awarded the Good Conduct Medal, Victory Medal, ETO, Occupation Germany and Expert Rifleman.

Memorable experience: As T5 Earl Ulrich and Van Buskirk were helping put up a PA system for General Eisenhower for his speech to the troops in Munich, they had to return a second day to finish their work. At that time there were several Generals present plus Ike, as they started to go about their way, he was approached by a full colonel. MP, he drew his side arm and demanded him to stop, wanting to know what he was doing there. He explained but he was almost shot by him. Talk about being scared. There were also many numerous adventures by too long to go into. Quite an experience.

Married Marge June 15, 1973 and they have children: Annita, Vickie, Denise, Scott, Laura, Andrea, Tom and Jeff; 27 grandchildren and three great-grandchildren. Employed as heavy equipment operator, road building and logging. Retired 1973.

BERNARD JAMES (VAN) VANLANDINGHAM, born Nov. 19, 1927, Fruitplain, joined the US Army Dec. 14, 1945, Richmond, VA.

Joined RA December 1945. Basic training, Ft. Bragg, NC, 1945-46. Replacement depot, LeHavre, France to Bamberg, 1946; 66th Armd. FA Bn., 66th Constab. Sqdn., 3rd Bn., 6th Armd. Cav. Regt. 1946-1953, Germany; 3rd Armd. Cav. Regt., Camp Pickett, VA 1953, Ft. Meade, MD 1954, Germany 1954-57, Ft. Meade, MD 1957-61, Germany 1961-63, 3rd Bn. of 3rd Cav. became 2nd Bn., of 11th Cav., Ft. Meade, MD 1963-65.

Held commands as first sergeant, 3rd, 6th, 11th A/C Regt. Achieved the E8, first sergeant. Discharged Dec. 1965.

Awarded Army Commendation Medal, Good Conduct and 6 Loops, Army of Occupation, European Theater, Victory Medal, National Defense, Civil Service Medals.

Memorable experiences: refusing direct commission 1951, raid on the Dandue River, Germany.

Married Bessie Elliot Sept. 12, 1949 and they have three children: Michael, Betsy, Deborah and four grandchildren. Employed WG 9 Civil Service, Ft. Meade, MD.

FRANCIS VIGLIOTTI JR., born June 14, 1929, Rochester, NY, enlisted RA June 30, 1948, basic training Ft. Dix, NJ.

Duties: US Constab., Strauving, Germany, October 1948-September 1952; Camp Drum, NY (278 RCT) October 1952-April 1953; Korea (5 RCT) May 1953-August 1954; Ft. Jackson, SC (101st Abn. Div.) September 1954-June 1955; Ft. Knox, KY (3rd Armd. Div.) July 1955-May 1956; Germany (3rd Armd. Div.) June 1956-May 1960; Ft. Lewis, WA (2/8 Cav.) June 1960-May 1963; Germany, (2/64 Armor) June 1963-May 1966; Ft. Carson, CO (5 Mech Div.) June 1966-June 1968; Vietnam, (5 Mech Div.) July 1968-July 1969; Ft. Lewis, WA (3 ACR) August 1969-October 1970; Vietnam (MACV) November 1970-November 1971; Santa Monica, CA (Advisor CA NG) December 1971-August 1973; Boise, ID (Advisor ID NG) September 1973-February 1975. Retired from active duty March 1, 1975 at Boise, ID.

His first constabulary assignment with Trp. A, 25th Constab. Sqdn. which was redesignated Tank Co., 1st Bn., 6th Armd. Cav. Some of the officers with whom he served in the Constabulary. Capt. Hugh M. Brown Jr., 1LT Guy K. Troy, 1LT John D. Conant, 2 LT Hal B. Richardson Jr., 2LT George C. Hoffmeister Jr., 2 LT Alfred B. Hale, 1LT Owen O. Wright, 1LT Luther J. Dean, Capt. Thomas B. Hobson, Capt. Paul D. Stephenson.

Married Johanna Hugh, Dec. 28, 1951, in Germany; two sons and two daughters, four grandchildren. He has been a volunteer with AARP Tax-Aide Program for 15 years. His leisure time is spent reading, fishing, camping, hiking or firewood cutting.

Awards earned include: LOM, BSM w/OLC, ARCOM, GCM 8th Award, AOM, NDSM w/OLC, KSM w/Battle Star, VSM w/5 Battle Stars, RVN Gallantry Cross w/Palm, RVN Gallantry Cross w/Silver Star, UNSM, ROKPUC, RVN Staff Service Medal 2nd CL, RVN Armor Badge and Combat Infantry Badge 2d Award.

WILLIAM G. (BILL) VOGELE,
born Feb. 15, 1929, Fall City, NE, joined the service February 1946. Military locations and stations: Fussen, Augsburg, Germany, Ft. McCoy, Ft. Carson, USA. Served with D Trp., 35th and 42nd Sqdns., July 1946-December 1948.

Discharged Dec. 12, 1946 as sergeant. Battles and campaigns: Korean Conflict 1950-51. Recalled to active duty October 1950. Discharged August 1951.

Awards and medals include the ETO Occupation, Korean War 1951.

Memorable experiences: just returned from one month visit to Germany Jan. 28, 1998. A spectacular charge from 1946-48. Visited Allgau Kaserne (Fussen) Sheridan Kaserne in Augsburg.

Vogele is divorced and has children: Billy, Gary, Erika and Carla and grandchildren: Matthew, Augustine, Victor and Jack III.

Employed with the Pfizer Company as general supervisor after 33 years. Member Musicians Union #424, Pinole, CA. Retired Feb. 2, 1994.

RICHARD K. (DICK) VOGT,
born Aug. 24, 1930, Detroit Lakes, MN. Joined the 1st US Inf. Div., July 1947 C Btry., 7th FA, transferred HQ Btry., Radio September 1947, transferred as cadre to HQ 15th Regt. Constab. Fussen, Germany to become the 70th FA Bn. Fall of 48 Ansbach Radio School, Radio Cpl. T/5. Fall of 1949 promoted to radio sergeant. S/Sgt. E5 spring of 1950 Truman's Year Radar School Ansbach Plt. Sgt. Counter Mortar Radar Plt.

Spring of 1951 back to USA, Ft. Sill, OK, FARTC. Summer of 1951 transferred to 187 Obsn. Bn. Working with Dept. of Obsn. On Counter Btry. Fire Gun Registration, Flare drop techniques for small planes.

Spring of 1951 transferred to 235th Obsn. A Btry. Counter Mortar Plt. Sgt. Summer of 1952 235th Obsn. Bn. off to Korea. Game plane relieve 1st Obsn. Bn. which had been well pounded on. The plane to relieve the 1st Obsn. Bn. never happened. They helped out for a month or so then their equipment caught up with them and they went on line and stayed until the truce was signed in July.

They had the first counter mortar radar set built for that purpose, AN/TPQ10 with a automatic plotter. It worked real good 419 missions fired in 30 days.

Summer 1952 received three Battle Stars, Bronze Star w/Purple Heart in Battle of Outpost Harry. Truce signed on the way home. Fall of 1952 reported in for duty, 504th AAA Bn., Detroit, MI. Fall of 1955, 504th AAA Bn., converts over to Nike Ajax missiles; fall of 1956 Guided Missile School, Ft. Bliss, TX. Summer of 1957 transferred to 517th Missile Bn. Nike Herc w/Nuclear Warheads. 1960 evaluator McGregor range New Mexico.

1962 returned to Detroit. Fall of 1962 shipped out for Germany, 67th Missile Bn. Werthiem. Spring of 1965 returned to USA, Huntsville, AL. Liaison between major powder companies and 5th Special Forces Gp., Vietnam. June 1967 retired. Msg/E7 Richard K. Vogt.

Married Doris and they have eight grown children.

EDWARD H. WALKER JR.,
born Aug. 27, 1927, Chicago, IL, (raised in Des Moines, IA).

Joined the US Army April 23, 1945. Military locations and stations: IRTC Camp Hood, TX April-September 1945; Trans School, November 1945-March 1946; 81st Cav. Rcn. Sqdn., Fulda, Germany, March 1946-June 1946; 81st Constab. Sqdn., Fulda, Germany July 1946-July 1947; 91st and 22nd Constab. Sqdn. Hersfeld, Germany, July 1947-January 1948; 83rd Cav. Recon Sqdn., 3rd Armd. Div., Ft. Knox, KY; February 1948-November 1949; Armd School, November 1949-May 1951; Mil. Dist. WV, May 1951-December 1952, MAAG Formosa, January 1953-December 1954, AFSWP Sandia Base, NM, January 1955-December 1958; JUSMAC, Thailand, January 1959-December 1960; Office Secretary of Defense, Pentagon, Washington, DC, January 1961-January 1963; MAAG Portugal, January 1963-December 1964, Granite City, Army Department January 1965-December 1965.

Retired Dec. 31, 1965 as SFC E-7. Awarded the Army Commendation Medal, Good Conduct Medal 6th Award, Office Secretary of Defense Individual Medal.

Married to Rosa Lea and they have children: Edward H. III, Curtis D. and Rickey D. Employed as manager Universal Carloading, Des Moines, IA, January 1966-August 1972, Traffic Anglist, Massey Ferguson North American HQ, 1974-72. Retired Aug. 31, 1992.

JOSEPH W. WALKER,
born March 30, 1928, Louisiana and joined the service April 1, 1946, Shreveport. Retired December 1973. Military locations and stations: 1946-47, US Constab., 6th AFA 1947-49, HQ 773rd, Tk Bn., 1950-52, 4th Armd. Div., 1954-55, Vietnam, 1966-67 1969-70.

Walker is currently retired.

CHARLES EUGENE (GENE) WALLS,
born July 28, 1927, Posey County, Mt. Vernon, IN. Joined the US Army Feb. 9, 1946. Military locations and stations: Bayreuth, Bamberg, Germany. Served with B Trp., 13th Constab. Sqdn.

Discharged July 24, 1947 as T/5 Corp. Awarded WWII Victory Medal.

Memorable experiences: serving in a very highly respected unit - among the German people.

Married Madeline (Mickie) and they have four children; and five grandchildren. Retired from civilian employment April 1, 1983.

GEORGE N. WALLS,
born Nov. 18, 1928 in Suitland, MD, enlisted in the US Army Nov. 19, 1945 and was processed at Ft. Meade, MD, Nov. 28, 1945 and stationed at Ft. Bragg for eight weeks of Tank Destroyer Training. He arrived in Le Havre, France, March 27, 1946 and rode the "Forty & Eights" into Germany and was given assignment to the US Constab. at Bad Bruckenau. After Bad Bruckenau, he was assigned to the 27th

Sqdn. in Schweinfurt, June 1, 1946 where he worked patrol on the Russian border from Konighoffen in the winter of 1946 and 1947. From February 1922 to March 8, 1947 he attended Constabulary School in Sonthofen. After completion of training, he returned to Schweinfurt, back to patrol duty and also participated in the 100 mile hike. After more duty was turned over to the German police he went to Weiden to start-up the 94th AFA Bn. in July of 1947. After test firing has been passed was sent to Fussen as cadre to start-up 70th FA Bn. where he worked the radio net in Fussen and temporary duty at Group HQ in Sonthofen. He met his future wife Christa Dorr in March 1947 in Konigshofen. After two years of paperwork he finally married her June 20, 1949 in Fussen with Cpl. Perry Wiley as his best man. After 42 months, 11 days in Germany he was shipped home and discharged Oct. 13, 1949 where he entered the Army Reserves until March 21, 1953.

Attended Theater Signal School in Arnbach, Germany and in December 1946-May 1947-January 1948 Intermediate and High Speed Radio Operator School.

Awarded the WWII Victory Medal and Army of Occupation Medal.

Married and has seven children, eight grandchildren and two great-grandchildren. Owns and operates a family retail bakery and gift shop.

JOHN (JACK) WALSH,
born March 29, 1929, Brooklyn, NY, joined the Coast Guard, September 1946. Military locations and stations: (USCG St. New London), Ft. Bragg, Camp Kilmer, Germany, Ft. Hood, Ft. Lee, Ft. Dix, Mitchell Field, USAFR, Islip Airport, Army NG.

Unit served with: 6th Armd. Cav. 1st Armd. Div. (NY National Guard (Army) 42 Div.), Air Force Reserve; (Coast Guard Air-Sea Rescue).

When the Korean War broke out in 1950 he was stationed in Landshut, Germany with D Co., 2nd Bn., 6th Armd. Cav. Regt., a light tank company. They were alerted and sent to the Czechoslovakian border. On the first night our radio jeep broke down and the captain sent one of their tanks up to the OP. That night they heard a lot of movement across the river. The next morning they saw 12 heavy tanks on the Russian side.

Discharged June 1952 as SFC. Awarded WWII Victory, Army Occupation Germany, National Defense, AFRM-01, Korean Service, United Nations ARCAM-04 - ASR-1.

Married Dorothy and they have children: James, Carolyn and Diane; grandchildren, James and Joe. Employed as Mech. Con Edison, NY (Utility Co.). Retired from the US Army National Guard August 1989; Civilian March 1991.

ROBERT J. WALTER,
born July 1, 1926, Catawissa, PA, entered military service Oct. 10, 1944. Basic training, Ft. Knox, KY. Overseas 1945 on *Queen Mary* to service Co. 712 Tank Bn., 90th Inf. Div. Transported supplies. After war end transported troops on Burchestgarden tour. The end of July transferred to 2nd Cav. light tank troop 42nd Recon. Around Labor Day he started to transport Lipizzan mares, from Zweisel to Freising his part of trip until December 21, when General Patton died. Assigned to honor guard that went to General Patton's funeral. On January 1946 was assigned to Gen. Harmon T O & E group at Bad

olz as a runner. Then back to tank troop, in June to ›onthofen to instruct new arrivals on operation and main-›nance of the M-24 Tank. July 25 left for USA. Sepa-ated Aug. 7, 1946, Ft. Dix, NJ.

Married Nellie Myers, June 23, 1951. They have a ;irl and two boys, one went to West Point and served in ıe 2nd Cav. in Europe. His awards include the EAME `ampaign, WWII Victory Medal, Army of Occupation 1edal, Good Conduct Medal and several commendations.

CRNEST (ERNIE) WALTON, born June 15, 1926, irand Rapids, MI, joined July 48, RA. Military locations ınd stations: Ft. Knox, basic training, Germany. Discharged t. Leonardwood, MO. Attended NCO Academy 1951-52. erved with 22nd Constab., 24th Constab., 14th A/C.

Discharged July 1954 SFC. Campaigns border pa-rol with the 22nd and 24th Constab. Awarded the Good Conduct Medal and Army Occupation Germany.

Memorable experiences: Attending NCO Academy `th Army in Munich, Germany Stetten, Kaserne. There vere so many good friends. And know they have the asso-:iation so they meet again.

Married Edith Taylor Sept. 7, 1956 and they have :hildren: Sally Bowers and Stanley Walton; grandchildren, Kaitlyn M., Emmily Jean. Employed as Grant Public School, ›us maintenance, supervisor 25 years. Retired Dec. 31, 1991.

JOE DELL WARD, born Jan. 8, 1930 in Wichita Falls, TX, enlisted in the US Army Aug. 31, 1948. Basic train-ng at Ft. Ord, CA. Duties to Bremerhaven, Germany, Dec. 24, 1948. Assigned to 22nd Constab., later to the 24th Constab. B Trp. Attended second class of NCO Academy n Munich, Germany. Participated on Rifle Team 45 Cali-ber Pistol Team, Sqdn. Baseball team, and Softball Team. Served on border patrol in Schweinfurt, Germany and Bad Hersfeld, Germany as patrol leader.

Received Army Good Conduct Medal, Army of Occupation and Unit Citation Medal. Returned to the US for Operation Cadery April 1951. Discharged at Ft. Hood, TX June 20, 1952.

Married Dorothy William May 26, 1978. Has one daughter and two sons by a previous marriage. Retired from General Motors, Inc. in Arlington, TX with 32 years service. His hobbies are golfing with a seven handicap. He cattle ranch and work as an assistant manager at the Greenville Municipal Golf Course.

MICHAEL F. (MIKE) WASKO, born June 19, 1931, Scranton, PA, joined the US Army Aug. 24, 1948. Mili-tary locations and stations: Breckinridge, KY; Camp Kilmer, NJ; Ft. Dix, NJ; Indiantown Gap, PA; Bad Hersfeld, Germany. Served with the 24th Constab. Sqdn.

Discharged as corporal June 23, 1952. Awarded the Good Conduct and Occupation Medal Germany.

Married Ercel Wasko and was employed at Bendix Allied, South Montrose, Pennsylvania Material Handler. Retired July 2, 1996.

MUNSEY W. WEBB born Feb. 16, 1927, Allisonia, VA. Joined the service June 5, 1945, Fort Meade, MD. Stations and locations in-clude basic training at Fort Knox, KY and various places in Germany.

He was assigned to the 6th U.S. Cavalry, 1946, U.S. Constabulary. Dis-1arged Dec. 2, 1946. mong his medals are the WII Victory Medal and the ›od Conduct Medal.

Married Hazel and they have one daughter, Margo W. Moretz. Webb has writ-ten a book that has sold over 2,000 copies so far.

DON M. (BUZZ) WEIRICH, born July 5, 1923, Lancaster, PA, McCaskey High, joined the US Army Feb. 11, 1943. Military locations and stations: Camp McCain, MS, 1943; Ft. Jackson, SC, early 1944; Devon England, June-July 1944. Served with C Btry., 336th FA Bn., 87th Div., Feb 1943-May 1944 USA. Held commands with A Btry., 773 FA Bn., 20th Corp., 3rd Army, June 44 - Nov 45.

Discharged Nov. 5, 1948 as corporal. Battles and campaigns: ETO, Northern France, Ardennes, Rhineland, Central Germany, Colmar Pocket Vosges, Operation Nordwind Alsace, January-February 1945.

Awarded Good Conduct, American Campaign, ETO w/4 Bronze Battle Stars, WWII Victory Medal and Army of Occupation w/Bar.

Memorable experiences: Also E Trp., 27th Constab. Sqdn., 14th Regt., July 1, 1946; A Trp., 1st Constab. Sqdn., 15th Regt., September 1948.

Married Violet and employed Armstrong World In-dustries postal position, retired July 1, 1988.

FRANCIS R. (FRANK) WEISS, born Aug. 5, 1931, Vera Cruz, PA, joined the US Army Aug. 29, 1949. Mili-tary locations and stations: Ft. Dix, NJ (training); Ft. Belvoir, VA; Patch Kaserne, Merrill Kaserne, Augsburg, Germany, Nurnberg, Germany.

Served with HQ and HQ Co., 2 A/C Regt., 656th Engr. to Po Bn., Ft. Belvoir, VA. Held command as Sup-ply and Arms Room (Merrill Kaserne).

Discharged June 6, 1955 as corporal. Awarded Oc-cupation Medal and Good Conduct Medal. Motor vehicle operator school, Ft. Belvoir, VA; typing and Quartermas-ter School (Lenggries Germany).

Memorable experiences: border patrol duty and the two things that could and sometimes did happen. Com-peting for soldier of the month and receiving a three day pass. He would rent a Lambretta scooter for $10.00 and head for the Bavarian Alps. August Fest and Oktober Fest were always memorable, being Penn. German, talking and understanding most of the language.

Spending time and giving gifts to the children in the orphanage at Christmas.

Married to Theresa H. Weiss for 41 years and have two children, Keith and Kevin Weiss; grandchildren, Philip, Shanna, John, Ashley and Amanda (triplets, five years). Employed as presser dry cleaning 11 years. Trac-tor trailer drive 28 years; Matlack Inc. and MTS Inc. (both in Northampton, PA). Retired June 1988 from Teamster Local 773, Allentown, PA.

JOHN M. WELK, born Jan. 9, 1926 Lancaster, PA, inducted Feb. 18, 1944, New Cumberland, PA; 12 week training, Camp Stewart, GA. Further training Camp Cook, Camp Irwin and Camp Hahn, all California. Went to Camp

Shenk's, NY. For overseas Scotland, to England later to France. Joined 815 AAA AW Btry. at Metz, attached 76 Div. and 3rd Army. Saw death camps. War ended. Returned to Germany from Czechoslovakia. To Antwerp Belgium, 10/ 31/45. Reenlisted for 15 month, three month furlough in USA. Returned to Europe March 1946. Sent to Berlin on 6th Cav. in Lauf, near Nurnburg. Later to Coburg, July 1, 1946. Patrolled Russian-American border met Melanie Forster. Married came to USA 1948. They have two daugh-ters, one son, five grandchildren, seven great-grandchildren.

Melanie died January 1966. He was discharged Feb-ruary 1947 worked for Packard Motor Co. 1947-59. Worked for Armstrong World Inds. 1959-89. Retired April 1989. Spend's time hunting, restoring old motorcycles, stock car races. Joined VFW, AmVets, American Legion, Mason's.

Married Janet Summers December 1978. Joined Constab. after 6th Cav. Reunion in Chattanooga, TN. Re-ceived Battle Stars, Citations and Ribbons from WWII. Was in first group when Constab. was started.

JACK R. WHEATON, born April 22, 1929, Erie, PA, joined the US Army, July 1, 1948. Military locations and stations: basic 9th Inf., Ft. Dix, NJ.

Served with D Trp., 15th US Constab. Discharged as private first class July 7, 1950.

Memorable experiences: served with the greatest men in the world.

Widowed and has children: Larry, Jacklyn, Pam, Glenda, Dawn and seven step-children; grandchildren: 16 grandchildren and three great-grandchildren. Employed as house painter and paper hanger. Retired April 22, 1983.

RICHARD G. (DICK) WHITAKER, born Sept. 30, 1927, Monroe, MI. Joined the Army Oct. 10, 1945. Mili-tary locations and stations: basic training, Ft. Knox, KY; 35th Med. Tk. Bn., April-June 1945; 35th Constab. Sqdn., C Trp. Landshut, Germany; 42nd Constab. Sqdn. CTRP Augsburg, Germany and various outposts. Held commands as tank commander, driver, command sergeant, platoon sergeant and scout leader.

Retired USAF Feb. 1, 1976 as SMS (E-8). Battles and campaigns: Chinese Comm Intervention, Operation Killer, Chipyong-Ni, Spring 1951 offensive.

Awarded the Silver Star, Commendation Medal, Meritorious Service, Presidential Unit Citation, Korean Service Medal w/4 Battle Stars.

Married Margit I. Whitaker (nee: Rother) and they had son, Richard H. Whitaker and granddaughter, Kristen J. Whitaker. Employed with USAF Civil Service (QS-12), instructor training manager, Computer Maintenance 33 years total 1960-93. Retired April 1993 (Civil Service).

WILLIAM ALLEN WHITE, born July 18, 1916, Sutter Creek, CA, drafted Sept. 4, 1944, OCS 1945 Class. Duties: US Constabulary January 1946 to July 1948. Dis-charged from Army July 1948. Recalled October 1950, Ft. Lewis Training Unit. Sent to Korea August 1951 to 1st Cav. Div. Division sent to Hokkaido, Japan January 1952. In October 1953 ordered to Camp Irwin, CA. Was motor officer for the training center. Took part in the atomic test razor on armored vehicles at Desert Rock Atomic Test Center 1954. 8th Inf. Div., 41st Armd. Bn., 1959 to 1962, 1st and 2nd Armd. Bn., Ft. Hood, TX. 1963 to 1966

USERUR NATO School, Oberammergau, Germany, post commander. 1966 to 1969 Presidio of San Francisco in DCSOP individual and unit training. Retired as LTC February 1969. Received several medals and ribbons during his career to include the Combat Infantry Badge and Commendation Medal with OLC as well as a medal from the German forces. Married Helen Davidson 1945, daughter Joan by previous marriage.

Director Retiree Activities Office (RAO) 1985 to 1995 at McClellan AFB, Sacramento. Still active with the RAO. Plays golf.

DR. JAMES OLIVER WHITTAKER,
born Sept. 27, 1927, Rochester, NY, enlisted in the RA, Feb. 20, 1946. Basic training, Ft. McClellan, AL. Discharged July 31, 1947.

Duties: US Constab. HQ Bamberg, Germany G-3, 1946; Heidelburg, Germany 1947; T/5. Medals include WWII Victory Medal, US Army of Occupation (Germany) Medal. Served in Vietnam 1966 for DOD (ARPA). Education: BA Texas Christian 1950; Summers, Harvard 1948 and 1949; MA University of Pennsylvania, 1952; PhD Social Psychology, University of Oklahoma, 1958.

An internationally known social psychologist, Dr. Whittaker's 16 books have been used by over a million university students in every country in the Western Hemisphere and throughout the world. Retired as full professor at Penn State 1987.

Married Sandra J. Oshel, Aug. 16, 1957. They have a son and a daughter.

WARREN D. WILCOX,
born Feb. 13, 1927, Warwick, RI, joined the Army July 2, 1945. Military locations and stations: Armored Tank Training July 1945-November 1945, Ft. Knox, KY, 42nd Cav., 42nd Constab. Sqdn., Freising, Germany November 1945-December 1946. Section Sgt.; 705th AA Gun Bn.

Served with 42 Cav., 6981 Inf. Rifle Co., 2nd Regt., 42nd Constab., 705th AA Gun Bn., 102nd AA Gun Bn. Member of 705 AA 90MM Gun Bn. RI National Guard. Unit activated for federal service Aug. 14, 1950. Discharged April 7, 1952. Duties: engaged in the training of replacement troops; 90mm AA etc. at Camp Stewart, GA.

Discharged Dec. 31, 1946 as master sergeant. Discharged the second time April 7, 1952. Awarded Army of Occupation and WWII Victory Medal.

Married Olga C. and they have children: Theresa, John and Rachel; grandchildren: Carrie, Nathan, Candice, Kyle and Jason. Employed as commercial fisherman 1952-57; November 1957-Feb. 13, 1989; Rigger 15 years and nuclear quality control w/structural 16 years. Electric boat Div. Gen. Dynamics Corp. Retired Feb. 13, 1989.

PERRY A. WILEY,
born June 10, 1927, Louisville, IL, joined the US Army Sept. 12, 1945. Military locations and stations: Camp Roberts, CA; Ft. Benning, GA; A Trp. and D Trp., 53rd-70th FA.

Honorably discharged as E-4 Feb. 30, 1951. Memorable experiences: two other troops and Wiley were installing a ham radio antenna in Graffenwohr when it came in contact with overhead high voltage lines. Troopers, Cherry, Walls and Wiley narrowly missed being electrocuted.

Married Clara and they have a daughter, Kelly and grandchildren, Jennie and Jason. Employed as supervisor quality control, General Motors Corporation. Retired Nov. 30, 1982.

DONALD L. (DON) WILLIAMS,
born Aug. 3, 1927, Portsmouth, OH, joined the US Army Aug. 3, 1945. Military locations and stations: Ft. Hayes, OH; Camp Atterbury, IN; Camp Robinson, AR; Camp Pickett, VA; Ft. Dix, NJ; various German cities.

Served with 2nd Armd. Cav. Regt., 2nd Constab. Regt., 42nd Constab. Sqdn.

Discharged as private first class March 30, 1947. Awarded Good Conduct Medal, ETO Medal, Victory Medal, Occupation Medal and Expert Infantry Badge.

Memorable experiences: In February, 1946 he arrived in Freising, Germany and was put in the 2nd Armd. Cav. Regt. which later became the 2nd Constab. Regt. under the command of Gen. Harmon. In May, 1946 while stationed in Freising, their whole unit was taken into the Alps Mountains, some 120 miles away, near Burchesgarden, Germany after SS troops had been spotted in the mountains. They never found them but they did find evidence of them being there.

On Oct. 16, 1946 their regiment stood Honor Guard for General Eisenhower when he was leaving the Army and returning to the US. They were issued scarves made from German parachutes that were dyed yellow to wear for this occasion. Ike said they were the sharpest outfit in the ETO. Later on the rest of the Army adopted scarves as part of their uniform.

While in the Constabulary they were stationed two Army men to a jeep and a German policeman who acted as an interpreter. They had six hour patrols where they went from town to town, checked in with the police and checked all crimes and to see how the civilians were doing. In the fall of 1946 near Wasserburg they had to investigate a murder with the CIC where a husband and wife and their maid were murdered. That was a very bad sight. Later, they had to attend the autopsy that was performed on all three victims.

Another time they picked up a war criminal at the Displaced Persons Camp in Moosburg and escorted him to Dachau.

While in Germany he played on the 42nd Constab. basketball team where they traveled throughout the American zone and played different outfits. At Daggendorf, there were not enough players for the opposing team and they were asked if they minded if the chaplain played for them. Of course they didn't mind until they got beat. They later found out the chaplain had played for the University of Indiana.

Williams married Wanda Jean and they have children: Georgia, Don Jr., Vickie, Dwight and Robert; grandchildren: Kim Frost, Kevin Frost, Kurt Frost, Ryan

Schmidt, great-granddaughter, Shalimar Allen. Employed with Frigidaire Div., GMC, job setter, retiring Oct. 1, 1977.

FREDERICK DAVID WILLIAMS,
born June 25, 1925 Niagara Falls, NY. Fred's parents, who were British, went back to England in 1930. When WWII broke out, when he was old enough, thinking he was English, tried to enlist in the British Navy. He also tried the RAF and finally the Army, none of them would accept him, although he passed all the exams.

He finally found out the reason was because of his American birth certificate. In December 1945 he was sworn in as a US citizen and drafted Feb. 12, 1945. Re-enlisted in the RA May 13, 1946.

Duties: 3071st QM Ref. Co. (Mbl) June 1945-May 1946; Camp Lee, VA, May 1946-November 1946. D Trp., 16th Constab. Sqdn. (Sep) Berlin, Germany November 1946-July 1948. A Co., 36th Armd. Inf. Bn., 3rd Armd. Div. Ft. Knox, July 1948-May 1949.

Married Gloria Durnford Aug. 25, 1951. They have one son, one daughter and three grandchildren. Retired from Pacific Bell Telephone Company in 1981 and they now live in Kingman, AZ.

R.C. WILLIAMS,
born Oct. 3, 1930, Williamston, NC, enlisted RA Feb. 18, 1948. Basic training, Ft. Jackson, SC. Retired 23 years service December 1969, Ft. Sill, OK.

Job assignments: FA, Nike Hercules and Pershing Missiles Communications and survey chief and detail platoon sergeant.

Assignments: 4006th Sta Comp. Unit Ft. Sam Houston, TX 48-49; 49-54 C Btry., 70th FA Bn. Fussen and Nurnberg Germany, US Constab.; 55 short tour Ft. Lewis, WA, 555th FA Bn.; 55-57, Hanau Germany, 765th FA Bn. Fliegerhorst Kaserne; 58-62 Dachau, Germany 2/37th FA Bn.; 62-63 Ft. Bliss, TX 62nd Nike Hercules Missile Bn. 63-65, Ft. Sill, OK activating 3/84th Pershing Missile Bn., 65-68, 3/84th deployed to Neckarsulm, Germany; 68-69, Ft. Sill, OK and retirement from 1/44 Pershing Missile Bn.

Married Nurnberg Germany 1953 to wife Christa raised two daughters and a son during his Army career. They also have five grandchildren: Christina, Ryan, Steve Nickalous and Amanda.

ROBERT J. WILLIAMS,
born March 11, 1927, in Youngstown, OH, was the son of the late Howard and Irene (Lentz) Williams.

Served in the Army with the 4th Cav. in WWII. Attended Ohio State University after discharge from the Army.

He was a lifetime member of VFW Post 2506 and McSherrystown Home Association; member of American Legion Post 14, the Republic Club of Hanover, US Constab., US Horse Cavalry Association, US Forces in Austria, Hanover Cavalry Club and NAARP.

Williams died March 1, 1997 at his home. He was the husband of Anna K. (Thaler) Williams and father of three children: Toni Wagaman, Kurt Williams and William Williams; four granddaughters and great-granddaughter.

JAMES E. WILSON, born Nov. 4, 1926, Woodruff, SC, joined the Army Sept. 21, 1945. Military locations and stations: Ft. Jackson, Ft. Bragg, Camp Robinson, AR; Camp Pickett, VA; Camp Kilmer, NJ; Camp Phillip Morris; Stuttgart, Bad Wimphen, Moss Bach, Schwiezingen, Sonthofen. Served with C Trp. 15th Cav. RC 15th Constab Sqdn.

Discharged March 16, 1947 as sergeant. Awarded Atlantic, Pacific, WWII Victory, Army of Occupation and Good Conduct.

Married Eveline and they have a daughter, Dorothy Jean and retired from civilian employment March 9, 1990.

LOUIS ALEXANDER WILSON, born March 30, 1927, Kosse, TX, drafted into the Army June 1945. Took basic training at Ft. Hood, TX. Sent to Germany December 1945. Joined 78th Div., 309th Anti Tank Co. in Berlin. Drove a jeep for CP.

Formed the 16th Constab. Separate Co C, in 1946. Went to HQ and HQ Co. as a mechanic in 2nd Echelon Shop. They worked on jeeps to the M8s.

Became motor pool sergeant and served during the Berlin Blockade until 1948. Stationed at Ft. Dix, NJ as motor pool sergeant.

He was released in 1949 and recalled in 1950. Trained again at Ft. Hood, 2nd Armd. and sent to Korea 559 MP.

Drove a truck for a guard duty then went to 2nd Echelon Shop as motor pool sergeant.

Returned to states and released September 1951 after serving 11 months in Korea 23 Div., 1st Logistic Command.

Married in 1948 and they have one son, three daughters and eight grandchildren. Member of US Constabulary and VFW 912.

WILLIAM J. (WILLIE) WOOTEN, born Jan. 31, 1930, Galax, VA. Joined the US Army Feb. 8, 1947. Military locations and stations: Landshut, Germany, 1948-52; Korea; Ft. Pickett; Camp Kilmer; Ft. Knox; Ft. Gorden. Served with Tank Co., 6th Armd. Cav. Constab. Held commands as platoon sergeant, first sergeant, sergeant major. Discharged 1974 as sergeant major.

Awards include the American Campaign, American Defesne, Army Good Conduct, Armed Forces Expeditionary, National Defense, EAME, Korean Service Airborne, Combat Service Badge, WWII Occupation Service, United Nations Service, Good Conduct, Unit Citation (Blue), Meritorious Citation (Red).

Married Cora Wooten and they have children: Danny Wooten, Scottie Wooten, Jesse Wooten and Larry Wooten; grandchildren: Tina Wooten, Lester Wooten, Justin and Andrew. Employed with Twin County Tire, retiring in 1998.

KENNETH T. (KEN) WRAGG, born Oct. 20, 1928, Shenandoah, PA, joined the US Army Feb. 9, 1951. Military locations and stations: Ft. Dix, NJ; Hersfeld, Germany. Served with 24th Constab. Discharged Dec. 24, 1952 as private first class. Awarded Army of Occupation-Germany.

His wife Marie is deceased. They had daughters, Barbara and Carol; grandchildren: Jeff, Nancy, Bobby and Katie. Employed at various locations of American Water Works Co. Started 1949 as utilityman, made manager in 1951 and continued until retired March 1, 1991.

CHARLES WERNER (CHARLEY or CW) WRATCHFORD JR., born Jan. 26, 1927, Ellamore, Randolph County, WV. Joined the US Army March 30,

1945. In Ft. Ord in California he was discharged to join RA and shipped to Germany in 29th Inf. Regt. under SHAEF HQ. In 1946 he returned to US and discharged November 24. He attended classes at Baltimore Technical Institute under GI Bill. Reenlisted in Army Nov. 19, 1947 and returned to Germany with and assigned to 22nd Constab. Sqdn. in Schweinfurt. Later assigned to Trp. B, 24th Sqdn. in Hersfeld. In 1952 when Constabulary broke up he was discharged at Ft. Meade, Jan. 11, 1952. On Feb. 10, 1954 reenlisted in the Army Security Agency and served in Alaska. Discharged Feb. 8, 1957 at Ft. Bragg, NC.

Married to Barbara and has children: Charleen, Kathleen and Julia. In 1958 got position in Civil Administration as electronic technician at Washington National Airport. Transferred to Elkins, WV airport in 1973. Retired October 1983 with 34 years, eight months not counting 11 months sick leave.

Currently quartermaster of VFW Post 3647. Also service officer and youth activities chairman. Service officer at American Legion Post 29. Commander and service officer of DAV, West Virginia Chapter 1. Hospital chairman for Military Order of Cooties Pup Tent 7. Senior vice commander of VFW District 7 and Voice of Democracy chairman. Their chapter of DAV has a 15 passenger van which serves VAMC in Clarksburg.

EVERETT E. WRIGHT, JR., born in Meriden, CT Jan. 27, 1928, moved to East Hampton, CT 1929. April 1946 he was drafted into the Army. After one day as a draftee he volunteered for 18 months in the RA. Took basic training in Amarillo, TX at the Amarillo AB. After basic he went to Scott AF in Illinois to go to teletype school or cable splicing school.

With one year of service left, instead of school, he was sent to Tokyo, Japan for a year, stationed with the Far East AF doing MP duty and motor pool maintenance. Discharged in October 1947 he received the WWII Victory Medal and the Occupation of Japan Medal.

After 1 1/2 years out of the service he reenlisted in 1949 for three more years. After eight weeks at Ft. Dix, NJ he was sent to A Trp., 24th Constab. Bad Hersfeld, Germany. His duties were machine gun operator, machine gun operator, machine gun jeep driver and driving the radio jeep on border patrol. He served in Germany 38 months. His nickname was "Woody Woodpecker." He was a drinker in the service, now he hasn't had a drink 44 years and quit smoking 31 years ago. He was discharged in November 1952 and received the German Occupation Medal. Returned to East Hampton, CT.

He worked for Pratt and Whitney Aircraft from 1966 and retired, after a heart attack, in 1986.

He is the father of three sons. He travels around the US riding his motorcycle. He's covered 38 states on his motorcycle. The furthest was to Yellow Stone Park, WY. Now he's sticking around home and riding his motorcycle around the eastern states and enjoying his retirement.

EDWARD J. YETSKO, born Feb. 14, 1932, Binghamton, NY, joined US Army March 1, 1950 at Binghamton. Discharged March 26, 1953, Camp Kilmer

Took basic training Ft. Dix with 9th Inf. Div. Shipped to Germany serving in Degerndof and Regenburg. From June 1950 to March 1953 served with Tank Co., 3rd Bn., 6th ACR. Attained the rank of staff sergeant and served as

tank commander and platoon sergeant. Graduated NCO Academy, Munich and other schools while in the Constabulary.

Holds the Good Conduct, Occupation and National Defense Medals.

In civilian life worked for IBM for over 30 years. He was a department manager in production control. Retired May 1987. Married Elizabeth Lucas November 1954. Two sons, one daughter, seven grandchildren. Resides Vestal, NY.

One of original "Dirty Dozen" who formed the USCON Association. Was the first National Vice Commander, is now national adjutant and adjutant Outpost 2.

Member American Legion and VFW.

SAMUEL (SAM) YOUNG, born Feb. 11, 1930, Lawrence County, KY, joined US Army June 1948. Military and locations: Ft. Jackson, SC; Berlin, Germany; Camp Polk, LA.

Served with 16th Constab. Sqdn. Discharged July 1952 as private first class. Battles and campaigns: Berlin airlift.

Awarded the Berlin Airlift Medal, Humane Medal, Army of Occupation Medal, Good Conduct Medal, Expert Marksman on Small Weapons.

Memorable experiences: Berlin Airlift and helping the German people; being married two times on the same day, Civil and military.

Married Sybille who was born and raised in Germany. They have children: Christina, Pearson and Marianna Young. Employed as tinsmith. Retired September 1982 General Motors Corp.

BURTON THOMAS YOUNT, born June 12, 1923, Hickory, NC, enlisted in US Army in 1940, Charlotte, NC.

Duties: 19th Inf. Schofield Barracks, HI, 9th Signal during Pearl Harbor attack. After four years returned to US 1944. Occupation duty in Germany Dec. 20, 1946. First sergeant, 820th Constab. MP Co., Bamberg. Accepted commission December 1946. Assigned 759th MP Bn., Berlin Germany, rotated to US December 1947; Sandia Base, Albuquerque, NM January 1948. Married German war bride Karin Trenina, interpreter for US Constab. Provost Marshal's office, Bamberg, Germany.

Transferred to Lompoc, CA as ROTC instructor to St. Ignatius High School, San Francisco, CA, Camp Roberts, CA.

May-November 1952 enclosure commander UN POW command Koje-Do, Korea. 1952-54, 16th Corps MP Plt. Co., Sendai, Japan, joined by his family. 1954-56 Oakland Army Base, CA 1956-58 Provost Marshall, Ft. Mason, San Francisco, CA, 1958-October 1960. CO MP Co., Office Ft. Eustis, VA. Capt. Yount retired from US Army in 1960 after more than 20 years of active service.

September 1961-65 received BS and masters degree in business administration, San Diego City College. Has been on hemodialysis since January 1984 due to kidney failure. Died Jan. 30, 1993 after kidney transplant.

Among numerous medals awarded Bronze Star for meritorious service in Korea, Army Commendation Medal and 11 other awards. Survived by his wife, three children and five grandchildren.

Note: at the time Burton Young applied for permission to marry his wife, a German national, the non fraternization law just had been lifted. The marriages in Germany were not allowed. It took six months of screening and investigating his wife's character and records at the US Consulate, Munich, in order to obtain permission to marry an US Lt., Burt also had to post $500 bond for her, pay her ticket and marry her under a special War Brides law which remained effect until 1952.

SAM ZAFRAN, born Feb. 5, 1928, Kings County, Brooklyn, NY. Enlisted Reserve Oct. 5, 1944. Active duty Jan. 14, 1946. Basic training,  Camp Joseph T. Robinson, Little Rock, AR. Served overseas European Campaign, 6th Armd. Inf. until March 1946. Volunteered at Marburg, Germany for the US Constab. Forces. Served in E Trp., 12th Constab. Sqdn., Neustadt Germany; A Trp., 12th Sqdn., Neustadt and A Trp., 10th Constab. at Fritzlar Germany. Reassigned to HQ 1st Constab. Bde., Wiesbaden, Germany until May 1949.

Stateside with I&R Plt., HQ 14th Inf. Regt., Camp Carson, CO. Returned back to Germany and served a brief stint with the 759 MP Bn. (Berlin). Transferred back to HQ 1st Bde. until June 1951, when unit started to disband and finished European tour with 4th Sig Co., 4th Inf. Div., Frankfurt, Germany.

Other duties with 278th Regt. Combat Team, 1st Recon Co., 1st Inf. Div., HQ CCB, 1st Armd. Div., 876th FA (280 Heavy Gun); 1st Sig. Co., 1st Inf. Div., HQ Btry., 5th Arty. (RKT/HOW) Bn.; A Co., 13th Sig. Bn., 1st Air Cav. (RVN).

Married Dorothea Wenninger, Nov. 8, 1958 and they have two sons, two daughters, five grandchildren and two great-grandchildren. Retired Oct. 1, 1973, Ft. Riley, KS.

WALTER S. ZOMBEK, born April 21, 1928, Wheeling, WV, joined the US Army, Oct. 3, 1946-Jan. 16, 1953. Stationed in Germany 1947-1952, Message Center, US Constab. Attended Signal School (3rd Plt.), US  Constab. stationed in Seckenheim near Mannheim, 15th Regt., March 1947, Darmstadt, 14th Constab. Sqdn.; Ansbach, July 1947; Karlsruhe-Knielingen, August 1947-48, Message Center, 1st Constab. Sqdn., 10th Constab. Regt.; Schweinfurt, 1948-49, (unit transfer); Heidelburg, October 1949-August 1952; Camp Pickett, VA, discharged January 16, 1953.

Married April 1952 in Karlsruhe/Germany to Juliana Schuehle. Attended University of West Virginia through 1957. Accepted position as aeronautical engineer with Convair/General Dynamics, San Diego, CA. He had two son, Thomas and Mark Zombek. Zombek died May 1972 in San Diego.

Color Guard on parade in 1947.

Horse Plt. 16th Constabulary Sq. Departing Templehof Airfield Berlin 1947.

Index

A MAGAZINE FOR THE GROUND COMBAT FORCES

INFANTRY JOURNAL

FEBRUARY 1949

40¢

B Troop 2d Sq. 20th Regiment

Review of 2nd Regiment. Munich 14 October 1946.

'CIRCLE C COWBOYS'

COLD WAR CONSTABULARY

BY DAVID COLLEY

Graffenwhor Germany - September 6, 1947, Labor Day Parade.

Brigadier General George W. Smythe as he prepares to sign up for the first war bond in the highly successful bond drive by the troopers of the United States Constabulary.

FUSILIER

A QUARTERLY FOR MILITARY HISTORIANS
Volume 2, Number 2

$1.50

Newsweek

THE U. S. MAGAZINE OF NEWS SIGNIFICANCE

BRITISH ISLES
DENMARK . . . . . . 1.25 kr.
EGYPT . . . . 7 pt.
FRANCE 40
GERMANY
GREECE 250
IRELAND
ITALY
LUXEMBOURG
NETHERLANDS
NORWAY
PALESTINE
PORTUGAL
SOUTH A
SWEDEN
SWITZ
SYRI
TU
U

Berlin: 'We Will Not Be Coerced'

U.S. CONSTABULARY

In Occupied Germany

Date: July 1946

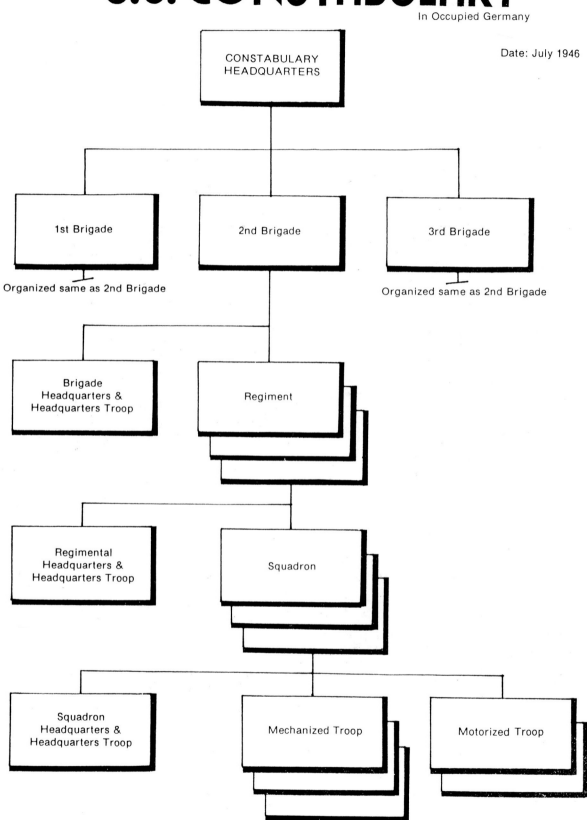

CONSTABULARY HEADQUARTERS

1st Brigade

2nd Brigade

3rd Brigade

Organized same as 2nd Brigade

Organized same as 2nd Brigade

Brigade Headquarters & Headquarters Troop

Regiment

Regimental Headquarters & Headquarters Troop

Squadron

Squadron Headquarters & Headquarters Troop

Mechanized Troop

Motorized Troop